Comparison–Shopping Services and Agent Designs

Yun Wan
University of Houston–Victoria, USA

INFORMATION SCIENCE REFERENCE

Hershey · New York

Director of Editorial Content:	Kristin Klinger
Senior Managing Editor:	Jamie Snavely
Managing Editor:	Jeff Ash
Assistant Managing Editor:	Carole Coulson
Typesetter:	Amanda Appicello
Cover Design:	Lisa Tosheff
Printed at:	Yurchak Printing Inc.

Published in the United States of America by
Information Science Reference (an imprint of IGI Global)
701 E. Chocolate Avenue, Suite 200
Hershey PA 17033
Tel: 717-533-8845
Fax: 717-533-8661
E-mail: cust@igi-global.com
Web site: http://www.igi-global.com/reference

and in the United Kingdom by
Information Science Reference (an imprint of IGI Global)
3 Henrietta Street
Covent Garden
London WC2E 8LU
Tel: 44 20 7240 0856
Fax: 44 20 7379 0609
Web site: http://www.eurospanbookstore.com

Library of Congress Cataloging-in-Publication Data

Comparison-shopping services and agent designs / Yun Wan, editor.

   p. cm.

 Includes bibliographical references and index.

 Summary: "This book investigates the effects of the evolution of comparison-shopping techniques and processes with the ready availability of online resources over the past few years"--Provided by publisher. ISBN 978-1-59904-978-6 (hardcover) -- ISBN 978-1-59904-979-3 (ebook) 1. Consumer education. 2. Shopping--Computer network resources. 3. Intelligent agents (Computer software) I. Wan, Yun, 1974-

  TX335.C633 2009 381.3'3--dc22

                              2008043760

British Cataloguing in Publication Data
A Cataloguing in Publication record for this book is available from the British Library.

All work contributed to this book is new, previously-unpublished material. The views expressed in this book are those of the authors, but not necessarily of the publisher.

Table of Contents

Detailed Table of Contents

Yun Wan, University of Houston-Victoria, USA

This chapter provides an overview of comparison-shopping services. Four research topics are covered: How to design a good shopbot? How Shoppers using the comparison-shopping services? What is the strategic use of comparison-shopping as a new channel by online vendors? And what is the impact of comparison-shopping on existing price equilibrium and electronic market structures? Emerging research topics like mobile comparison as well as comparison in health information are also discussed.

Maria Fasli, University of Essex, UK

The huge growth of e-commerce has had a profound impact on users who can now choose from a vast number of options online. Inevitably, as the number of choices has increased, so has the need for tools to help users organize, manage and utilize information on these for better decision-making. Comparison shopping agents or shopbots can help users decide what to buy and enhance their online shopping experience. However, despite the high expectations, the immense potential of shopbots has not been fully realized. In this chapter, the authors identify the limitations and drawbacks of current shopbots, in particular, with regard to the underlying technology for building such systems. They then discuss how these technical limitations can be overcome by making use of the Semantic Web and Web Services. They also consider how shopbots can truly serve the user by providing personalized, impartial and flexible services.

Hongwei Zhu, Old Dominion University, USA
Stuart E. Madnick, Massachusetts Institute of Technology, USA

Global comparison services facilitate easy comparison of product offerings around the world. To offer such services, one has to address the semantic heterogeneity problems that often arise when data is collected from sources around the world. In this chapter, the authors use examples to illustrate three types of semantic heterogeneity problems that a global comparison service may encounter. Then they present a mediation architecture as a solution to addressing these problems. The feasibility of using the architecture to enable global comparison is demonstrated with a prototype application. An evaluation of the solution shows that it is scalable due to its capability of automatically generating necessary conversions from a small set of predefined ones.

This chapter examines how product price, product complexity and product durability influence consumers' comparison shopping process. Frequently comparison shopping is equated only to price comparisons. However, comparison shopping is becoming far broader than finding the cheapest price over the internet. Nowadays a vast variety of products are sold over the Internet. Some are relatively simple products such as books and movie DVDs. Others are more complex such as computer related products, travel reservations and real-estate properties. As the number of key product attributes increases, consumers apply different kinds of decision making rather than just looking for the cheapest price. Consumers also use different decision making tactics between durable and non-durable products. This chapter looks into the implications of such differences for consumers and product sellers. It concludes with managerial implications and future research agendas.

The aim of this chapter is to analyse antecedents of search engines use as prepurchase information tools. Firstly, there is a literature review of the factors influencing search engines use in online purchases. Then, there is an empirical analysis of a sample of 650 Spanish e-shoppers. Logistical regression is used to analyse the influence of demographics, surfing behaviour and purchase motivations on willingness to use search engines for e-shopping. Data analysis shows that experience as Internet user and as Internet shopper are negative key drivers of search engine use. Most of the utilitarian shopping motivations analyzed predict comparison shopping behaviour. Demographics are not determinant variables in the use of search engines in online purchases. This research enables companies to know the factors that potentially affect search engine use in e-shopping decisions and the importance of using search engines in their communication campaigns.

Online trust is a critical element to the success of electronic commerce (e-commerce). Indeed it reduces the level of uncertainty that arises because of the lack of face-to-face interactions with vendors. In e-commerce purchaser-vendor interactions are subject to uncertainty, anonymity, and communication means reliability. This chapter discusses how some trust models have been developed to address these issues. Some models promote familiarity and competitiveness as part of the exercise of assessing online trust. This assessment uses fuzzy logic-based techniques.

Chapter VII

Electronic markets are expected to facilitate consumer information search and product comparison to the extent that consumers are able to accumulate nearly perfect information. The authors present an analysis of search patterns based on a laboratory experiment on product search processes. They identified three types of search patterns in our experiment: sequential, agent search, and iterative search. They studied the factors affecting the choice and the outcome of agent search pattern compared to the other search patterns. They found that the employed search pattern has an impact on search cost and the efficiency of search measured with purchase price and the time used for searching. Agent search seems to combine low search costs with high efficiency. Sequential search still emerged as the dominant search pattern even though it leads to the most expensive purchase. Iterative search pattern was the slowest of them all.

The use of online shopping agents has increased dramatically in the last ten years, as a result of e-commerce development. Despite the importance of these online applications, very few studies attempted to identify and analyse the main factors that influence the users' perception regarding the service quality of online shopping agents, and consequently, the elements that determine the users' choice of online shopping agents. The present study attempts to fill this literature gap, identifying on the basis of primary data analysis, the various circumstantial or personal factors that can determine the choice of a specific searching strategy and shopping agent

Chapter IX

Wen-Jang (Kenny) Jih, Middle Tennessee State University, USA

Technological advancements in Wireless communication and Internet capabilities are rapidly converging to provide an unprecedented level of convenience for online shopping. Despite much discussion regarding the unique capabilities of mobile commerce in supporting online shopping via unprecedented convenience, the relationship between mobile commerce service features and convenience perception remains an unanswered issue from both the vendor and customer points of view. Although the concept of consumer-perceived convenience has been extensively discussed in marketing and consumer behavior literature, in the context of mobile commerce, however, these discussions are subject to systematic validation with empirical data to be convincing. This study conducted a field survey to investigate how mobile commerce service features and customer perception of convenience are correlated. It also examined the effect of convenience on customers' intention of shopping via their mobile communication devices. The primary data collected in Taiwan were used in the analysis. It was found the service features and customer convenience perceptions are significantly correlated. It also showed a significant relationship between the convenience perception and shopping intention. Further, there was a positive effect of convenience perception on shopping intention. The findings may have practical implications for mobile commerce strategists by providing more understanding of the mobile commerce success factors from a consumer behavior point of view.

Chapter X

Călin Gurău, GSCM–Montpellier Business School, France

Comparison-shopping is becoming the mainstream marketing channel for B2C ecommerce. More and more small online vendors are using shopbots to bring in customers. There are mainly two types of shopbots: those general shopbots that provide product comparison cross multiple heterogeneous product categories (like shopping.com) and the specialized shopbots that provide comparison within a single or a few highly-related product categories (like addall.com on books and music CD). The effectiveness of shopbot selection strategy by small online vendors is the focus on this chapter. By analyzing data from shopbots and online vendors, the authors found there is significant positive correlation between the number of shopbots an online vendor participates and its traffic rank, which indicates the general effectiveness of using shopbots as a marketing channel. They also found that for online vendors competing on a niche product like college textbook, participating specialized shopbots brings in higher traffic. For competing in mainstream market, there is less significant correlation between participating general shopbots and higher traffic rank for vendors. They conclude that using general shopbots is a reactive strategy for small online vendors while using proper specialized shopbots could provide an edge for small online vendors.

Chapter XI

Patricia T. Warrington, Texas Christian University, USA
Adam Hagen, Purdue University, USA
Richard Feinberg, Purdue University, USA

Customer satisfaction/dissatisfaction can occur at/after the store, on the telephone, on the internet, after a catalog purchase. Customer satisfaction leads to repurchase/loyalty. Customer dissatisfaction leads to lower repurchase/loyalty. However, no research has looked at how satisfaction/dissatisfaction (S/D) in one channel affects the repurchase/loyalty in the same or different channels and the same/different stores. While S/D will increase/decrease the S/D in the same channel it does not always affect S/D in other channels the same way. In addition, S/D in a channel in one retailer may affect S/D in that same channel but in a different retailer.

Chapter XII

Changsu Kim, Yeungnam University, Korea
Robert D. Galliers, Bentley College, USA, & London School of Economics, UK
Kyung Hoon Yang, University of Wisconsin–La Crosse, USA
Jaekyung Kim, University of Nebraska–Lincoln, USA

This article offers a theoretical analysis of evolutionary processes in WBSS strategies. For that purpose, we propose a research model that shows strategy patterns. Based upon the model, we identified several types of strategies. In our research model, WBSS are classified into four types: (1) general-direct-sales (GDS); (2) general-intermediary-sales (GIS); (3) specialized-direct-sales (SDS); and (4) specialized-intermediary-sales (SIS). On the basis of these four categories of WBSS, we analyze the characteristics of WBSS and suggest five evolution strategies for WBSS, which have implications for both theory and practice. Amazon.com's strategic movements, such as product line expansion through alliance and acquisition, provide an exemplary case of the evolution of WBSS strategy. We expect that this research will serve as a guide for Internet businesses and as a catalyst for new research agendas relevant to Web-based shopping and electronic commerce.

Chapter XIII

Maria Madlberger, Vienna University of Economics and Business Administration, Austria

Multichannel retailing can offer a wide range of synergies for retailers when their distribution channels accommodate consumers' preferences and buying behaviors. Among the large number of retail types, mail-order companies are well-suited to benefit from electronic commerce. Not only can they use their infrastructure and experience with direct selling, but they also seek to use the Internet to attract new target groups in order to increase their typically small, narrow customer bases. Currently, we do not know enough about the antecedents of channel choices, especially in the mail-order sector. This article addresses this issue and draws special attention to exogenous (i.e., independent of the retailer) factors that influence online shopping behavior. These variables include perceived convenience and perceived security of online shopping in general and consumers' attitudes toward the catalog as the existing distribution channel. One endogenous factor—attitude toward the online shop—is assumed to influence buying behavior at the online shop. In order to examine relationships between the catalog and the online shop, 2,363 consumers who were familiar with both distribution channels of a mail-order company were surveyed online. The structural equation model developed reveals that attitudes toward the printed catalog most strongly influence attitudes toward the online shop. Further, the analysis showed that antecedents of buying behavior at the online shop are moderated by gender. Shopping behaviors of men are influenced by their attitudes toward the catalog, while shopping behaviors of women are determined by their attitudes toward the online shop.

Chapter XIV

Research on online shopping has taken three broad and divergent approaches viz, human-computer interaction, behavioral, and consumerist approaches to examine online consumer behavior. Assimilating these three approaches, this study proposes an integrated model of online shopping behavior, with four major antecedents influencing online purchase intent: Web site quality, customer concerns in online shopping, self-efficacy, and past online shopping experience. These antecedents were modeled as second-order constructs with subsuming first-order constituent factors. The model was tested using data from a questionnaire survey of 214 online shoppers. Statistical analyses using structural equation modeling was used to validate the model, and identify the relative importance of the key antecedents to online purchase intent. Past online shopping experience was found to have the strongest association with online purchase intent, followed by customer concerns, Web site quality, and computer self efficacy. The findings and their implications are discussed.

An exploratory study was conducted to investigate consumer adoption of online purchase using a survey data set. Based upon the theory of innovation and self-efficacy theory, risk aversion, online proficiency, shopping convenience, and product choice variety were proposed to influence consumer intention to shop online, which, in turn, affects online purchases. Results of regression analyses revealed that all but shopping convenience were significant predictors of consumer intention to purchase online. In addition, consumer intention directly determines consumer purchases online. Finally, consumer intention to purchase online mediates the relationship of risk aversion, shopping convenience, and product choice variety to online shopping. Research and managerial implications of the findings were discussed.

Trust is a major issue in e-markets. It is an even more prominent issue when online shoppers trade with small, less-established e-vendors. Empirical studies on Web seals show that small e-vendors could promote consumers' trust and increase Web sales by displaying Web seals of approval. This article takes a theoretical approach to examine online trading when seals are used in e-markets. We establish an online shopper's decision-making model to reveal the online shopper's decision-making criteria. Criteria include when to trade with a well-established e-vendor and when to trade with a small, less-established e-vendor, with or without a Web seal. Based on our analysis of the research results, we reveal the price effect, the seal effect, the reputation effect, and their impact on a shopper's decision-making process. Meanwhile, a social welfare analysis is conducted to further demonstrate the positive impact of Web seals on small, less-established e-vendors.

Preface

From the BargainFinder experiment in 1995 to the now popular comparison-shopping destinations like Shopping.com, Web-based comparison-shopping as an e-commerce innovation has been enriching our online shopping experience for more than a decade.

Different from other electronic commerce innovations, comparison-shopping as an emerging e-commerce sector is shared by multiple players from its inception. This multiple-player environment allows both competition and mutual learning in a much faster pace compared with other ecommerce sectors. Thus, we found numerous incremental innovations of shopbot technologies in the past decade initiated by different shopbots. These innovations keep perfecting user experiences and eventually lead comparison-shopping into one of the top three B2C ecommerce shopping modes.

The existing research on comparison-shopping can be organized into three different domains: the technical design of shopbots, the comparison-shopping user behaviors, and the economics of comparison-shopping.

The first domain is the design of shopbots. Research on the technical design of shopbots started before 1995 and mainly focuses on how to retrieve data from heterogeneous data sources. Later, when comparison-shopping became popular, how to optimize the data retrieval algorithm and improve the consumer experience became the research trend. It also overlapped with user behavior research in the second domain.

Comparison-shopping user behavior is the second major research domain. Psychologists used controlled or semi-controlled experiment to explore the impact of comparison-shopping information display and functions. Major findings include the confirmation of shopbot efficacy as well as choice overload phenomenon.

Shopbots and comparison-shopping services are also being explored from economics perspective, which is the third domain. In this domain, the impact of comparison-shopping on market equilibrium and pricing strategy of vendors are investigated. Theoretical analysis, empirical data analysis, as well as simulations are three main methodologies. Empirical data collected from comparison-shopping services are used. It was found that comparison-shopping more or less decreased the equilibrium price in many commody and service sectors though evidence is not conclusive and the effects are not consistent.

As indicated above, though we there exist a considerable number of studies on comparison-shopping services, they are largely disintegrated from each other and failed to achieve synergy. On the other hand, comparison-shopping services or shopbot is both a Web-based technology and an innovative B2C ecommerce model. It is difficult to separate its technical design from its business model innovation. They are influenced by each other as indicated in the first chapter of this book.

In light of this situation, the goal of this book is to provide a cross-discipline summary of existing research on comparison-shopping, as well as online shopping in general. So researchers in their own disciplines like computer science, information system, marketing as well as psychology and economics could get inspirations from other disciplines and conduct more fruitful research in the future. Following is a brief explanation of each chapter of this book.

OVERVIEW

Chapter I gives an overview of comparison-shopping services and shopbot design. The explanation of comparison-shopping services and shopbot design is followed by a brief account of the evolution of comparison-shopping in the last 13 years. Then four important research topics are discussed. They are the design of shopbots, the behavior of online shoppers when using the services, comparison-shopping as a new channel for small online vendors to reach consumers, and the impact of comparison-shopping on the pricing structure of the market. Comparison-shopping for travelling and health services is also discussed.

Infrastructure and Shopbot Design Issues

Chapter II to IV provided us three frameworks for the design and application of comparison-shopping services.

Chapter II first identifies the limitations and drawbacks of the current design of shopbots, in particular, with regard to the underlying technology for building such systems. It then discusses how these technical limitations can be overcome by making use of the Semantic Web and Web Services and how shopbots can truly serve the user by providing personalized, impartial and flexible services. This chapter will be especially useful for shopbot developers who are considering integrating Web services into their design.

Chapter III addresses how to accommodate the semantic heterogeneity problems that arise when data is collected from different information sources around the world. In this chapter, authors use examples to illustrate three types of semantic heterogeneity problems that a global comparison service may encounter. Then they propose agent architecture to mediate between the heterogeneous data sources and the users (or user applications). This agent architecture provides three services: data access, entity resolution, and context mapping. The feasibility of using the architecture to enable global comparison is demonstrated with a prototype application. An evaluation of the solution shows that it is scalable due to its capability to automatically generate necessary conversions from a small set of predefined ones. This chapter will be especially useful in light of current expansion of comparison-shopping services across country boundaries so the same product offered by vendors in different countries could be compared together.

Chapter IV investigates the search pattern of online shoppers for a specific product. The authors identify three search patterns, sequential, agent search and iterative search. Comparison-shopping is one type of agent search pattern. They examine the factors affecting the choice and the outcome of agent search pattern compared to the other search patterns. They found that agent search seems to combine low search costs with high efficiency. Sequential search still emerges as the dominant search pattern even though it leads to the most expensive purchase. The iterative search pattern was the slowest of them all.

Theoretical Analysis of Comparison-Shopping

Chapter V to VI presented a few theoretical models for the study of comparison-shopping as well as online shopping in general.

Chapter V explores the relationship between the complexity of products and services and their implications for comparison-shopping for both consumers and vendors. Products and services are different in terms of complexity and convenience for evaluation. Thus, we may expect that online shoppers anticipate a different set of comparison information when buying a book compared with buying a computer. For the former, all they need is overall price and expected delivery time. For the latter, a good comparison site should provide side by side function comparison for similar configurations but different manufacturers.

Chapter VI presents a fuzzy logic to human reasoning about electronic commerce (e-commerce) transactions. It uncovers some hidden relationships between critical factors such as security, familiarity, design, and competitiveness about using ecommerce. It explores how some trust models have been developed to address these issues. Some models promote familiarity and competitiveness as part of the exercise of assessing online trust. It also analyzes the effect of these factors on the human decision process and how they affect the Business-to-Consumer (B2C) outcome when they are used collectively. Finally, it provides a toolset for B2C vendors to access and evaluate a user's transaction decision process and also an assisted reasoning tool for the online user.

Empirical Investigation of Comparison Shopping

Chapter VII to XI is a series of empirical investigations of comparison shopping as well as consumer behavior in electronic market.

Chapter VII investigates the comparison-shopping market from a vendor perspective. Here, comparison-shopping services become a new marketing and sales channel for small online vendors to compete with brand name online portals. Online vendors have a wide range selection of comparison-shopping services to participate. There are mainly two types of shopbots for them to choose: those general shopbots that provide product comparison across multiple heterogeneous product categories (like shopping.com) and the specialized shopbots that provide comparison within a single or a few highly-related product categories (like addall.com on books and music CD). The chapter then examines the effectiveness of small online vendors' shopbot selection strategy. By analyzing data from shopbots and online vendors, the authors found that there is significant positive correlation between the number of shopbots an online vendor participates and its traffic rank, which indicates the general effectiveness of using shopbots as a marketing channel. They also found that for online vendors competing on a niche product like college textbooks, participating specialized shopbots brings in higher traffic. For competing in the mainstream market, there is less significant correlation between participating general shopbots and higher traffic rank for vendors. The conclusion is that using general shopbots is a reactive strategy for small online vendors while using proper specialized shopbots could provide an edge for small online vendors.

Chapter VIII explores factors that influence the use of comparison-shopping search engines. The authors conducted a survey of 650 Spanish online shoppers. They use logistical regression to analyze the influence of demographics, surfing behaviour and purchase motivations on willingness to use search engines for online shopping. Data analysis shows that experience as an Internet user and an Internet shopper are negative key drivers of search engine use. Most of the utilitarian shopping motivations analyzed predict comparison shopping behaviour. Demographics are not determinant variables in the use of search engines in online purchases. This research enables companies to know the factors that potentially affect search engine use in online shopping decisions and the importance of using search engines in their communication campaigns.

Chapter IX explores acceptance of mobile shopping from a consumer perception prospective. Mobile shopping has been an emerging shopping mode in recent years. It provides many conveniences for shoppers to compare and purchase products in different locations. This chapter explores if perceived convenience, the most important feature of mobile shopping, is conducive or could positively influence the shopping intention of consumers. This has been extensively discussed in marketing and consumer behavior literature, but is not empirically validated in the context of mobile commerce. College students in Taiwan were used as subject. The data were analyzed to examine the relationship between perceived convenience and shopping intention. The result shows a significant relationship between the two variables, and a positive effect of convenience perception on shopping intention. The findings have practical implications for mobile commerce strategists by providing more understanding of the mobile commerce success factors from a consumer behavior point of view. It also provides useful information for mobile comparison-shopping service providers.

Chapter X identifies and analyzes the main factors that influence the users' perception regarding the service quality of online shopping agents, and consequently, the elements that determine the users' choice of online shopping agents. The various circumstantial or personal factors that can determine the choice of a specific searching strategy and shopping agent were tested. One hundred and twenty one people from the United Kingdom that have direct experience of using the shopping agents took the face to face interview regarding their use of shopping agents and their perception about the quality of shopping agents.

Chapter XI explores how multi-channel retailers utilizing an e-CRM approach stand to benefit in multiple arenas by providing targeted customer service as well as gaining operational and competitive advantages. To that end, it is apparent that multi-channel retailers better understand how satisfaction—a necessary condition for building customer loyalty—influences consumers' decisions to shop in one retail channel or another. The purpose of this study was to examine the influence of shopping experience on customers' future purchase intentions, both for the retailer and for the channel. Using a controlled experimental design, United States and European subjects responded to a series of questions regarding the likelihood of making a future purchase following either a positive or negative shopping encounter. Results suggest that shopping intentions vary based on the shopping channel as well as on cultural differences.

We also include a carefully selected reading list of comparison-shopping related research. It could be used both as a good reference and a starting point for new researchers in this field.

Yun Wan
University of Houston-Victoria, USA

Chapter I
Comparison–Shopping Services and Agent Design:
An Overview

Yun Wan
University of Houston-Victoria, USA

ABSTRACT

This chapter provides an overview of comparison-shopping services. Four research topics are covered: How to design a good shopbot? How Shoppers using the comparison-shopping services? What is the strategic use of comparison-shopping as a new channel by online vendors? And what is the impact of comparison-shopping on existing price equilibrium and electronic market structures? Emerging research topics like mobile comparison as well as comparison in health information are also discussed.

INTRODUCTION

Comparison-shopping was introduced into the World Wide Web in 1995 as the third mode of B2C ecommerce after online retailing and online auction. Shopbots became a popular shopping aid. They evolved from providing mere price information to offering a combination of product and vendor review as well as ratings for functions for a particular product or service. The vendor attitude towards comparison-shopping also evolved from doubt and refusal to complete acceptance and paying to participate.

Daily life is also influenced by this service. More and more people visit one of the major comparison-shopping sites before make any important purchase online. Cell phone users found they could be informed about online prices for the same product while they are shopping in a local store, and all they needed to do was to key in the barcode.

The concept of Web-based comparison-shopping was extended into the public domain too. Several state governments set up comparison-shopping websites to allow their residents to compare the service quality of hospitals and physicians as well as prescription drugs.

Web-based comparison-shopping seems also to have increased the general welfare of the society. We found term life insurance rates dropped around 8 to 15 percent because of the use of comparison-shopping sites.

The research in the field of comparison-shopping, however, is relatively scant. This book aims at providing a summary and general reference for existing research in this field.

WHAT ARE COMPARISON-SHOPPING SERVICES AND SHOPBOTS?

Comparison-shopping services refer to the Web-based service online shoppers use when they try to find product, price, and other related information aggregated from multiple vendor sites. Instead of visiting each vendor site offering the same product, online shoppers can view the prices from the comparison-shopping site and make shopping decisions. Once they made the decision, they will be redirected to the chosen vendor site to complete the purchase.

Shopbots is a term that refers to the software agent on the backend of the comparison-shopping service. Though there are variations in design and implementation for different services, shopping basic functions include data collection, storage, and presentation. It is the data collection methodology that differentiates most shopbot technologies, which could roughly be divided into two categories: data wrapping and data feeding.

Shopping.com is a typical comparison-shopping service. A shopper may use a keyword to locate a product or browse to find a product from existing categories. Once a product has been identified, the shopbot displays the prices from multiple vendors. In addition to prices, it also provides product review and vendor rating information to the shopper. On the back end, a sophisticated

shopbot technology was used to allow vendors to feed their product price information into the Shopping.com database. Meanwhile, these data are matched with product review and other cost information to be presented to shoppers upon request.

Shopping.com is only one example of comparison-shopping services. In other business categories like online travelling, comparison-shopping had already been the preferred business approach, even before the Web era, and their transformation to the Web was more challenged by existing business model than by technology.

Consider the so called "big three" in online travelling: Expedia.com, Travelocity.com, and Orbitz.com. All of them offer one-stop comparison-shopping for integrated services, including airfare, hotel, and car rental. Because of the maturity of such business categories, derived comparison-shopping services like Kayak.com also emerged to allow shoppers to compare offers provided by different comparison-shopping services. In personal finance, comparison-shopping services like bankrate.com allow individuals to find the best loan rate offered by different financial institutions for their mortgage and other financial needs.

Apart from pure online comparison-shopping services, in recent years, mobile comparison-shopping services have also emerged and have been adopted gradually. All these innovations have important implications for the future evolution of comparison-shopping services.

Compared with the explosive growth of comparison-shopping services and shopbots, research in this field is relatively limited. We classify the existing research in this field into following topics:

1. **Agent design:** How to design a good shopbot?
2. **User:** How shoppers use the comparison-shopping services?
3. **Vendor:** How online vendor use comparison-shopping strategically as a new channel?

4.   **Impact:** What impact comparison-shopping has on existing price equilibrium and electronic market structures?

Next, we first briefly illustrate the evolution of comparison-shopping services and then give a brief account for each above research topic.

A SHORT HISTORY OF COMPARISON-SHOPPING

The Emergence of Comparison-Shopping Services

Though it is widely believed that the BargainFinder experiment in 1995 was the first shopbot in the public domain, at least two successful comparison-shopping services preceded or went online at about the same time as the BargainFinder experiment: Killerapp.com and Pricewatch.com.

Motivated by finding the best price for computer accessories, Ben Chiu, a young Taiwanese immigrant to Canada, developed Killerapp.com to allow shoppers to find the price of a computer part from his website. The prices data were initially collected manually from computer-related trade journals and catalogs. Later, as a gifted programmer, Chiu coded a shopbot to collect price data from online vendors directly. Killerapp.com became a hit in 1997 and then was sold to CNET and integrated into its CNET shopper system in 1999.

During the same time period, a similar comparison-shopping service, Pricewatch.com, was also launched by a San Antonio entrepreneur, though it used a different approach to get the price data: instead of searching vendor sites or getting prices from magazines, it asked interested vendors to register with Pricewatch.com and then provide price data to the service.

The aforementioned two comparison-shopping services soon became established but received rel-atively little public attention and media exposure compared with the BargainFinder experiment.

BargainFinder was an agent designed for a phenomenal experiment conducted by then Andersen Consulting and Smart Store Research center in 1995. The intent of this experiment was not to test how an effective comparison-shopping service could assist consumers in online shopping; Instead, it was designed to test the impact on online vendors of the price arbitrage behavior of online shoppers.

When electronic commerce was in its infant age in 1995, online vendors doubted the Return on Investment or ROI of providing a premium site with rich product information. It was argued that online shoppers might take advantage of the rich product information provided by premium sites like Amazon and then purchase the actual product from another online vendor charging a lower price. This behavior may lead to a situation called Cournot equilibrium (Cournot, 1838), in which online vendors compete solely on price and compromised the online shopping experience, a ruinous outcome for both online retailers and consumers. The emergence of comparison-shopping services might aggravate the situation. Thus, to test the reactions of consumers and online vendors when such technology was available, BargainFinder was built and deployed on the Web for public trial.

The basic interaction mode between Bargain-Finder and online shoppers defined the style for all subsequent comparison-shopping agents:

"[BargainFinder] takes the name of a particular record album, searches for it at nine Internet stores, and returns to the user a list of the prices found. After the search, the user can select one of the stores and be taken electronically into it and directly to the album. He then has the option of getting more information, looking for other albums, or buying the product" (Krulwich, 1996).

It turns out that even though BargainFinder was a very primitive agent, most online shoppers would like to use it at least occasionally, according to the survey conducted during the experiment by the research team. Also, as expected, 90% BargainFinder users clicked on the cheapest price in the list.

The responses from online retailers diversified. Some refused to be contacted by the team or even blocked BargainFinder's access while others sought collaboration with BargainFinder and hoped the agent could search their sites too.

The initial reactions of both online shoppers and online retailers represented typical behaviors later experienced by subsequent comparison-shopping services. Though lasting only a short time, the BargainFinder experiment provided valuable information about the early attitudes of online shoppers and vendors when faced with the convenience (for shoppers) and challenges (for vendors) brought by comparison-shopping services.

Early Services and Shopbots

The popularity of the BargainFinder experiment motivated many techno-entrepreneurs. Hence, a large number of more sophisticated services emerged between 1996 and 1998. Some notable ones included Pricescan, Jango, Junglee, ComparisonNet, and mySimon.

Pricescan.com was launched in 1997. Like BargainFinder, Pricescan can search and aggregate price information from multiple online retailers for computer products. It could also provide nifty features like displaying high, low, and average price trends over the past several weeks for each product. Pricescan.com emphasized its pro-consumer position in providing price comparison information. According to David Cost, its co-founder, Pricescan did not charge online retailers to be listed in its database. In addition, to bring consumers the best prices, it obtained pricing information not only from vendor web

sites, but also from off-line sources like magazine ads. Pricescan.com survives through the revenue generated from the banner advertisements on its website.

Jango.com or NETBot was based on the prototype of a comparison-shopping agent designed by three researchers at University of Washington (Doorenbos, Etzioni, & Weld, 1997). A notable feature of Jango was that it could automate the building of a wrapper for a specific online vendor. Like BargainFinder, Jango was a research project-like agent and it was soon acquired by Excite for $35 million in stock in October 1997.

Junglee was the nickname of a comparison-shopping technology called virtual database (VDB) created in 1996 by three Stanford graduate students. The core of Junglee is an improved wrapper technique that made it easier to search for complex product information online (Gupta, 1998). Instead of having its own Web presence, Junglee.com provides search service to multiple online portals like Yahoo.com. Junglee.com was acquired by Amazon.com for $230 million in 1998.

CompareNet.com was founded by Trevor Traina and John Dunning in 1996 and backed by venture capitals like Media Technology and Intel. It provided comparison information on rather diverse categories like electronics, home office equipment, home appliances, automobiles, motorcycles, sporting goods, and software and computer peripherals. It was acquired by Microsoft in 1999.

MySimon.com was founded in 1998. It used its own proprietary wrapper technology ("Virtual Agent") to collect information from almost every online store. MySimon.com was noted for its easy-to-use interface and was acquired by CNET in 2000. Though being acquired, the brand name was kept and the service remained independent. It has became one of today's remaining major comparison-shopping agents.

As indicated above, from 1996 to 1998, we experienced the first booming of comparison-shopping services in the commodity market and they were characterized by innovative data wrapping technologies. However, many of them were subsequently acquired by major Web portals. Meanwhile, according to one estimation (Baumohl, 2000), there were only about 4 million online shoppers who used comparison-shopping agents in October 2000, less than 1% of the Internet users in the United States at that time. Thus, it was not a coincidence that few of the comparison-shopping services could take hold by amassing a large enough online shopper base.

The Service Became Established

By the end of 1999, the first boom of comparison-shopping agents came to its end due to acquisitions by established ecommerce portals. Another dampening factor was that many ecommerce portals could not strategically synthesize these technologies into their existing infrastructure. As a result, many excellent technologies and burgeoning brand names were abandoned and became obsolete. The acquisition of Junglee by Amazon was one example. The crumbling of Excite@Home in 2001 also ended the further development of Jango.com.

Thus, the comparison-shopping category in the B2C ecommerce market experienced its first reshuffling from 1999 to 2001. Meanwhile, the second generation of comparison-shopping services emerged with an emphasis on improved business models and alternative information retrieval technologies, the data feeding.

Since 2000, a new generation of comparison-shopping services has emerged and has become increasingly popular. If technical innovation characterized the first generation shopbots, business model innovation distinguished the second generation services. The top three are shopping.com (renamed from dealtime.com), PriceGrabber.com, and Shopzilla.com.

Shopping.com was founded in 1997 with Dealtime.com as its name. Together with CNET

Networks' mySimon.com, Shopping.com was among the first group of comparison-shopping service to use intensive marketing efforts to build the concept of Web-based comparison-shopping among consumers (White, 2000). With only three years development, Shopping.com managed to rank fourth (behind eBay, Amazon and Yahoo Shopping) among U.S. multi-category e-commerce sites in terms of unique monthly visitors.

PriceGrabber.com was another major comparison-shopping agent that emerged in 1999. It improved its service by incorporating tax and shipping costs into the price comparison as well as the availability of the product from vendors, though this innovation was soon emulated by other services.

Shopzilla.com was transformed from Bizrate.com in 2004. Bizrate.com was an online vendor rating service launched in 1996. Like other first generation ecommerce startups, Bizrate.com found the comparison-shopping service an attractive category and thus made a natural transformation to comparison-shopping since it already possessed an important element, the rating on online vendors.

Sensing the challenges from new startups and observing the opportunities of exponential growth in traffic, established online portals also began to add or transform their shopping channel into a comparison-shopping mode. By 2004, we found comparison-shopping services like Froogle by Google, Yahoo! Shopping by Yahoo, and MSN Shopping by Microsoft, etc.

In addition to online retailing, comparison-shopping was already established in online travel due to the travel industry's well-developed technology infrastructure, which dated back to the 1950s. In this category, we observed not only well-established services like Expedia.com, Orbitz.com, and Travelocity.com but also the agents of agents like Kayak.com, which aggregated and re-packaged information collected from existing comparison-shopping agents.

Comparison-shopping service was also a natural adaptation for finance and insurance businesses that are essentially broker-coordinated. In this category, most comparison-shopping agents served as an additional channel parallel to human brokers interacting with consumers, thus increasing customer experience, e.g. lendingtree.com.

Except in some unique cases (like Pricescan. com), almost all comparison-shopping agents that emerged in this period adopted a cost-per-click (CPC) business model, the model that evolved from Pricewatch.com. The CPC model allows startup agents like shopping.com and pricegrabber.com became profitable without an initial capital infusion by large venture capitals.

Consolidated Comparison-Shopping Services

Starting in 2003, major comparison-shopping services began to acquire more service features in order to compete with each other (Wan, Menon, & Ramaprasad, 2007).

The most notable case was Dealtime's acquisition of resellerratings.com and epinion.com in February and March 2003 respectively. Dealtime. com was mainly focused on price comparison. Resellerratings.com was one of the earliest agent services that focused on collecting ratings about online vendors. Epinion.com specialized in collecting product review information. When these three services merged, online shoppers could obtain in one search almost all they wanted regarding a product and making a shopping decision.

The popularity of comparison-shopping also has spread across national boundaries. In Europe, Kelkoo, which launched in 2000, the same year as Dealtime, experienced multiple mergers with other small Shopbots like Zoomit, Dondecomprar and Shopgenie. Within a few years, it became Europe's largest e-commerce website after Amazon and eBay and the largest e-commerce advertising platform both in the UK and Europe. It was acquired by Yahoo in 2004. Microsoft acquired another leading European comparison shopping service, Ciao, in 2008.

In online traveling, Expedia.com, Travelocity. com, and Orbitz.com became the top 3 consolidators. They integrated the airline, hotel and car rental information into their offerings. As a result of these consolidations, a more mature market structure was formed.

THE DESIGN OF THE SHOPBOTS

Comparison-shopping services are powered by shopbots. The core function of a shopbot is to retrieve data from multiple data sources, aggregate them, and then present them to online shoppers in certain ways so that shoppers can make shopping decisions efficiently.

Existing research on the design of shopbots mainly has two directions: data retrieval and data presentation.

When BargainFinder first emerged on the Web in 1995, price data retrieval and presentation were all integrated. The shopbot was activated by a query from users for a specific music title. The shopbot then searched a few pre-selected online music stores for this title with a pre-coded wrapper. Once it retrieved prices from these sites via the wrapper, it aggregated them. The results were then processed and presented in html format as a response to the user.

This straightforward method was sufficient for a light version service that only crawled a few online vendors, but it was inadequate for aggregating price information from a large number of vendors and complex site and web page structures.

Compared with the simple design of Bargain-Finder, Killerapp used a database to temporarily store the price data and then update it from time to time. Pricewatch asked its vendors to update its database directly. The latter two represented two distinctive methods of data retrieval: data wrapping and data feeding.

Data Extraction and Wrappers

Even before the emergence of shopbots on the Web, people were already exploring how to retrieve data from the Web. It turns out the biggest challenge was *how to automatically retrieve and integrate information from multiple and heterogeneous information sources in HTML format.* There is a historical limitation in HTML design: the tags used in the programming language are semi-structured, and they only describe how to *display* the data but not what the data is about. For example, the price of a product on an HTML page may have a tag to describe what font style and size should be used to display it in a browser, but there is no way to indicate whether this data is a price and whether it is a price for iPod or something else.

This design limitation posed a considerable challenge for intelligent software to identify a specific piece of information from different websites. Manual configuration of an agent was only applicable to a limited number of websites; thus, there was no scalability. An ideal agent has to automatically search the Web, identify the data organizing patterns, and then retrieve and transform them into a fully structured format. Hence, considerable research efforts were directed on the design of a perfect "wrapper" that could perform these tasks.

Based on the degree of automation, we have three types of wrappers: manual, semi-automatic, and fully automatic (Firat, 2003). The manual wrapper was designed and customized for a specific data source structure; thus, it cannot be used in other places. It also needs to be revised once the data source structure is changed. The semi-automatic wrapper needs manual indication of the structure of the information on Web page, and then the program generates corresponding rules to automatically retrieve the data for similar pages. The fully automatic wrapper uses inductive learning and other artificial intelligence methods to learn and retrieve information from the web

page directly. The learning stage usually involves training cases.

Though data wrapping is an independent way for shopbots to retrieve and present information for shoppers, the scalability of this method was limited because of the inconsistency of HTML page design as well as the demand for more complex data that could not be easily analyzed via full automation. Thus, few established comparison-shopping services could expect to expand based on this method only. Most services were using a mixture of both data wrapping and data feeding, as we explain in the next section.

Data Feeding

The data feeding method is essentially allowing or encouraging online vendors to provide their product price data to Shopbots in a specific data format defined by the comparison-shopping service provider. Data feeding technology is simpler than data wrapping, but there is a social challenge in it: online vendors may hesitate to list their goods on a comparison-shopping site to compete with their peers merely on price. This used to be a major concern and also led to some legal issues (Plitch, 2002).

The data feeding method can also be regarded as an online version of the catalog business model. Pricewatch.com was probably the first comparison-shopping services using this method. Back in 1995, instead of crawling the Web, it invited computer vendors to feed the data into its database using its proprietary DataLink system, which was essentially a data feeding system aggregating vendor data input.

The data feeding method is advantageous to comparison-shopping service providers. By using a pre-defined data input format, many errors in data retrieval can be avoided. Also, shopbots can receive more comprehensive information from vendors regarding the product, not only price but also shipping cost, inventory level, discount, as well as other information.

There are also advantages to vendors. They had more control over their presence in comparison-shopping. They could update their price whenever they wanted. Actually with the increasing number of comparison-shopping sites to participate and products to upload, vendors soon found the need to use a specialized data feed management service. Such needs fostered a niche business in managing data feeding to multiple comparison-shopping sites. And it was led by companies like *SingleFeed* and *FeedPerfect*. These companies allowed a vendor to upload the product data to their site, and then they would publish the data in all those leading comparison-shopping sites. Vendors then could manage their data from a single point instead of logging into each shopbot. More sophisticated services like ChannelAdvisor provided solutions for a vendor to monitor the ROI of its listings so the whole selling process could be more efficient.

The limitation of the data feeding solution is mainly the impact on online shoppers. By asking the participation of online vendors or even charging a fee from online vendors to participate, the comparison-shopping site essentially transforms itself from a buyer's agent into a seller's agent. So the welfare of consumers may be compromised.

Though data extraction and data feeding are two different technology tracks, most established comparison-shopping services use both technologies to optimize their offering. Data feeding is generally the major data retrieval method while data wrapping is complementary. This mixed solution trend is dominant currently.

Data Presentation

Regarding how to present the comparison data in a most effective way, there are several important findings since 2000.

First, the current data presentation style may overload online shoppers by too many choices. The popularity of comparison shopping among online shoppers has attracted many online vendors to participate. As a result, we consumers experienced an increasing number of offerings for the same product from the popular comparison-shopping sites. It is not uncommon for a shopper to get more than one hundred selections for one popular electronic product when searching a comparison-shopping site.

Screening and making a decision become more and more stressful in such situations, and consumers may be overloaded by so many choices. Indeed, in one research by Iyengar and Lepper (2000), they found that when exotic jam was offered to customers in a local grocery store, the probability that a customer would buy one was negatively related to the number of different choices presented to them. In other words, the more choices available, the less likely they were to make the purchase. Wan (2005) designed an experiment to test similar symptoms in a Web-based comparison-shopping environment. It was found that when the number of choices and/or number of attributes for each choice exceeded certain limits, the decision quality decreased dramatically.

Though choice overload could be a big hurdle for current techno-business models of comparison-shopping services, the solution is restricted by service providers' incentives to list more products and generate more revenues. This leads to the second question: Are more listings always good for service providers?

Depending on your own judgement, the answer is probably "no" because it may reduce the purchase rate and eventually decrease their competitiveness compared with other online channels.

In a related study by Montgomery, Hosanagar, Krishnan, and Clay (2004), they assume a scenario in which a shopbot searches all available vendors and retrieves all results to the shopper. However, because there is a waiting time cost to the shopper as well as redundant or dominant choices being unnecessarily presented, the utility of the shopper was compromised. Thus, they proposed that shopbot designs can be improved by developing a utility model of consumer purchasing behavior. The shopbot could utilize this model to decide which stores to search, how long to wait, and which offers to present to the user. Because this utility model considers the intrinsic value of the product and its attributes, the disutility associated with waiting, and the cognitive costs associated with evaluating the offers retrieved, it could increase the utility of the user. They use six months of data collected from an online book comparison shopping site to demonstrate the effectiveness of their model.

Empirically, by intelligently filtering the choices and removing those obviously dominated choices, comparison-shopping service providers could save response time, reduce overhead traffic, and mitigate the choice overload impact on shoppers. Eventually, such design may improve the purchase probability and thus increase the revenue as well.

HOW SHOPPERS USING THE COMPARISON-SHOPPING SERVICES

Though shopbots are being implemented in different technologies, sometimes as far from each other as complete data feeding is from data extraction -- from consumer perspective, such differences are transparent. For most online shoppers, comparison-shopping services decreased their search cost and thus potentially increased the welfare of the consumer.

However, certain shopper behaviors prevent consumers from fully utilizing the characters and features of comparison-shopping services. Thus, more research is needed in this area to help us better understand the interaction pattern between shoppers and shopbots.

We review this topic by first explaining how online retailing is different from its brick and mortar counterpart. Then we review existing research on user behavior when interacting with shopbot-like agents. After that, we review major theories that can be used to further explore this issue.

The Significance of Online Retailing

The emergence and commercialization of Internet provides a completely new channel for consumer shopping – online shopping. Compared with traditional channels, this online channel has two distinctive features: a low entry barrier and almost unlimited shelf space.

As described in the seminal book *"Information Rules"* (Shapiro & Varian, 1998), the online channel has an unprecedented low entry cost for potential retailers. Nowadays, any individual can launch an ecommerce site by uploading the product data to a template provided by ISPs with only slight customization of the interface. As a result, there are an increasing number of small online retailers that are operated by only one or two individuals.

Online retailers also have the unique privilege of almost unlimited shelf space. For example, Wal-Mart, the world's biggest brick-and-mortar chain store, at any one time has 100,000 items available on the shelf in a typical Supercenter. However, Amazon.com, the biggest online store can already offer as many as 18 million unique items even without the consideration of third-party vendors who utilize the platform provided by Amazon to sell their own customer base.

These two features have led to an exponential increase in product offerings online in the past 10 years, which have enriched our shopping experience. However, with so many vendors available online, finding them and the products they offer is not as easy as expected unless one is very savvy in searching the Web. In most cases, online shoppers eventually make their purchase from a few established online portals like Amazon.com. Thus, comparison-shopping services have become a necessity for helping consumers locate the best price from the inside of the Web.

Theories on User Shopping Behavior

To design an interface of shopbots that could accommodate the decision-making behavior of shoppers, the following theories have been used in research on shopping behavior by many existing studies and maybe useful.

Multi-Attribute Utility Theory

Generally speaking, any individual decision task that involves choosing from several alternatives can be considered as a preferential choice problem. The normative theory to explain such a process is multi-attribute utility theory, or MAUT (Raiffa & Keeney, 1976). Early applications of MAUT focus on public sector decisions and public policy issues. These decisions not only have multiple objectives but also involve multiple constituencies that will be affected in different ways by the decision. Under the guidance of Ralph Keeney and Howard Raiffa, many power plant decisions were made using MAUT. The military also used this technique because the design of major new weapons systems always involves tradeoffs among cost, weight, durability, lethality, and survivability.

MAUT assumes the decision-maker can subjectively assign a weight to each attribute and calculate the utility of each choice by multiplying the weight and value of each attribute then adding them together. As a result, each alternative has a corresponding utility. Comparison can be performed and a decision can be made by choosing the alternative that has the highest utility. MAUT is a normative decision-making theory in the sense that it tells us what we "ought" to act based upon measurements of our utility for different criteria and combinations of them.

It turns out the default design for many comparison-shopping services is based upon MAUT. For example, most shopbots list their offerings in a tabular format and allow customers to compare choices by their aggregated utilities. Some experiments indicated that using a shopbot designed on this principle could increase the efficiency and effectiveness of decision-making in general circumstances (Haubl & Murray, 2003; Haubl & Trifts, 2000).

However, empirical research also found that consumers do not always make decisions based on MAUT because of its relative high demand for cognitive efforts. This is especially true when online shoppers are making trivial shopping decisions, e.g. buying a $10 paperback bestseller. In such cases, when consumers have to choose from many alternatives, instead of making thoughtful comparisons as described in MAUT, they may use heuristics.

Heuristic and Heuristic Strategies

Heuristics are frequently observed in humans' decision-making process due to a lack of complete information as well as limited cognition (Simon, 1955, 1956). While Simon's model was widely accepted by decision-making researchers, it was too general to answer specific questions about why a decision-maker opts for one particular choice over others. Research on cognitive heuristics and adaptive algorithms provides a better explanation.

Payne, Bettman, and Johnson (1993) proposed a contingency model of decision-making and conducted a series of experiments to examine how decision-makers use heuristics when being presented a decision task with many similar choices. Based on Herbert Simon's "bounded rationality" theory, Payne and his colleagues regard the human mind as a "limited-capacity information processor" with "multiple goals" for a specific decision-making problem. Because of the limitations of the human mind, decision-makers tend to use various heuristic strategies to make decisions. These heuristic strategies can be roughly divided into two categories: compensatory and non-compensatory. Compensatory strategies are normative strategies that emphasize the consideration of all relevant attributes for each choice, while non-compensatory strategies are heuristics that emphasize saving efforts and only focus on relevant attributes. Among these, elimination-by-aspects (EBA) or "row-based" elimination strategy (Tversky, 1972) is probably the best match to shoppers' behavior when using comparison-shopping services.

When decision-makers or shoppers face many choices, they usually switch from compensatory strategies to non-compensatory strategies (Einhorn, 1970; Tversky, 1972). But most non-compensatory heuristics could eliminate potentially high-quality choices. Thus, when online shoppers are provided with an increasing number of choices by shopbots, the quality of their decision may decrease. As mentioned in the previous section, a better design of the shopbot could mitigate this problem. But fundamentally, the data feeding business model motivated the service provider to cram as many options as possible into the response page for consumers. A better solution might lie in the revision of both the technology and the business model.

The Least Effort Principle

If consumers are provided with better designed shopbots and comparison tools, will they be able to use them to make a better choice?

As discussed in previous sections, in the rational view, decision-makers should always use strategies that optimize the decision outcome. In reality, heuristics are frequently used when people make choices. These heuristic behaviors are usually not the strategies that lead to optimal outcome, but they are quicker and easier to perform. This phenomenon was probably first systematically

observed by Zipf (1949), who used the term *principle of least effort* to describe it.

According to Zipf's least-effort principle, the decision-maker adopts a decision strategy not solely based on the decision quality the strategy produces but also intuitively considers the effort a strategy demands. As long as the minimum decision quality is met, the strategy that requires the least cognitive effort will be adopted—usually those very familiar and fully routinized heuristic strategies. The least-effort principle tells us that human beings always try to minimize their effort in decision-making as long as the decision quality meets the minimum criteria.

The least-effort principle was observed in experiments conducted by Todd (1988) and Todd and Benbasat (1992, 1999). In their experiments, when provided with both compensatory and non-compensatory tools in a shopbot-like interface with decision tasks, consumers chose to use non-compensatory tools, though the compensatory tools would have generated higher quality results. Subjects merely chose a satisfying result and reserved effort for harder decisions.

The Cognitive Process of Decision-Making

Online shoppers' behavior with comparison-shopping services may also relate to their own shopping experience and their familiarity with the product or services.

From this perspective, it is generally believed that there are three types of consumer decision-making modes. They are routinized response behavior (RRB), limited problem solving (LPS), and extensive problem solving (EPS) (Howard, 1977). From RRB to EPS, consumers become less familiar with the products so they need more effort and routines to conduct the decision-making task. In the RRB mode, decision-makers are very familiar with the product they are looking at; they are more concerned with impersonal information (price, after-sale service quality, etc.). In EPS mode, decision-makers are very unfamiliar with the product, so a lot of additional cognitive effort is invested in forming the concept of the product, in addition to processing impersonal information.

So far there is little research that addresses the familiarity and experience issue in comparison-shopping.

COMPARISON-SHOPPING AS A NEW SALES CHANNEL

With the popularity of comparison-shopping, more and more small vendors found it an effective channel to reach more price sensitive customers. Thus, they have the incentive to use the shopbots proactively as new sales channels. Because of this, those established comparison-shopping services could command a premium participation fee as well as a referral fee from small online vendors.

Because of the competition pressure from peers, many vendors found it important to list their product on not only one comparison service but all those used by their competitors. On the other side, there is a fixed cost for each participation and a variable cost for each referral that may or may not lead into a sale. Thus, if we consider each comparison-shopping site as a channel to reach consumers, it is important for an online vendor to formulate a viable channel selection strategy. It could be identifying one most profitable channel or a combination of channels.

From a sales and marketing channel perspective, there are two types of comparison-shopping services, those general ones that provide comparison-shopping for multiple categories of commodities or even services (e.g. shopping.com or pricegrabber.com); and those specialized ones that provide comparison service for a single or a few closely related commodity categories (e.g. book

price comparison site addall.com or computer and accessories comparison site pricewatch.com).

Depending on the business, choosing a general or a specialized comparison-shopping service or a combination of sites may have different effects on the business's sales performance.

THE IMPACT OF COMPARISON-SHOPPING SERVICES

How will comparison-shopping influence and shape the landscape of electronic commerce or the economic status quo in general?

Empirically, comparison-shopping has established its position among the top 3 online shopping options, together with online retailing and online auction. Since 2003, the traffic rank for the leading comparison-shopping service provider, shopping.com, has been right after Amazon and eBay among major B2C ecommerce portals, as measured by comScore and other Internet Information Providers.

Comparison-shopping also significantly changed the pricing structure of certain service sectors. For example, in an empirical study by Brown and Goolsbee (2002) on comparison-shopping sites for life insurance policies, they found that with micro data on individual insurance policies and with individual and policy characteristics controlled for, increases in Internet use significantly reduced the price of term life insurance. Such increase did not happen before the comparison sites began, nor for insurance types that were not covered by these sites. They also found that such usage reduced the term life price by 8 to 15 percent.

However, the impact of comparison-shopping is also limited by other product and service factors. For example, Brynjolfsson and Smith (2000) found that when consumers use price shopbots to search for price information on books and CDs, instead of picking the online book vendor offering the lowest price, they tended to choose the branded vendor who charged the lowest premium price. As a result, even faced with price competition from small online vendors via comparison-shopping services, branded online vendors like Amazon. com could still command a premium price on products.

Thus, we may conclude that though there are impacts of comparison-shopping on the pricing structure of products and services, exactly how such impacts work out on different products and services needs to be explored separately. It depends on many factors like the complexity in evaluating the quality of the product or service.

In a forward look, Kephart and his colleagues simulated a software bot-enabled electronic commerce market where "billions of software agents exchange information goods with humans and other agents," of which, shopbots is one important software agent category (Kephart & Greenwald, 1999, 2000; Kephart, Hanson, & Greenwald, 2000). Through simulation on different pricing behavior of Shopbots, it was found that both beneficial and harmful collective behaviors that could arise in such system, which could lead to undesired phenomena.

COMPARISON-SHOPPING IN ONLINE TRAVELLING AND HEALTH CARE

In addition to the commodity market, comparison-shopping is also widely adopted in many service sectors like online travelling and health care.

Because of the existence of agents in many service sectors, computerized comparison information was already available before the emergence of the Web. For example, the SABRE system of American Airlines began to provide airfare comparison service for its agents back in the 1960s. So for those already computerized

service sectors, migration to the Web is largely a shift for consumers to get information from comparison-shopping agents instead of the traditional human agents.

Travelling

Unlike online retailing, which has been a relatively new innovation since 1994, the travel industry was "wired" much earlier and has more sophisticated information aggregation and comparison technology except that it is the agent, not consumers, who can access the information. This was especially the case for the airline industry.

Back in the late 1950s and early 1960s, due to the tremendous growth of the number of air travelers and increasing size of airplanes, the traditional manual reservation and ticket inventory checking solution could no longer keep up with the demand. As a result, major airline companies began to develop fully automated airline reservation systems like SABRE with the technical assistance of IBM and other IT companies. The main purpose of these systems was to connect the reservation with the seat inventory information so people could check the availability of seats in real time and make reservations on the spot. Once these systems became stable, major airlines realized that they could outsource the ticket booking function to travel agents. Thus a new competition emerged between major airlines to compete for travel agents to use their systems. Small airlines also decided to join such systems so their flight and ticket information could also be accessed by agents. SABRE and Apollo became two major systems, and they were called consolidators. Gradually, agent-oriented comparison-shopping infrastructures were established within such systems.

With the introduction of the Web, many travelling companies found they could sell directly to customers. Thus, the agent-mediated market structure was transformed, and traditional agents were dis-intermediated. The debut of Expedia.com by Microsoft in 1996 ushered the travel industry into this new competition age. SABRE also launched Travelocity.com in the same year in order to compete. With the integration of car rental and hotel information systems, the so-called Global Distrubtion Systems were formed. Currenlty, the three major competitors are Expedia.com, Travelocity.com and Orbitz.com.

Meanwhile, shopbots was also characterized by continuous innovations. The most notable one included the derivative comparison-shopping agents, like Kayak.com, that could retrieve information from existing comparison-shopping services (Wan et al., 2007); and the ITA software, which focuses on calculating optimal travel routes.

Health Services

The scenario of health services is different from online travel.

On one side, services like health insurance were transformed on the Web very early. Comparison-shopping on the best insurance rates was available in the mid 90s, if not earlier. This is because insurance industry is coordinated by brokers and it is a natural extension for brokers to set up a Web presence, basically another channel for attracting consumers.

On the other side, comparison services on in-patient/operation cost, hospital/clinic/doctor evaluation information, and pharmacy cost, etc. are lagging behind and only became available recently.

Pharmeutical cost was the second comparable information category available on the Web. Major players include destinationrx.com and price-rx.com. The in-patient/operation cost information as well as evaluation information for hospital and doctors are probably the most important health information a consumer needs to know.

One reason for pharmeutical cost lagging behind is that information is only available via

non-profit organizations or government agencies like the US Department of Health and Human Services (www.hospitalcompare.hhs.gov), which provides comparison information on hospitals, and the Joint Commission (www.jcaho.org), which provides information on hospitals as well as other health care service providers. The latter is responsible for accreditation and certification of hospitals, which allows it to get such information on quality of services during evaluation.

Recently, some state governments began to provide evaluation information for hospitals and doctors. Massachusetts Health Quality Partners (MHQP), for example, is an independent state agency that monitors the quality of health services in Massachusetts. It provides side-by-side comparisons to its residents on the quality of service of clinics in the state.

Recently, a few commercial sites began to integrate this information and provide their users a comprehensive comparison-shopping environment. Vimo was probably the first one. According to the site launched in 2006:

"Vimo is the nation's first integrated comparison-shopping portal for healthcare products and services. On January 24, 2006 we launched a website that allows businesses and consumers to research, rate and purchase health insurance plans and Health Savings Accounts (HSAs), and choose doctors from across the country. Vimo brings together a variety of private and public data sources so that shoppers can find a physician and compare hospital prices for medical procedures. Vimo users can read and post reviews about any of the services or products available." Source URL: http://www.vimo.com/html/about.php

It turns out that collecting feedback from patients about hospitals, doctors and dentists is not a technical challenge for most heath-related sites. There are many Websites that help people find doctors, hospitals, dentists, etc. But few of them ask the patient to provide feedback. It is understandable that such sites survive on referral fees paid by doctors, but they may not realize that by accumulating feedback information from consumers, they become the Amazon of health care. In contrast, established online portals do not have such conflict-of-interests concerns so the feedback features are added naturally on their health-related site, like the recently launched local dentist evaluation in Live Search by Microsoft.

With the information revolution in health services, comparison-shopping would become easier and more efficient in this sector. We expect more research in the future on this topic.

FUTURE RESEARCH

There are many interesting directions for the future research of comparison-shopping services and the design of shopbots.

Mobile Comparison

With the ubiquitous of Web-enabled mobile devices like iPhone, comparison-shopping services could be extended into the brick-and-mortar store. Services like Frucall already allow consumers to comparison-shop a product in a store with the same product offered by online stores. All customers need to do is provide the bar code or ISBN of the product via their mobile device.

There is another innovation to provide a comparison for a product between online and local offerings. For example, ShopLocal.com provides product price comparisons from popular online stores as well as local stores based on a zip code provided by the user.

It is probably a natural move for future services to combine both mobile comparison and local comparison so consumers can get price quotes on the spot from both online and nearby brick and mortar stores.

We expect such services may not only change the price structure but also the product portfolio for both online and local stores.

Bundled Comparison

Though comparison-shopping has been around for 13 years, there is still relatively little progress in bundled comparison. That is if a consumer wants to buy several products, he may wish to compare bundled offers instead of comparing each individual piece. A simple example is buying textbooks at the beginning of the semester: students may want to buy all textbooks from one book store that offers the best price instead of comparison-shopping each one separately.

Currently, a UK-based comparison-shopping service, mySupermarke.co.uk, does provide bundled comparison for groceries. Shoppers could select multiple groceries and put them into their online shopping cart. The service could calculate which local grocery store could offer the best price for them, and the shopper could be redirected to the grocery website to complete the transaction. Around 2006, the company claims an average online grocery cart includes approximately 50 items, with a total cost of between $160 to $220. Consumers could save an average 20 percent per cart.

How to design such agents to provide bundled comparisons for other commodities and services could be an interesting challenge.

Feature and Function Comparison

Most comparison-shopping services focus on price comparison on the same product offered by different online vendors. A few provide limited feature and function comparison across similar products. There is no comparison across product categories. On the other side, new products are being invented every day. Many of them serve the same function needs but belong to different product categories. Thus, it will be helpful if a comparison-shopping service could allow consumers to select products based on a specific feature or function.

CONCLUSION

In this overview, we covered several major topics of comparison-shopping service and agent design. We demonstrated that though comparison-shopping services have developed into a popular online shopping channel, there are many issues that need to be investigated about this new phenomenon. In addition, the innovation on comparison-shopping service and shopbots design is still far from satisfactory. We expect this book could provide some aspirations for new research and innovation in this area.

REFERENCES

Baumohl, B. (2000). Can you really trust those bots? *TIME Magazine, 156,* 80.

Brown, J. R., & Goolsbee, A. (2002). Does the Internet make markets more competitive? Evidence from the Life Insurance Industry. *Journal of Political Economy, 110*(3), 481-507.

Brynjolfsson, E., & Smith, M. D. (2000). The great equalizer? consumer choice behavior at Internet shopbots. *Working Paper.*

Cournot, A. (1838). *Researches into the Mathematical Principles of the Theory of Wealth.* New York: Macmillan.

Doorenbos, R. B., Etzioni, O., & Weld, D. S. (1997). *A scalable comparison-shopping agent for the World Wide Web.* Paper presented at the International Conference on Autonomous Agents, Marina del Rey, California.

Einhorn, H. J. (1970). The use of nonlinear, noncompensatory models in decision making. *Psychological Bulletin, 73*(211-230).

Firat, A. (2003). *Information integration using contextual knowledge and ontology merging.* Massachusetts Institute of Technology, Cambridge, MA`.

Gupta, A. (1998). *Junglee: integrating data of all shapes and sizes.* Paper presented at the Fourteenth International Conference on Data Engineering, Orlando, FL.

Haubl, G., & Murray, K. B. (2003). Preference construction and persistence in digital marketplaces: The role of electronic recommendation agents. *Journal of Consumer Psychology, 13*(1&2), 75-91.

Haubl, G., & Trifts, V. (2000). Consumer decision making in online shopping environments: the effects of interactive decision aids. *Marketing Science, 19*(1), 4-21.

Howard, J. A. (1977). *Consumer Behavior: Application of Theory.* New York: McGraw-Hill.

Iyengar, S. S., & Lepper, M. R. (2000). When Choice is Demotivating: Can One Desire Too Much of a Good Thing? *Journal of Personality and Social Psychology, 79*(6), 12.

Kephart, J. O., & Greenwald, A. R. (1999). *Shopbot economics.* Paper presented at the International Conference on Autonomous Agents, Seattle, Washington, United States.

Kephart, J. O., & Greenwald, A. R. (2000). When Bots Collide. *Harvard Business Review, 78*(4), 17-18.

Kephart, J. O., Hanson, J. E., & Greenwald, A. R. (2000). Dynamic pricing by software agents. *Computer Networks, 32*(6), 731-752.

Krulwich, B. (1996). The BargainFinder Agent: Comparison Price Shopping on the Internet. In J.

Williams (Ed.), *Bots, and Other Internet Beasties* (pp. 257-263). Indianapolis: Macmillan Computer Publishing.

Montgomery, A. L., Hosanagar, K., Krishnan, R., & Clay, K. B. (2004). Designing a Better Shopbot. *Management Science, 50*(2), 189-206.

Payne, J. W., Bettman, J. R., & Johnson, E. J. (1993). *The adaptive decision maker.* Cambridge: Cambridge University Press.

Plitch, P. (2002). E-Commerce (A Special Report): The Rules --- Law: Are Bots Legal? --- Comparison-shopping sites say they make the Web manageable; Critics say they trespass. *Wall Street Journal, 240*(54), R.13.

Raiffa, H., & Keeney, R. L. (1976). *Decisions with Multiple Objectives.* New York: Wiley.

Shapiro, C., & Varian, H. R. (1998). *Information Rules: A Strategic Guide to the Network Economy.* Cambridge, MA: Harvard Business School Press.

Simon, H. A. (1955). A behavioral model of rational choice. *Quarterly Journal of Economics, 69*(1), 20.

Simon, H. A. (1956). Rational choice and the structure of the environment. *Psychological Review, 63*, 129-138.

Todd, P., & Benbasat, I. (1992). The Use of Information in Decision Making: An Experimental Investigation of the Impact of Computer-Based Decision Aids. *MIS Quarterly, 16*(3), 373-393.

Todd, P., & Benbasat, I. (1999). Evaluating the Impact of DSS, Cognitive Effort, and Incentives on Strategy Selection. *Information Systems Research, 10*(4), 356-374.

Todd, P. A. (1988). *An Experimental Investigation of the Impact of Computer Based Decision Aids on the Process of Preferential Choice.* The University of British Columbia, Vancouver.

Tversky, A. (1972). Elimination by aspects: A theory of choice. *Psychological Review, 79*(281-299).

Wan, Y. (2005). *The Impact of Web-based Product Comparison Agent on Choice Overload in Online Individual Decision-Making.* University of Illinois at Chicago, Chicago.

Wan, Y., Menon, S., & Ramaprasad, A. (2007). A Classification of Product Comparison Agents. *Communications of the ACM, 50*(8), 65-71.

White, E. (2000). E-Commerce (A Special Report): The Lessons We've Learned --- Comparison Shopping: No Comparison --- Shopping 'bots' were supposed to unleash brutal price wars. Why haven't they? . *Wall Street Journal*, R.18.

Zipf, G. K. (1949). *Human Behavior and the Principle of Least Effort: An introduciton to Human Ecology.* Cambridge: Addison-Wesley Press.

KEY TERMS

BargainFinder Experiment: In 1995, a shopbot named BargainFinder was launched by a group of researchers in then Andersen Consulting to test the reaction of consumers and online vendors. It received major media coverage and became one of the first shopbots that came into public attention.

Bundled Comparison: A feature of comparison-shopping service that allows shoppers to compare price for multiple products as a whole offered by different online vendors.

Choice Overload: A scenario when a consumer is being overwhelmed and hesitating to make decisions when facing with too many choices.

Comparison-Shopping Services: The Web-based services that online shoppers use when they try to find product prices and other related information aggregated from multiple vendor sites.

Data Feeding: A data retrieval technique that allow users to feed information into a shopbot database in a pre-defined format. Data feeding was widely used in popular shopbots.

Data Wrapping: A data retrieval technique that can be either automatically or manually created to identify information contained in a HTML web page and then transform them into a consistent format for further processing. Data wrapping technology was widely used in early shopbots.

The Least Effort Principle: A decision-making theory that human beings always try to minimize their effort in decision-making as long as the decision quality meets the minimum criteria.

Mobile Comparison: A feature of comparison-shopping service that allows a shopper to interact with shopbot via mobile devices.

Multi Attribute Utility Theory: A decision-making theory that assume human beings can subjectively assign a weight to each attribute and calculate the utility of each choice by multiplying the weight and value of each attribute then adding them together. As a result, each alternative has a corresponding utility. Comparison and a decision can be made by choosing the alternative that has the highest utility.

Shopbot: The software agent powered the comparison-shopping service. Though there are variations in design and implementation for different services, the basic functions include data gathering, storage, and presentation. There are two main data retrieval methods: data wrapping and data feeding.

Chapter II
The Next Generation of Shopbots:
Semantic Interoperability and Personalization

Maria Fasli
University of Essex, UK

ABSTRACT

The huge growth of e-commerce has had a profound impact on users who can now choose from a vast number of options online. Inevitably, as the number of choices has increased, so has the need for tools to help users organize, manage and utilize information on these for better decision-making. Comparison shopping agents or shopbots can help users decide what to buy and enhance their online shopping experience. However, despite the high expectations, the immense potential of shopbots has not been fully realized. In this chapter, the author identifies the limitations and drawbacks of current shopbots, in particular, with regard to the underlying technology for building such systems. She then discusses how these technical limitations can be overcome by making use of the Semantic Web and Web Services. She also considers how shopbots can truly serve the user by providing personalized, impartial and flexible services.

INTRODUCTION

The phenomenal growth of the Internet has had a profound impact on the way organizations and individuals conduct business. In particular, the nature of business-to-consumer commerce (B2C)

has changed dramatically over the last decade. Businesses and organizations have recognized the potential of the Internet and the World Wide Web as the means to reach potential customers on a scale never before possible or imaginable. To begin with, users were wary of online shopping and reluctant to provide personal and financial information (credit card details, date of birth, bank accounts etc.). This was mainly due to fear of fraud and loss of privacy. But with the recent advances in security and cryptography (Stallings, 2003), users have gradually become more familiar with the technology and more willing to engage in e-commerce activities. As a result, e-commerce sites abound offering a wide range of services and products. Online users can now shop from the privacy of their homes for almost anything ranging from groceries to holidays and cars (Fasli, 2006). Hence, slowly but steadily, the traditional shopping trip has been transformed into a virtual one: instead of having to visit a conventional shopping mall, a user may now visit virtual shopping malls which may be operating from a different city, state, country or even continent than the one the user is physically located.

Reflecting the changing consumer attitudes, online transactions have increased dramatically over the last few years (Forrester Research, 2002; Shop.org, 2007). Retail e-commerce sales in the U.S. have risen steadily since 1999 (when

e-commerce sales were first tracked) as can be seen in Figure 1. The estimated U.S. retail e-commerce sales for the second quarter of 2008 (figures are adjusted for seasonal variation, but not for price changes) was $34.6 billion which amounts to 3.3% of the total sales figure. This is an approximate increase of 9.5% from the second quarter of 2007.

In January 2008 Nielsen (Nielsen Media Research, 2008) reported that the number of users that have shopped online was up 40% in two years amounting to 875 million. According to the Nielsen report the most popular commodities purchased online are (1) books; (2) clothing, accessories and shoes; (3) DVDs, games and CDs; (4) airline tickets; and (5) electronic equipment such as cameras, computers and computer parts.

But this abundance of products, services and information, has made it all the more difficult for users to decide what to buy and where from. Inevitably, as the number of choices has grown, so has the need for tools to help users organize, manage and utilize this information for better decision making. Agent technology can help us-

Figure 1. Estimated quarterly U.S. retail e-commerce sales as a percent of total quarterly retail sales between 4th quarter 1999 – 2nd quarter 2008 (source: (US Census Bureau News, August 2008))

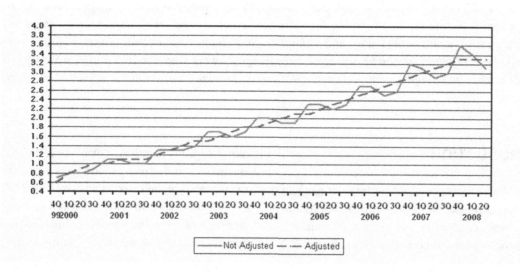

ers sift through information and find what they require. Unlike traditional software, agents are semi-autonomous, proactive, reactive and continuously running entities (Guttman et al., 1999) that can assist the user in a variety of contexts. In particular, the potential for agents in e-commerce is immense – e-commerce is considered by some researchers and technology analysts as the prospective killer application for agents (Ulfelder, 2000). The term comparison shopping agent or *shopbot* has been coined to describe systems that can help users decide what to buy and enhance their shopping experience. A shopbot is an agent that operates online, receives requests from users for products and services and then can query vendors and providers and retrieve and compare relevant information such as price, delivery options, warranty etc.

Shopbots can alleviate the significant burden of finding products and services and comparing prices and other attributes, ultimately enhancing the users' shopping experience while saving them time and money. However, despite the high expectations (Edwards, 2000), the immense potential of shopbots has not been fully realized. This is primarily due to current technical limitations as shopbots cannot 'understand' the information that they retrieve and moreover, they cannot discover and query vendors dynamically. This chapter discusses the current limitations of shopbots as well as how these can be addressed through the use of Semantic Web technologies and Web Services. In addition, we also discuss a number of issues that need to be taken into account in creating the next generation of shopbots that will truly serve the needs of the user and enhance their shopping experience.

The chapter is organized as follows. Next we discuss how shopbots can enhance the user's online shopping experience. The following section presents a concise literature review of characteristic shopping agents and comparison shopping sites. The current technological limitations are also discussed. Section 4 provides a brief overview of the technologies behind Semantic Web Services. Next we present our vision of the third generation of shopbots and how semantic interoperability can be facilitated. The penultimate section describes the next step in the evolution of shopbots – personalization – and discusses the issues that need to be addressed in order for shopbots to truly work for the user. The chapter closes with a summary and the conclusions.

ENHANCING THE ONLINE SHOPPING EXPERIENCE

Users looking for products online can currently visit sites that they have previously identified, or use a standard search engine and keyword retrieval to identify potential vendors. In each site that the user visits, she has to search for the product and find out the price, product specification and other related information. This simple approach has a number of shortcomings (Meczer et al., 2002). First, there may be hundreds of vendors selling the same or very similar products. Unless the user has knowledge of specific vendors selling the desired products, she is faced with the problem of which of these to visit and when is it that enough have been visited to acquire the necessary information. Visiting multiple vendors requires considerable time, but not visiting enough may lead to a suboptimal decision. Second, identifying vendors using classical search engines and keywords may not be the best way to go about it, as the returned set of vendors may be biased in favor of larger sites, which may not necessarily offer the best prices. Third, if the user requires several items, there may be no single site that caters for all her shopping needs, which increases the search time for each new product category. Finally, every time a new site is visited the user has to get acquainted with new interfaces which again increases the search time and unavoidably hinders impulse shopping.

To help customers stay informed vendors may allow them to sign up to receive alerts and notifications for instance, when the price of a product changes or it becomes available. Such services are not personalized. Users typically have to complete long surveys describing their interests and preferences. Furthermore to receive email notifications they are also required to reveal part of their identity. As a result, the users' privacy is weakened, and users may be reluctant to sign up for such services.

Hence, although information on different products and services is at one's fingertips, users increasingly require assistance, guidance and support in the vast information space of the Internet (Fasli, 2006). There is simply too much information for an individual to process; information overload is an undisputed fact. Consequently, tools that will allow users to manage and utilize information for better decision making are essential. This is the role that software agents are called upon to play. Agents are pieces of software (and/or hardware) that exhibit a number of characteristics such as autonomy, pro-activeness, reactiveness and the ability to collaborate and coordinate with other (human or software) agents (Fasli, 2007a; Wooldridge and Jennings, 1995). They may also be able to learn and adapt. Such 'smart' pieces of software represent the user and act on her behalf. Comparison shopping agents or simply shopbots are agents that can help users decide what to buy and enhance their shopping experience. Shopbots operate online, receive requests from users for products and services and then can query vendors and providers and retrieve and compare (these are *differentiation* and *evaluation* agents according to (Wan et al., 2003)) relevant information such as price, delivery options, warranty etc. More specifically, shopbots can:

- Find product information such as specifications and reviews;

- Compare products, vendors and services according to user-defined criteria;
- Find the best value products or services;
- Monitor online shops for product availability, special offers and discounts and send alerts;
- Recommend services and products;
- Identify new products of potential interest to the user based on her preferences and purchase history.

Delegating such tasks to shopbots who can scour the Web on the users' behalf has significant advantages. The user saves time as a shopbot can search a number of vendors much faster than its human counterpart would. As a shopbot can query many more vendors, it may also query vendors that the user has no knowledge of and yet they may be offering better deals. Furthermore, shopbots may be able to uncover special deals that the user would otherwise be unaware of (when commodities are being offered for instance as part of a bunch). Another potential benefit is that of psychological burden-shifting (Rajiv and Aggarwal, 2002). Users are often uncertain about buying a product. By employing a shopbot, they can often shift some of the psychological cost of making a decision to the agent. If the decision turns out to be not a very good one, the shopbot can be blamed, thereby minimizing the psychological risk in the purchase decision. In addition, when deploying shopbots users may not even be aware if the recommendation is only suboptimal. Shopbots may also help protect the users' privacy as the search for product information can be anonymized. Finally, shopbots can lead to more efficient marketplaces. As shopbots provide the means for users to compare the prices and services offered by many vendors, the competition in the marketplace increases. Smaller vendors offering competitive prices can be accessible to the user, thereby reducing the larger vendors' monopoly.

LITERATURE REVIEW

Shopbots made their appearance in the mid 1990s and technology analysts at the time were predicting that they would have a huge impact on vendors and the way business would be conducted in the years to come (Edwards, 2000). In the following sections we conduct a concise literature review of shopbots and related technologies and discuss their current technical and other limitations. We divide these systems into two generations: shopping agents and comparison shopping sites.

Shopping Agents: The First Generation

The first generation of shopbots includes systems such as BargainFinder, PersonaLogic, and Shop-Bot among others.

The first shopbot for price comparisons was BargainFinder which was developed by Andersen Consulting (Krulwich, 1996) and was released in 1995. BargainFinder allowed users to compare prices of music CDs from up to nine online stores. Despite its popularity among users, many retailers started blocking access to the agent, as BargainFinder simply evaluated vendors based on the offered price and ignored all other features that online music retailers had built into their sites. Eventually, BargainFinder ceased operating.

PersonaLogic (Guttman et al., 1999) helped users who described their tastes make decisions on products and services that fitted their needs and preferences. The system created profiles that enabled the identification of products with features important to the users. For example, if the user was interested in an MP3 player, she would have to tell the system her budget, desired features, etc. PersonaLogic would then provide the user with a list of models that best fit the given information. However, PersonalLogic required vendors to provide an interface that explicitly disclosed the features of the products in a way that could be matched against the user profiles. Hence, vendors

that had not provided that interface could not be queried, although they could be offering the desired products and at better prices. PersonaLogic was acquired in 1998 by AOL and the system was withdrawn from the market.

ShopBot (Doorenbos et al., 1997) was an agent that could learn to submit queries to e-commerce sites and parse the results to extract information on products. ShopBot used an automatic process for building 'wrappers' to process semi-structured HTML documents and extracted features such as product description and price. The mechanism exploited a number of properties that characterize the layout of e-commerce sites. ShopBot was later renamed to Jango and was acquired and commercialized by Excite in 1997. Jango avoided the problem that BargainFinder faced as product information requests originated from the user's browser, not from the agent's server.

A more recent example of a comparison shopping agent is IntelliShopper (Menczer et al., 2002). IntelliShopper observed the user's actions and unobtrusively attempted to learn her preferences and help her with her shopping. IntelliShopper consisted of three different agents: a Learning, a Monitor and a Privacy agent. The Learning agent observed the user, learnt her preferences and handled the user's requests for information on products. The Monitor agent monitored various vendors on behalf of the user and periodically checked for product availability or any other pending request. The Privacy agent looked after the user's privacy. IntelliShopper preserved the user's privacy through concealing her IP address by passing requests through one or more anonymizer servers. In addition, shopping personas were used to hide all information about the user from the IntelliShopper server. A persona reflected the mode of use of a particular user and its purpose was two fold: to guarantee the user's privacy as no data about the user were revealed to the server and to allow the user to take on different personas, i.e. shopping characteristics, for different shopping needs. Logic about the different vendors that the IntelliShopper dealt with was stored in modules which specified how a vendor could be queried and how to interpret the results and extract the information required by the user from the returned HTML pages.

Technological Limitations

First generation shopbots such as those described in the previous section, operate in a similar way to meta-search engines and retrieve information from different vendors through a form of 'screen-scraping' (Singh, 2000). The location of the vendors' e-commerce sites is usually identified by humans who then feed it into the system in the form of static links. Shopbots typically permit buyers to sort product and vendor information along some desired dimension such as price. Essentially, they interact with a vendor through HTML pages that are designed and generated to be read and understood by humans and not to be processed or manipulated by programs. They submit queries to vendors and attempt to process the resulting HTML pages by parsing them and searching for the name of the item of interest to

the user and then the nearest set of characters that has a currency sign, which presumably is the item's price. Shopbots rely on a number of regular characteristics in the layout of an e-commerce Website to retrieve such information (Doorenbos et al., 1997):

- navigation: e-commerce sites are designed so that users can easily navigate through them and find what they need;
- uniformity: the Web pages of a site are designed so that they have a similar look and feel;
- vertical separation: white spaces are customarily used to separate products and each new product description starts in a new line.

In fact, the information that shopbots are looking for is stored in a machine-processable and well-structured format in the vendor's database. But shopbots cannot query a vendor's database directly. They can only gain access to the database indirectly through retrieving and parsing the Web pages that have been generated from the database as illustrated in Figure 2. Consequently, devel-

Figure 2. How current shopbots work

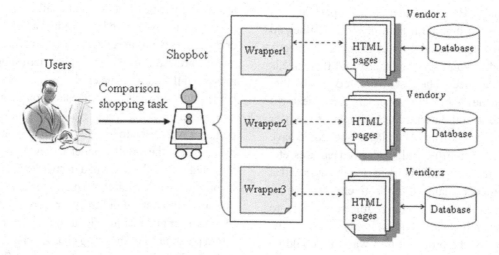

opers are required to develop 'smart' heuristics that will enable them to process Web pages and extract the original well-structured data from the implicit information contained in the pages. But such heuristics are inevitably ad-hoc, difficult and time-consuming to develop and prone to errors, while they are only able to retrieve limited information. In addition, they must be updated every time the layout of the vendor's site changes. This makes the development of shopbots cumbersome and the resulting systems inflexible and vendor-specific. Methods that can extract information from one e-commerce Website may not be directly applicable to others. One of the most significant disadvantages of 'screen-scraping' techniques is that new vendors cannot be discovered and queried at runtime: they first have to be identified and then tailor-made methods for retrieving information from their Web pages need to be developed.

As current techniques take advantage of the underlying regularities in the design of e-commerce sites and rely predominantly on syntax, shopbots can only retrieve limited information from vendors and ignore attributes such as warranty and shipping options which are harder to retrieve. This is a severe limitation. Although price is often the most important factor in deciding what to buy and where from, other attributes may affect the buying decision such as the delivery and payment options, or the vendor's reputation. Crucially, these value-added services may be what differentiates vendors that otherwise may be offering the same price. Naturally, vendors object to the idea of being compared on price alone as this does not necessarily reflect the full range of services and value for money that they offer. This is the most important reason why many vendors block price requests from shopbots thus restricting their ability to make comparisons among multiple vendors and assist the user in finding the best deal around.

This limitation has further consequences on the accuracy of the information retrieved. Often there are discrepancies between the prices reported by shopbots and those listed at the vendor's site. As shopbots do not understand the content of the retrieved Web pages, they cannot distinguish between vendors that include shipping charges and taxes in their prices and those that do not. Shopbots therefore appear unable to provide accurate information on vendors and products.

Comparison Shopping Sites: The Second Generation

The aforementioned problems have led to the demise of vendor-independent shopbots such as the ones described in the previous sections and the emergence of comparison shopping sites (CSS). These comparison shopping sites may operate as part of portals, for instance such as Yahoo!Shopping (Yahoo!Shopping, 2008), or as independent systems such as for instance PriceGrabber (PriceGrabber, 2008). Such sites usually rely on vendors to provide the necessary information on catalogues and products, or operate as meta-search engines and perform searches on the vendors' sites.

Sites like MySimon (MySimon, 2008) and Shopping.com (Shopping.com, 2008) collate catalogues of products which are provided by the vendors themselves who pay to be listed on the site. If vendors are using more than one CSS, then significant effort must be exerted on optimizing the data feeds provided for each individual CSS. Furthermore, as each CSS may be using a slightly different system for product categorization, a vendor would also need to take this into account.

Comparison sites that operate as meta-search engines such as Kayak (Kayak, 2008) and Side-Step (SideStep, 2008) may have either informal or formal relationships with vendors. Vendors may simply allow such shopping sites to access and retrieve information from their Web sites or form explicit partnerships and pay a commission for each hit made to the vendor's site as a result of the listing, or for sales resulting from clickthrough purchases or alternatively they place advertisements.

Google's Product Search, originally named Froogle, (Google Product Search, 2008), indexes products from multiple e-commerce sites in two ways:

1. Sellers can submit information on the products that they would like to list in Google Product Search directly;
2. Google Product Search identifies Web pages that offer products and services while Google searches and indexes the Web.

Typically, comparison shopping sites are not actually agents as described earlier as they lack the characteristics that are often ascribed to agents.

Although CSSs do allow comparisons among multiple vendors, they may not necessarily offer impartial advice. Vendors that have formal relations with such CSSs (i.e. they pay to be listed) usually appear on the top of the returned list, whereas those that do not have a formal relationship are usually listed towards the bottom of the page or in subsequent pages. At the same time, there may be other vendors that offer competitive prices that are not included in a CSS's listings at all.

CSSs provide comparisons usually on price alone and not on attributes such as warranty, delivery options etc. (although such information may be listed, it is not explicitly compared). Depending on how often the data feeds are received or the vendors' sites are searched, information on product availability may be inaccurate. Unless a CSS is somehow connected to a vendor's inventory management system, listings cannot be automatically updated once a product is out of stock (or back in stock).

Nevertheless CSSs have been growing in popularity, in particular as the numbers of Web users and online transactions have increased. Hitwise (Hitwise.com, 2008), a leading online competitive intelligence service, reported a 48% increase in CSSs' market share of visits in December 2007

compared to December 2006. More recently in July 2008 Hitwise (Hitwise.co.uk, 2008) reported a 37% increase in the UK of traffic to their Shopping and Classifieds: Rewards and Directories category which comprises mainly comparison shopping sites, affiliates and voucher sites. This reflects the growing need for comparison shopping systems that enable Web users to find as well compare products and services.

SHOPBOTS AND THE SEMANTIC WEB

Despite the high expectations about the impact of shopbots on retail markets, their true potential has not been fully realized. This is mainly due to the technique used to extract information, i.e. screen-scrapping, and its inherent shortcomings. Consequently, this places limitations on the information that can be retrieved and the type of comparisons that can be performed using shopbots – typically only based on price. But even comparisons based on price may not always be accurate as some vendors include shipping and taxes in their listed prices whereas others do not.

These problems could be alleviated if the Web pages were to be marked up not only with presentation details, but also with a separate representation of the meaning of their contents which could be read by a program. This is in essence the vision of the Semantic Web: to enrich Web pages with meaning so that programs such as software agents can understand, process and manipulate (Berners-Lee et al., 2001). Shopbots would then be able to extract the required information on price or other attributes even if the layout of the Web page had been changed since they would be able to 'understand' the content. In other words, vendors would have to offer their catalogues in a machine-processable form which shopbots could understand by consulting explicit and shared ontologies describing the underlying domain.

A second very promising avenue to tackling the problems faced by shopbots is offered by Web Services.

Web Services

Web Services is the emerging paradigm in distributed computing which promises to change the way businesses interact with each other. Accordingly, applications are no longer deployed on individual machines, but they comprise a number of software components which are distributed across many different machines and are programmatically accessible over standard protocols. The power of Web Services lies in that they interact seamlessly and transparently with each other to produce combined functionality (Huhns and Singh, 2005).

A Web Service is a software program that encapsulates a collection of functions and is identified by a Uniform Resource Identifier (URI). It is published on the network and can be accessed by other programs through its exposed programmatic interface. The interface description of a service includes information on the operations that can be performed on the service (i.e. its functionality), the message exchange during a typical interaction (inputs and outputs), as well as the physical location of ports where information should be exchanged (binding). For instance, a Web service for providing the conversion of a given temperature from degrees Celsius to Fahrenheit would have an operation *getFahrenheitDegrees* with one input of type float (degrees in Celsius) and one output of type float (degrees in Fahrenheit). The binding information of the service would describe the physical machine and ports where the messages should be sent.

A typical usage scenario for Web services includes three entities: a service provider, a service requester and a registry. The providers of services can describe and register them in registries or directories whose purpose is to facilitate the discovery of services by requesters as well as Web

service composition. When a requester requires a particular service, it can search the registry by browsing or querying it. Once an appropriate service is found, the requester can invoke it through standard protocols.

The standards for enabling the description of, discovery and interaction with Web services are based on XML. The Universal Description, Discovery and Integration protocol (UDDI) standard specification (UDDI, 2006) describes a mechanism for registering and locating services. Knowing the location of a service, a requester can use the Simple Object Access Protocol (SOAP) (SOAP, 2003) to invoke the service with its parameters.

The UDDI specification provides structural templates for representing information about businesses and their services which consist of four data types:

1. *businessEntity*: information about businesses and providers;
2. *businessService*: descriptive information about services. A *businessEntity* may have more than one *businessServices*;
3. *tModel* (technical model): technical information about a service;
4. *bindingTemplate*: links a *businessService* element with one or more *tModels*.

The *businessEntity* and *businessService* elements can be directly associated with *tModel* elements through a *categoryBag* element. For a more detailed description of the UDDI the interested reader is referred to (UDDI, 2006). The concept of a *tModel* is similar to that of metadata which contain information about the objects that are being represented. Each service can have one or more *tModels* that describe its attributes and characteristics. A *tModel* can refer to either technical specifications, for instance a WSDL representation, or to taxonomy schemes, such as the North American Industry Classification System (NAICS) and the United Nations Standard

Product and Services Classification (UNSPSC) System. The Web Services Description Language (WSDL) (Christensen et al., 2001), which is an XML-based language, can be used to describe the programmatic interfaces to Web services. The description of a service includes the input and output parameters and their data types, the format of messages that can be exchanged, the service's operations, its network address, and protocol bindings. Notably, a UDDI *tModel* does not contain the actual WSDL specification, but the URL of where that specification can be found.

UDDI allows a number of ways to search for a service: by business name, service name, category or by *tModel*. For instance, one can search for "Car Rental Services" according to the UNSPSC taxonomy. However, UDDI search facilities do not go beyond keyword-based matches and this has a number of inherent limitations (Paolucci and Sycara 2003; Verma et al., 2005). First, UDDI does not support any inference based on the taxonomies referred to by the *tModels*. For instance, searching for "Limousine hire" would not produce any results, despite the fact that "Limousine hire" is a subtype of "Car Rental Services". Second, UDDI does not support capability-based search. For instance, in the above example, if one was only interested in retrieving car rental services that accept credit cards, or can arrange a car drop-off at one's home, such services would not be retrieved. As another example, a search in a UDDI registry for vendors (their services) that can ship to the U.K. is not possible as UDDI would not be able to represent such a capability. Although such information may be represented in the *tModels* (in WSDL for instance), UDDI does not facilitate such search. Third, syntactic search may fail to identify potential matches. For instance, searching for "Van hire" may not yield any results if the corresponding services are described under "Truck rentals".

Semantic Web Services

In order to overcome the limitations of UDDI, both richer descriptions of Web services and the means to process such descriptions are required. One way to enhance service descriptions is by using ontology languages. Ontology languages are able to describe the attributes and characteristics of services as well as their capabilities, and facilitate ontological reasoning in order to infer new relations.

OWL (OWL, 2006) is an ontology language that can formally describe the meaning of terminology used in Web documents. OWL extends and is a revision of the DARPA Agent Markup Language+Ontology Inference Layer (DAML+OIL) Web ontology language. OWL builds on the Resource Description Framework (RDF) and proposes a specific vocabulary that provides selected frame and description logic primitives to capture ontologies. Hence, it provides an enriched vocabulary which allows for describing classes and properties, including relations between classes (e.g. disjointness), cardinality (e.g. exactly one), equality, richer typing of properties, characteristics of properties (e.g. symmetry), and enumerated classes.

OWL provides three sublanguages with increasing expressiveness and decreasing computational guarantees: OWL Lite, OWL DL and OWL Full. An OWL specification document, which is an XML file, defines classes, and relationships among those classes. For instance, the following is a fragment of a transportation ontology which asserts that there is a class named Automobile and that there is another class called Limousine which is a subclass of Automobile.

```
<owl:Class rdf:ID="Automobile">
<rdfs:label>Automobile </rdfs:label>
<rdfs:comment>Automobile class</rdfs:comment>
</owl:Class>
<owl:Class rdf:ID="Limousine">
<rdfs:subClassOf rdf:resource="#Automobile"/ >
```

```
<rdfs:comment>Class Limousine is a subclass of Automo-
bile</rdfs:comment>
</owl:Class>
```

The Ontology Web Language for Services (OWL-S) is based on OWL and is a language for describing the capabilities of services (OWL-S, 2004). A Web Service in OWL-S is described by three interrelated sub-ontologies. The *ServiceProfile* describes the capability specification of a service which is essential in determining whether or not it meets the requester's needs. The *ServiceModel* describes how a requester can use the service, how to ask for it and what happens when it is executed. The *ServiceGrounding* specifies the communication protocol, message formats and other service-specific details such as port numbers used in contacting the service.

Hence, languages such as OWL-S can be used encode semantically rich descriptions of Web Services. The selection of providers using such enhanced descriptions requires a type of registry that enables search based on semantics which is not currently offered by UDDI and several approaches have been proposed in this direction (Srinivasan

et al., 2004; Verma et al., 2005). Returning to the example in section 4.1, using OWL-S descriptions of services one would be able to infer that a limousine is a type of car or automobile and return such services when requested.

SHOPBOTS: THE THIRD GENERATION

The third generation of shopbots is envisioned to resolve some of the pertinent issues associated with the first and second generations, namely the inability to provide comparisons on attributes other than price and unbiased services. In addition, third generation shopbots will also be able to offer personalized services to users. Figure 3 illustrates our vision of the third generation of shopbots which is described in more detail in the next section.

Semantic Interoperability

The fundamental problem with shopbots is that they cannot have direct access to a vendor's da-

Figure 3. Shopbots: Making use of the semantic Web and Web services

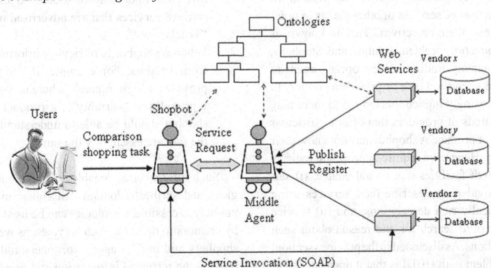

tabase. This can be resolved if vendors provide Web Services to facilitate retrieval as is illustrated on the right side of Figure 3. In essence, shopbots can use Web services as gateways to vendors' sites since services can provide the means of retrieving information directly from the vendor in machine-processable form. Although such practices are not widespread among vendors yet, the leading efforts of retailers such as Amazon are notable. Amazon (Amazon, 2008) offers Web services that allow programs to perform operations such as retrieving information about products and adding items to a shopping cart.

Shopbots can potentially access a very large number of vendors provided that the latter make available the programmatic interfaces to facilitate the retrieval of the required information. But finding vendors that offer products or services on a network the size of the Internet is a non-trivial problem. (Note: The term *service* is used in this section to describe two different things: (i) services offered by vendors as in a car hire service or a flower delivery service; and (ii) services being software components that encapsulate functionality, such as for instance allowing access to a vendor's other sub-systems (e.g. product catalogue or database). The use of the term should be clear from the context.)

Generally speaking, agents may need to locate and use the services of other agents in order to achieve their objectives. This is known as the *connection* problem (Huhns and Stephens, 1999), namely finding an appropriate agent to perform a required task or provide a service. In an increasingly interconnected world there may be hundreds of providers that offer a particular service or product. A shopbot may not know their location. Hence, we require appropriate registry and search facilities that would enable: (i) service providers to describe their services using semantically rich descriptions; and (ii) service requesters to search for and reason about such descriptions. As discussed in the previous section, the problem with UDDI is that it does not repre-

sent service capabilities and thus cannot facilitate the automatic location of Web services based on capability specifications. Richer languages such as OWL-S should be used to describe services and their capabilities.

To facilitate discovery, middle or broker agents can be used that act as ontology-based search engines and take into account semantics. The role of the middle agent in this context is to match a requester's request for service with one or more providers (middle of Figure 3). This process is simply referred to as *matching* (Wong and Sycara, 2000). Middle agents specialize in making connections and they store, maintain and provide connection information. Vendors can publish/register their Web services with middle agents, and shopbots can then enquire middle agents when receiving requests from users to find products or services (left side of figure 3).

Using semantically rich languages that provide the necessary techniques for reasoning about the concepts being described, facilitates semantic interoperability. This semantic interoperability is necessary at two distinct levels:

1. When middle agents process requests from requesters (such as shopbots) about services. For example, if a requester is asking for "Van hire", the middle agent should be able to retrieve services that are advertised under "Truck rental".

2. When a shopbot is retrieving information from vendors. For example, if vendor x provides a "guarantee" whereas vendor y provides a "warranty" for product A, a shopbot should be able to understand that the two are essentially the same.

Such inferences are enabled through ontologies that describe the domain of discourse and are publicly accessible. Ontologies can be used both by creators to describe Web services, as well as shopbots and middle agents to understand and process the retrieved information and present it to the user/requester.

Having an understanding of the information being retrieved will enable meaningful comparisons to be made not only based on price, but on various other attributes. For instance, understanding that the terms "guarantee" and "warranty" describe the same concept would enable a shopbot to place a vendor who offers a 1-year warranty higher in the returned list of results than a vendor offering a 6-month guarantee (provided everything else is the same).

For shopbots to achieve their full potential, the matching between a request for service and potential providers needs to take into account semantics and capability specifications and also needs to be done in context. To summarize our vision of the third generation of shopbots: Vendors can facilitate access to their sites and database/catalogues in a pre-determined way by developing Web services which they publish/register with middle agents. Users delegate the task of finding and comparing products to shopbots. Shopbots contact middle agents who identify and return a set of providers offering the service along with information on how to contact and interact with the service. This is subsequently used by the shopbot to invoke the service and retrieve information. In such a setting, shopbots would be able to dynamically retrieve information from a variable number of vendors and not depend on static links that may be unreliable. Shopbots could also cashe the locations of Web services for common requests thereby improving efficiency. Having access to machine-processable information and being able to 'understand' this information, shopbots are then in a position to make meaningful comparisons in a systematic way based on user-defined criteria. The end result would be easily digestible information that the user can use to make the final purchasing decision.

To allow shopbots to retrieve semantic information on products and services from vendors the following main technical challenges need to be addressed:

- registries that include capability descriptions;
- efficient algorithms for matching requests with Web services;
- efficient ontology services including ontology consolidation services;
- reasoning mechanisms that enable shopbots to perform true comparison shopping based on the user's preferences, the retrieved information and the underlying ontologies.

Although standardizing ontologies to describe certain parts of the retail sector would be ideal, standardization cannot be easily enforced. That is why shopbots and middle agents need to be able to reason with and compare multiple ontologies.

Work on shopbots that are able to retrieve information on vendors through Web services has been so far rather limited. A recent approach is (Kim et al., 2005) where a meta-search and comparison system for products is described. The Intelligent Product Information Search (IPIS) system assumes that shopping malls offer Web services that describe the products and goods available. On receiving a request from a user the system is able to use the services to retrieve information. Such an approach is along the lines described above, though the concept of a middle agent as an intermediary is not used.

Offering Personalized and Impartial Services

Agent technology can greatly assist users sift through information and find what they require in a range of application domains. Shopbots that can collate information on products, services as well as vendors can be a very valuable tool for users as they can help them avoid drowning in choices. However, for the user to truly benefit from the deployment of such agents, the offered services need to take into account the user's needs.

Addressing the technical limitations that were described in the previous sections through

Semantic Web technologies and Web Services will enhance the functionality of shopbots with regard to two important aspects: impartiality and flexibility.

Impartiality is one important requirement for shopbots. To provide the best possible services to the user, a shopbot needs to remain independent from vendors. Shopbots need to be impartial and perform wide searches and take into account as many vendors as possible when for instance looking for a particular product, as opposed to only searching a small number of preferred vendors such as those sponsoring the agent. Using multiple middle agents to search for services offered by vendors would enable a shopbot to perform wide searches and hence look at a significant proportion of the market before returning the comparison results to the user. Offering impartial services will increase the users' confidence and as a result the use of shopbots. But given the current mode of operation, this also requires reconsidering current business models for such agents. Typically, shopbots and comparison shopping sites make commissions in three different ways (Markopoulos and Kephart, 2002): (i) for each hit made to a vendor's site as the result of a shopbot's recommendation; (ii) for sales that result from clickthrough purchases; or (iii) for a favorable placement on the generated recommended lists. If shopbots are to offer impartial services, then the third source of revenue may have to be abandoned altogether. But extra revenue can be generated through advertisements.

Ideally, a shopbot should be able to make comparisons not based on the attribute of price alone. Although price is usually the most important factor in deciding where to buy from, other factors may affect the buying decision such as warranty, delivery and payment options, possible extras and the vendor's reputation. Using Semantic Web technologies such as ontologies, information from different vendors can be retrieved and used to make meaningful comparisons among multiple attributes that the user may be interested in.

Perhaps, the most crucial step in the evolution of shopbots is addressing the issue of personalization. At the time being, shopbots (and comparison shopping sites) typically perform searches and comparisons for the cheapest products available without taking into account any other user-expressed preferences or any user profiles. But third generation shopbots are expected to offer an enhanced shopping experience to users. Maintaining user profiles may allow a shopbot to filter the results for products and services. For example, a user residing in the U.K. searching for cameras, will only be provided with vendors who *can* ship to the U.K. Furthermore, the agent can learn the user preferences by observing her actions while shopping. When users consider the items available at e-commerce sites, they indirectly provide relevance feedback, i.e. submitting queries for products or browsing catalogues provide implicit information about the user's preferences (Kelly and Teevan, 2003; Kim et al., 2000). The agent can utilize this feedback to infer the user's preferences and apply such acquired knowledge in taking the initiative for future searches, and in predicting when a user might be interested in an item. Hence, shopbots can proactively help the user for instance by checking periodically for new product information and notifying them when new products of potential interest have arrived in store.

Personalization is inadvertently closely related to privacy. Generally speaking, deploying software agents to represent the user in e-commerce carries a number of risks (Fasli, 2007b) as the user's privacy may be compromised if information is not appropriately managed and protected. Users need to be told explicitly and agree to data about them being gathered while they are interacting with the shopbot and they also need to know how such information is subsequently used (Fasli, 2007a). Users should also have access to this information and be able to amend or delete it. The issue of acquiring and maintaining user profiles through observing the users' actions should be carefully monitored so as to avoid such user profiles being used in price discrimination schemes or push-marketing. A lot of information can be mined out of user profiles, such as habits or spending power. For instance, by tracking the number of holidays and the value of each, a system can infer the spending power of a user. The next time that the user requests information on holidays, the shopbot could offer luxury packages only or use specific hotel chains.

Maintaining the user's privacy while searching for products is also important. Users may not want to reveal their identity or other information about their shopping patterns when searching for products as this information can be used by vendors in price discrimination schemes or for push-marketing purposes (Vulkan, 2003). The privacy of the user needs to be protected by concealing her identity and behavior as for instance in the IntelliShopper system (Menczer et al., 2002), i.e. through concealing the IP address of the origin of the user's request when submitting queries to vendors. But, protecting the user's privacy should be conditional and should be selectively revoked if the user abuses it.

CONCLUDING REMARKS

Shopbots have the potential to have a major impact on both brick-and-mortar and purely Internet vendors and ultimately lead to more efficient marketplaces as well as enhance the users' shopping experience. The transition to the Semantic Web and Web Services would alleviate the problems associated with current shopbots and comparison shopping sites. In particular, Web services allow for the retrieval of additional attributes apart from price. As shopbots would have an understanding of these attributes, they would be able to offer comprehensive information to users and uncover deals that are differentiated not only by price, but also other attributes. Such information can be presented in a uniform way. Vendors can

be discovered and queried dynamically depending on the user's request through middle agents. Fundamentally, shopbots no longer have to be dependent on specific vendors and thus can offer impartial advice. As vendors can be compared on additional attributes and not on price alone, they have an incentive to provide programmatic interfaces to their sites to enable shopbots to locate them thereby increasing their visibility. Although this inevitably increases competition, overall market efficiency improves. Smaller vendors can increase their visibility and benefit from the large volumes of traffic that pass through the shopbot (Iyer and Pazgal, 2003). Larger vendors with a bigger customer base and more loyal customers may have less of an incentive to join or allow access to a shopbot. Nevertheless, some will choose to do so in order to increase their customer base even further.

Shopbots can also facilitate anonymity on the Web as the requests for product information can be processed without revealing the user's identity. Price discrimination schemes would be difficult to apply as vendors cannot know the identity of the user requesting information. Furthermore, shopbots can use reputation systems to filter out unreliable vendors. Reputation systems collate information on vendors by aggregating feedback on past transactions from users (or agents) and then measuring the vendor's trustworthiness via some means (Resnick et al., 2000). Shopbots may be able to steer users away from dubious vendors and can help tackle market fraud. Finally, users could interact with shopbots indirectly through their personal agents. Users could delegate the task of finding products to their personal agents who in turn may enlist the help of a shopbot. The user's personal agent can filter the information returned by the shopbot even further by considering additional user preferences or other restrictions.

This chapter concentrated in the application of shopbots to B2C markets. But shopbots can also benefit organizations in business-to-business (B2B) markets. A shopbot can perform searches and comparisons not for consumer goods and products, but for suppliers and components on behalf of businesses and organizations as in a supply chain. Shopbots would be able to quickly locate the cheapest suppliers or those that can satisfy certain conditions, e.g. delivery deadlines. The same infrastructure as described above would enable interactions between parties in B2B markets reducing costs and improving the overall market efficiency. Furthermore, shopbots could also facilitate the identification of potential business partners in the creation of virtual organizations (Petersen et al., 2001). In today's fast-evolving business world, organizations need to be agile and innovative to be able to withstand competition and respond to the changing needs of the customer force. A virtual organization (VO), often referred to as virtual enterprise (VE) or agile enterprise, consists of a number of independent partners that forge a consortium dynamically in order, for instance, to exploit a niche in the market, meet customer demand, offer new improved services or added value. Businesses looking for potential partners to provide a particular service can delegate the task of identifying the most suitable partners to shopbots who can then compare the service descriptions as these are stored in middle agents. The creation of such virtual organizations would therefore be greatly enhanced and to a significant extent automated as the initiator and the potential partners can themselves be represented by software agents in this process.

Third generation shopbots will only realize their true potential if they utilize the power of the Semantic Web and Web Services and address the user needs by offering impartial, flexible and personalized services.

ACKNOWLEDGMENTS

An earlier version of this work appeared in "Shopbots: A Syntactic Present, A Semantic Future" by Maria Fasli which appeared in IEEE Internet Computing, November/December 2006, 10(6): 69-75, © 2006 IEEE.

REFERENCES

Amazon. (2008). See http://www.amazon.com.

Berners-Lee, T., Hendler, J. & Lassila, O. (2001). The Semantic Web. *Scientific American*, May 2001, 29-37.

Christensen, E., Curbera, F., Meredith, G., & Weerawarana, S. WSDL. (2001). Web Services Description Language. See http://www.w3.org/TR/wsdl.

DAML. (2006).The DARPA Agent Markup Language. See http://www.daml.org.

Doorenbos, R. B., Etzioni, O., & Weld, D. S. (1997). A scalable comparison-shopping agent for the World-Wide Web. In *Proceedings of the First International Conference on Autonomous Agents (Agents-97)* (pp.39-48).

Edwards, J. (2000). Is that your best offer? Shopbots search the Web for bargains. CIO Magazine. See http://www.cio.com/archive/110100/et.html.

Fasli, M. (2006). Shopbots: A syntactic present, a semantic future. *IEEE Internet Computing*, *10*(6), 69-75.

Fasli, M. (2007). *Agent Technology for e-Commerce*. Chichester: John Wiley and Sons.

Fasli, M. (2007). On Agent Technology for E-commerce: Trust, Security and Legal Issues. *Knowledge Engineering Review*, *22*(1), 3-35.

Forrester Research. (2002). See http://www.forrester.com/ER/Press/ForrFind/0,1768,0,00.html.

Google Product Search. (2008). See http://www.google.com/products.

Guttman, A. G., Moukas, R. H., & Maes, P. (1999). Agent-mediated integrative negotiation for retail electronic commerce. In *Agent Mediated Electronic Commerce, First International Workshop on Agent Mediated Electronic Trading (AMET'98)* (pp. 70-90). Berlin: Springer.

Hitwise.com. (2008). Hitwise US holiday 2007 retail recap report. See http://www.hitwise.com.

Hitwise.co.uk. (2008). See http://www.hitwise.co.uk.

Huhns, M. N., & Stephens, L. M. (1999). Multiagent Systems and Societies of Agents. In G. Weiss, (Ed.), *Multiagent Systems: A Modern Approach to Distributed Artificial Intelligence* (pp. 79-120). Cambridge, MA: The MIT Press.

Iyer, G., & Pazgal, (2003). A. Internet shopping agents: Virtual co-location and competition. *Marketing Science, 22*(1), 85-106.

Kayak. (2008). See http://www.kayak.com.

Kelly, D., & Teevan, J. (2003). Implicit feedback for inferring user preference: A bibliography. *SIGIR Forum, 37*(2), 18–28.

Kim, J., Oard, D., & Romanik, K. (2000). *Using implicit feedback for user modeling in internet and intranet searching.* Technical Report, College of Library and Information Services, University of Maryland at College Park. Available at http://www.clis.umd/edu/research/reports/.

Kim, W., Choi, D., Kim, J., & Jin, J. (2005). Development of a meta product search engine with Web services. In *Proceedings of the Second Asia Information Retrieval Symposium (AIRS 2005)* pp.571-576. Berlin: Springer.

Krulwich, B. T. (1996). The BargainFinder agent: Comparing price shopping on the Internet. In J. Williams (Ed.), *Bots and other Internet beasties* (pp. 258-263). Indianapolis, IN: Sams.

Markopoulos, P. M., & Kephart, J. O. (2002). How valuable are shopbots? In *Proceedings of the First*

International Joint Conference on Autonomous Agents and Multiagent Systems, AAMAS'02 (pp. 1009-1016). New York, NY: ACM.

Menczer, F., Street, W. N., & Monge, A. E. (2002). Adaptive Assistants for Customized E-Shopping. *IEEE Intelligent Systems, 17*(6), 12-19.

MySimon. (2000). See http://www.mysimon.com.

Nielsen Media Research. (2008). Over 875 million consumers have shopped on line. See http://www.nielsenmedia.com. January 2008.

OWL-S. (2004). Semantic Markup for Web Services. See http://www.w3.org/Submission/OWL-S/.

Paolucci, M., & Sycara, K. (2003). Autonomous Semantic Web Services. *IEEE Internet Computing, 7*(5), 34-41.

Petersen, S. A., Divitini, M., & Matskin, M. (2001). An Agent-based approach to modelling virtual enterprises. *Production, Planning and Control, 12*(3), 224-233.

PriceGrabber. (2008). See http://www.pricegrabber.com.

Rajiv, V., & Aggarwal, P. (2002). The impact of shopping agents on small business ecommerce strategy. *Journal of Small Business Strategy, 13*(1), 62-79.

Resnick, P., Kuwabara, K., Zeckhauser, R., & Friedman, E. (2000). Reputation systems. *Communications of the ACM, 43*(12), 45-48.

Shop.org. (2002). See at http://www.shop.org/learn/stats_usshop_general.asp.

Shopping.com. (2008). See http://www.shopping.com.

Sidestep (2008). See http://www.sidestep.com.

Singh, M. P. (2000). The Service Web. *IEEE Internet Computing, 4*(4), 4-5.

Singh, M. P., & Huhns, M. N. (2005). *Service-oriented computing: Semantics, Processes, Agents.* Chichester: John Wiley and Sons.

Srinivasan, N., Paolucci, M., & Sycara, K. (2004). An Efficient Algorithm for OWL-S Based Semantic Search in UDDI. In *Semantic Web Services and Web Process Composition, First International Workshop, SWSWPC 2004, Revised Selected Papers* (pp. 96-110). Berlin: Springer.

SOAP. (2003). Simple Object Access Protocol. See http://www.w3.org/TR/soap/.

Stallings, W. (2003). *Network Security Essentials: Applications and Standards.* Upper Saddle River, NJ: Prentice Hall.

UDDI. (2006). Universal Description, Discovery and Integration protocol. See http://www.uddi.org/.

U.S. Census Bureau News. (2008). Quarterly retail e-commerce sales 2nd quarter 2008. See http://www.census.giv/mrts/www/data/html/08Q2.html, August 2008.

Ulfelder, S. (2000). Undercover Agents. Computer World, See http://65.221.110.98/news/2000/story/0,11280,45452,00.html, June 2000.

Verma, K., Sivashanmugam, K., Sheth, A., Patil, A., Oundhakar, S., & Miller, J. (2005). METEOR-S WSDI: A scalable P2P infrastructure of registries for semantic publication and discovery of Web services. *Information Technology and Management, 6*(1), 17-39.

Vulkan, N. (2003). *The Economics of E-commerce.* Princeton, NJ: Princeton University Press.

Wan, Y., Menon, S., & Ramaprasad, A. (2003). A classification of product comparison agents. In *Proceedings of the Fifth International Conference on Electronic Commerce, ICEC'03* (pp.498-504). New York, NY: ACM.

Wong, H. C., & Sycara, K. (2000). A taxonomy of middle-agents for the Internet. In *Proceedings of the Fourth International Conference on MultiAgent Systems, ICMAS-00* (pp.465-466). Washington, DC: IEEE Computer Society.

Wooldridge, M., & Jennings, N. R. (1995). Intelligent Agents: Theory and Practice. *Knowledge Engineering Review, 10*(2), 115-152.

Yahoo!Shopping. (2008). See http://shopping.yahoo.com.

Chapter III
A Mediation Architecture for Global Comparison Services

Hongwei Zhu
Old Dominion University, USA

Stuart E. Madnick
Massachusetts Institute of Technology, USA

ABSTRACT

Global comparison services facilitate easy comparison of product offerings around the world. To offer such services, one has to address the semantic heterogeneity problems that often arise when data is collected from sources around the world. In this chapter, the authors use examples to illustrate three types of semantic heterogeneity problems that a global comparison service may encounter. Then they present a mediation architecture as a solution to addressing these problems. The feasibility of using the architecture to enable global comparison is demonstrated with a prototype application. An evaluation of the solution shows that it is scalable due to its capability of automatically generating necessary conversions from a small set of predefined ones.

With the global reach of the Internet, every business can be a global business. In this environment, it is often desirable to know how things are selling in various parts of the world – vendors need to price their products strategically and consumers want to find the best deals around the world. This need can be facilitated by a global price comparison service. Although there have been numerous regional comparison services which compare prices of vendors in a particular country, there have not been many global comparison services. This is partially due to the problems of *semantic heterogeneity*: what seems to be the same data (e.g. price data) has different meanings in different sources (e.g., prices in USD without taxes on one web site vs. prices in Swedish krona with 25%

taxes included on another). A global comparison service has to make data from worldwide sources meaningful to diverse end users. For example, for users in South Korea, all price data should be in thousands of South Korean won with taxes and shipping charges excluded, regardless of how prices are reported in the original sources.

Comparison service providers are also known as *comparison aggregators* for their capability of transparently aggregating information from multiple web sources (Madnick and Siegel, 2000). They are also called *price comparison agents*, *shopping agents*, and *shopping robots* (or *shop-bots* for short) elsewhere; we will use these terms interchangeably in the rest of the chapter.

In this chapter, we use examples to illustrate the semantic heterogeneity problems. Then we present a mediation architecture for solving these problems. We show the feasibility of the architecture using a prototype implementation. Although we use price comparison as an example, the architecture is applicable for comparison of other characteristics, such as product dimensions and weights.

MOTIVATING EXAMPLE

Imagine for the moment you are from Sweden and interested in buying a pocket sized digital camcorder. After some research on the Web you decide to buy a SONY MICROMV DCR-IP5, which records video in MPEG format for easy editing on computers and weighs only 0.336 kilograms (i.e., 12 ounces). You use your favorite comparison service *Kelkoo* (at www.kelkoo.se) to find the best deals and it returns information as shown in Figure 1.

Among the vendors found, 18,082 Swedish krona (SEK) is the lowest total price (see the Totalpris column in Figure 1). Is this the best deal, or is there a substantially better deal, on a global basis? If you plan to use the camcorder while on an upcoming trip to several countries, is it better to buy it in Sweden before the trip or buy it at the first stop (say, the U.S.) on your arrival? Without a global comparison service, this can only be done manually by visiting numerous regional comparison aggregators available in other countries. Our manual exercise found one vendor in the U.S. sells

Figure 1. Price data displayed by a comparison aggregator in Sweden

Produkt	Butik	Märke	Pris	Lev.tid	Fraktpris	Totalpris	
DCR-IP5 Visa mer	FOTO ELEKTRONIK Butiksinfo	SONY	kr 19,495	2-5 D	kr 115	**kr 19,610**	Mer
DCR-IP5 Visa mer	Lars Bengtsson Ljud Video Butiksinfo	SONY	kr 19,900	3-7 D	kr 75	**kr 19,975**	Mer
Sony DCR-IP5 Visa mer	alfadigi.com Butiksinfo	SONY	kr 17,983	1-3 D	kr 99	**kr 18,082**	Mer
Sony DCR-IP5 (E) Visa mer	CYBERPHOTO Butiksinfo	SONY	kr 19,115	1-3 D	kr 99	**kr 19,214**	Mer
Digital videokamera DCR-IP5. Visa mer	OnOff Butiksinfo	SONY	kr 21,994	4-5 D	kr 95	**kr 22,089**	Mer

the product for $999.99, and you can add $100 to have it shipped to you in Sweden.

Between 18,082 SEK and $1,099.99, which is the better deal? Additional information such as 1 US dollar is approximately 10 SEK (at the time) will be useful in answering the question, but such information usually is not readily available from a regional aggregator. After this information is obtained, for example by querying a currency conversion service, such as www.oanda.com, we can use it to convert the prices into the same currency. Only after all these steps have been done do we know that the Swedish offer is 64% more expensive than the U.S. offer.

As seen in the example, there are certain "inconveniences" when comparing prices globally: a user has to visit and collect data from multiple sites, determine if the data needs to be converted to reconcile the differences (e.g., currencies and inclusion or exclusion of taxes), and perform the conversions to make the comparison meaningful. This process is time consuming and error prone. A global comparison service could alleviate the user from these tedious tasks. Such a service provider would need to ensure that the information is properly processed so that data coming from different parts of the world can be correctly interpreted by users who are also geographically dispersed around the world. The users of such services can be consumers (looking for the best deals), vendors (developing competitive pricing strategies), manufacturers (monitoring vendor pricing behaviors), arbitragers (buying low at one place and selling high at another), and economists (studying the global markets).

TECHNOLOGY CHALLENGES

Characteristics and Deficiencies of Existing Price Comparison

A number of price comparison service providers have emerged since the introduction of the first online price comparison agent, which was implemented as an internal project of Anderson Consulting in 1995 (Smith, 2002). Other examples include *BizRate, mySimon, Dealtime, Shopper, PriceRunner, PriceGrabber, Kelkoo, Kakaku,* and Google's Product Search service (which used to be called *Froogle*). A main characteristic of these aggregators is that they only compare prices of vendors within a country. This is the case even for those that have an international presence. For example, *Kelkoo* currently operates in 11 countries; each *Kelkoo* country-specific site is considered as a regional aggregator. *AddAll.com* is the only site that we know to compare book prices in different countries.

Most existing regional price comparison services use information extraction techniques (Chang et al., 2006) to extract data from web sources. These techniques often rely on the syntactic structures of web pages (Fasli, 2006) to obtain the raw data from multiple web sites. When these techniques are used for regional comparison services, the direct use of raw data from multiple sites usually does not create a problem of understanding or comparing the data because the sources usually report data using the same convention that is understood by the customers in the region. For example, online vendors in the U.S. list prices in USD with taxes and shipping charges excluded, while those in Sweden list prices in krona with domestic taxes and shipping charges included. But when the service is provided on a global basis, there will be significant difficulties in understanding the data because the sources from different parts of the world use different conventions to report data, whereas the users of such a global system are familiar with their local conventions only. To make the information from diverse sources meaningful to equally diverse customers, a comparison service provider must address the data semantics issues that we will discuss next.

Semantic Heterogeneity of Multiple Data Sources

We have seen in the motivational example that currency needs to be converted to make sensible comparison for the Swedish user. Many other such issues also exist. Let us illustrate these issues with an example of information about laptop computers from several web sites of Sony, summarized in Table 1. We will ignore most language differences in the following discussion.

First to note is that not all information is available at a single source. In this case the thickness information is not immediately available from the U.K. sources (it is buried in a PDF document). If an aggregator takes the information from the U.S. source and directly reports it to German users, 1.09" probably would not be helpful to the users who are not familiar with the English units of measurement. In addition to different units being used (lbs vs. kilograms, inches vs. centimeters, US dollars vs. British Pounds, etc.) there are other representational differences, such as symbols for thousands separator and decimal point.

There is another subtle difference in the price data reported in Table 1: different sources use different definitions for *price* in terms of what is included in the price. The U.S. source does not indicate if taxes are included but they are probably not included according to the convention, whereas the U.K. source indicates the price includes VAT. All listing prices must be converted to the same definition for meaningful comparison. A classic example of this problem is given in McCarthy and Buvac (1994), where different prices of the same GE aircraft engine are perceived by different organizations, such as the U.S. Air Force and U.S. Navy depending on whether the price includes spare parts, warranty, etc.

Another problem not explicitly shown in Table 1 is how the aggregators identify the same product from different sources. In the process of manually composing the Table, we noticed that the model numbers are different between laptops in the U.S. and those in Europe. We recognize their similarity (in this case identical except for the model numbers) by examining the configurations (e.g., CPU speed, hard disk capacity, weight, etc.). It is a common practice that manufacturers often market the same product with different labels in different regions (Bergan, et al., 1996). For example, a Pentax IQ Zooms in the U.S. is labeled as Pentax Espios elsewhere. This practice makes it difficult for the aggregator to recognize the same product.

Conversely, when models with different features are named the same or slightly differently in different regions, aggregators sometimes cannot recognize the distinction. In the Sony DCR-IP5 case study we found that some vendors labeled the product as DCR-IP5E to indicate that it is an international model compatible with the PAL standard rather than the NTSC standard in the U.S. What makes it worse is that most vendors use DCR-IP5 for both the NTSC model and the PAL model. Although this does not cause big problems because of its common MPEG recording format, for other types of products this could be an issue.

Table 1. Information from multiple sources

	U.S.	**U.K. (in English)**	**U.K. (in German)**
Weight	2.76 lbs	1.26 kg	1,26 kg
Thickness	1.09"		
Price	$2,029 plus $25 shipping	1,699.00 GBP incl. VAT	1.699,00 GBP inkl. MwSt.

The preceding discussions can be summarized into three issues, which we call IDR, related to semantic heterogeneity:

- **I**dentification – same entity being named or described differently, e.g., Pentax IQ Zooms vs. Pentax Espios,
- **D**efinition – a general concept having different definitions, e.g., base price vs. tax-included price; and
- **R**epresentation – the same information being represented differently, e.g., using different currencies and different thousands delimiters.

A global comparison service provider has to reconcile the IDR differences between the data sources and the data users. The provision of the reconciliation is an n^2 problem because when n different parties attempt to exchange data, $n(n$-1), which is O(n^2), conversion programs are needed to ensure each party can interpret the data from all the other parties. Traditionally, theses conversions are hand-coded as computer programs. This is not a scalable solution because the number of conversions to be provided and maintained grows quickly as n becomes large.

ENABLING TECHNOLOGY

The adoption of XML data standards (Madnick, 2001) and the emergence of Web services (Curbera, et al., 2003) will make it much easier to obtain the raw data from various sources. But semantic heterogeneity will continue to exist because of cultural diversity and different user preferences (e.g., prices will be quoted in local currencies until a global currency is adopted, which will not happen in any foreseeable future). The Semantic Web (Berners-Lee, et al., 2001) initiative aims to develop an architecture of the future Web and a set of technologies to represent and reason with data semantics. But the development and wide

deployment of Semantic Web technologies will take some time. Furthermore, the Semantic Web does not directly address the n^2 problem. Thus we need a near-term solution to address the issues identified in the previous section.

Mediation Architecture

The concept of mediation was introduced more than a decade ago (Wiederhold, 1992) to enable applications to use heterogeneous data sources. A mediation architecture is well suited for enabling global price comparison. Below we present a mediation architecture (see Figure 2) and discuss how it can be used for global comparison.

A software system known as a mediator exists between the data sources and the users (or user applications) to provide three services with which the users can obtain information from data sources: data access, entity resolution, and context mapping. Each service may or may not use a certain data model to facilitate its task.

Data access. This service provides the other mediation services with a uniform access to heterogeneous data sources and is responsible for obtaining data from sources using source-specific protocols or extraction rules. A data model, usu-

Figure 2. Mediation architecture

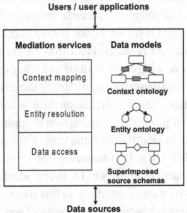

ally in the form of a data schema (e.g., a relational schema), can be superimposed to each source to provide a uniform view of the data in various sources. The superimposed schemas are needed because sources can have different schemas, or they may not have an explicit schema, such as in the case of semi-structured or unstructured sources (e.g., web pages). The superimposed schemas are usually application specific. Source-specific extraction rules can be provided manually as in Cameleon (Firat et al., 2000) and TSIMIS (Garcia-Molina et al., 1995), semi-automatically as in STALKER (Muslea et al., 2001), or automatically as in RoadRunner (Crescenzi et al., 2001). The increasing adoption of web services has made data access on the web much easier. The software components that implement the data access service are considered as wrappers to the original data sources.

Entity resolution. This service addresses the identification issue. Information about the same entity (e.g., a person) or the same kind of entity (e.g., a SONY DCR-IP5 camcorder) often appears in different forms in disparate sources, making it difficult to identify and link them. The service of entity resolution, also known as record linkage or inter-database instance identification (Madnick and Wang, 1989), uses a software component to identify data about the same entity in disparate sources. Many entity resolution techniques measure a certain similarity (or conversely a certain distance) of different records referring to the same entity (Winkler, 2006; Birzan and Tansel, 2006). Recent research has explored the use of an entity ontology (a collection of known entities and their attribute values) to identify these records (Michelson, 2005; Michelson and Knoblock, 2007). For purpose of comparison shopping, it is desirable to identify the same kind of entity (e.g., any SONY DCR-IP5) instead of the same entity (e.g., a particular SONY DCR-IP5 identifiable perhaps by a serial number). In this paper, we do not distinguish between "same entity" and "same

kind of entity", and loosely use "same entity" to refer to both cases.

Context mapping. This service addresses the definition and representation issues. Both the sources and the users often make different semantic assumptions that affect the interpretation of data, in which case we say the sources and the users are in different *contexts*. For example, in one context, the price may be reported in USD, using dot (.) as the decimal point, and not including taxes or shipping charges, yet in another context the price may be reported in Euros, using comma (,) as the decimal point, and including 15% taxes but not including shipping charges. The context mapping service takes the semantic assumptions into account to appropriately transform data from source contexts to the user context.

Figure 3 illustrates how this mediation architecture can be applied to implementing global price comparison services.

Users and sources. Different users, shown in the top portion of Figure 3, have different needs. For illustration purposes, we show two users: one wants prices, in USD, of a product represented using a black dot, the other wants prices, in South Korean won, of a product represented using a hollow circle. The sources, shown in the bottom portion of Figure 3, can be from anywhere in the world and in different forms (e.g., HTML web pages, web services, or relational databases, etc.). The users and the sources may share the same context or be in different contexts.

Wrappers. Within the mediator, a wrapper is created for each source. The wrappers communicate with the sources using source-specific protocols. The output of the wrappers uses a uniform data schema (e.g., a relation of three attributes: <I, V, P>, which correspond to <product_item, vendor, price>). The schema is instantiated with data extracted from each source. The extracted data, although organized according to the uniform schema, is still its original form without any semantic transformation (e.g., if the source reports

Figure 3. Mediation architecture for global comparison service

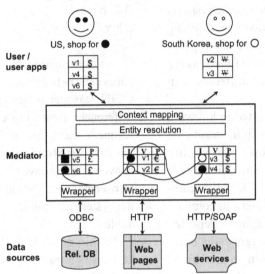

prices in Euros, the extracted prices are in Euros regardless of user preference).

Entity resolution. In Figure 3, we use different symbols to represent different entities. The actual representations of an entity can be different across sources (e.g., using "Sony DCR-IP5", "DCR-IP5", or "MicroMV IP5" to represent a SONY MICROMV DCR-IP5). The entity resolution service identifies these different representations for the same entity and establishes the linkage of these records.

Contexts and context mapping. To simplify explication, we only show different currencies used for price in Figure 3. Later we will introduce more context differences. Different contexts need to be recorded only once before using the service or if there is a context change. When the mediator receives a user request, it compares source and user contexts; if there is a mismatch, it invokes a conversion to reconcile the difference (e.g., using a currency conversion to convert prices from Euros to USD or South Korean won). This mediator service ensures that the users always receive data that can be correctly interpreted

in their contexts, without the need to manually consult other data sources and perform manual data conversions. In the example, the user in the USA receives price data in USD (thanks to the context mapping service) for the desired product (thanks to entity resolution service), similarly for the user in South Korea.

Prototype Demonstration

We have developed a prototype to demonstrate the feasibility of the proposed architecture. The prototype uses the COntext INterchange (COIN) technology (Goh et al., 1999; Firat, 2003) to implement the context mapping service, and the Cameleon web wrapper engine (Firat et al., 2000) to allow web sources to be queried using SQL. Data sources used in the prototype are regional price comparison aggregators, such as those mentioned earlier. To a large extent, regional aggregators have performed entity resolution tasks for various products offered by different vendors. Therefore, we did not include an entity resolution component in the prototype.

In this demonstration, we focus on price data, which may have different contexts in such aspects as domestic and international taxation, shipping charges, and currency. Example contexts are given in Table 2. In addition, conversion functions are provided to deal with potential differences in each aspect.

The Swedish buyer is interested in knowing the total cost of the camcorder from worldwide vendors. For illustration purposes, we simplify the data schema of the wrappers to only include <seller, price> for the SONY DCR-IP5 camcorder. The buyer can issue a query to compare prices of vendors in multiple countries reported by regional price comparison aggregators (such as kelkoo, pricerunner, etc.) using a predefined SQL, *compare_all*:

Select seller, price from kelkoofrance union
//French source
Select seller, price from pricerunnersweden union
//Swedish source
Select seller, price from pricerunneruk union
//UK source

Select seller, price from cnetshopper union
//US source
... //etc.

As illustrated in the sample contexts, differences exist between the sources and the user. The COIN reasoner is designed to determine these differences (from the context definitions) and reconcile them by rewriting the original query into a mediated query that incorporates necessary conversions to convert data from source contexts to user context. Some of the conversions that the system automatically generates are given in Table 3.

Within the COIN system, the original input SQL query is translated into a DATALOG (Ceri et al., 1989) query representation which the reasoner operates upon to generate the mediated query, also in DATALOG. The mediated DATALOG query can be translated back a SQL query for inspection. Assuming that multiple sources are to be used, the mediated query is divided into sub-queries, one for each source, which, when possible, are executed in parallel by the executioner. The fol-

Table 2. Contexts for price in global compassion

		Currency	Tax	Shipping[+]
Source context	**France**	Euro	Included, 19.6%	Domestic: 15 Int'l: 80
	Sweden	Krona	Included, 25%	Domestic: 20 Int'l: 800
	UK	Pound	Included, 17.5%	Domestic: 10 Int'l: 35
	US	USD	Excluded	Domestic: 50 Int'l: 100
Receiver context	**Sweden, Cost**	Krona	Include 25% tax regardless	int'l shipping accordingly
	US, Base	USD	Excluded	Excluded
	US, Cost	USD	If domestic vendor, no tax; otherwise, add 3% import tax	Include domestic or int'l shipping accordingly

[+]: *Assume vendors only distinguish between domestic and interchange shipping charges. This can be refined to use online shipping inquiry services to calculate shipping costs by supplying product's dimensions and weight.*

lowing shows the final mediated query, in SQL format, generated by the system to answer the user's initial query. We hope that readers can examine this and be convinced that all necessary conversions are indeed performed by the following query. In order to accomplish the conversions, sometimes auxiliary data sources are used. In this example, olsen (a wrapper for www.oanda.com) is an auxiliary online source that provides current and historical currency exchange rates; the system uses current date (*i.e.*, date when the query is issued).

```
//French source. Deduct 19.6% French tax;
add 25% Swedish tax;
//add €80 int'l shipping; convert Euros to Krona
select kelkoofrance.seller,
    ((((kelkoofrance.price/1.196)+((kelkoofrance.price/
1.196)*0.25))+80)*olsen.rate)
from   (select seller, price
        from  kelkoofrance) kelkoofrance,
        //find exchange rate using auxiliary source
        (select 'EUR', 'SEK', rate, '11/01/02' from  olsen
        where  exchanged='EUR'
        and    expressed='SEK'
        and    date='11/01/02') olsen
union

//Swedish source. Add 20 Krona domestic shipping
select pricerunnersweden.seller, (pricerunnersweden.
price+20)
from   (select seller, price
        from  pricerunnersweden) pricerunnersweden
union
```

```
//UK source. Deduct 17.5% UK tax; add 25% Swedish tax;
//add £35 int'l shipping; convert Pounds to Krona
select priceruuneruk.seller, ((((priceruuneruk.price/
1.175)+((priceruuneruk.price/1.175)*0.25))+35)*olsen.rate)
from   (select seller, price
        from  priceruuneruk) priceruuneruk,
        //find exchange rate using auxiliary source
        (select 'GBP', 'SEK', rate, '11/01/02' from  olsen
        where  exchanged='GBP'
        and    expressed='SEK'
        and    date='11/01/02') olsen
union

//US source. Add 25% Swedish tax; add $100 int'l shipping;
//convert USD to Krona
select cnetshopper.seller, (((cnetshopper.price+(cnetshopper.
price*0.25))+100)*olsen.rate)
from   (select seller, price
        from  cnetshopper) cnetshopper,
        //find exchange rate using auxiliary source
        (select 'USD', 'SEK', rate, '11/01/02' from  olsen
        where  exchanged='USD'
        and    expressed='SEK'
        and    date='11/01/02') olsen
union
...
```

An excerpt of the query execution results is shown in Table 4 (reformatted from prototype output). All prices have been converted into the context of the Swedish user, who can easily compare them on the same basis.

Table 3. Appropriate conversions for reconciliation of context differences

Source	Conversion
France	Deduct 19.6% French tax, add 25% Swedish tax, add €80 international shipping, convert euros to krona
Sweden	Add 20 krona domestic shipping
US	Add 25% Swedish tax, add $100 international shipping, convert USD to krona
UK	Deduct 17.5% UK tax, add 25% Swedish tax, add £35 international shipping, convert pounds to krona

We demonstrated the case showing how the application works for one particular receiver context. The application also works for any user whose context is one of the example source or receiver contexts in Table 2. We will not show the other cases to save space.

Prototype Implementation Using COIN

Below we provide an overview of the COIN technology and show how it is used to implement the global comparison service demonstrated earlier. We also discuss how it solves the n^2 problem.

The COIN mediator consists of application specific as well as generic components, as shown in Figure 4. The application-specific components are created only once during initial configuration of an application, or when a new user/source is added or context of a user/source has changed. After this has been done, a user can query the sources as if all sources were in the user context. The generic components intercept user queries, compare the user contexts with the contexts of the sources involved; if there is any difference, they rewrite user queries to generate mediated queries that incorporate necessary conversions to reconcile context differences, and execute the mediated queries to extract data from the sources

and transform the data into the user context. The generic components can be used for other applications when it is supplied with the corresponding application-specific components. Below we briefly describe each component.

Shared ontology. It models the application domain using a collection of semantic types (which correspond to the high level concepts in the domain, e.g., *price*) and their relationships. Figure 5 gives a graphical representation of the ontology used in the prototype. A semantic type can be related to another in three ways: 1) as a subtype or supertype (e.g., *price* is a subtype of *monetaryValue*); 2) as an attribute (e.g., *price* is the *prodPrice* attribute of *product*); and 3) as a modifier or contextual attribute, whose value is specified in context descriptions and can functionally determine the interpretation of instances of the type that has this modifier (e.g., *monetaryValue* type has a *currency* modifier). There is a modifier-free type *basic* that serves as the supertype of all the other types in the ontology. To avoid clutter, the subtype-supertype relationship between all the other types and the *basic* type is not shown in Figure 5. A subtype recursively inherits the attributes and modifiers of its supertypes.

Context descriptions. They are the declarative descriptions of the representational and definitional variants of the high level ontological

Table 4. Excerpt of results in user's context

Source	Seller	Price (*i.e.* total cost in krona)
Sweden	Foto & Elektronik AB	15815
	Expert Citybutiken/Konserthuset	16015
	...	...
	Click ontime	23470
...	...	
US	Bridgeviewphoto.com	10255
	PC-Video Online	10594
	...	...
	Circuit City	14933

Figure 4. COIN mediator applied to global comparison

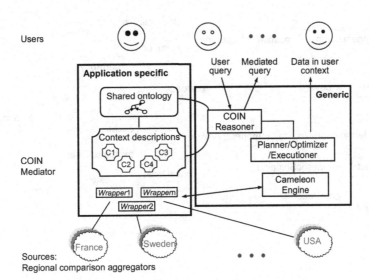

concepts (e.g., *price* can be quoted in different currencies). The descriptions can also include implicit assumptions (e.g., domestic tax rates) made by the data sources and the data receivers (which can be users or user applications). A context, identified by a unique ID (e.g., C1), is a set of specifications of all modifiers in the ontology. Two contexts are different if there is at least one modifier that has different values. In addition, the context descriptions also include conversion rules for each modifier between different modifier values (e.g., rules that specify how to convert price from one currency to another). We call such conversions *component conversions*.

The correspondence between the data elements (i.e., the table fields) in the data sources and the ontological concepts are established via declarations. Each data element is also associated with a context via declarations. These declarations as well as the ontology and the context descriptions are expressed using a logic formalism of the F-logic (Kiffer, et al., 1995) family. An example component conversion for currency modifier is shown below; it is parameterized with context Cx

and Cy and can convert between any currencies (see Box 1):

Wrappers. The wrapper specifications consist of source-specific schema declarations and data extraction rules for each data element. Details of wrapper specification can be found in Firat, et al. (2000). The actual wrappers are produced by the Cameleon engine (discussed later) using the wrapper declarations.

COIN reasoner. This is a query rewriting engine that allows users to issue queries against sources without concerning context differences. The query it generates, called the mediated query, incorporates necessary conversions to reconcile context differences between the sources involved and the user. Context differences are determined by comparing the modifier assignments between the source context and the user context for each concept involved.

Planner/Optimizer/Executioner (POE). It takes the mediated query as the input, generates a query execution plan that considers source capability constraints, optimizes the plan by imposing

Figure 5. Lightweight ontology for global price comparison

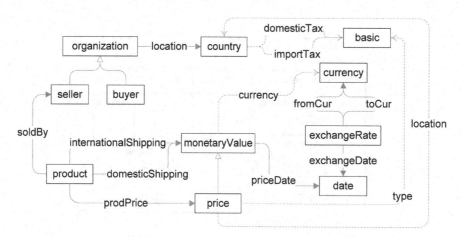

Box 1.

$$\forall X : price \vdash$$
$$X[cvt(currency, Cy)@Cx, u \rightarrow v] \leftarrow$$
$$X[currency(Cx) \rightarrow C_f] \wedge X[currency(Cy) \rightarrow C_t] \wedge x[dataOf \rightarrow T] \wedge$$
$$olsen\_(A, B, R, D) \wedge C_f \overset{Cy}{=} A \wedge C_t \overset{Cy}{=} B \wedge T \overset{Cy}{=} D \wedge R[value(Cy) \rightarrow r] \wedge v = u * r.$$

an execution order of sub-queries and employing parallel execution when possible, and subsequently executes the plan to produce the dataset interpretable in the user context. Details of POE can be found in Alatovic (2002). The parallelism significantly reduces the execution time. In the prototype, the execution time is determined by the regional aggregator with the longest response time, and it is not dependent on the number of regional aggregators used.

Cameleon engine. It uses the wrapper specifications to produce the source-specific wrappers and provide an SQL interface to other components that use the wrappers.

The COIN approach solves the n^2 problem by using a lightweight ontology and a reasoner that can dynamically compose composite conversions using a small number of component conversions. We briefly describe these mechanisms here, the details of which can be found in Zhu and Madnick (2006a).

A lightweight ontology includes only high level concepts (e.g., *price*) as opposed to their well-specified variants (e.g, "price in USD not including taxes or shipping charges", "price in Euros including 15% taxes but not including shipping charges", etc.). Imagine how big the ontology would be had we included all possible variants of *price* in Figure 5. As an artifact, a lightweight ontology is much easier to create than a well-specified ontology. The ambiguity of the high level concepts is removed by the context descriptions. In other words, the well-specified ontology can be derived from the lightweight ontology and the context descriptions.

The lightweight ontology provides the vocabulary and a structure for describing contexts. The reasoner exploits the structure to dynamically compose conversions. As mentioned earlier, the conversions specified for each modifier between different modifier values are called *component conversions*. An ontological concept may have multiple modifiers. A *composite conversion* is composed by the reasoner to incorporate the component conversions, if necessary, of all modifiers of a concept.

The dynamic composition of composite conversions is illustrated in Figure 6, where the triangle symbol on the left represents the price concept in the source context, and the circle symbol on the right represents the price concept in the receiver context. For the data in the source context to be viewed in the receiver context, they need to be converted by applying the appropriate composite conversion. In the illustration, we assume that *price* has *currency* and *scaleFactor* modifiers, and their corresponding component conversions $\mathrm{cvt}_{currency}$ and $\mathrm{cvt}_{scaleFactor}$ have been provided. The dashed straight arrow represents the composite conversion that would have been implemented manually in other approaches.

With the COIN lightweight ontology approach, the composite conversion can be automatically composed using the predefined component conversions. As shown in Figure 6, the composition will first apply the component conversion for *currency* modifier (represented by $\mathrm{cvt}_{currency}$), then apply the component conversion for *scaleFactor* modifier (represented by $\mathrm{cvt}_{scaleFactor}$).

The composition algorithm is described in Figure 7 and is implemented using abductive constraint logic programming (ACLP) (Kakas, et al., 2000) and constraint handling rules (CHR) (Frühwirth, 1998).

In the worst case scenario, the number of predefined component conversions required by the COIN approach is:

$$\sum_{i=1}^{m} n_i(n_i - 1)$$

where n_i is the number of unique values that the ith modifier has in all contexts, m is the number of modifiers in the lightweight ontology.

While the formula appears to be n^2, it is fundamentally different from the approach that requires the manual creation of *comprehensive conversions* between each pair of the parties engaging in data

Figure 6. Composite conversion composed using component conversions. Without composition, one would hand-code a direct conversion to convert the price in 1000's of KRW to the price in 1's of USD; this conversion illustrated by the straight dashed arrow. With COIN, this composite conversion can be derived from the component conversions for currency (cvt$_{currency}$) and scale factor (cvt$_{scaleFactor}$).

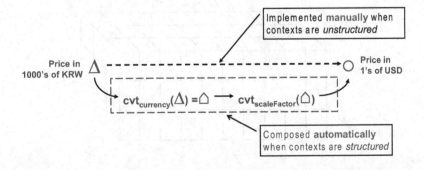

exchange. The supplied conversions needed in COIN are only the component conversions, which are much simpler than the comprehensive conversions that consider the differences of all data elements in all aspects between two parties.

Furthermore, the number of component conversions is significantly smaller than the number of pair-wise comprehensive conversions. Consider a scenario we have studied where there are 50 data sources, each having its own context, and the users share contexts with their preferred data source. In the lightweight ontology in Figure 5, the *price* concept has three modifiers. Concept

country also has two modifiers, but no component conversions are needed fro them because they are used to describe the tax rates, which are used by the component conversions of *location* modifier. Assume the 50 sources are located in 10 countries with different currencies, and there are four *types* of prices (e.g., base price, price with domestic taxes included, price with domestic taxes and shipping charges, and price with all taxes and shipping charges). The pair-wise approach requires 2450 (i.e., 50*49) predefined comprehensive conversions, the COIN approach requires only 192 (i.e., 10*9+10*9+4*3) component conversions.

Figure 7. Conversion composition algorithm

```
Input: data value V, corresponding concept C in ontology,
       source context Cx, target context Cy
Output: data value V (interpretable in context Cy)

Find all modifiers of C
  For each modifier m
      Find and compare m's values in Cx and Cy
      If different: V=cvtm(V, Cx, Cy); else, V=V
Return V
```

Figure 8. Intuition of scalability of COIN approach. Component conversions are provided along the modifier axes. Composite conversions between any cubes in the space can be automatically composed.

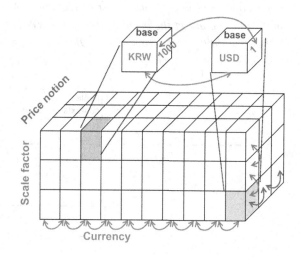

All the 2450 comprehensive conversions can be composed dynamically, as needed, using the 192 component conversions by the COIN reasoner. As explained in (Zhu and Madnick, 2006a), the actual number of component conversions can be considerably less if they can be parameterized – for example, the olsen web source can be used to create a general conversion between any two currency values.

We use Figure 8 to further explain the intuition of the scalability result.

The modifiers of each ontological concept span a context space within which the variants of the concept exist. Each modifier defines a dimension. In the figure, we show the space spanned by the three modifiers of *price* concept. The component conversions required by the COIN approach are defined along the axes of the modifiers. With the composition capability, the COIN approach can automatically generate all the conversions between units (e.g., the cubes in a three-dimensional space, as sown in Figure 8) in the space using the component conversions along the dimensions. In contrast, the approaches that suffer from the n^2 problem require the conversions between any two units in the space to be supplied.

RELATED WORK

Most existing commercial price comparison services are provided only regionally and regional sources usually do not have representational and definitional semantic problems that are pervasive in global data sources. The service providers use a product catalog, which can be considered as an entity ontology, to address the identification problem. We have mentioned a few commercial providers and used them as the data sources in the global comparison prototype. Brief reviews of other commercial providers can be found in Smith (2002) and Fasli (2006).

There have been a few research prototypes of price comparison. As in the commercial case, the research prototypes that we are aware of do not address the semantic heterogeneity issues discussed here. The PriceBot agent (Doorenbos, et al., 1997) uses inductive learning techniques to learn how to extract product and price data from web sites about a certain category of products. The WhereBuy shopping broker (Santos, et al., 2001) uses product catalogs to identify the products offered by different vendors; it subsequently extract the prices (the raw data) for price comparison. The IPIS (Intelligent Product Information Search) system (Kim, et al., 2005) focuses on the product identification issue. It uses ontology matching techniques to rewrite queries to match products of vendors that may use different category schemes (e.g., Television vs. TV&HDTV) and different attribute names (size vs. diagonal). Assuming all sources are accessible via web services, Fasli (2006) presents a similar architecture where the middle agent serves as the mediator.

We have focused on price comparison in this paper. But comparison can involve other dimensions to serve different purposes (e.g., compare other features, such as size and weight, compare vendor reputation, or assist buyers to make decisions). A classification scheme of different comparison agents can be found in Wan, et al., (2003).

In addition to the technical issues discussed here, there are other issues that concern various stakeholders of price comparison. These issues, some of which are summarized in Smith (2002), include the strategy of comparison service providers (Madnick and Siegel, 2002), vendor pricing strategies (Koças, 2005), data reuse regulations (Zhu and Madnick, 2006b).

DISCUSSION

We have presented a mediation architecture to address data semantics issues in global comparison and demonstrated its feasibility using a prototype global aggregator. There are certain limitations of the prototype. For example, the wrapper specifications are manually created and need to be updated when there are changes at the web sources. The entity resolution task has mainly relied on the underlying sources. However, the mediation architect is not subject to such limitations. For example, the wrappers can be generated using any automatic methods developed in recent research, e.g., RoadRunner (Crescenzi et al., 2001). Entity resolution can be implemented using techniques such as those in Michelson (2005) and Kim et al. (2005).

Certain other limitations may not be resolved in practice using any technology. For example, in general, there is no reliable means to obtain data from changing and uncooperative sources. Even when all sources use web services, a source can change its API's without notification. Conversion for subjective measures can be problematic. Consider the star ratings of different sites: the same product may be given different ratings at different sites; site may use different maximum number of stars for top ratings (e.g., 3-star vs. 5-star). There are generally no all-agreed-upon conversions among these different ratings.

To use the mediation architecture for global comparison in practice, knowledge about the contexts of various sources and receivers need to be collected. Then the shared ontology should be developed, which will be used to encode the context knowledge. During these knowledge acquisition and ontology development stages, tools such as Protégé (protege.stanford.edu) are useful. An extension to Protégé has been developed (Tan et al., 2004) so that Protégé can be used develop COIN ontology and create context descriptions.

Overall, the mediation architecture and the technologies demonstrated can be used to enable global comparison aggregation services. These new services will benefit a variety of users. They can help consumers find the best deals around the world; they can also assist researchers and policy makers to systematically and efficiently collect global market data at low cost; manufacturers can also use the services to find out the actual retail prices of their products around world, with which they can better assess demand and set appropriate wholesale and suggested retail prices. The emergence and the wide usage of global comparison services will make the web the truly efficient platform for e-business.

REFERENCES

Alatovic, T. (2002). *Capabilities aware planner/optimizer/executioner for context interchange project*. M.S. thesis, MIT.

Berners-Lee, T., Hendler, J., & Lassila, O. (2001). The semantic Web. *Scientific American, 284*(5), 34-43.

Bergan, M., Dutta, S., & Shugan, S.M. (1996). Branded variants: A retail perspective. *Journal of Marketing Research, 33*(1), 9-19.

Birzan, D.G., & Tansel, A.U. (2006). A survey of entity resolution and record linkage methodologies. *Communications of the IIMA, 6*(3), 41-50.

Ceri, S., Gottlob, G., & Tanca, L. (1989). What you always wanted to know about Datalog (and never dared to ask). *IEEE Transactions on Knowledge and Data Engineering, 1*(1), 146-166.

Chang, C.H., Kaye, M., Girgis, M.R., & Shaalan, K.F. (2006). A survey of Web information extraction system. *IEEE Transactions on Knowledge and Data Engineering, 18*(10), 1411-1428.

Crescenzi, V., Mecca G., & Merialdo, P. (2001). RoadRunner: Towards automatic data extraction from large web sites. *Proceedings of the 27th International Conference on Very Large Databases (VLDB 2001)*, (pp. 109-118).

Curbera, F., Khalaf, R., Mukhi, N., Tai, S., & Weerawarana, S. (2003). The next step in Web services. *Communications of the ACM, 46*(10), 29-34.

Doorenbos, R.B., Etzioni, O., & Weld, D.S. (1997). A scalable comparison-shopping agent for the World-Wide Web', *Proceedings of the First International Conference on Autonomous Agents* (*Agents'97*), (pp. 39-48).

Fasli, M. (2006). Shopbots: A syntactic present, a semantic future. *IEEE Internet Computing*, *10*(6), 69-75.

Firat, A., Madnick, S., & Siegel, M. (2000). The Cameleon Web wrapper engine. *Proceedings of the Workshop on Technologies for E-Services*, September 14-15, 2000, Cairo, Egypt.

Firat, A. (2003). *Information integration using contextual knowledge and ontology merging*. Ph.D. thesis, Sloan School of Management, MIT.

Frühwirth, T. (1998). Theory and practice of constraint handling rules. *Journal of Logic Programming*, *37*(1-3), 95-138.

Garcia-Molina, H., Hammer, J., Ireland, K., Papakonstantinou, Y., Ullman, J., & Widom., J. (1995). Integrating and accessing heterogeneous information sources in TSIMMIS. *AAAI Symposium on Information Gathering*, Stanford, California, (pp. 61-64).

Goh, C. H., Bressan, S., Madnick, S., & Siegel, M. (1999). Context interchange: New features and formalisms for the intelligent integration of information. *ACM Transactions on Information Systems*, *17*(3), 270-293.

Kakas, C., Michael, A., & Mourlas, C. (2000). ACLP: Integrating abduction and constraint solving. *Journal of Logic Programming*, *44*(1-3), 129-177.

Kiffer, M., Laussen, G., & Wu, J. (1995). Logic foundations of object-oriented and frame-based languages. *Journal of the ACM*, *42*(4), 741-843.

Kim, W., Choi, D., & Park, S. (2005). Product information meta-search framework for electronic commerce through ontology mapping. *The Semantic Web: Research and Applications, LNCS 3532,* 408-422

Koças, C. (2005). A model of internet pricing under price-comparison shopping. *International Journal of Electronic Commerce*, *10*(1), 111-134.

Madnick, S.E. (2001). The misguided silver bullet: What XML will and will NOT do to help information integration. *Proceedings of the Third International Conference on Information Integration and Web-based Applications and Services* (IIWAS2001), September 2001, Linz, Austria, (pp. 61-72).

Madnick, S. E., & Siegel, M. D. (2002). Seizing the opportunity: Exploiting Web aggregation', *MISQ Executive*, *1*(1), 35-46.

Madnick, S. E., & Wang Y. R. (1989). The interdatabase instance identification problem in integrating autonomous systems. *Proceedings of the Fifth International Data Engineering Conference*, February 1989, Los Angeles, CA.

Maier, P. (2005). A "Global Village" without borders? International price differentials at eBay. Netherlands Central Bank Working Paper, #044.

McCarthy, J., & Buvac S. (1994). *Formalizing context (expanded notes)*. Stanford University.

Michelson, M. J. (2005). *Building queryable datasets from ungrammatical and unstructured sources*. M.S. thesis, University of Southern California.

Michelson, M. J., & Knoblock, C. A. (2007). An automatic approach to semantic annotation of unstructured, ungrammatical sources: A first look. *IJCAI'07 Workshop on Analytics for Noisy Unstructured Text Data*, January 8, Hyderabad, India, (pp. 123-130).

Muslea, I., Minton, S., & Knoblock, C. (2001). Hierarchical wrapper induction for semistructured information source. *Journal of Autonomous Agents and Multi-Agent Systems, 4*(1-2), 93-114.

Santos, S. C., Angelim, S., & Meira, S. R. (2001). Building comparison-shopping brokers on the Web. *Proceedings of the Second international Workshop on Electronic Commerce* November 16-17, L. Fiege, G. Mühl, and U. G. Wilhelm, Eds. *LNCS 2232,* 26-38.

Smith, M. D. (2002). The impact of shopbots on electronic markets. *Journal of the Academy of Marketing Science, 30*(4), 446-454.

Tan, P., Madnick, S. E., & Tan, K. L (2004). Context mediation in the semantic Web: Handling OWL ontology and data disparity through context interchange. Processing of Semantic Web and Database (SWDB), (pp. 140-154).

Wan, Y., Menon, S., & Ramaprasad, A. (2003). A classification of product comparison agents. *Proceedings of International Conference on Electronic Commerce* (*ICEC'03*), Sept. 30 – Oct. 3, Pittsburgh, PA.

Wiederhold, G. (1992). Mediators in the architecture of future information systems. *Computer, 25*(3), 38-49.

Winkler, W.E. (2006). Overview of Record Linkage and Current Research Directions, Research Report, Statistics #2006-2, US Census Bureau, available at http://www.census.gov/srd/papers/pdf/rrs2006-02.pdf.

Zhu, H. (2002). A technology and policy analysis for global e-business. M.S. thesis, Massachusetts Institute of Technology.

Zhu, H., & Madnick, S. (2006a). A lightweight ontology approach to scalable interoperability. *VLDB Workshop on Ontologies-based techniques or DataBases and Information Systems* (*ODBIS'06*), September 11, 2006, Seoul, Korea.

Zhu, H., & Madnick, S. E. (2006b). Reutilization and legal protection of non-copyrightable database contents. *Proceedings of the Fourth IASTED International Conference on Law and Technology* (*LawTech'06*), October 9-11, Cambridge, MA, USA.

Chapter IV
The Efficiency of Different Search Patterns in Electronic Market

Theresa Lauraeus-Niinivaara
Helsinki School of Economics, Finland

Timo Saarinen
Helsinki School of Economics, Finland

Anne Sunikka
Helsinki School of Economics, Finland

Anssi Öörni
Helsinki School of Economics, Finland

ABSTRACT

Electronic markets are expected to facilitate consumer information search and product comparison to the extent that consumers are able to accumulate nearly perfect information. The authors present an analysis of search patterns based on a laboratory experiment on product search processes. They identified three types of search patterns in the experiment: sequential, agent search, and iterative search. They studied the factors affecting the choice and the outcome of agent search pattern compared to the other search patterns. The results show that the employed search pattern has an impact on search cost and the efficiency of search measured with purchase price and the time used for searching. Agent search seems to combine low search costs with high efficiency. Sequential search still emerged as the dominant search pattern even though it leads to the most expensive purchase. Iterative search pattern search pattern.

INTRODUCTION

Consumer's pre-purchase information search is an essential part of consumer decision making process (Bettman 1979; Bettman et al. 1990; Engel et al. 1990; Howard and Sheth 1969; Olhavsky 1985, Schmidt and Spreng 1996). In recent years, there have been many studies into consumer search behavior in a digital environment (Chiang 2006, Jansen 2006, Jansen and Pooh 2001, Johnson et al. 2004, Lauraeus-Niinivaara et al. 2007, Lauraeus-Niinivaara et al. 2008, Smith and Spreng 1996, Spink et al. 2005, Öörni 2002, Öörni 2003) in the context of search attributes (Johnson et al. 2004, Smith and Spreng 1996).

Recently, there has been research into internet-based market efficiency (Hogue and Lohse 1999, Wu et al. 2004, Öörni 2003) and search costs (Biswas 2004, Jansen 2006, Wu et al. 2004, Öörni 2003). In a digital environment, consumer information pre-purchase and search behavior might differ from the traditional search behavior (Jansen and Pooh 2001, Johnson et al. 2004, Öörni 2002).

There are nearly 60 factors that have been found to influence the consumer pre-purchase information search (Schmidt and Spreng 1996; Srinivasan and Ratchford 1991). In the past decades, some researchers have modeled the relationships among these 60 factors influencing the consumer search behavior (Kulviwat et al. 2004, Schmidt and Spreng 1996, Srinivasan and Ratchford 1991, Punj and Staelin 1983). Consumer information search has been one of the most enduring literature streams in consumer research (Beatty and Smith 1987). Marketing and consumer behavior researchers have been examining consumer's pre-purchase information seeking behavior since at least 1917 (Copeland 1917) and even today most consumer information processing and decision making models include pre-purchase information search as one of the key components (Bettman 1979, Bettman et. al 1990, Engel et al. 1990,

Howard and Sheth 1969, Olshavsky 1985). The research of consumer behavior in electronic markets and consumer choice of distribution channels is in need of sound theoretical frameworks that enable researchers to integrate electronic markets research with adjacent fields of study.

Consumer search is the main method, besides advertising, for acquiring information necessary for making purchase decisions. Consumers look for products with desired qualities and sellers offering these products at competitive prices in an attempt to decide what, when, and from whom to purchase. Markets are dynamic, which results in information becoming obsolete (Stigler 1961). Changing identity of sellers and buyers, and also fluctuations in supply and demand, result in uncertainty. Identification of prospective products and sellers is often the dominant motive of search. Another, yet related, cause is consumers' inability to ascertain product quality and seller reliability before the purchase decision (Stigler 1961, Moorthy et. al. 1997, Bakos 1997, Öörni 2003).

Information search precedes many consumer decisions (Newman and Staelin 1971, Bettman et. al 1990, Moorthy et. al. 1997, Punj and Staelin 1983, Beatty and Smith 1987, Smith and Spreng 1996). However, information search is often costly (Stigler 1961, Wu et al. 2004, Öörni 2002). The main cost factor is typically the opportunity cost of the searcher's time (Wu et al. 2004, Öörni 2003). Search costs depend on consumer's ability to search, which heavily impacts the pattern of search one can adopt (Öörni 2002).

We have three claims in our work: 1) Consumers employ different search patterns in their pre-purchase search (H1), 2) Age, gender and knowledge have an effect on choosing a search pattern (H2), 3) Different search patterns influence the outcomes of search activity (H3). In the body of this paper, we will first discuss the prototypical search patterns identified in consumer behavioral literature; sequential and agent search. This work connects the search pattern to the outcomes of search, i.e. purchase price and time. We set up a laboratory experiment in which the subjects searched for compact discs. We observed the resulting search process, identified the prototypical patterns of search, and studied the impact of the patterns on the outcomes of search. Further, we uncovered a few demographic variables and personal characteristics that seem to shape the search along with the uncertainties. Finally we will discuss the outcomes of search.

INFORMATION SEARCH BEHAVIOR

There have been three major theoretical streams of consumer information search literature (Smith and Spreng 1996). The first is the *psychological / motivational approach*, which incorporates the individual, the product class, and the task related variables such as beliefs and attitudes (Beatty and Smith 1987, Duncan and Olshavsky 1982) and involvement (Beatty and Smith 1987). The second is the *economics approach*, which uses the cost-benefit framework to study information search (Smith and Spreng 1996). The economic theory of search states that consumers weigh the cost and benefits of search when making search decisions. The third one is the *consumer information processing approach* which focuses on memory and cognitive information processing theory (Smith and Spreng 1996).

A search is often characterized by the locus of search activity. Information search behavior can be defined as "the motivated activation of knowledge stored in memory or acquisition of information from the environment" (Engel et al. 1990). As the definition suggests, information search can be either internal or external. *Internal search* is based on the retrieval of knowledge from memory. *External search* consists of collecting information from the marketplace (Engel et al. 1990).

It is generally believed that consumers tend to acquire information as a strategy of certain

risk reduction efforts in the events of identified uncertainty regarding the outcome of an action (McCleary and Whitney 1994) and in the events of identified discrepancy between external information and prior product knowledge to protect themselves and to maximize their satisfaction (Bettman 1979). However, consumers' information search behavior is likely to be influenced by the perceived cost of information search. Jansen and Pooh (2001) report that the internet seekers use different search characteristics from traditional seekers. Consumers are likely to search for information as long as they believe that the benefits of acquiring information outweigh the cost of information search as indicated in "the economics of information" (EoI) theory of Stigler's seminal paper 1961. Consumers are often searching the web for information on more than one topic concurrently, and multitasking web search sessions are longer (Spink et al. 2005).

As a measure of search behavior we followed the Kiel and Layton's retail search factors (Kiel and Layton 1981). Search behavior can be measured by the *actual shopping time* (AST), and we used actual minutes spent on search. In addition, we noted the *price of the product*. Sub-constructs of search behaviour are the width and depth of search, meaning the extensiveness of search. The *width of search* can be defined as the number of alternatives considered. The *depth of search* describes how many attributes of a product or alternative are evaluated.

The Costs of Consumer Information Search

Cost of information search in the theoretical framework is presented by three dimensions: financial cost, time spent and cognitive effort required (Bakos 1997, Öörni 2003). Each dimension of cost represents a different perspective of cost. Financial cost represents the amount of money spent to acquire the necessary information. Time spent refers to the amount of time required for information search. Effort refers to the amount of cognitive effort required to process the information. The first dimension of the proposed cost of information search construct, financial cost, was first proposed by the Stigler (Stigler 1961) in the EoI theory. The other two dimensions of the cost of information search; time spent, and effort required, are mostly utilized in consumer behavior studies (Bettman and Sujan 1987, Jansen 2006, Wu et al. 2004, Lauraeus-Niinivaara et al. 2008).

Search theory is rather uniform in its definition of the implications of search costs on consumer behavior and price dispersion (Öörni 2002). Stigler (Stigler 1961) proposed that high search costs will lead value maximizing consumers to limit their pre-purchase search, which results in less than perfectly informed purchase decisions. Since consumers vary on their market knowledge and search costs, relatively wide price dispersions persist in many consumer markets. The very basis of search theory (Stigler 1961) suggests two of the most profound measures of search costs: the amount of search and price dispersion for products of comparable quality. These are the two key measures that this work examines in an attempt to determine whether electronic consumer markets have positively affected pre-purchase consumer search (Lauraeus-Niinivaara et al. 2008, Öörni 2003).

Determinants of Search

There are nearly 60 factors that have been found to have an influence on consumer pre-purchase information search (Schmidt and Spreng 1996; Srinivasan and Ratchford 1991). According to Srinivasan and Rachford (1991), the factors can be divided into three dimensions: Environmental factors, situational factors and factors of consumer characteristics. However, we concentrate mainly on consumer characteristics in our study.

Age and Gender

According to earlier literature, age should have an impact on search behavior. In addition, it is generally assumed that males are more interested, and thus more experienced users of the internet.

Experience

Prior knowledge is presented by two components: familiarity and expertise within the "dimensions of prior product knowledge" (Alba and Hutchinson 1987). Experience or expertise works through both subjective and objective knowledge. The multi-dimensional prior knowledge construct was initially developed by Alba and Hutchinson (1987) in order to better define and understand the construct itself and the effects on consumer decision making and information search behaviour.

Information search behavior can be divided into internal and external search. Internal information search occurs when consumers use information already stored in their memory – knowledge from previous search, experience with products, or passively acquired information during normal daily activities. Earlier studies of knowledge used a single construct of prior knowledge. In later studies, the construct of prior knowledge has been divided into objective and subjective knowledge (Brucks 1985, Park et al. 1994, Spreng and Olshavsky 1993, Schmidt and Spreng 1996), and the experience works through both of those (Park et al. 1994, Schmidt and Spreng 1996). Because objective knowledge presents what is actually stored in memory, it can also be called expertise or the ability to perform product-related tasks (Alba and Hutchinson 1987). It has been found that subjective and objective knowledge are highly related (Brucks 1985, Spreng and Olshavsky 1990). Brucks (1985) showed that objective knowledge compared to subjective knowledge has a different influence on search behavior: objective knowledge leads to deeper search behavior (more attributes searched), whereas subjective knowledge had no influence on the depth of search.

Objective Knowledge

As objective knowledge represents expertise or ability to perform product-related tasks (Alba and Hutchinson 1987), the construct is measured with frequency of the internet usage and knowledge of web sites that the researchers thought would be beneficial in accomplishing the tasks efficiently.

In our study, the item measuring objective knowledge and experience with the internet was the hours of internet usage per week. Experience with search engines and record shops were measured with the number of either search engines or music record shops familiar to the respondents.

Subjective Knowledge

Subjective knowledge is described as including both knowledge and confidence in the adequacy of one's knowledge level (Brucks 1985), and research has shown that people's self-assessments of knowledge do not always match their actual knowledge levels (Brucks 1985). Subjective knowledge is strongly related to a consumer's past experiences about a product domain (Alba and Hutchinson 1987, Bettman and Sujan 1987) and may be closely related to confidence (Park and Lessig 1981). According to Ducan and Olshavsky (1982), high subjective knowledge means that consumers have confidence in their ability to perform product-related tasks including information search.

In our study, the self estimation of the ability to search in general on the internet environment, and in particular, the ability to search music on the internet, was measured. The self-estimation scale was from four to ten.

THE SHAPE OF THE SEARCH PROCESS

The main search related cost factor is typically the opportunity cost of the searcher's time. Search costs depend on consumer's ability to search, which heavily impacts the pattern of search one can adopt. Exhaustive consumer search, or at least a radical increase in the size of the consideration set, could be attained if a simultaneous (agent) search pattern prevailed in the electronic markets. We next describe the two dominant search patterns, sequential and simultaneous (also agent) search, found in the literature. These patterns are portrayed in Figures 1 and 2.

Sequential Search

Sequential search occurs when a consumer consecutively visits or contacts sellers. Each visit is composed of an information gathering and a buying decision phase. The consumer familiarizes her/himself with the products available and decides whether to purchase a product or to visit the next store. The consumer can compare the products in various stores, yet s/he has to resort to her/his memory as a source of product information to evaluate those products not in the current store.

Agent Search

Product comparison could be more efficient if the consumer were able to evaluate more available products side by side. This is the essence of simultaneous, in the other words, agent search. All information needed for the evaluation is readily available, and the consumer has no need to resort to secondary information sources. Thus, there are only two phases in the process: information gathering and buying decision. Whinston et al. (1997, p. 267) suggest that online search technol-

Figure 1. Sequential search pattern (adapted from Whinston et al.1997, p. 266)

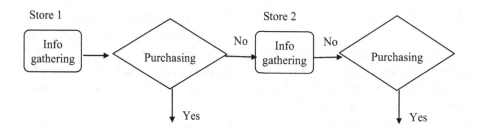

Figure 2. Simultaneous (agent) search process (adapted from Whinston et al.1997, p. 266)

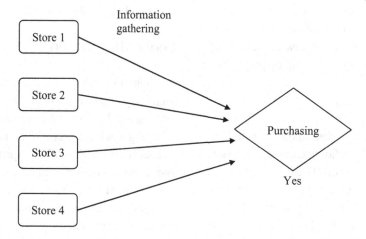

ogy may automate the search process and enable consumers to execute more sophisticated and efficient searches.

According to Stigler (1961), search takes place when a buyer (or seller) wishes to ascertain the most favorable price, and must thus canvass various sellers (or buyers). Stigler developed the EoI theory on the assumption of the so called fixed sample size (FSS) searching, according to which an individual obtains all samples at once, and the commodity is purchased from the seller quoting the lowest price. In other than the economics literature, FSS searching is also called simultane-

ous or agent search. The essence of agent search is that a consumer is able to evaluate available products side by side.

In offline circumstances, a consumer might collect a simultaneous search sample based on either internal information formed by experience of repeated purchases (internal search), or by, for example, acquainting her/himself with special issues of consumer journals that compare products the consumer is interested in (external search). In online settings, a consumer can use various tools (for example, comparison sites, search engines or comparison agents) to collect information that is available on the internet on a particular product or service. According to Whinston et al. (1997), price search in a price database is an example of a simultaneous search in an online environment.

Electronic and agent search is given a definition by Öörni (2002, 2003) the characteristics of which are i) the information channel is electronic, ii) all the information is retrieved in a single stage iii) no human interaction is required. In his empirical research, Öörni (2002, 2003) found out that the use of electronic and agent search in the context of travel services was very rare at the beginning of 2000's.

Manning and Morgan (1982) stated that both agent search and sequential search may be considered special cases of a *general search pattern*, according to which a searcher obtains more than one sample at a time and then has to decide how many more times to sample. Agrawal et al. (2005) compared simultaneous search and sequential search, and concluded that simultaneous search allows for information gathering fast, though overinvestment in information gathering may occur (i.e. the simultaneous search sample might be too extensive). Sequential search, on the other hand, is slow, but avoids unnecessary information gathering. The optimal search pattern has been suggested to combine the speed of agent search with the flexibility of sequential search to avoid unnecessary costs (Agrawal et al. 2005).

Iterative Search

The possibility to return to price / product information that was previously searched but not chosen can be called iterative search. Iterative search allows back-and-forth-movement as consumers compare product and service offerings.

An iterative search begins just as a sequential query to the product information. The query results are compared to each other, and then outputs or results are reported or at least noted. The difference in the sequential search is that after finding the outputs, a consumer will make the query again, and the process is then repeated.

METHOD

The effect of individual differences and purchase situations on search behavior is complex, often interactive and difficult to interpret and generalize about. Therefore, we chose as similar and consistent a group as possible for our observation research. Our response group consisted of 12 - 15 year old teenagers from the same demographic area. Our observation situation was the same for every respondent, interactive purchase via internet without time limits.

The method used in this study is empirical observation. We chose this method in order to find out what people really do in a search and purchase situation, instead of just asking what they think they would do. The more specific description of our method can be found in is in our previous papers (Lauraeus-Niinivaara et al. 2007 and 2008). We observed and interviewed 56 pupils belonging to age groups from twelve to fifteen years studying in Espoo, Finland. We chose this target group because we felt that pupils have not established ways of searching information on the internet. We conducted observations during three days in April and May 2004 on the school's premises. There was always an observer present per pupil. All the observers had a PhD degree or were PhD students, and all of them had a full understanding of the research objectives and methods.

The observational study was conducted in the following way: The observer explained the purpose and objectives of the study to the pupils who were asked to follow the general principle of the observational research - to speak aloud, i.e. comment on all the moves and reasons for their choices while they were searching for information. Background information on the pupils was gathered with a formal sheet and we used a standardized form to note the answers of the pupils. After each interview, the respective observer went through the results with the Ph.D. student who inserted the data in a database. As the person to insert data was the same all the time it was ensured that every observation was understood in the same way.

The Design of the Experiments

We designed three assignments to measure the influence of knowledge and choice uncertainty on the search effort. The assignments were a simple product search and comparison tasks during which the subjects were asked to think aloud their actions and the reasons behind them. The three assignments were worded as follows:

Assignment 1: Buy a Christmas present CD for Your grandmother.
Assignment 2: Buy the Red Hot Chili Peppers' "By the way"- CD for a friend.
Assignment 3: Buy a CD yourself.

In the first assignment, knowledge uncertainty was high while choice uncertainty was low. The subjects were unlikely to be familiar with the music categories searched for the CD, yet, choice uncertainty was low since the risks related to an adverse choice were low – the subject would not be stuck with the record. The second assignment was designed to have both low knowledge and choice uncertainty. The music category should be familiar to most subjects and the task was narrowly framed to lower choice uncertainty. In the third assignment, knowledge uncertainty was low because the subjects were knowledgeable about the music genres of their choice. Choice uncertainty, on the other hand, was high since they had the chance to win the record and, therefore, were at some pressure to make a good choice.

RESULTS

Identification of Search Patterns

Three different search patterns were identified during the experiment thus confirming our first proposition on different search patterns that consumers employ in their pre-purchase search. Out of 168 units of analysis, sequential or iterative search was employed 110 times (65%) and agent search 58 times (35%).

The Impact of Age and Gender for Choosing Agent Search

Age has an impact on search behavior. It is assumed that younger consumers are quite flexible in their search behavior in comparison with older consumers who already have established ways of searching and purchasing. However, in our study, younger consumers, maybe because of their inexperience, resorted more to the sequential search pattern. According to our results, portrayed in Table 1, the slightly older pupils preferred agent search.

It is generally assumed that males are more interested, and thus more experienced users of the internet. This seems to the case in our study, too. Boys used more often agent search as depicted in Table 2.

The Impact of Knowledge and Experience for Choosing Agent Search

Objective Knowledge

In our study, the items that measured objective knowledge and experience with the internet were hours of the internet usage per week and knowledge of certain types of product sites on the internet. Experience with search engines and record shops were measured with the number of either search engines or music record shops familiar to the respondents.

The amount of internet usage (in hours per week) has an effect on choosing agent search. Those who use internet more are also more likely to use agent search when looking for information on the internet as Table 3 depicts.

*Table 1. The impact of **age** for choosing agent search*

	Search pattern	
	Agent search	**Other search**
Avg.	13.62	13.02
Std.Dev.	1.240	1.266
n	58	110
N	168	168
T-tests	t-value	p-value (2-tailed)
	2.93	0.0040**

*Significant at the .05 level
** Significant at the .01 level

*Table 2. The impact of **gender** for choosing agent search*

	Search pattern	
	Agent search	**Other search**
Avg.	0.31	0.49
Std.Dev.	0.466	0.502
n	58	110
N	168	168
T-tests	t-value	p-value (2-tailed)
	-2.32	0.0219*

Male = 0, female = 1
*Significant at the .05 level
** Significant at the .01 level

*Table 3. The impact of **internet usage per week** (in hours) for choosing agent search*

	Search pattern	
	Agent search	**Other search**
Avg.	13.36	8.58
Std.Dev.	15.034	12.455
n	58	110
N	168	168
T-tests	t-value	p-value (2-tailed)
	2.20	0.0293*

*Significant at the .05 level
** Significant at the .01 level

*Table 4. The impact of the **experience with search engines** for choosing agent search*

	Search pattern	
	agent search	other search
Avg.	4.19	3.38
Std.Dev.	2.395	2.512
n	58	110
N	168	168
T-tests	t-value	p-value (2-tailed)
	2.04	0.0432*

*Significant at the .05 level
** Significant at the .01 level

*Table 5. The impact of the **experience with record shops** for choosing agent search*

	Search pattern	
	Agent search	Other search
Avg.	1.10	0.67
Std.Dev.	1.252	1.050
n	58	110
N	168	168
T-tests	t-value	p-value (2-tailed)
	2.36	0.0193*

*Significant at the .05 level
** Significant at the .01 level

The experience with search engines has an effect on choosing agent search. Those who have more experience and recognize more search engines prefer using agent search as shown in Table 4.

The experience with record shops influences on choosing agent search. Those who have more experience and recognize more record shop sites chose agent search as depicted in Table 5.

Subjective Knowledge

In our study, the self estimation of the ability to search in general on the internet, and the ability to search music on the internet, in particular, was measured. The self-estimation scale was from four to ten.

Our results suggest that subjective knowledge has no effect on choosing agent search pattern. The values for *ability to search music* t-value is 1.07 and P –value 0.287. The values for *ability to search in the internet* are: t-value 0.80 and P –value 0.423. Thus subjective knowledge does not seem to have any impact on the used search pattern.

The Effect of Search Patterns on Outcomes of Search

Our third proposition suggests that search patterns influence the outcomes of search. We operationalized the impact of search pattern as the time spent for search. We formulated hypothesis 3 so that both search time and the price at which consumers were able to find a suitable product are dependent on the search pattern. Our null hypothesis is that the observed shopping time and the best prices found were equal over the tasks, i.e. the amount of uncertainties did not affect either.

$$H0 = \mu_1 = \mu_2 = \mu_3.$$
$$H1 = \mu_1 \neq \mu_2 \neq \mu_3$$

The actual shopping time varied between 4.49 minutes to 7.19 minutes. On average, the subjects spent most time when using iterative search strategy (7.19), and the least when using agent search (4.49 minutes). The difference in time used was statistically significant when agent search was compared with iterative search pattern (p = 0.0042). In addition, there was a statistical difference between the time used for searching with the sequential and iterative search pattern (p = 0.0068). However, there was no statistically significant difference when compared the time used for agent search and sequential search (p= 0.6180).

We found out in our earlier paper (Lauraeus-Niinivaara et al. 2008) that iterative search pattern is the slowest under any uncertainty, and the agent search is the most efficient under any uncertainty (choice or knowledge uncertainty). In summary, the agent search seems to be the most efficient search pattern when measured by time spent on search, and the iterative search pattern seems to be the least efficient way of searching, as depicted in Table 6.

The actual purchase price in different search patterns varied from 11.70 euros to 16.20 euros. The pupils spent the most money when searching with sequential pattern (16.20 euros), and the least when using agent search. The difference in purchase price was statistically significant (p<.0001) for agent search against sequential search. Judging by the result of our t-tests, the pupils spent the least amount of money when using agent search, and both sequential and iterative search patterns led to more expensive purchases. Our results suggest that agent search pattern has effect on purchase price as shown in Table 7.

We established in our earlier paper (Lauraeus-Niinivaara et al. 2008) that sequential search pattern seems to lead to the most expensive purchase under any uncertainty. Agent search, on the other hand, leads to most inexpensive purchase under any uncertainty.

Our observation may explain, at least in part, why electronic markets have not increased market efficiency, i.e. narrow price dispersion and low average prices, as expected. While the benefits of agent search strategy seem quite apparent, the majority of the subjects did not exploit them (65% of our sample). Consumers must adjust their behavior to the new environment to realize the potential benefits.

We also found that there is no statistical difference when compared various search patterns with variables like "searched alternatives", "searched attributes", or "quantity of visited stores". The values of *"searched alternatives"* are: t-value 0.85 and P–value 0.397. The values for *"the number of searched attributes"* are: t-value 0.95 and P–value 0.345. The values for *"the number of visited stores"* are: t-value 0.69 and P–value 0.494.

DISCUSSION AND CONCLUSION

In this paper, we have demonstrated that the employed search strategy and search pattern are concepts that can be used to explain the variation in the efficiency of consumer search in electronic markets. Previously the patterns and extent of consumer search have been explained by using

Table 6. The impact of chosen search pattern on **shopping time**

	Search Pattern		
	Agent search	Sequential	Iterative
Avg.	4.49	4.76	7.19
Std.Dev.	2.59	3.41	3.52
N	168	168	168
T-tests			
Pairs	t-value	p-value (2-tailed)	
Agent & Sequential	-0.50	0.6180	
Agent & Iterative	-3.08	0.0042**	
Sequential & Iterative	-2.92	0.0068**	

*Significant at the .05 level
** Significant at the .01 level
*** Significant at the .001 level

Table 7. The effect of search pattern on **purchase price**

	Search Pattern		
	Agent search	Sequential	Iterative
Avg.	11.70	16.20	14.00
Std.Dev.	5.46	4.93	5.18
N	168	168	168
T-tests			
Pairs	t-value	p-value (2-tailed)	
Agent & Sequential	-4.67	<.0001***	
Agent & Iterative	-1.89	0.0662	
Sequential & Iterative	1.79	0.0837	

*Significant at the .05 level
** Significant at the .01 level
*** Significant at the< .0001 level

concepts such as price, brand, and loyalty (e.g. Brynjolfson and Smidt 1987). While these concepts are valid, as such, they share little theoretical ground and it is not clear how they could be fitted into a framework encompassing the essential factors of consumer search. In addition, to the two prototypical search patterns, sequential and agent search, we used iterative searching pattern in our study. The sequential searching is still the predominant way of searching, even among with youngsters. In the following, we summarize the results of our experiment.

Consumers employ different search patterns in their pre-purchase search (H1)

According to our data, most people (110) used sequential or iterative search pattern (65%). Only 35 % of our sample used (58) agent search. It is possible that even the relatively young consumers have pre-existing, well developed search strategies and they are unable or reluctant to adjust their behavior to the new environment to realize the potential benefits. The finding that even relatively young people tend to adhere to sequential search rather than agent search on the internet indicates a need for consumer education.

Age, gender and knowledge influence the search pattern chosen (H2)

According to our results the majority of younger consumers prefer sequential search over agent search, and the tendency to benefit from agent search increases when the pupils become older. In addition, boys use agent search more often. Furthermore, the frequency of internet usage influences the chosen search pattern so that more active users tend to choose agent search. The experience with search engines and record shops also influence the search pattern chosen. Those who have more experience with search engines or record shops would rather choose agent search. In our study, the self estimation of the ability to search on the internet in general, and the ability to search music on the internet, in

particular, was measured. Our results suggest that subjective knowledge has not effect on choosing agent search pattern. Figure 3 below presents the results of our study.

Search patterns influence the efficiency of search (H3)

Our t-test shows that the actual shopping time varied between 4.49 minutes to 7.19 minutes according to the different search strategies. Our observations support the hypothesis (*H3*) that selection of search strategy has an impact on the efficiency of search when measured with the amount of time the subjects used for search. The actual purchase price according to the different search patterns varied from 11.70 euros to 16.20 euros. Our analyses tend to support the hypothesis (*H3*) and point to agent search strategy having an impact on the efficiency of search also when measured with purchase price.

Agent search seems to be the most efficient search pattern when measured by time spent on search; it seems to combine low search costs with high efficiency. The fact that it was not the strategy of choice for most of our subjects raises the question of the necessary preconditions to agent search. It is possible that electronic markets are less transparent when it comes to search related meta-information: where to find suitable search

Figure 3. Variables influencing the usage of agent search

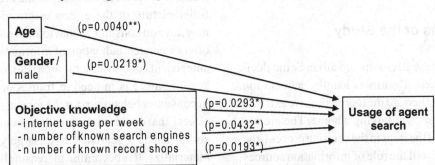

engines, comparison sites and how to use the tools in order to find necessary information. This knowledge must, for the large part, be extracted at a cost through on-going search.

Managerial Implications

It seems that search engines and comparison sites are perceived as difficult by most of the younger teenagers who encounter them for the first time. Hence, even though the teenager target group was chosen in order to examine how inexperienced information searchers and shoppers behave online, the results might be fairly typical for most of the inexperienced users of the internet, regardless of their age.

As agent search seems the most efficient search pattern, companies should incorporate the comparison facilities in their own websites in order to facilitate customers' search tasks. Comparison functionality should be as easy to use as possible to encourage novices to try the tools. Using search strategies that are not common in offline environment seems to require time, effort and significant others who inform the youngsters about new sites and new ways to search. Moving from sequential search to more efficient search patterns more suitable in online environment does not seem to come automatically. Companies might, however, be reluctant to provide search facilities that incorporate information from various product and service providers since there is always a danger that customers might find a cheaper or better quality offering from the competitor with the help of a search tool.

Limitations of the Study

Not all purchase decisions are alike. Some decisions are preceded by a more lengthy deliberation process than others. At the more extensive extreme lie decisions such as buying a home. The greater the distance of the steps in the decision process, the more diverse will the role of information sources

become. Our experiment captured the decision process for a relatively simple product class, the compact disc. As decisions grow in complexity, social information sources will become increasingly important and that mix of different types of information sources may result in decision processes and outcomes rather unlike the ones depicted in this paper. Therefore, to generalize our findings to purchase decisions at large, it would be necessary to test them against purchase processes involving decisions of higher complexity and longer periods of deliberation.

Future Research

Consumers' ability to use search agents will be increasingly important as the amount of information available for consumers increases. When Biswas (2004) compared the determinants of EoI in the traditional and in the internet environment, he concluded that expertise in web surfing and appropriate use of search agents lead to more efficient search. There are several interesting aspects to be studied in agent search, one being personalized search. For example, Google offers ways to personalize searching so that previously used searches and sites are kept in the memory of the Google tool.

In addition, uncertainty research offers interesting venues for future research. Uncertainty has been established as the motive of consumer search (Stigler, 1961). It is a concept that can be used to link electronic markets research to economic, consumer behaviour, and decision-making streams of research facilitating the creation of a fuller picture of the effects electronic markets may have on consumer behaviour. In particular, it offers a conceptualization of information related antecedents of consumer search. Electronic markets literature is in need of frames of reference in consumer behaviour, for the forecasted market effects that build on assumed rationality of the consumer as a searcher, have largely failed to materialize. It is becoming increasingly apparent that price or product attribute information alone cannot explain consumers' search behaviour and these measures should be augmented with informational goals that drive the search (uncertainty). The concept of uncertainty provides us with a coherent theoretical frame to explore consumer search in electronic markets. Uncertainty, on the other hand, is a concept well established as the foundation of consumer search. It is also the prime concept linking consumer search and decision-making theories. As decision-making is central to consumer search, it is hoped that uncertainty could be conceptualized further to create a theoretical frame that could be used to analyze any consumer search process in electronic markets.

REFERENCES

Agrawal M., Hariharan G., Kishore R., & Rao H. R. (2005). Matching intermediaries for information goods in the presence of direct search: an examination of switching costs and obsolescence of information. *Decision Support Systems, 41*(1), 20 – 36.

Alba, J. W., & Hutchinson, J. W. (1987). Dimensions of consumer expertice. *Journal of Consumer Research,* 13 March, 411-54.

Bakos, J. Y. (1997). Reducing buyer search cost: Implications for electronic marketplaces. *Management Science, 43*(12), 1676-1692.

Beatty, S. E., & Smith, S. M. (1987). External search effort: an investigation across several product categories. *Journal of Consumer Research,* 14 June, (pp. 83-95).

Berlyne, D. E. (1960). *Conflict, Arousal and Curiosity.* New York: McGraw-Hill.

Bettman, J. R. (1979a). *An Information Processing Theory of Consumer Choice.* Reading, MA: Addison-Wesley., (p. 218).

Bettman, J. R., & Sujan, M. (1987). Effects of Framing on Evaluation of Comparable and Non-comparable Alternatives by Expert and Novice Consumers. *Journal of Consumer Research, 14,* 141-154.

Bettman, J. R., Johnson, E. J., & Payne, J. W. (1990). A componential analysis of cognitive effort in choice. *Organizational Behaviour Human Decision Processes, 45,* 111-39.

Biswas, D. (2004), Economics of information in the Web economy towards a new theory? *Journal of Business Research, 57,* 724-733

Brucks. M. (1985).The Effects of Product Class Knowledge on Information Search Behavior, *Journal of Consumer Research,* June 1985, *12.*

Brynjolfsson, E., & Smith, M. D.(2000). Frictionless commerce? A comparison of Internet and conventional retailers. *Management Science 46,* 563-585.

Chiang K-P. (2006). Clicking Instead of Walking: Consumers Searching for Information in the Electronic Marketplace, *Bulletin,* December/January 2006

Copeland, M. T. (1917). Relation of consumers buying habits of marketing methods. *Harvard Business Review,* 1 April, 282-289.

Duncan, C. P., & Olshavsky, R. W. (1982). External search: The role of consumer beliefs. *Journal of Marketing Research,* 19 Feb, (pp. 32-43).

Engel, J. F., Blackwell, R. D., & Miniard, P. W. (1990). *Consumer Behavior.* Chigago: The Dryden Press, 6th edition.

Hoque, A. Y., & Lohse, G. L. (1999). An information search cost perspective for designing interfaces for electronic commerce. *Journal of Marketing Research, 36,* 387-394.

Howard, J. A., & Jadish, N. S. (1969). *The Theory of Buyer Behavior.* New York, NY: Wiley.

Jansen, B. J. (2006, July). Paid Search. *IEEE Computer.*

Jansen, B. J., & Pooch, U. (2001). Web user studies: a review and Framework for future work. *Journal of the American Society of Information Science and Technology, 52*(3), 235-246.

Johnson, E. J., Moe, W., Fader, P., Steven, B., & Lohse, J. (2004). On the depth and dynamics of online search behavior. *Management Science, 50,* 299-308.

Kiel, G. C., & Layton, R. A. (1981). Dimensions of Consumer Information Seeking Behavior. *Journal of Marketing Research,* 18 May, 233-239.

Kohn M. G., & Shavell, S. (1974). The theory of search. *Journal of Economic Theory, 9,* 93– 123.

Kulviwat, S., Guo C., & Engchanil (2004). Determinants of online information search: a critical review and assessment. *Internet research* 2004, *14*(3), 245-253.

Lauraeus-Niinivaara, T., Saarinen, T., & Öörni, A. (2007). Knowledge and Choice Uncertainty Affect Consumer Search and Buying Behavior. *HICSS Conference paper* 3.- 7.1.Jan.

Lauraeus-Niinivaara, T., Saarinen, T., Sunikka, A., & Öörni, A. (2008). Relationship between uncertainty and patterns of pre-purchase search in electronic markets. *HICSS Conference paper* (2008) 7.- 10. Jan.

Manning, R., & Morgan, P. (1982). Search and Consumer Theory. *Review of Economic Studies* 1982, XLIX, (pp. 203–216).

Marmorstein, H., Grewal, D., & Fishe, R. P. H. (1992). The value of time spent in price comparison shopping: Survey and experimental evidence. *Journal of Consumer Research, 9*(June), 52-61.

McCleary, K. W., & Whitney, D. L. (1994). Projecting western consumer attitudes toward travel to six Eastern European countries. *Journal of International Consumer Marketing, 6*(3/4), 239-256.

Moorthy, S., Ratchford, B., & Talukdar, D. (1997). Consumer information search revisited: theory and empirical analysis. *Journal of Consumer Research,* March, (pp. 263–77).

Newman, J., & Staelin, R. (1971). Multivariate analysis of differences in buying decision time. *Journal of Marketing Research,* 8 May, (pp. 192-8).

Olshavsky, R. W. (1985). Towards a more comprehensive theory of choice. In E. Hirschman and M. T. Holbrook (Eds.), *Advances in Consumer Research, 12,* 465-470.

Park, C. W., & Lessig, P. V. (1981). Familiarity and Its Impact on Consumer Decision Biases and Heuristics. *Journal of Consumer Research, 8*(2), 223.

Park, C. W., Mothersbaugh, D. L., & Feick, L. (1994). Consumer Knowledge Assessment. *Journal of Consumer Research, 21*(1), 71-82.

Punj, G., & Staelin, R. (1983). A Model of Consumer Information Search Behavior for New Automobiles. *Journal of Consumer Research,* March, 9.

Sieber, J. E., & Lanzetta, J. T. (1964). Conflict and Conceptual Structure as Determinants of Decision making Behavior. *Journal of Personality, 32*(4), 622-641.

Smith, J. B., & Spreng, R. (1996). A proposed model of external consumer information search, Journal of the *Academy of Marketing Science, 24,* Summer, 246-56.

Spink, A., Koshman, S., & Jansen, B. J. (2005). Multitasking on the Vivisimo Web Search Engine. *IEEE ITCC International Conference on Information Technology,* 2005, LA.

Spreng, R. A., & Olshavsky, R. W. (1993). A Desires Congruency Model of Consumer Satisfaction. *Journal of the Academy of Marketing Science, 21*(3), 169-177.

Srinivasan, N., & Ratchford, B. (1991). An Empirical test of a model of external search for automobiles. *Journal of Consumer Research, 18.*

Stigler, G. J. (1961). The Economics of information. *Journal of Political Economy, 69*(June), 213.

Urbany, J. E. (1986). An Experimental Examination of the Economics of Information. *Journal of Consumer Research, 13*, Sep 1986.

Urbany, J., Dickson, P., & Wilkie, W. (1989). Buyer Uncertainty and Information Search. *Journal of Consumer Research*, September 1989, *16.*

Whinston, A. B., Stahl, D. O. et al. (1997). *The Economics of Electronic Commerce.* Indianapolis, Macmillan Technical Publishing.

Wilkie, W. (1975). *How consumers use product information: An assessment of research in relation to public policy needs*, Washington, D.C.: National Science Foundation. 1985.

Wu, D., Ray, G., Geng, X., & Whinston, A. (2004). Implications of reduced search cost and free riding in e-commerce. *Marketing Science, 23*, 255-262.

Öörni, A, (2003). Consumer Search in Electronic Markets. *European Journal of Information Systems,* (2003) *12*, 30-40.

Öörni, A. (2002). Dominant search pattern in electronic markets: Sequential or agent search search, *HSE Working papers*, W-31

Öörni, A. (2002). *Consumer Search in Electronic Markets*, Dissertation in Helsinki School of Economics, Acta Universitatis Oeconomicae Helsingiensis, A-197.

ADDITIONAL READINGS

Biswas, D. (2004). Economics of information in the Web economy towards a new theory? *Journal of Business Research, 57*, 724-733

Brynjolfsson, E., & Smith, M. D. (2000). Frictionless commerce? A comparison of Internet and conventional retailers. *Management Science, 46*, 563-585.

Johnson, E. J., Moe, W., Fader, P., Steven, B., & Lohse, J. (2004). On the depth and dynamics of online search behavior. *Management Science, 50*, 299-308.

Lauraeus-Niinivaara T., Saarinen T., & Öörni A. (2007). Knowledge and Choice Uncertainty Affect Consumer Search and Buying Behavior, *HICSS Conference paper* 3.- 7.1. Jan. 2007

Lauraeus-Niinivaara, T., Saarinen, T., Sunikka A., & Öörni, A. (2008). Relationship between uncertainty and patterns of pre-purchase search in electronic markets, *HICSS Conference paper* 7.- 10. Jan. 2008

Marmorstein, H., Grewal, D., & Fishe, R. P. H. (1992). The value of time spent in price comparison shopping: Survey and experimental evidence. *Journal of Consumer Research, 9*(June), 52-61.

Moorthy, S., Ratchford, B., & Talukdar, D. (1997). Consumer information search revisited: theory and empirical analysis. *Journal of Consumer Research*, March, 263–77.

Park, C. W., Mothersbaugh, D. L., & Feick, L. (1994). Consumer Knowledge Assessment. *Journal of Consumer Research, 21*(1), 71-82.

Smith, J. B., & Spreng, R. (1996). A proposed model of external consumer information search. *Journal of the Academy of Marketing Science, 24*, Summer, 246-56.

Srinivasan, N., & Ratchford, B. (1991). An Empirical test of a model of external search for automobiles. *Journal of Consumer Research, 18.*

Öörni, A. (2003).Consumer Search in Electronic Markets. *European Journal of Information Systems,* (2003) *12,* 30-40.

KEY TERMS

Agent Search: In agent search, a consumer is able to evaluate more available products side by side, as is the situation in simultaneous search. In the electronic markets simultaneous search is often called agent search, because of the internet tools that makes information comparing available, is called search agents. In online settings, a consumer can use various tools (for example: comparison sites, search agents or comparison agents) to collect information that is available on the internet on a particular product or service.

Electronic Markets: Consists of the buying and selling of products or services over electronic systems such as the Internet. Other words: e-commerce, digital markets, virtual markets, online markets.

Information Search: Consumers look for information of products with desired qualities and sellers offering these products at competitive prices in an attempt to decide what, when, and from whom to purchase. Consumer's pre-purchase information search is an essential part of consumer decision making process (Bettman 1979; Bettman et al. 1990; Engel et al. 1990; Howard and Sheth 1969; Olhavsky 1985, Schmidt and Spreng 1996).

Iterative Search: An iterative search begins just as a sequential query to the product information. The query results are compared to each other, and then outputs or results are reported or at least noted. The difference in the sequential search is that after finding the outputs, a consumer will make the query again, and the process is then repeated. The possibility to return to

price / product information that was previously searched, but not chosen, can be called iterative search. Iterative search allows back-and-forth-movement as consumers compare product and service offerings.

Search Agent: We define, the internet tools that make information *comparing* available, for consumers purchase decision, search agents. Search agents are made to help consumers to make purchase decision most efficiently. Search agents include information of product prices and product qualities in the same internet site. In search agent site, information is in comparable form.

Search Behavior: In recent years, there have been many studies into consumer search behavior in a digital environment (Chiang 2006, Jansen 2006, Johnson et al. 2004, Lauraeus-Niinivaara et al. 2007, 2008, Smith and Spreng 1996, Spink et al. 2005, Öörni 2002, 2003). When we are writing about search behavior, we mean the situation when Consumers are seeking, or looking for, information of products for decision making purposes. There are nearly 60 factors that have been found to influence the consumer pre-purchase information search behaviour (Schmidt and Spreng 1996; Srinivasan and Ratchford 1991).

Search Engine: Web application that gathers information from the Web using different strategies (crawlers or spiders) and then performs the basic retrieval task, accepting a query, comparing a query with the records in a database, and producing a retrieval set as output.

Search Patterns: Search pattern means the shape of the consumer search process. In other words, search pattern is the search strategy consumer employed, when seeking for information for buying decision. Consumers employ different search patterns in their pre-purchase search. We identified three types of search patterns in the experiment: sequential, agent search, and iterative search.

Sequential Search: Sequential search occurs when a consumer consecutively visits or contacts sellers. Each visit is composed of an information gathering and a buying decision phase. The consumer familiarizes her/himself with the products available and decides whether to purchase a product or to visit the next store. The consumer can compare the products in various stores, yet s/he has to resort to her/his memory as a source of product information to evaluate those products not in the current store.

Simultaneous Search: Product comparison could be more efficient, if the consumer were able to evaluate more available products side by side. This is the essence of simultaneous search. All information needed for the evaluation is readily available, and consumer has no need to resort to secondary information sources. Thus, there are only two phases in the consumer decision making process: information gathering and buying decision. In the electronic markets simultaneous search is often called agent search, because of the internet tools that makes information comparing available is called search agents. In offline circumstances, a consumer might collect a simultaneous search sample based on either internal information formed by experience of repeated purchases (internal search), or by, for example, acquainting her/himself with special issues of consumer journals that compare products the consumer is interested in (external search).

Chapter V
Price, Product Complexity, and Durability in Comparison Shopping

Makoto Nakayama
DePaul University, USA

Norma Sutcliffe
DePaul University, USA

ABSTRACT

This chapter examines how product price, product complexity and product durability influence consumers' comparison shopping process. Frequently comparison shopping is equated only to price comparisons. However, comparison shopping is becoming far broader than finding the cheapest price over the Internet. Nowadays a vast variety of products are sold over the Internet. Some are relatively simple products such as books and movie DVDs. Others are more complex such as computer related products, travel reservations and real-estate properties. As the number of key product attributes increases, consumers apply different kinds of decision making rather than just looking for the cheapest price. Consumers also use different decision making tactics between durable and non-durable products. This chapter looks into the implications of such differences for consumers and product sellers. It concludes with managerial implications and future research agendas.

INTRODUCTION

For many, "comparison shopping" often means the search for the cheapest price on a product. Price is a universal quantitative measure that we can tell which "deal" is the best one, given the similar product quality. Not surprisingly many comparison shopping websites offer product prices as a key shopping criterion. Among many other, websites such as www.bizrate.com and www.

bestbookbuys.com use prices as a key, convenient purchase criteria for comparison shopping.

Today there are numerous comparison shopping websites. So much so, there are comparison websites for comparison shopping websites, such as www.pricingcentral.com that provides "180 listings of comparison shopping engines (124 active) and 320 listings of online stores (186 active)" as of July 5, 2008. In addition, the website claims to include "11757 user ratings of comparison shopping sites and 7309 ratings of online merchants."

While the above mentioned websites focus mainly on price offered online, there are other websites that provide a broad range of criteria and analyses for product purchasing by using data that is not directly available online. A well known example is www.consumerreports.org. Another example is www.pcmag.com which offers information technology (IT) related product reviews as an aid for comparison shopping.

Search engines are known to "offer" the leads for comparison shopping by showing links to the three types of comparison websites (comparison shopping websites, meta comparison websites, and comparison shopping aid websites). For example, one can enter "laser printers" as search words in www.google.com; the results include the links to numerous shopping websites and product shopping guides. This type should probably be called *involuntary* comparison shopping in a sense that comparison shopping is enticed even when the consumer has no comparison shopping in mind.

In short, online comparison shopping is not really a simple venue through which consumers just compare product availability and price. Rather, it is becoming a venue through which consumers voluntarily or non-voluntarily obtain "expert" assistance in the process of purchase decision making on simple to complex products. Such "expert" assistance includes not only product availability and price but also key product attributes, product reliability, post-purchase product service assessment, and expert as well as user overall product evaluations.

This chapter focuses on the complexity, durability and price range of products as key variables in the process of comparison shopping. We present a model that summarizes issues consumers face and tactics firms use in the process of online comparison shopping. A key message this chapter imparts is that comparison shopping goes far beyond price comparisons and that its main goal is the total fulfillment of satisfactory product purchase experience.

At the outset, the products that this chapter considers are consumer products often seen in comparison shopping websites. This chapter does not review academic concepts and theories. Rather, this chapter explores salient issues in the consumer comparison shopping process for consumers, sellers and researchers from a broader perspective based on first-hand observations.

In the following sections, we first discuss the process and different levels/types of comparison shopping. We then examine the concept of product attributes and their impact on comparison shopping. The next section presents a model of comparison shopping with propositions. Implications for consumers and sellers are discussed. The last part of this chapter considers future research directions followed by conclusions.

PROCESS OF "SHOPPING"

The term "shopping" is used casually to mean selecting a product for purchase. Comparison shopping often means the process in which determining the product to buy is the result of performing an assessment of products, especially their prices. In it, the focus is often on the moment of actually making the purchase decision. However, it is important to recognize that "shopping" is a process rather than just the decision moment. A general, five-stage model of consumer purchase decision process is commonly seen as: (1) problem recognition, (2) information search, (3) alternative evaluation, (4) purchase decision, and (5) post-purchase behavior, based on a so-called the EBK model (Engel, Blackwell, & Kollatt, 1978; Gay, Charlesworth, & Esen, 2007; Sandhusen, 2000). The actual process of this model can be brief or lengthy, and simple or complex. Also consumers are known to use different heuristics adaptively for their decision making (Payne, Bettman, & Johnson, 2003). Nevertheless, we set forth the following steps of comparison shopping process to examine what issues consumers need to assess specifically for online comparison shopping:

Step 1: Defining the needs and requirements (e.g., functionality, budget) for the product purchase

Step 2: Understanding the general nature of the product

Step 3: Recognizing product attributes of the product

Step 4: Assessing the impact of post-purchase requirements (service & support)

Step 5: Identifying sellers of products

Step 6: Assessing the reputation of these sellers

Step 7: Constructing purchase criteria

Step 8: Assessing the purchase criteria vis-à-vis product price and, if any, additional fees

Step 9: Purchasing the product from a chosen seller

This is a generalized conceptual model It is important to note that consumers assess not only the products but also the sellers of these products (Girard, Silverblatt, & Korgaonkar, 2002). Particularly relevant for consumers is the overall reputation of sellers in terms of product quality assurance, product return policy, payment security, product delivery options, to name a few. Given that consumers use adaptive decision making strategies, the sequence of the above decision making steps can more often than not be iterative rather than linear. In addition, some steps in the process are done concurrently. For example, a consumer can research product attributes and sellers at the same time. A consumer can change her mind on the purchase requirements after she assesses product attributes; she then re-assesses the purchase requirements and can re-do the purchase decision making process partially or entirely.

The above process model assumes that consumers are rational. However, consumers are often not rational and/or they lack resources (especially, time) to follow each step of the process completely. This often leads to the "expedited" shopping process in which consumers depend on the reputation of products and sellers, such as in compulsive purchases (Faber & Christenson, 1996). In this "expedited" shopping process, comparison shopping is used more or less to confirm the validity of such "expedited" actions.

Figure 1. Product purchase decision steps for comparison shopping

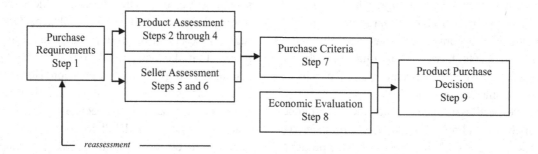

Indeed, a study shows that online shoppers are more conscience of brand and their actual purchase reflects such brand dependency (Danaher, Wilson, & Davis, 2003). Also online stores that build on repeat, loyal customers attain higher profitability (Kocas, 2002). Therefore, we have another level, or an indirect type if you will, of comparison shopping.

PRODUCT ATTRIBUTES

According to American Marketing Association ("Resource Library - Dictionary," 2008), product attributes are defined as: "The characteristics by which products are identified and differentiated. Product attributes usually comprise features, functions, benefits, and uses." To compare and contrast, we will use two products with simpler and more complex product attributes. A movie DVD, for example, has the following product attributes:

Title: Top Gun (Widescreen Special Collector's Edition)
Language: English
Format: Widescreen, NTSC
Region: U.S. and Canada only.
Features: 6-part documentary on the making of the film, 4 music videos

In case of movie DVDs, the product attributes are relatively simple and do not vary across different sellers.

One of the most popular online purchase items, personal computers, in contrast, have considerably more complex product attributes. For example, part of the product attributes of a PC includes:

Product name: Compaq Presario Desktop with Intel® Celeron® D Processor 356
Model: SR2150NX
Warranty terms: 1 year limited (parts), 1 year limited (labor)

Processor speed: 3.33 GHz
RAM: 512 MB (with upgrade options)
Hard drive type: SATA (7200 rpm)
Graphics: ATI RADEON XPRESS 1100
Video memory: 64 MB up to 128 MB
Audio: Integrated (6-speaker support)
USB2.0 ports: 4 USB 2.0 (2 front, 2 rear)
Operating System: Windows Vista Home Basic
Software Included: Microsoft Works 8; Adobe Reader 7.0; Roxio Creator; DVD Play

There are several key differences in the product attributes between movie DVDs and PCs. First, the number of product attributes usually is below 10 for movie DVDs and well above 10 for PCs. Second, some of a PC's product attributes are variable; consumers can configure them for their needs. Third, the boundary of a stand-alone product is somewhat obscured for PCs in that PCs are usually sold with accessories such as a monitor, a printer, cables, speakers, a surge protector, a web cam, software applications, just to name a few. In fact, many sellers offer discounts for accessories for a PC purchase. Some sellers even define different package deals on the same product as "new" (bundled) products. Fourth, the use of product or the context of product use varies significantly more for products with complex product attributes than it is for products with simple product attributes. For instance, the context of PC use can be office personal use, basic home use, home entertainment use, and so forth whereas the use of movie DVDs presumably is personal use at home.

PRODUCT ATTRIBUTES AND PURCHASE DECISION PROCESS

A product with simple product attributes usually has a few fixed, clear bases for product purchase criteria. For example, when we want a movie DVD for a weekend, we usually look for only a small portion of product attribute details; after selecting a particular move title, we don't usually look into other product attributes (except for the DVD format in case one is purchasing the DVD from a non-US seller). In the comparison shopping process (Figure 1), the first four steps can be pretty much "expedited." Key issues in the comparison shopping process are to identify who offers competitive product prices (including shipping and handling charges) and to assess their potential for fulfilling any post-purchase service requirements such as the product return policy.

In contrast, additional challenges for products with complex product attributes are how to understand individual product attributes and how to assess the product through these attributes. The other challenge is how to integrate the individual product attributes or how to prioritize them. The study by Lee and Lee shows that the number of attributes and attribute level distribution are good predictors of consumer information overload (Lee & Lee, 2004). In theory, a consumer knows which product is best by ranking the sum of the utilities for individual product attributes. In marketing research, we have a well-known statistical technique such as conjoint analysis (Dolan, 1990, 2001) in which the valuation of a product is assessed through finding out our preferences on a small subset of products to predict relative preferences for any products given the product attributes already considered. In this regard, a comparison shopping website can leverage the conjoint analysis for a particular product type and for a particular consumer. Two practical challenges for consumers are the finding such a website and then evaluating that website's reliability.

In the following sections, we present six informal propositions on product price, product complexity and product durability. We discuss them through a few product purchase examples and the implications for both consumers and product sellers. The intent of these informal propositions is to explore our future research directions and/or questions.

PRICE AND PRODUCT COMPLEXITY

If we define product complexity as the number and intricacy of product attributes, how then does product complexity relate to product price – the frequent focus in comparison shopping?

A key issue is the consumer's decision making process. In the aforementioned examples of movie DVDs and PCs, the product price is more salient for movie DVDs than PCs for product selection. For a movie DVD, there aren't many product variations in the first place once you are interested in a particular movie title. On the other hand, it is more difficult to identify and compare PCs with similar specifications (product attributes). Price comparison becomes relevant only when you can compare products based on some ranking scheme(s).

Once you select a product, in contrast, price comparison seems quite the same between simple and complex products. For example, we can use a model name "SR2150NX" in the Google search and easily obtain a list of PC prices that certain sellers offer. In this case, price comparison is possible because many PCs come with their manufacturer standard specifications. Once product specifications (or product attributes) are fixed, we can look at a set of product attributes – however complex they may be – as a package or a bundled unit.

Past studies provide some support for the above line of reasoning. First, the more product attributes a product has, the more likely consumers face information overload (Lee & Lee, 2004). Yet in contrast, the principle of least effort (Mann, 1987; Zipf, 1949) implies that consumers have a tendency to avoid information overload and go with a short-cut or with heuristic decision making. This applies to even simple price search; many consumers spend less time for price search than the economics-of-information theory predicts (Grewal & Marmorstein, 1994). If a product has more complex attributes, consumers are likely to face more challenges in assessing the overall value of the product in relation to its price. On the other hand, all other things being equal, price tends be more salient when a product is a simple one. Therefore, we propose the following informal propositions:

(I) The more complex the product attributes, the less significant the product price becomes for an online product selection. Instead, more sought is the integrative expert advice in using comparison shopping websites.

(II) The less complex the product attributes, the more significant the product price becomes for a seller selection in using comparison shopping websites.

Implications to consumers. Based on the above, when a consumer wants to buy a complex product, the key success factor is how to understand complex product attributes and how to prioritize the assessment of the product attributes that matter most for that consumer. For this, a consumer should get the information from vendor neutral comparison shopping websites like ConsumerReports.org (Figure 2). In case of PCs, comparison shopping is possible through search engines (e.g., Google, Yahoo), IT related news websites (e.g., CNET, eWeek), IT magazines (e.g., PC Magazine, PC World) and general shopping websites (e.g., Shopzilla.com, Shopping.com, and PriceGrabber.com) (Figure 3). It is common knowledge, however, that many of these websites offering product selection assistance have a sponsor relationship with vendors. Thus, consumers should always obtain information from multiple sources and compare the recommendations and their rationale.

For simple products, price is certainly a salient indicator for choosing a seller. However, consumers should be wary of hidden benefits and costs such as shipping fees, rebates, and conditional discounts. Therefore, the purchase

decision should be based on the total price rather than the list price.

Implications for sellers. For complex products, sellers can use several strategies. For a low-cost strategy (Porter, 1980), sellers can offer only a limited number of select products with competitive prices. Using market segmentation and focus analyses will guide the selection of such products. Another possible strategy is a differentiation strategy (Porter, 1980) where a seller offers greater variety of products with slightly higher prices. This strategy can be accompanied with a product bundling strategy in which a seller purposefully blur the boundaries of standard products by changing their products attributes. Offering optional and/or complementary products with discounts goes along this

Figure 2. Example of product selection guide

©*2008 by Consumers Union of U.S., Inc. Yonkers, NY 10703-1057, a nonprofit organization. Reprinted with permission from ConsumerReports.org® for educational purposes only. No commercial use or reproduction permitted. www. ConsumerReports.org.*

line. Rebates are another popular tactic to blur price levels, and it can be used with the product bundling strategy.

For simple products, consumers' natural focus is on product prices. For better or worse, search engine agents usually index product prices along with product prices that competitors offer. Then, sellers have two strategies to counter consumers' price focus. Sellers can either be the price leader, or they can "redefine" simple products with product bundling and/or discount/rebate policies. The first strategy is not feasible unless the seller enjoys economies of scale to offer lower prices, or the seller wants to use those products as "baits" to direct consumers' website access.

For both simple and complex products, sellers want to explore the opportunities for an alliance with search engines and comparison shopping websites that offers expert advice and/or consumer ratings.

Figure 3. Example of a seller product guide

Reproduced with permission of Yahoo! Inc. ® 2008 by Yahoo! Inc. YAHOO! and the YAHOO! logo are trademarks of Yahoo! Inc."

PRICE AND PRODUCT DURABILITY

Next to the price of a product, the durability of the product is an important buyer consideration. Typical durable consumer goods include automobiles, real-estate properties, household equipment, and entertainment equipment. The U.S. Bureau of Labor Statistics ("Producer Price Indexes Introduced for the Wholesale Trade Sector—NAICS 423, 424, and 425120," 2006) defines durable goods as "new or used items generally with a normal life expectancy of 3 years or more."

Interestingly, one of the shorter inventory cycles recognized for a durable good is 40 months or 3-1/3 years (Kitchin, 1923). As an example of technology-related goods that seem to evolve rapidly, "Prepackaged software has an average service life of 3 years and is depreciated geometrically at a rate of 0.55 per year; custom and own-account software have average service lives of 5 years and are depreciated geometrically at a rate of 0.33 per year" (Herman, 2000).

Durable goods are also called hard goods. Non-durable goods have shorter life spans than durable goods. Examples of non-durable goods include food, apparel, footwear, books, magazines, and drugs.

While there is a wide range of consumer products, Figure 4 shows how some durable and non-durable products are classified by their level of durability and price in four quadrants of the 2 by 2 matrix. The level of durability is classified "high" with a normal life span of 3 years or more and "low" when less than 3 years. While there is no definitive cut-off price level, Figure 4 places products whose top price range is somewhere around $2,000 to $3,000 in the "low" price range, whereas products whose top price range exceeds that price as "high." As a rationale for this cutoff, the U.S. national average weekly wage in 2008 is $580, according to the U.S. Department of Labor ("Office of Workers' Compensation Programs (OWCP)," 2008). Based on this figure and using the standard 4.3 weeks for a month, the average monthly wage thus is $2,494.

In the upper-left quadrant, we have products whose prices are relatively low but whose durability is relatively high. Vacuum cleaners can last for three to five years. Washing machines and central air conditioners often last for ten years or more. Some additional considerations on these two durable products are (a) initial installation (including delivery) costs and (b) ongoing service and maintenance costs. The longer the product life span is, the more likely that maintenance and repairs for the project becomes a critical factor. Moreover, many durable products are complex products.[a] The maintenance of such products is usually beyond the capability, and/or economies, of lay people. This means that labor costs of experts are expected. Thus the consumer needs to make an effort to research and estimate these service and maintenance costs. This type of research, unfortunately, cannot always be done with a quick Google search; the consumer frequently must rely on the first-hand experience from neighbors, friends, and coworkers. Critical

issues are product reliability and particularly the availability and quality of local service agencies or agents.

Products in the upper-right quadrant tend to be even more complex products that the consumer needs carefully examine the long-term product reliability, future service and maintenance requirements, the availability and access to trustworthy service and maintenance agents. Therefore, the longer the product is likely to last, the more likely a buyer will make an effort to do research on the future service requirements and costs, rather than just comparing the product prices from different sellers. Indeed, even prior to the internet age, a study found that consumers had higher purchase satisfaction when they use Consumer Reports for durable goods (Engledow, Anderson, & Becker, 1978). Currently product reviews by third-parties and consumers are quite readily available via comparison shopping websites and various online forums.

One interesting case in Figure 4 is the purchase of home. While a home itself has many product attributes (e.g., style of construction,

Figure 4. Durability vs. price of consumer products

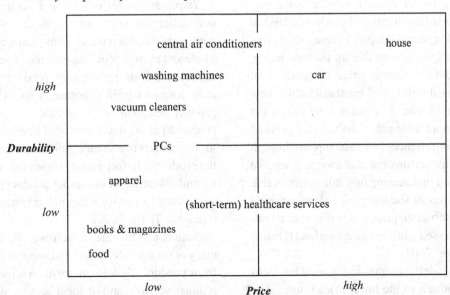

81

specifications of each room, land, utilities, equipment, zoning regulations, taxes), the process of a home purchase is usually complex involving the search, selection and contractual management of legal, real-estate, home inspection, insurance and financial services (cf. www.hud.gov/buying). The purchase of automobiles, too, is rarely just the search, selection and purchase, but purchase also includes dealings with service maintenance contract, insurance and financial services.

(III) The longer the product durability, the product price and product seller selection become less significant when using comparison shopping websites. Instead, the information on product service and support become more important.

In general, marketing strategies assume that commodity goods are more price sensitive than specialty goods (Jain, 1990). Many common goods we need regularly have price sensitivity (or price elasticity) of around 1.0 whereas goods we don't need often tends have higher numbers (Anderson, McLellan, Overton, & Wolfram, 1997).[b] In the context of online comparison shopping, whether and how comparison shopping websites alter consumer price sensitivity across many different types of goods is indeed an important long-term, empirical research theme. Nevertheless, we assume that for the time being, the traditional consumer price perceptions of goods are still valid until contradicted by new empirical evidence. In addition, the internet is providing more information on not only product prices but also product service and support through various online forums and chat rooms. Thus, we are interested in assessing how consumers value different types of shopping related information when the internet supplies more information than can be processed – information overload (Drake, 2003; Kantor, 2007).

The lower-left quadrant in Figure 4 has nondurable products in the lower price range. The utility of those products is expected to be shorter. The post-purchase service and maintenance requirements are usually not significant. Then, if we consider the initial product purchase price to include any shipping and delivery charges, the initial purchase price is relatively more pronounced item for the total economic commitment the consumer has to make.[c]

(IV) The shorter the product durability period, the more significant the product price becomes when using comparison shopping websites in selecting the product to purchase and its seller.

Implications to consumers. When buying a durable product, consumers need to assess the availability and quality of long-term product support systems. They need to find out which comparison websites provide such information and evaluate any completeness, fairness and bias issues. For purchasing non-durable products, consumers need to be aware of all charges relating to purchases, shipping and delivery. Another critical area is the return policy. Consumers want comparison websites that sufficiently cover all these issues.

Implications for sellers. For complex products, sellers can use several strategies. Often the vendors of durable products provide the consumer guide and even product support packages. Often durable products are complex products. In this case, a seller can incorporate in its website the product selection tools provided by a vendor (Figure 5) or can develop similar interactive tools for consumers to enhance their understanding of the products. In fact a study shows that the quality and efficiency of consumer product purchase significantly improve with such interactive tools (Haubl & Trifts, 2000).

Sellers can include in their website the summary of the available guide and support packages from vendors. Sellers can form an alliance with product vendors and/or local service providers to provide the "life-long" care of products. A well-known example is Greek Squad (www. geeksquad.com) at Best Buy (www.bestbuy. com)." Some comparison shopping websites do recognize and evaluate the availability and quality of such service.

For non-durable products, sellers can focus primarily on total price that includes product price, shipping and handling charges with delivery options. While the sales of non-durable products are one-time events, sellers should be fully aware that their long-term success depends on repeat purchases and word-of-mouth (WOM). Therefore, implementing a customer retention strategy is critical.

PRICE AND ECONOMIC COMMITMENT

The previous two sections discussed the implications of product complexity and product durability. In these discussions, we note that price level comes into play directly or indirectly. For example, PCs are more complex consumer products than movie DVDs. The price level of PCs is usually ten times or even higher than that of movie DVDs. Some durable products such as automobiles and houses have highly complex product attributes and have comparatively much higher price levels. Thus, product complexity, product durability and price may relate to each other. Yet, how much does the level of price influence a consumer's purchase decision making process?

A study shows that consumers have lower expectations in an online environment than in a traditional sales channel (Karlsson, Kuttainen, Pitt, & Spyropoulou, 2005). From the standpoint of comparison shopping, how much weight do consumers give price over the perceived benefits of key product attributes when selecting products and their sellers? In other words, do consumers appreciate "feature comparisons" more than "price comparisons" in using comparison shopping websites? It probably depends on how much products are differentiated. For the commodity types of products, price sensitivity is usually high so that comparison shopping websites emphasize product prices as a key purchase decision criterion. But is this different for expensive and inexpensive products?

Figure 5. Product selection guide used by Ford Motor Co.

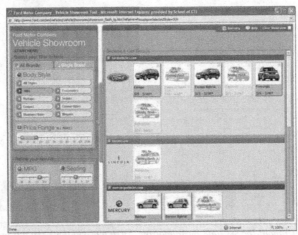

By and large, so-called commodity products are inexpensive whereas expensive products are usually more differentiated. For expensive products, consumers make a significant economic commitment. Consumers need to balance perceived benefits against economic sacrifices. These differentiated, expensive products tend to last longer, such as cars and homes. It is therefore the long-term economic impact assessment that consumers most appreciate from comparison websites.

For example, Figure 6 shows a 5-year cost estimate of owning a car including depreciation, fuel costs, insurances, and even opportunity costs. This is meaningful information for consumers as they have to live with their purchase decision over an extended time period with non-marginal economic commitment.

Before the Web emerged, such a comparison feature was rarely available to consumers. When such comparison shopping was available, consumers had to pay for it and had difficulty accessing the information. Now numerous comparison shopping websites have emerged. Such information is as readily available as price comparison information.

(V) With online comparison shopping, the higher the product price, the more search time is used and the cost-benefit analysis is more detailed when selecting a product and its seller.

Figure 6. Example of a comparison website showing a log-run economic analysis

In contrast, inexpensive products are usually less durable. Therefore, consumers are making a one-time decision that has a less significant economic commitment. Figure 7 is an example of a website that lists total cost comparisons on a book. This website also incorporates seller evaluations by consumers.

(VI) The lower the product price, the more significant in search time and decision impact the price comparison becomes for selecting a seller in the context of online shopping.

While empirical examination of the two informal propositions above is important to do, there are a few previous studies that looked at a related construct in the context of service goods. These studies do not directly assess price level impact but use a construct "sacrifice," which captures price (monetary factor) and time/effort (non-monetary factors) at the same time. One study (Cronin, Brady, & Hult, 2000) focus on a set of relatively inexpensive services (spectator sports, participation sports, entertainment, healthcare, long distance carriers, fast food). It does not find a significant tradeoff between service quality and sacrifice although the literature then "clearly" predicts such a tradeoff. That means, the service value consumers get given a sacrifice level does not change in relation to how much sacrifice they

Figure 7. Example of a comparison shopping website showing price comparisons

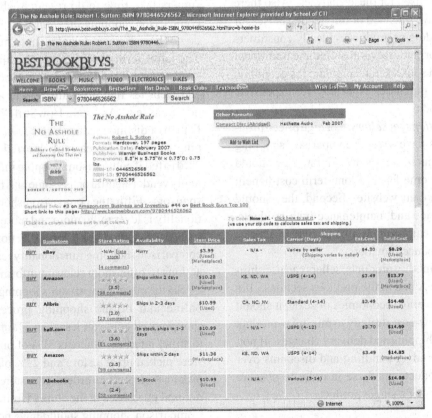

make. However, a more recent study (Hackman, Gundergan, Wang, & Daniel, 2006) that examines online service goods does find such a tradeoff. If consumers' economic sacrifice has a negative impact on service value, consumers have a greater motivation to look into the price level of services, especially when their price levels go higher.

Implications to consumers. When consumers purchase a product with a significant price level, they need to assess the long-term economic impacts. Such assessment needs to examine not only one-time costs but also value appreciation/ depreciation, service and maintenance costs and ongoing expenses over the expected life span of the product. Finding comparison shopping websites with such an assessment capability is a good starting point. A caution should be placed, however, on any cost-benefit analyses presented by those websites. There are certain explicit/implicit assumptions used for these analyses. Also there may well have intended or unintended biases for certain vendors or products. Ideally consumers want to incorporate several online and traditional information sources to triangulate the economic payoff of a purchase, especially for expensive, durable goods.

Implications for sellers. For high priced products, sellers have several comparison shopping venues for increasing sales. First, they should implement some form of long-term cost-benefit analyses on their website. Second, they should bundle service and maintenance with products. Third, they can form an alliance with a service and maintenance provider.

For commodity products, sellers can use similar strategies cited in the previous sections. If a seller can leverage economies of scale, it should focus on a low-cost strategy to minimize product prices and shipping and delivery changes. If not, it can use product bundling and discounts over multiple products purchase in order to obscure the boundary of a single product.

LOOKING FOR THE FUTURE

Online comparison shopping is a "wild west" for consumers, retailers, product vendors, industry media, and researchers. First, the level of sophistication is evolving continuously. For example, a comparison shopping website like BizRate (Figure 8) incorporates all the functionalities to address the issues we've discussed in this chapter. Second, more and more comparison shopping functionality is seen not only in standalone comparison shopping websites (voluntary comparison shopping) but also is embedded in search engines, online media websites and even websites providing personal web spaces (involuntary comparison shopping).

Third, comparison shopping is taking both full-fledged and expedited forms. That is, some websites offers the functionality in which consumers take time to do research whereas some comparison shopping sites aim at consumers who do not have time or do not want to make efforts. The latter form can often be seen in the search result pages in search engines (e.g., Google, Yahoo) and websites that offer answers to a variety of questions (e.g., Ask.com, HowStuffWorks.com). Fourth, a distinction between comparison shopping and ads is increasingly blurred. It often is hard to tell if comparison shopping information is really vendor-neutral or has some bias from vendor sponsors. Fifth, the comparison shopping functionality is leveraging more and more interactive tools. Consumers take certain actions, and the comparison shopping functionality reacts to their actions to offer more relevant information.

Sixth, more comparison shopping integrates online and offline shopping process. Online shopping accounts for less than 7% at traditional (offline) retailers, whereas 31% of online orders were picked up at a store and 27% of those who picked their online orders at a store made additional purchases at the store (Timiraos, 2006). Comparison shopping should have no boundary between online and offline shopping. Seventh,

Figure 8. A comparison shopping website showing relatively complex products

BizRate.com ®, a Shopzilla Company

there are mergers and acquisitions between comparison shopping websites, search engines, and websites are occurring. The resulting firms can now offer some form of comparison shopping (such as industry media websites). Lastly, we are starting to see more meta-comparison shopping websites like sidesteps.com, websites that summarize the information available in comparison shopping websites.

While the frontier of comparison shopping is evolving rapidly, we believe that practitioners and researchers need some anchors to base their perspectives. This chapter considers the impact of product price levels, product complexity and product durability as anchoring variables. Because there is a wide spectrum of product variations and consumer types, it is not feasible to create and examine empirically a general model that applies to every product and consumer type. However, it seems quite possible to examine the actual behaviors of consumer purchase using comparison shopping by focusing a few types of durable and non-durable products with some product complexity levels.

REFERENCES

Anderson, P. L., McLellan, R., Overton, J. P., & Wolfram, G. (1997). *The Universal Tuition Tax Credit: A Proposal to Advance Parental Choice in Education*. Retrieved July 9, 2008, from http://www.mackinac.org/archives/1997/s1997-04.pdf.

Cronin, J. J., Brady, M. K., & Hult, G. T. M. (2000). Assessing the effects of quality, value, and customer satisfaction on consumer behavioral intentions in service environments. *Journal of Retailing, 76*(2), 193-218.

Danaher, P. J., Wilson, I. W., & Davis, R. A. (2003). A Comparison of Online and Offline Consumer Brand Loyalty. *Marketing Science, 22*(4), 461-476.

Dolan, R. J. (1990). *Conjoint Analysis: A Manager's Guide, Note 9-590-059*. Boston, MA: Harvard Business School.

Dolan, R. J. (2001). *Analyzing Consumer Preferences, Note 9-599-112*. Boston, MA: Harvard Business School.

Drake, M. A. (2003). *Encyclopedia of Library and Information Science*. New York, NY: Marcel Dekker.

Engel, J., Blackwell, R., & Kollatt, D. (1978). *Consumer Behavior*. Hinsdale, IL: Dryden Press.

Engledow, J. L., Anderson, R. D., & Becker, H. (1978). Comparative Product Tests in the Consumer Decision Process: Correlates of Use and Impact on Satisfaction. *Decision Sciences, 9*(4), 627.

Faber, R. J., & Christenson, G. A. (1996). In the mood to buy: Differences in the mood states experienced by compulsive buyers and other consumers. *Psychology & Marketing, 13*(8), 803-819.

Gay, R., Charlesworth, A., & Esen, R. (2007). *Online Marketing: A Customer-led Approach* New York, NY: Oxford University Press.

Girard, T., Silverblatt, R., & Korgaonkar, P. (2002). Influence of Product Class on Preference for Shopping on the Internet. *Journal of Computer-Mediated Communication, 8*(1).

Grewal, D., & Marmorstein, H. (1994). Market price variation, perceived price variation, and consumers' price search decisions for durable goods. *Journal of Consumer Research, 21*(3), 453-460.

Hackman, D., Gundergan, S. P., Wang, P., & Daniel, K. (2006). A service perspective on modeling intentions of on-line purchasing. *The Journal of Services Marketing, 20*(7), 459.

Haubl, G., & Trifts, V. (2000). Consumer Decision Making in Online Shopping Environments: The Effects of Interactive Decision Aids. *Marketing Science, 19*(1), 4-21.

Herman, S. W. (2000). Fixed Assets and Consumer Durable Goods. Retrieved July 10, 2008, from http://www.bea.gov/scb/account_articles/national/0400niw1/maintext.htm

Jain, S. C. (1990). *Marketing Planning & Strategy* Cincinnati, OH: Thomson South-Western.

Kantor, A. (2007, June 14). Internet suffering from information overload. *USA Today*.

Karlsson, T., Kuttainen, C., Pitt, L., & Spyropoulou, S. (2005). Price as a variable in online consumer trade-offs. *Marketing Intelligence & Planning, 23*(4/5), 350.

Kitchin, J. (1923). Cycles and Trends in Economic Factors. *The Review of Economics and Statistics, 5*(1), 10-16.

Kocas, C. (2002). Evolution of prices in electronic markets under diffusion of price-comparison shopping. *Journal of Management Information Systems, 19*(3), 99.

Lee, B.-K., & Lee, W.-N. (2004). The Effect of Information Overload on Consumer Choice Quality in an On-Line Environment. *Psychology & Marketing, 21*(3), 159-183.

Mann, T. (1987). *A Guide to Library Research Methods*. New York, NY: Oxford University Press.

Office of Workers' Compensation Programs (OWCP). (2008). Retrieved July 12, 2008, from http://www.dol.gov/esa/owcp/dlhwc/NAWWinfo. htm

Payne, J. W., Bettman, J. R., & Johnson, E. J. (2003). *The Adaptive Decision Maker*. New York, NY: Cambridge University Press.

Porter, M. E. (1980). *Competitive Strategy*. New York, NY: Free Press.

Producer Price Indexes Introduced for the Wholesale Trade Sector—NAICS 423, 424, and 425120. (2006). from http://www.bls.gov/ppi/ppi-wholesale.htm

Resource Library - Dictionary. (2008). Retrieved April 4, 2008, from http://www.marketingpower. com/_layouts/Dictionary.aspx?dLetter=P

Sandhusen, R. L. (2000). *Marketing*. Hauppauge, NY: Barron's Educational Series.

Timiraos, N. (2006, December 23). Web Can Pay Off for Traditional Retailers. *Wall Street Journal*.

Zipf, G. K. (1949). *Human Behaviour and the Principle of Least Effort: An Introduction to Human Ecology*. Cambridge, MA: Addison-Wesley.

ENDNOTES

[a] It is important, however, that we distinguish between product complexity and product durability. For instance, durable goods like home furniture, sporting goods and jewelry are relatively simple.

[b] A study done by Erdem et al. (2008) shows how ads can influence consumers' price sensitivity on certain products.

[c] It is interesting to note that some books are considered durable goods. One interesting study is done by Chevalier and Goolsbee (2004).

Chapter VI
Evaluation of Fuzzy Models to Support Online–Trust Assessment

Fahim Akhter
Zayed University, Dubai, UAE

Zakaria Maamar
Zayed University, Dubai, UAE

ABSTRACT

*Online trust is a critical element to the success of electronic commerce (e-commerce). Indeed it reduces the level of uncertainty that arises because of the lack of face-to-face **interactions** with vendors. In e-commerce purchaser-vendor interactions are subject to **uncertainty, anonymity**, and communication means reliability. This chapter discusses how some trust models have been developed to address these issues. Some models promote **familiarity** and **competitiveness** as part of the exercise of assessing online trust. This **assessment** uses **fuzzy** logic-based techniques.*

INTRODUCTION

The relationship between **trust** and commerce goes back to ancient times. First comes good bartering; a **transaction** was always in person, and the goods carried their individual intrinsic values. For example, someone might give away clothing and obtain food in return. The next type of commerce involved the exchange of precious coins, which derived value from the metals they were made of. Then paper money came, issued by governments, and financial institutions. Just as the first means of commerce (bartering) relied on trust between individuals, e-commerce equally depends on trust between people and online businesses (Ahuja, 2000). In the early years, bartering was the main process for the exchange of goods and services. Furthermore, it overcame the problem of lack of currencies. Nowadays, bartering still continues but in different ways, despite the existence of several currencies and the progress of humanity from the Stone Age to the Byte Age (Maamar, 2003). Mainly, money is given to pay for the goods purchased and the services used. Notwithstanding the various technologies that could be involved, undertaking commerce transactions can be associated with one of the following exchanges (Liand and Huang, 2000): bargaining, bidding, auctioning, and clearing. The first two exchanges are bilateral and the last two exchanges are trilateral.

E-commerce has unique features as compared to regular commerce, which allows consumers and businesses to interact with each other on favorable terms and conditions. E-commerce is ubiquitous, meaning that it is available almost everywhere, which enables customers to shop any time from home, work, just to cite a few. E-commerce has extended the market beyond conventional boundaries so that transactions could take place from anywhere. It is enabling business transactions to cross cultural and national boundaries far more easily and cost effectively than regular commerce. E-commerce enables a vendor to establish an interactive mode of access with customers even in a remote area with the help of text, video, and audio, which is not possible with regular commerce. During this interactive process, e-commerce allows for two-way interactions between vendor and consumer in ways similar to face-to-face experience in traditional commerce. The cost attached to a transaction process has been reduced and the quality improved by the widespread of technology. Internet reduces the overhead of storage, processing, and communication while improving the accuracy and timeliness of information. Online vendors can target their products or services to specific individuals/communities by adjusting the sales pitch with regard to customers' preferences and cultural norms. This level of

personalization of messages and customization of products and services does not so readily exist in regular commerce. E-commerce has a potential to be used to generate higher profits, improved communications, reduce operating cost, and improve customer service due to be open all the time.

During **online shopping**, a user often relies on common sense and applies vague and ambiguous terms when making a buying decision. The main problem currently faced by vendors is not the availability of information, but the possession of appropriate levels of knowledge to take the right decisions (Casillas et al, 2009). A typical online customer normally develops some sort of ambiguity, given the choice of similar alternative products and services (Mohanty and Bhasker, 2005). Decisions to buy or not to buy online are often based on users' human intuitions, common sense, and past experiences, rather than on the availability of clear, concise, and accurate data. Fuzzy logic is used for reasoning about inherently vague concepts (Lukasiewicz, 1970), such as "online shopping is convenient", where level of convenience is open to interpretation.

While a number of studies have examined browsers' concerns over trust, confidentiality and security, few have sought to identify gender-related differences in respect of e-business infrastructure. There is now substantial evidence that the Internet has changed the way in which customers conduct online transactions in respect of their culture norms (Akhter & Kaya 2008). Though many factors influence the decision process of online transactions such as ease-of-use, pricing, convenience, and security (Akhter et al, 2003), the perception of an influencing feature is more important than the actual level of the feature itself. For example if the perceived security level is higher than its actual implementation then that will contribute positively to the online transactions. There may be cases where the reverse is true as well, but for such cases a high level of persuasion will be needed to alter the perception level.

TRUST ASSESSMENT IN ELECTRONIC COMMERCE

In e-commerce, consumers have access to substantial amount of online information for making informed decisions. However they could easily become overwhelmed by this information, much of which many not be relevant (Vahidov and Fazlollah, 2004). Due to this overload of vague and ambiguous information consumers find the decision-making process hard (Chiu et al., 2004). Vahidov and Fazlollah's (2004) solution was to use a web-based technology, which they argued could prove a productive tool for rendering decision support in e-commerce. Bhargava and Power (2001) supported this recommendation by arguing that web-based technologies have a major impact on design, development, and implementation processes for all types of decision support systems (DSS).

A Model of Trust in E-Commerce (MoTEC) is presented in Egger's (2003). The model classifies the online factors that affect a consumer's judgment of a vendor's credibility. Egger's model comprises four components: pre-interactional filters taking place prior to any online interaction, the interface properties of the web site, the information content of the web site, and relationship management. The strength of this model is that it covers the entire buyer–seller interaction process. Egger emphasized the importance of trust from the perception of the consumer especially where consumers are more directly involved in the commercial exchange. Here users use their own equipment, provide sensitive information about themselves as individuals, and spend their own money. Therefore, consumers look forward seeing some trustworthiness signs and the vendor's assistance at the beginning of the interactions, which could lead them to buy or acquire services from the particular vendor. Preston (1998), also believes that trustworthiness and co-operation favor long-term stability and success for organizations. Egger focused on factors of trust for

initial contact. He recognized that trust could be built through iterative transactions, so he called his work "trustworthiness." Egger believed it imperative to show that benefits of ecommerce significantly outweigh potential risks. He considered the efficacy of privacy seals such as TRUSTe, but pointed out that US based seals were not significant for users in other countries. He believed the users' level of trust fluctuates during interaction with the website, but that there is an initial trust value even before accessing a website. Egger's view is supported by the exploration and commitment trust model of McKnight (2002), and the impressionistic judgment and dynamic cognitive evaluation model of Briggs (2003).

Jarvenpaa et al.'s (2000) study analyzes the major factors that encourage consumer trust in geographically scattered websites. They discussed the issue of how to cultivate trust in a consumer when that consumer might be located in another country and had no prior experience with the website. Their findings could be skewed due to the young age of respondents, lack of online experience, and cultural homogeneity of the sample in the target countries. The results might have been different if they had chosen a mix of websites instead of focusing only on bookstore sites. They found that the consumer perceived websites more to be trustworthy based on reputation rather than size of websites, especially in the case of travel websites. Jarvenpaa et al.'s (2000) study represents that there are factors besides size and reputation among heterogeneous consumers that affect trust in websites. These factors are website layout, ease-of-use, appearance, and the local language. For example, level of usability could reflect the vendor's concern for consumers. They have revealed that beside trust inducing interface cues of the websites, other factors could also foster trust among consumers. They advised that inclusion of personalization of the website for the customer, hyperlinks to other websites, and the presence of endorsements from well-known sites could affect consumer-purchasing decision.

An interesting point noticed in their research was that consumers prefer trial periods before making the final purchase and appreciate small gifts from the vendor. Their research mentioned that trust might be transferred from other people who have positive experience with the particular websites. In future research, all these interesting claims could be quantitatively validated. Jarvenpaa et al (2000) believe that affective and social components that affect trust are diverse among countries. Brengman et al., (2005) also stress that a single trust definition or measurement of trust could not be applied to different cultures simultaneously. The empirical results of this study cautiously support that while attractive prices might attract overseas consumers on the website, trust could still be a leading factor for online shopping.

Gefen (2000) developed a research model that includes familiarity with online vendors. In this model an individual's natural disposition to trust was defined as "the confidence a person has in his or her favorable expectations of what other people will do, based, in many cases, on previous interactions" and as "the belief that the other will behave as one anticipates" (Gefen, 2000). He had examined the effects of consumers' familiarity with an online vendor and its processes as well as the consumers' trust in the vendor. Gefen also assumed that familiarity and trust would positively affect a consumer's purchasing intentions from the specific websites. The proposed model reveals that both trust in a vendor and familiarity with the vendor and its procedures influence two distinct aspects of e-commerce; inquiry and purchase. Trust was affected by familiarity, whereas intended purchase and intended inquiry were both significantly affected by how much trust there is in the e-commerce vendor. The findings reveal familiarity as an additional antecedent of e-commerce that has not previously been emphasized. Gefen used a well-known website to collect data; it is unclear whether the results can be generalized to lesser-known websites.

There are many vague steps involved in shopping online, such as customers not physically being able to inspect products, and not knowing what the vendor will do with the personal information that is collected during the shopping process; both of these cause a low level of trust among customers. To reduce this vagueness and uncertainty, the consumer relies on antecedents such as cultural background and prior interactions with the online vendor to serve as a mechanism to cope with uncertainty. Lee and Turban (2001) presented a model that consists of four main antecedents influencing consumer trust in a website. These antecedents are: trustworthiness of the vendor; trustworthiness of the internet shopping medium: this includes technical competence of the medium, reliability of the medium, and medium understanding of the consumer; infrastructural factors: this includes perceived effectiveness of third party certification and perceived effectiveness of the security infrastructure, and last but not least the other factors that do not fall into the three previous types of antecedents such as company size. According to Lee and Turban, (2001) consumers' trust in Internet shopping is "the willingness of a consumer to be vulnerable to the actions of an internet merchant in an internet shopping transaction, based on the expectation that the internet merchant will behave in certain agreeable ways, irrespective of the ability of the consumer to monitor or control the internet merchant". Lee and Turban tested six hypotheses using multiple linear regression analysis. The objective of this testing was to assess the effect of perceived ability, perceived integrity, and perceived effectiveness of third-party recognition on trust and the moderating effect of trust propensity on perceived integrity, perceived competence, and perceived effectiveness of third-party recognition. The results backed only two of the six hypotheses, namely: the moderating effect of propensity to trust on perceived integrity, and the results further indicated a direct effect of perceived integrity on consumer trust in internet shopping The other hypotheses were found to be statistically insignificant. It was notable that Lee and Turban (2001) considered the perception of the medium itself as a crucial element of trust in e-commerce, while most researchers seems to neglect the role of Internet itself and only emphasize on creating trust between consumer and vendors.

EVALUATION OF FUZZY MODELS

Wang et al. (2006) present a model of an intelligent negotiation agent based on **fuzzy logic** methodology in order to alleviate the complexity of negotiation. The proposed negotiation agent model is particularly suitable for open environments such as the Internet. The conventional methods, such as game theory, are incapable of handling an open environment where the information is sparse and full of uncertainty, while fuzzy logic-based approaches are suitable to elegantly deal with this problem. The fuzzy logic based intelligent negotiation agent, presented in Wang et al. (2006), is able to interact autonomously and consequently reduce the negotiation burden on humans. The aim of modeling a **negotiation** agent is to reach mutual agreement efficiently and intelligently. The negotiation agent is able to negotiate with other such agents, over various sets of issues, on behalf of the real-world parties they represent, i.e. it can handle multi-issue negotiation. Wang et al. (2006) focus on modeling multi-issue, one-to-one negotiation agents for a third party driven virtual marketplace. They have argued that during building autonomous negotiation agents, which are capable of flexible and sophisticated negotiation, three broad areas need to be considered:

- **Negotiation protocols:** The set of rules which govern the interaction,
- **Negotiation issues:** The range of issues over which agreement must be reached,

- **Agent reasoning models:** The agents employ to act in line with the negotiation protocol in order to achieve their negotiation objectives.

Wang et al. (2006) proposed a model for fuzzy logic based intelligent negotiation agent. The proposed FINA agent is suitable for an agent based e-marketplace. An offer evaluation block has been implemented by using Microsoft .NET and fuzzy approaches. By analyzing the results from the Windows .NET test application and the MATLAB solutions, they concluded that their proposed offer evaluation blocks are acceptable, implementable, extendable, and scalable.

Metaxiotis et al., (2004) discussed the possibility of incorporating fuzzy logic into DSSs for the benefit of online consumers who have to make buying decisions. Metaxiotis et al. presented an overview of fuzzy logic modeling techniques and their applications to diverse areas such as the business medical, telecommunication, marketing, and e-commerce sectors and described the procedures for constructing a fuzzy logic model.

Liu et al., (2005) proposed a method that introduces interactive fuzzy logic to assist consumers in gaining a higher satisfaction level when purchasing products and services online. They introduced a notion of serving different online consumers based on their preferences and requirements. Their prototype system allows users to make initial selections from the available options and then the system will compute the satisfaction score for the specified product based on the fuzzy inference system. If consumers are satisfied with the satisfaction score, the system will display all the products in the selected range for consumers. Otherwise, they can always go back and change their selection.

Ngai and Wat (2004) adopted a fuzzy decision support system (FDSS) to assist e-commerce managers to evaluate the risks associated with e-commerce development. They developed a Web-based prototype system to assist managers in identifying potential risk factors and evaluating the corresponding e-commerce development risk. Ngai and Wat have adopted a five-stage system development methodology that incorporates the use of fuzzy logic for risk analysis. These stages are: construction of fuzzy risk analysis model, development of system architecture, analyzing and designing of the system, beginning of the prototype, and evaluation of the system. Ngai and Wat argued that their prototype is compatible with Windows 2000 server platform and could run on Internet Explorer. The results showed the benefits of using the systems: risks associated with e-commerce development are identified; overall risk of the project could be predicted at the beginning. The results of the evaluation process support the fuzzy logic approach using fuzzy sets, and demonstrated the feasibility of evaluation e-commerce project risk. It would be very beneficial for e-commerce managers to observe the system's effectiveness and usability once it is used in real life e-commerce projects.

Nyongesa et al., (2003) developed a web portal to support online shopping, using fuzzy logic in order to improve consumers' shopping experience. They deployed fuzzy logic in their prototype as the mechanism for modeling consumers' behaviors to generate appropriate user interfaces. They collected information about consumers to facilitate interface personalization and adaptation, and fuzzy logic was then used to implement these processes. Nyongesa et al. argued that fuzzy logic could handle ambiguous data related to consumers' online shopping preferences. In addition they created two inputs and one fuzzy output in their system like what Ngai did in his thesis (2004). Nyongesa et al., (2003) evaluated their prototype from the perspectives of usability, feature design, navigation, and functionality of the user interface. They adopted a questionnaire for the evaluation purposes and selected five knowledgeable users to answer the questions. The results of the evaluation showed that most users agreed with the functions of ease of use. However, the search

function was considered a weak factor because it was showing unwanted results. The adoption of fuzzy logic approach has helped them achieve a high degree of adaptation in unpredictable user behavior. Yuan (2009) has presented a model that utilizes experts' knowledge, employs the fuzzy set concept to handle imprecision, and then to establish a fuzzy logic-based system for managers to access and evaluate the cost-volume-profit decision making process, and finally to make the right decision.

Sugumaran (2007) has presented a system based on fuzzy logic to support the evaluation and the quantification of trust in e-commerce. Although the system has addressed many issues that other systems did not such as taking into account the fuzzy nature of trust, Sugumaran (2007) argued that the system can be improved in many ways. As stated in many trust models, there are other aspects that contribute to the completion of online transactions. This includes price, scarcity of the item, and experience of customers. In order to develop an effective decision support system, future development should include some if not all of these aspects. The price of an item is certainly an important variable as it is shown in many studies that if the price is reasonably low, customers are ready to take the highest risk to purchase the item. Online transactions also depend on customer's experience and personality. Some customers may value some variables more than others. Hence Sugumaran (2007) argued that future systems should allow customers to rank trust variables according to their own perception and experience. Sugumaran (2007) argued that Kasiran and Meziane (2002) developed a trust model for business-to-consumer (B2C) e-commerce that is based on the kind of information customers are looking for on a vendor's Website to help them decide whether to engage in a transaction or not. The model identified four major factors that need to be present on a merchant's Website to increase customers' trust when shopping online. These factors are: existence, affiliation, policy, and fulfillment. The information the customer needs to collect to satisfy the existence factor include physical existence, such as the merchant's telephone number, fax number, postal address, mandatory registration, and people existence. These are known as variables. The affiliation factor looks at third-party endorsement, membership and portal and the policy factor looks at information with regards to customer satisfaction policy, privacy statement, and warranty policy. Finally, the fulfillment factor looks at delivery methods, methods of payment and the community comments. Hence, a total of 12 variables have been identified.

Given the large amount of information the model (Meziane & Kasiran, 2002) requires, an information extraction system has been developed to automate the data collection process (Meziane & Kasiran, 2003, Meziane & Kasiran, 2005). Indeed it has been reported that users struggle to identify specific information on websites (Center for the Digital Future, 2004). In addition, they do recognize that users may not be able to make proper use of the collected information. For this purpose, they developed tools to evaluate the trustworthiness of an e-commerce website based on the collected information. Two models have been developed by them for evaluating the trust factor; the linear model and the parameterized model. However, for both models they recognized that this is not the natural way customers adopt to evaluate their trust towards online merchants or make the decision to buy or not. As with any other business transactions, customers develop in their mind some sort of ambiguity and uncertainties when purchasing online (Mohanty & Bhasker, 2005). A customer may wish to classify merchants using different preferences or take into accounts other parameters such as the cost or the brand of the product. The decision to buy or not to buy online is often based on user's human intuitions, common sense, and experience rather than on the availability of clear, concise, and accurate data (Akhter, Hobbs, & Maamar, 2005).

PROPOSED FUZZY-LOGIC MODEL

Our research is based on the rationale that actual level of any **B2C** transaction is based on two factors, namely: what is the level of Trust (T) of the given website, and how competitive (C) is this site for purchasing purposes. Therefore we propose to investigate into the truthfulness of the following relationships:

1. $T = f(S, F, D)$
2. $L_{B2C} = g(T, C)$

Where S is the level of **security**, F is the level of familiarity, and D is the level of design layout of the B2C site. The premise is that the factors determining the level of Trust T are a function of these three parameters. Therefore any degree of B2C transaction will be based on the level of *Trust* (T) and the *competitiveness* (C) of the website. The three premises represented in figure 1 are values for fuzzy sets such as Low, High and Good; representing state information for linguistic variables security, familiarity and design. These sets represented by their values as shown in the figure from the fuzzification process. Therefore, the operators are executed on the fuzzified values as follows: Result: min (0.7, max (0.0, 0.8)) = 0.7. The implication is therefore for this rule that trust is Low with a degree of 0.7. This outcome is presented because of implication, which is graphically represented by cutting off the fuzzy set for degree greater than 0.7.

In order to analyse the impact of human decisions on the level of e-commerce transactions, it was organise and categorise the factors that are significant to the decision processes linked to conducting the B2C transaction. The Table 1 displays the user's preferences for B2C level based on their perceived level of trust and competitiveness.

The rules describing the basis for a given Trust level was based on degrees of security, familiarity and design. These degrees were formulated in terms of their linguistic variables such as low, mod-

Figure 1. Fuzzy rule with three premises and one implication forming the conclusion

| | Antecedent | | | | Consequent | |

Table 1. Formation of B2C rules

Rule	Trust	Competitiveness	B2C level
No	Linguistic	Linguistic	Linguistic
	Value	Value	Value
1	HT	Fairly	low
2	HT	Highly	high
3	HT	Moderate	moderate
...	...	...	...
...	...	...	...
13	VLT	Fairly	low
14	VLT	Highly	low
15	VLT	Moderate	low

VLT = *very low trust,* **HT** = *high trust,*
MT = *moderate trust* **LT** = *low trust*

Table 2. Formation of trust rules

Rule	Security	Familiarity	Design	Trust
No	Linguistic	Linguistic	Linguistic	Linguistic
	Value	Value	Value	Value
1	High	High	Good	VHT
2	High	High	Moderate	VHT
3	High	High	Poor	H T
4	High	Low	Good	HT
...	...	...	...	...
...	...	...	...	...
23	Moderate	Low	Moderate	LT
24	Moderate	Low	Poor	LT
25	Moderate	Moderate	Good	MT
26	Moderate	Moderate	Moderate	LT
27	Moderate	Moderate	Poor	LT

VHT = *very high trust,* **HT** = *high trust,*
MT = *moderate trust* **LT** = *low trust*

erate and high. The degree for Design level was expressed in terms of poor, moderate and good. Similarly the degree for a Trust level was ranging from very low to very high, in five distinct fuzzy sets. These rules were derived from the survey data after a thorough organization and analysis and represent the users views of the Trust level of a given website based on the given factors. A rule from the Table 2 can be extracted as: If (security = high) **and** (familiarity = low) **and** (design = moderate) **then** (trust = moderate trust).

Trust is given in terms of five fuzzy sets whilst the competitiveness and B2C level is represented in terms of three linguistic labels for fuzzy sets. A given rule from the table 1 can be expressed as:

If (trust = low trust) **and** (competitiveness = highly) **then** (B2C level = moderate)

There were a total of 27 rules for Trust deduced from the survey as shown in Figure 2. Similarly

Figure 2. Shows the GUI for the rule editor

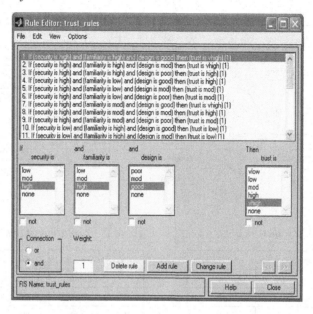

the rules disclosing the B2C level for various inputs were found to be 15. These rules form the basis of the compounded inference system consisting of two separate, but interconnected systems to postulate a B2C level for given values for security, familiarity, design and competition levels of the website.

CONCLUSION

The capturing of human thought and evaluation processes in a fuzzy expert system will be of great advantage to B2C vendors in accessing the level of acceptance of their products / services amongst the consumer base. The proposed model will assist consumers and vendors in quantifying the trust level of any given site. Consumers will be able to quantify the human reasoning processes of evaluating security, privacy, customer services and so on. In this chapter we provided an overview of the use of fuzzy logic in e-commerce with focus on trust assessment. Trust can be seen from two

perspectives. From a customer perspective, trust means that a customer's details and request would be dealt with according to her personal preferences and requirements. Indeed not all customers would like to see their recent purchasing requests shared with other parties without their approval. From a provider perspective, trust means that a provider expects dealing with collaborative customers who do not want to ``harm'' their resources. Because of the uncertainty, vagueness, and anonymity that feature e-commerce transactions, assessing trust during these transactions require advanced models that could be built on fuzzy logic. These models promote important factors such as user familiarity and provider fairness during this assessment.

REFERENCES

Ahuja, V. (2000). Building Trust in Electronic Commerce. *IT Professional, 2*(1), pp. 61-63.

Akhter, F., & Kaya, L. (2008). Building Secure e-Business Systems: Technology and Culture in the U.A.E. *In E-Business Applications Track of ACM SAC.* Fortaleza, Brazil, March 16-20.

Akhter, F., Hobbs, D., & Maamar Z. (2005). A fuzzy logic-based system for assessing the level of business-to-consumer (B2C) trust in electronic commerce. *Expert Systems with Applications, 28,* 623–628.

Bhargava, H., & Power (2001). Decision support systems and web technologies: a status report. *Seventh Americas Conference on Information Systems.*

Brengman, M., Geuens M., Weijters, & Swinyard, W. (2005). Segmenting Internet shoppers based on their Web-usage-related lifestyle: a cross-cultural validation. *Journal of Business Research, 58*(1), 79-88.

Casillas, J., & Martínez-López, F. J. (2009). *Expert Systems with Applications, 36*(2) PART 1, 1645-1659

Center for the Digital Future (2004). *USC Annenberg School, The digital future report.* www. digitalcenter.org/downloads/ DigitalFutureReport-Year4-2004.pdf

Chiu, Y. C., Shyu, J. Z., & Tzeng, G. H. (2004). Fuzzy MCDM for evaluating e-commerce Strategy. *International Journal of Computer Applications in Technology, 19*(1), 12-22.

Egger, F. N. (2003). Deceptive Technologies: Cash, Ethics & HCI. *SIGCHI Bulletin, 35*(2). ACM Press.

Gefen, D. (2000). E-Commerce: The Role of Familiarity and Trust. Omega. *The International Journal of Management Science, 28*(6), 725-737.

Jarvenpaa, S. L., Tractinsky, N. M., & Vitale, M. (2000). Consumer trust in an Internet store. *Information Technology and Management,* (pp. 45–71).

Kasiran, M. K., & Meziane, F. (2002). An information framework for a merchant trust agent in electronic commerce. In H. Yin, N. Allinson, R. Freeman, J. Keane, &Hubbard S. (Eds), *Intelligent data engineering and automated learning,* (pp. 243-248). Springer

Lee, M. K. O., & Turban, E. (2001). A Trust Model for Consumer Internet Shopping. *International Journal of Electronic Commerce, 6*(1), 75-91.

Liand, T. P., & Huang, J. S. (2000). A framework for applying intelligent agents to support electronic trading. *Decision Support Systems, 28*(4).

Liu, F., Geng, H., & Zhang, Y. (2005). Interactive Fuzzy Interval Reasoning for smart Web shopping. *Applied Soft Computing, 5*(4), 433-439.

Lukasiewicz, J. (1970). Philosophical remarks on many-valued systems of propositional logic. Reprinted in Selected Works, ed. Borkowski, Studies in Logic and the Foundations of Mathematics (North-Holland, Amsterdam, 1970) (pp. 153-179).

Maamar, Z. (2003). Commerce, E-Commerce, and M-Commerce: What Comes Next? *Communications of the ACM, 46*(12).

McKnight, D. H., Choudhury. V., & Kacmar, C. (2002). The impact of initial consumer trust on Intentions to transact with a website: A Trust building model. *Journal of Strategic Information Systems, 11,* 297-323.

Metaxiotis, K., Psarras, J., & Samouilidis, J. (2004). New applications of fuzzy logic in decision support systems. *International Journal of Management and Decision Making, 5*(1), 47 – 58.

Meziane, F., & Kasiran, M. K. (2003). Extracting unstructured information from the WWW to support merchant existence in e-commerce. In A. Dusterhoft & B. Thalheim (Eds.), *Lecture Notes in Informatics, Natural Language Processing and Information Systems, GI-Edition,* (pp. 175-185). Bonn, Germany.

Mohanty, B. K., & Bhasker, B. (2005). Product classification in the Internet Business: a fuzzy approach. *Journal of Decision Support Systems, 38*, 611-619.

Ngai, E., & Wat, F. (2005). *Fuzzy decision support system for risk analysis in e-commerce development.*

Nyongesa, H., Shicheng, T., Maleki-Dizaji, S., Huang, S. T., & Siddiqi, J. (2003). Adaptive Web Interface Design Using Fuzzy Logic. *IEEE/WIC International Conference on Web Intelligence, 13*(17), 671- 674.

Preston, D. (1998). Business Ethics and Privacy in the Workplace. *ACM Computers and Society,* (pp. 12-18).

Sugumaran, V. (2007). *International Journal of Intelligent Information Technologies, 3*(4), *Support Systems, 2*(40), 235-255. IGI Global.

Vahidov, K., & Fazlollahi, R. (2004). Multi-agent DSS for supporting e-commerce decisions. *Journal of Computer Information Systems, 44*(2).

Xin, W., Xiaojun, S., & Georganas, N. D. (2006). A Fuzzy Logic Based Intelligent Negotiation Agent (FINA) in Ecommerce. Electrical and Computer Engineering, Canadian Conference (pp. 276–279).

Yuan, F.-C, (2009). *Expert Systems with Applications, 36*(2), PART 1, 1155–1163.

Chapter VII
Comparison–Shopping Channel Selection by Small Online Vendors:
An Exploratory Study

Yun Wan
University of Houston - Victoria, USA

Nan Hu
Singapore Management University, Singapore

ABSTRACT

Comparison-shopping is becoming the mainstream marketing channel for B2C ecommerce. More and more small online vendors are using shopbots to bring in customers. There are mainly two types of shopbots: those general shopbots that provide product comparison cross multiple heterogeneous product categories (like shopping.com) and the specialized shopbots that provide comparison within a single or a few highly-related product categories (like addall.com on books and music CD). The effectiveness of shopbot selection strategy by small online vendors is the focus on this paper. By analyzing data from shopbots and online vendors, the authors found there is significant positive correlation between the number of shopbots an online vendor participates and its traffic rank, which indicates the general effectiveness of using shopbots as a marketing channel. They also found that for online vendors competing on a niche product like college textbook, participating specialized shopbots brings in higher traffic. For competing in mainstream market, there is less significant correlation between participating general shopbots and higher traffic rank for vendors. They conclude that using general shopbots is a reactive strategy for small online vendors while using proper specialized shopbots could provide an edge for small online vendors.

INTRODUCTION

The expansion of the B2C electronic market keeps attracting brick and mortar vendors to join in the online market. However, it is not easy for new online vendors, especially small online vendors, to compete effectively with behemoths like Amazon.com or WalMart.com by using traditional Web advertising strategies like banner ads. Nor do small online vendors have the deep pockets to invest heavily in website design to enhance consumer experiences.

Recently the emergence of comparison-shopping services, like shopping.com and mysimon.com, provides a relatively cost-effective way for most small online vendors to use their most important advantage over established portals– the lower price and flexible product offering. As a result, we observed an increasing number of online vendors participating comparison-shopping in the last four years.

Sensing the opportunity in Shopbots, private equities flooded into this market and various comparison-shopping services have mushroomed since 1997. Among them, the most popular Shopbots include Shopping.com, Shopzilla.com, and PriceGrabber.com. Established players also began to provide their comparison-shopping services like Yahoo Shopping, MSN Shopping and Froogle by Google.

Thus, we are observing an increasingly dynamic market consisting of online shoppers, online vendors, and shopbots. In this market, channel selection by small online vendors, or how small online vendors select shopbots as their new channel to bring in online shoppers, is important for our understanding of this market as we will explain in more details in subsequent sections.

Due to the dynamic nature of online retailing and the comparison-shopping market, we lack comprehensive statistics in this domain. Web technology already enables a one-man-store to be set up in one hour and, at the same time, intensive competition could make a large number of such stores disappear overnight. Since tracking the full details of this fast-changing new market, including individual vendor strategies, is almost impossible, we take a step back by studying a "snapshot" of this dynamic and share some preliminary findings in this direction.

Subsequent sections are organized as follows: In part I, we introduce the new online channel of comparison-shopping and then review the current status of and existing studies on comparison-shopping. In part II, we propose our study's methodology, research model, and hypotheses. We also explain our data collection procedure. In part III, we present our findings by analyzing the obtained data. In part IV, we draw our conclusion and propose future research directions.

LITERATURE REVIEW

Background of Shopbots and Comparison-Shopping Services

Shopbots, an Internet innovation also called comparison-shopping agents, aggregators, or recommendation agents, refers to those Web-based Business-to-Consumer (B2C) electronic decision aids that can collect product and service information – especially price-related information – from multiple online vendors, aggregate them, and process them into easy-to-compare formats for online shoppers to assist their shopping. Comparison-shopping services are provided by Shopbots.

Comparison-shopping services first caught media attention via the BargainFinder experiment in 1995. Developed by several researchers in the, then, Andersen Consulting's research lab and smart store center, BargainFinder is a Web-based intelligent application that could automatically gather prices of CDs from up to nine online music stores based on a query from the user. Though BargainFinder is a very limited comparison-shopping test site, it received enormous positive responses from consumers and media alike. Within one week of its public release on June 30, 1995, it received an average of 2,000 visits per day (Krulwich, 1996).

Since the BargainFinder experiment, several more sophisticated comparison-shopping services like Jango, Junglee, and CompareNet emerged from1996 to 1998. However, few of them could secure a large enough market share before being acquired by established portals. Jango was acquired by Excite for $35 million in October 1997, Junglee by Amazon in 1998, CompareNet by Microsoft in 1999, and mySimon.com by CNET in 2000. Only a few shopbots, like Pricescan.com, remained independent after the acquisitions. Due to bad strategy by some of these portals, many of these promising comparison-shopping technologies were not further developed and some were tweaked and then abandoned quickly (Gimein, 1999). Consequently, comparison-shopping service experienced a temporary stagnant stage between 1999 and 2000.

In 2000, there came another round of boom time for comparison-shopping services and new shopbots. A distinctive feature of this round was the consumer market development for using Web-based comparison-shopping. Israel-based Dealtime.com (now shopping.com) and CNET Network's mySimon.com were among the first to use traditional media like TV advertisement to reach customers and build the concepts of comparison-shopping in consumers (E. White, 2000). They extended major efforts in popularizing the concepts of comparison-shopping and eventually brought comparison-shopping services into mainstream B2C ecommerce.[a] In the period from 2000 to 2005, new Shopbots like shopping.com, pricegrabber.com, shopzilla.com (transformed from Bizrate.com), and pronto.com came into being and established themselves quickly.

The popularity of comparison-shopping began to again draw the attention of established players and investors. In 2005, the second round of shopbots acquisition by eBay and other conglomerates

further increased the public awareness of this new online shopping channel.

Comparison-Shopping Services as a New Online Marketing Channel

From the marketing perspective, shopbots and the comparison-shopping services they provide could be regarded as an online marketing channel similar to catalog retailing in traditional B2C business. According to the Electronic Market Hypothesis, shopbots facilitate transactions in the electronic market by reducing the transaction cost, or more specifically, the information searching cost and partial information processing cost incurred to online shoppers (Malone, Yates, & Benjamin, 1987). As a result, more small online vendors are able to enter the market because of the lower cost of attracting a large enough number of customers for a viable business.

This new online marketing channel has three constituents: the online shoppers, the online retailers, and the Shopbots (Figure 1).

A highly simplified description for the dynamics of this channel can be summarized by two marketing flows: the information flow and the revenue flow. These two intertwined flows link the three elements that form the market. The information flow starts with online vendors. Product and service information from online vendors are either fed into or extracted by Shopbots. Subsequently, Shopbots aggregate the information from multiple vendors, process them in a value-added way, and present them to online shoppers. After reviewing the information presented by Shopbots, online shoppers select their preferred choice, which generates a utility for them, and then are led to the online retailers to finalize the purchase. The revenue flow runs in the opposite direction. It originates from online shoppers. When online shoppers finalize the purchasing, their payments are sent to the online vendors as revenue. Online vendors then split the revenue to share with Shopbots as the referral charge, or the

Figure 1. The constituents of comparison-shopping market

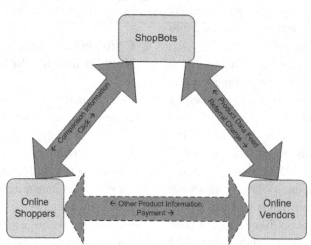

so-called cost-per-click (CPC). With a continuing replenishment of revenue from online vendors, the Shopbots are able to maintain the information aggregation and other routine operations.

There have been several major studies on the impact of this new channel on price equilibrium. Early findings showed that Web-based comparison-shopping could increase the welfare of consumers by lowering product or service price. For example, Brown and Goolsbee (2002) found that the rise of comparison shopping sites reduced average insurance prices by as much as 5 percent in the 1990s while prices were not reduced for insurance types that were not covered by the comparison websites.

However, this impact was not consistently observed in other product and service categories. Iyer and Pazgal (2003) collected pricing data from up to seven comparison-shopping sites for homogeneous products like CDs and books. They found that the availability of this new channel did not lead to intensive pricing competition among online businesses because the purposes of participating comparison-shopping among online businesses varied.

Smith and Brynjolfsson (2001) found similar patterns after evaluating thousands of data points obtained from a book comparison-shopping site: online shoppers were not absolute bargain-finders; many visitors to the website chose to buy from the brand name stores instead of those unknown stores though the unknown stores offered the lowest price. Based on Smith and Brynjolfsson's calculation, brand name bookstores on average commanded a \$1.41 price premium over unbranded retailers for each book in this online channel.

Based on previous research on the comparison-shopping market for books, Markopoulos and Kephart (2002) found that the information provided by shopbots for a book's price can be about 6% to 10% as valuable as the book itself for online shoppers.

The above findings greatly increased our understanding of the complexity of this new online channel's impact from a price equilibrium perspective, an aggregated influence. To further explain such impacts and identify new influences, we need to look deeper into the interactions among the three constituents of comparison-shopping markets: Knowledge is still limited in how they influence the evolution of each other. So far, we only have moderate advancement in the interaction between online shopper and shopbots, like our understanding of how online shopper using these shopbots (Haubl & Murray, 2003; Haubl & Trifts, 2000; Tan, 2003), how to design a better shopbots to accommodate comparison-shopping uses(Ariely, 2000; Montgomery, Hosanagar, Krishnan, & Clay, 2003), and what is the shoppers' online comparison-shopping behavior for specific products like books or wines (Smith & Brynjolfsson, 2001). Even in this interaction, we still have major issue unresolved like the risk in over-provision of shopping choices (Schwartz, 2004).

In this research, we increase our understanding on another aspect of the interactions among these three constituents by extending the study of online marketing channels into the interaction between online vendors and shopbots with a focus on the channel selection by small online vendors.

Online Vendor's Channel Selection in Comparison-Shopping Market

In marketing literature, a channel is defined as *a set of interdependent organizations involved in the process of making a product or service available for use or consumption* (Coughlan, Anderson, Stern, & El-Ansary, 2001). Online vendors are part of the marketing channel for product manufacturers. In the comparison-shopping market, shopbots and their host, the comparison-shopping service providers, can be considered as the marketing channel for online vendors or as an indirect channel for product manufacturers and service providers[b]. Two reasons made the study of comparison-shopping channel selection by small online vendors meaningful and important.

First, channel selection by small online vendors is an outcome of market evolution. There used to be two ways for shopbots to collect vendor information: data extraction or data feeding. In late 90s, when early shopbots emerged, most of them used a data extraction method. A data extraction method allows a shopbot to aggregate the product price information from online vendors by using a screen scalping algorithm, or the so-called wrapper. A wrapper can automatically collect information from the html page from a designated website (Doorenbos, Etzioni, & Weld, 1997). Since this method did not require any action from the vendor side, online vendors do not have an active channel selection strategy, though they may choose to refuse to be searched by shopbots. However, this method has gradually lost its popularity since 2000 due to its technical limitation[c] and potential lawsuits from online vendors (Plitch, 2002). Gradually, data feeding technology became the standard way for most shopbots and vendors to participate comparison-shopping – vendors have to upload their product price information to shopbots and pay to be listed. Thus, how to select the most effective comparison-shopping channels in a cost-benefit framework became an important business strategy for vendors.

Second, not all vendors are created equal; there is a great distinction in strategy between top online vendors and small online vendors. In the comparison-shopping market, small online vendors do not have much bargaining power in terms of participating comparison-shopping. In contrast, top online vendors like Amazon.com not only have the bargaining power when participating comparison-shopping but also may refuse to be listed in shopbots[d] because of top online vendors' premium price is not competitive with small online vendors. However, shopbots may still want to collect information from these established online vendors to give shoppers a full-spectrum selection. So the channel selection for comparison-shopping for top online vendors is different from channel selection for small online vendors[e]. In light of this difference, this research focuses on those small online vendors that have to treat the cost of participating comparison-shopping as given and formulate an appropriate channel selection strategy to optimize their profit.

In the still-limited literature on vendor strategy in the comparison-shopping market, researchers mainly focused on the pricing strategy of online vendors. For example, through the collection of the daily price data of uVision, a comparison-shopping agent for CDs, Crowston (1997) found that most small businesses might not benefit from comparison-shopping because a few retailers consistently provide the lowest product price for all products. Later, Crowston and MacInnes (2001) confirmed the "cheapest-for-all" phenomenon when online vendors feeding their data to comparison-shopping sites.

There are few studies on the empirical interaction between online vendors and Shopbots except the simulation research by Kephart and his colleagues (Kephart, Hanson, & Greenwald, 2000; Markopoulos & Kephart, 2002). However, understanding the *empirical* interactions and their impact on the formation of this emerging electronic comparison-shopping market is important for at least two reasons.

First, from an academic perspective, the existing electronic market was not all driven by rational software agents but by an interactive influence of both software agents and human beings. The bounded rationality of human beings, here the online vendors and consumers, made the evolution of their strategy and the market not strictly follow a rational way (Simon, 1956). Empirical investigation will adjust our prediction to make it more or less follow the actual evolutionary path.

Second, with the popularity of comparison-shopping, there are an increasing number of online vendors and Shopbots entering the market; the interactions between these two types of elements largely determined the market structure. Both incumbents and prospective institutional players and industry analysts in this market want to know the way the interaction unfolds. Consultancy wise, our understanding in this area is important.

For the remainder of this paper, we first propose the research question, hypothesis, and model about channel selection in comparison-shopping market.

Then we analyze the collected data to verify the hypothesis. Finally we discuss the research outcome and its implications for future studies.

THE RESEARCH QUESTION, HYPOTHESES, AND RESEARCH MODEL

As elaborated in previous sections, our research question is how small online vendors using comparison-shopping, a new online marketing channel, and the impact of such strategies on their site traffic.

We start from two most intuitive hypotheses based on conventional business strategies. Through the data collection and analysis, we gradually identify new findings related to our hypotheses and the research question in general. Again, this approach is due to the explorative nature of this research and the novelty of this emerging market.

From an online vendor perspective, comparison-shopping as an online marketing channel consisting of essentially two types of shopbots: the general shopbots listing products in multiple categories (Shopping.com) and the specialized shopbots listing product for one or a few closely-related product category (AddAll.com for Media products, including books, CDs and DVDs). For the convenience of expression, we borrow a marketing concept, *niche*, to describe the second type of shopbots though the original concept covers more focused product categories[f].

Each type corresponds to one marketing channel. The general shopbots provide a *mainstream channel* and the niche shopbots provide a *niche channel*.

We hypothesize that the strategic goal for small online vendors is to bring in as much traffic as possible from the aggregated comparison-shopping channels with minimum overall cost. This hypothesis is in accordance with the general consensus of the industry[g].

With the goal and the two basic channel categories for selection, we try to use a descriptive model to identify an intuitive channel selection strategy by small online vendors. We hypothesize a positive correlation exists between the number of shopbots a vendor selects and the traffic the vendor receives. This is a natural assumption because adding individual shopbots would generate more traffic for online vendors when all other things are equal. Thus, more shopbots bring in more aggregated traffic. So we have hypothesis 1:

Hypothesis 1: There is a positive correlation between the number of shopbots an online vendor participates, and the traffic this online vendor receives, regardless of the types of shopbots and the product the vendor sells.

When engaging in the comparison-shopping market channel, a small online vendor might adjust the participation strategy. This adjustment is influenced by several factors.

If the vendor is in a niche market, the vendor has the option of choosing both general shopbots and niche shopbots or just one of them for the online site. Comparatively, for mainstream market, though, a vendor only has the option of choosing general shopbots. The vendor still has the option of deciding how many and how popular the general shopbots it wants to participate. But what exactly is the influence of these different strategies on generating traffic for a vendor site?

For example, *winner takes all* is the typical philosophy and practice in B2C electronic commerce and has been verified by established portals like eBay and Amazon.com. Does this approach imply using the most popular shopbots will guarantee traffic for small online vendors in a mainstream market? Also, since most niche shopbots are far less popular and known only by the niche market customers, is participating niche shopbots worthwhile and do niche shopbots generate comparatively more traffic than participating

general shopbots for a small online vendor in a niche market?

Based on these questions, we propose the following hypothesis:

Hypothesis 2a: Participating most popular general Shopbots is positively correlated with the higher traffic rank for small online vendors.

Hypothesis 2b: Compared with participating general shopbots, participating niche Shopbots is positively correlated with higher traffic rank for small online vendors that sell niche products.

Before we proceed to analyze the correlation between comparison-shopping channel selection strategy and the site traffic rank, we realize that other characters of the site might influence its traffic rank. Since the subject of our research is small online vendors, we can assume that the major advertising method for such sites is via click through from other sites. In other words, we can safely exclude impact from other advertising channels like TV and other media advertisement as major advertising channels due to the limited budget of small online vendors.

To have a relatively comprehensive consideration of various factors, here we use a set of factors identified and collected by Alexa.com. Alexa.com, a company owned by Amazon.com, is engaging in site traffic ranking and consumer behavior analysis. The site variables they collect are considered authoritative from an industry perspective, thus they serve our purpose for this research. The variables and the rationales for their inclusion are listed here:

Existence Time (ExistenceTime), the length of time since an online retailer established its Web presence. For online vendors, early entrants to a market usually have a competitive advantage over later entrants in accumulating customer base, which in turn affects how an online vendor chooses the participation of comparison-shopping and its revenue structure. So the *existence time* for an online vendor may correlate with its participation strategy to influence the revenue it generates.

Number of LinkSites (#LinkSites) refers to the number of other sites linked to the online retailers', which indicates its hyperlinked status with the Web. Since the success of Google, the number of hyperlinks to a site from other sites becomes an important factor in deciding the importance of the linked site for a query by search engines (Brin & Page, 1998). Also, having more links to a site, whether they are via banner ads from other sites or organic links, could naturally generate more traffic to the site (hence more revenues), so #LinkSites is another critical factor that may correlate with participating strategies for online vendors.

Response Speed (Speed) refers to site's loading time of the site in response to requests from online shoppers. The Existence of Pop Up (popup) refers to the existence of pop up windows on the vendor site. Both response time to online query and pop up advertisement could affect the user satisfaction and thus influence the traffic of the site. So we also include speed and popup as additional factors in the model.

For a dependent variable in the model, we use Traffic Rank (TR) of a site as a proxy to measure the comparative impact on traffic of different channel selection strategies. The Traffic Rank is based on three months of aggregated historical traffic data from millions of Alexa Toolbar users and is a combined measure of page views.[h]

With above independent and dependent variables, we measure the impact of the number of comparison-shopping channels a small online vendor subscribed (#Shopbots) via equation (1):

$$TR = f(ExistenceTime, \#LinkSites, Speed, Popup, \#Shopbots) \qquad (1)$$

DATA COLLECTION

We have followed four steps in the data collection. In the first step, we identified two representative product categories for mainstream and niche markets; in the second step, we identified representative Shopbots in each market and then collected online vendor participation information for the two representative products we identified in step 1; in the third step, we aggregated the online vendors information in step 2 and collected the individual vendor characteristics information, like existence time, etc. from Alaex.com. Finally, we brought all these data together for analysis.

Identification of Product Categories

As discussed previously, we included two types of product categories in the research, the mainstream product and niche product. We selected one product in each category: *digital camera* in the mainstream product category and *college textbook* in the niche product category.

We chose *digital camera* as the representation of a mainstream product because "digital camera" is consistently ranked the most frequently searched query in all major search engines and it is being purchased by all age groups regardless of profession, genders, or nationality. It is also a product category that is covered by all major online shopping portals. During our data collection period, digital camera comprised of 25%~30% of the top 20 sellers in the electronics category of Amazon.com. Considering millions of electronic product being sold in Amazon, digital cameras are most representative of mainstream products.

We chose *college textbook* as the representative of a niche product because college textbooks are almost exclusively used by college students through a relatively small yet highly specialized supply chain. Also, because of its standardization level, *book* is one of the earliest searchable products from Shopbots. College students are more price-sensitive and Internet-savvy compared with other online shopper groups. Considering these factors all together, the college textbook market becomes a perfect mature niche market in comparison-shopping for analysis.

We also identified specific representative products for each category. For *digital camera*, we selected the top three most popular digital cameras on Amazon during our data collection period. They are Canon PowerShot SD110, S500, and S410. For *college textbooks*, we selected three popular computer science and information system textbooks the authors are familiar with: *Artificial Intelligence* by Stuart Russell and Peter Norvig (2002), *Computer Networks* by Andrew Tanenbaum (2002), and *Modern System Analysis and Design* by Jeffrey Hoffer, Joey George, Joseph Valacich (2004). All these textbooks are returned as first entry in Google if one types the query with a combination of the textbook name and keyword "textbook."

Identification of Shopbots Online Vendors Participate

Since it is very difficult to track all Shopbots an online vendor participates, which is usually confidential, we try to obtain an approximation of their participation strategy. Because of the power law distribution of the Web (Adamic et al., 2000), such approximation does not skew too much from the actual situation as long as we explore all major Shopbots in the market and sampled the remaining less known ones. For example, Yahoo Shopping, Shopping.com, bizrate. com (now Shopzilla.com), and PriceGrabber.com are considered the top four comparison-shopping marketing channels in the mainstream market. So an online vendor participating all these Shopbots indicates a strategy distinct from the strategy of an online vendor who participates only one of them, even though we do not know their other selection for those less known Shopbots.

Thus, we classify the Shopbots into three levels based on their popularity. Each level contains 1~3 Shopbots that share similar a level of popularity based on their overall traffic load.

The Shopbot list for *digital camera* in mainstream market includes Yahoo Shopping as the top level; Shopping.com, Pricegrabber.com and Bizrate.com as the second level; mySimon.com and Pricescan.com as the third level. For *college textbook,* in the niche market, based on their traffic rank, we classified Shopping.com and Pricegrabber.com as the top level; mySimon.com and Pricescan.com as the second level; Addall. com and Bestbookdeal.com as the third level. Here AddAll.com and Bestbookdeal.com are both niche Shopbots.

Collection and Aggregation of Data

We collected the online vendor participation data from Shopbots listed in each category for three times from the last week of March 2005 to the second week of April 2005. In each product category, we collected online vendor data for the three popular products, as mentioned above. Meanwhile, we collected the vendor features data from Alexa. com three times, too. After we completed the data collection, we cleaned them and conducted the pre-processing work by aggregating the vendor lists for similar products in each category to get the complete participation set for each online vendor in each product category.

DATA ANALYSIS

Table 1 shows how many online retailers subscribe to each Shopbot in the *digital camera* and *college textbook* categories.

In the digital camera category, we can observe a more even distribution for the number of online vendors in each Shopbot. In the college textbook category, the numbers of online vendors in each Shopbot are significantly different. The most

Table 1. Distribution of online vendors for each product category for different shopbots

Digital Camera	Yahoo Shopping	Shopping	BizRate	PriceGrabber	PriceScann	MySimon
# online vendors	56	58	47	59	36	45
College Textbook	Shopping	PriceGrabber	MySimon	PriceScan	AddAll	BestBookDeal
# online vendors	27	34	27	77	50	93

popular one is besebookdeal.com with 93 online retailers subscribing to it while the least popular one is shopping.com with only 27 subscribers, even though shopping.com is a much more popular Shopbots in the mainstream market.

After aggregating the number of online vendors distributed in each level for both categories as we described in the previous section, a chi-square test of goodness-of-fit was performed to determine whether the numbers of vendors over these three levels of shopbots really depends on the product categories. The significant chi-square result (N = 169, Chi-square= 30.7308, and P <.0001) indicates that vendors in mainstream and niche markets use different channel selection strategies, with a significantly large percentage of online vendors in the college textbook category (niche market) participating niche shopbots (low level).

To explore if there are significant correlations between participating more Shopbots and higher traffic rank, we transformed model 1 into a parameterized model (2) and estimated both textbook and digital camera categories by using Ordinary Least Squares (OLS) analysis.

We identified influential observations using recommended cutoffs for leverage points, studentized residuals, the DFFITS measure, and standardized influence of observations on the covariance of estimates (Belsley, Kuh, & Welsch, 1980). Observations were excluded from the analysis if any one of the four cutoffs was exceeded. Residual plot confirmed the normality assumption. White's test (H. White, 1980) was used for checking the heteroskedasticity.

$$TR = \alpha + \beta_1 Speed + \beta_2 Popup + \beta_3 ExistenceTime + \beta_4 \#Shopbots + \beta_5 \# LinkSites + \varepsilon_{i,t} \qquad (2)$$

As we can see from table 3 and 4, for both niche and mainstream products, the more Shopbots the online vendor participates, the higher its traffic rank (p_{TR} = 0.0001 and p_{TR} = 0.0255 respectively). This indicates a positive correlation between the number of Shopbots an online vendor participates and its revenue size, which confirmed hypothesis one.

Even though the number of shopbots an online vendor participates increases its internet visibility,

Table 2. Aggregated distribution of online vendors

Categories\Levels	Top Level	Mid-Level	Low Level
# online vendor for Digital Camera	56	164	81
# online vendor for College Textbook	61	104	143
Chi-Square: 30.7308; DF: 2; Asymptotic Pr > ChiSq <.0001;			

combined with the findings in Table 1, it becomes evident that vendors in the mainstream market and the niche market might use different strategies for comparison-shopping participation.

To further explore the differences between these two sets of strategies and to verify our hypothesis 2, we ran a factor analysis to examine how individual online vendors in these two electronic markets prepare their "portfolio" of Shopbots to participate and then how that related to their other features.

Since participating comparison-shopping is equivalent to generating dynamic links to a retailer's site, static links from other sites (#LinkSites) may play a similar role here, so we add the total number of static links (#LinkSites) to an online vendor in the analysis of Shopbot "portfolio" for the same vendor. Interestingly, through the factor analysis, we identified two factor groups in each market.

For the college textbook market, we identified two factors with eigenvalue bigger than 1 (one is 1.90, the other one is 1.45). Table 5 shows that factor 1 is composed of #LinkSites, Mysimon.com, PriceGrabber.com, and Shopping.com; Factor 2 includes AddAll.com, BestBookDeal.com, and PriceScan.com. Variance explained by

factor 1 is 2.05, for factor 2 is 1.30. And the total communality is 3.35.

For the digital camera category, we also identified two factors. Table 6 shows that factor 2 is composed of #Linksites and Yahoo Shopping; Factor 1 includes all the other five Shopbots. Variance explained by factor 1 is 2.04, by factor 2 is 1.25. And the total communality is 3.29.

When we sorted the Shopbots in the college textbook category based on their traffic rank, we found that factor 1 include the top three Shopbots in ranking, while factor 2 includes the last three Shopbots in ranking. For the category of digital camera, factor 1 includes the last five Shopbots in ranking, while factor 2 includes the top Shopbot in ranking (Yahoo Shopping). So what is the specific impact for each factor on the TR for online vendors in each category? To explore this question, we use OLS again on following modified model,

$$TR = \alpha + \beta_1 Speed + \beta_2 Popup + \beta_3 ExistenceTime + \beta_4 Factor1 + \beta_5 Factor2 + \varepsilon_{i,t} \qquad (3)$$

We found that in the niche market represented by *college textbook*, both factor 1(general shopbots) and factor 2 (niche shopbots) have significant

Table 3. Regression results of college text book (niche product) category

Variables	Traffic Rank (TR)	
	Parameter	P-Value
Speed	-257553	0.0001*
Popup	-603.48	0.4721
Existence Time	-21.80	0.0168*
#Shopbots	-10500	0.0001*
#LinkSites	0.23	0.2878
Stat	N=136	Adj R²=0.3361

Table 4. Regression results of digital camera (mainstream product) category

Variables	Traffic Rank (TR)	
	Parameter	P-Value
Speed	1281.65	0.8445
Popup	-2745.50	0.9793
Existence Time	-3.98	0.1307
#Shopbots	-12126	0.0255*
#LinkSites	-1.56	0.1713
Stat	N=83	Adj R²=0.1402

Table 5. Rotated factor pattern of college textbook category

Items	Factor 1	Factor 2
#LinkSites	0.5256*	0.0353
AddAll	0.2473	0.5132*
BestBookdeal	0.1274	0.7091*
MySimon	0.7629*	-0.1433
PriceGrabber	0.7027*	0.2764
PriceScan	0.3825	-0.6532*
Shopping	0.5695*	0.4020

Table 6. Rotated factor pattern of digital camera category

Items	Factor 1	Factor 2
#LinkSites	-0.0939	0.6891*
Mysimon	0.6096*	0.2833
PriceGrabber	0.5877*	-0.0397
PriceScan	0.6427*	-0.2180
Bizrate	0.6937*	0.1940
Yahoo Shopping	-0.1111	0.7825*
Shopping	0.6359*	0.01223

impact on TR, and factor 2 (niche shopbots) has a relatively significant bigger impact compared with factor 1(general shopbots) (table 6). This means for online vendors in a niche market, there are stronger positive correlations between the number of niche Shopbots they participates and their traffic rank even though participating popular general Shopbots also has some positive influences.

However, in the mainstream market represented by *digital camera*, only factor 2 (major general shopbot) has significant impact (table 7). This indicates for online vendors in a mainstream market, the only significant positive correlation between participating comparison-shopping and their traffic rank is associated with the most popular Shopbot, Yahoo Shopping in this case.

Both findings are interesting, and we will discuss them in detail in the next section.

DISCUSSION

The emerging electronic comparison-shopping market is one of the most fascinating areas to explore. This paper examined one aspect of this market, the channel selection strategy of small online vendors.

For small online vendors, finding the effective comparison-shopping channel is an important

competition strategy. However, due to the emerging nature of this market, small online vendors do not have enough reference information when making their selections, except the general popularity information about shopbots and the product categories shopbots cover. As a result, small vendors have to use the trial and error method when exploring this market – they may choose their first comparison-shopping channel based on the two aspects above. If it turns out the channel is worth the cost being charged, they stay with their selection and expand their channels to new shopbots; if it does not justify the cost, they switch to another one or simply quit this market. The collective decision by small online vendors and their evolving strategy based on trial and error outcomes reveal the existing picture of this emerging market as we explored in this paper.

Through initial analysis, we found that there are significant differences in the distribution of small online vendors among Shopbots between the niche product market (*college textbook*) and mainstream product market (*digital camera*), which implies distinctive channel selection strategies by small online vendors. In the niche market, online vendors have a tendency to participate niche Shopbots (like BestBookDeal and AddAll) or shopbots that charge a low or zero fee (PriceScan). While in the mainstream market, online

Table 7. Regression result of college textbook category by using factor scores

Variables	Traffic Rank (TR)	
	Parameter	P-Value
Speed	-2072	0.0001*
Popup	-604.70	0.5221
Existence Time	-11.06	0.2899
Factor 1	-34969	0.0002*
Factor 2	-40686	0.0003*
Stat	N=136	Adj R2=0.3216

Table 8. Regression result of digital camera category by using factor scores

Variables	Traffic Rank (TR)	
	Parameter	P-Value
Speed	5514.78	0.2923
Popup	-97279	0.2300
Existence Time	-3.94	0.0464
Factor 1	-5491.64	0.3921
Factor 2	-12886	0.0338*
Stat	N=83	Adj R^2=0.1744

vendors tend to participate all popular Shopbots with no particular preference.

The selection of niche shopbots could be a proven strategy after the initial trial by small online vendors when they enter this market because the latter could provide more profitable customers via a higher conversion rate, though niche shopbots are less popular compared with mainstream Shopbots. However, this is not the case for Shopbots in the mainstream market. The online vendors in this market, big or small in size, not yet have formed their consistent comparison-shopping participation strategies. This is understandable in this initial stage of market formation, because for an online vendor, its participation in comparison-shopping is more of an arbitrary trial and error exploration than a systematic approach supported by experiences that can only be accumulated from a relatively mature market. In addition to this, most general Shopbots may not be stable in performance in their start-up stage by attracting customers, which might be another reason that it could not lead to aggregated effects when online vendors participate more of them.

To verify the above explanation, we analyzed the comparison-shopping participation strategy in detail. By using factor analysis, we identified some significant patterns in each market that are consistent with our explanation.

In a niche market, for online book vendors, selecting the lowest three ranked Shopbots to participate contributes significantly to their TR (p_{TR} = 0.0003). These three Shopbots are PriceScan, BestBookDeal and AddAll. And two of them are niche Shopbots (BestBookDeal and AddAll). Though these two niche shopbots have low traffic rank themselves and some even have lower rank than the vendors that participate them, the effectiveness of this strategy is significant (p_{TR} = 0.0003) from their correlation with vendors' traffic rank. This strategy could be justified from online vendors' perspective because though niche shopbots have low overall popularity, the online shoppers they bring in are savvy customers and have a higher chance of purchasing the product. Thus, the overall cost of acquiring a customer via a niche channel is higher than in a mainstream channel.

Another significant pattern in this market is selecting general shopbots to participate, which also contributes significantly to an online book vendor's TR (p_{TR}=0.0002) though the *magnitude* of their contribution is much lower than selecting niche shopbots as described previously.

In the mainstream market, we found there was only one significant correlation between participating comparison-shopping and higher TR (p_{TR}=0.0338): participating Yahoo Shopping.

Because this factor also includes another variable, the number of linked sites (#LinkSites) to online vendor, we can not attribute the significance in correlation to Yahoo Shopping only. This pattern supports our analysis that the participation of the mainstream comparison-shopping market is still in the emerging status with new shopbots and online vendors joining. The effectiveness of individual general shopbots still needs to be identified in this market.

Generally speaking, comparison-shopping in the electronic market emerged from the niche market 10 years ago. (It proved its effectiveness in leveling the competition between well-known online vendors and those new small online vendors in the niche market, too.) The findings in the niche market in this research confirmed this. However, for the mainstream market, the proven strategy for small online vendors seems not yet clear (at least from the findings in this research). This uncertainty is partially due to the emerging nature of this channel, for which there are no service standards and proper rating mechanisms to provide feedback. It may also be due to the competition from other online marketing channels for small vendors like online auctions (eBay). In the near future, when this market is more solid in structure, we should expect some new patterns.

LIMITATIONS

There are several major limitations of this study. First, when collecting data about individual vendors' comparison-shopping channel selection strategy, we used a data sampling method, so the results are only an approximation of the actual strategy a small online vendor might use. Second, the data we collected revealed the correlation between the comparison-shopping channel selection strategy by small online vendors and their traffic rank; however, we could not justify a causal relationship. For example, if a small online vendor enjoys higher TR, it usually has a better

reputation, so it has a higher chance of attracting online shoppers when being compared with other vendors. Conversely, if an online vendor selects an appropriate comparison-shopping channel, it will attract more online shoppers, thus increasing its traffic rank. Third, the online vendor character data is collected via Alexa.com, and in turn, is collected from its toolbar subscribers. So the external validity of this research result is limited by the online-shopper population it represents. In the future, when a more comprehensive data set is available, we expect better models will be developed for such research.

CONCLUSION AND FUTURE RESEARCH

This is exploratory research aimed at identifying the effectiveness of online vendors' comparison-shopping channel selection strategy.

Through data collected from hundreds of small online vendors in two different product categories (*digital camera* and *college textbook*), we first demonstrate that comparison-shopping as a new marketing channel has significant correlation with the traffic rank of a small online vendor site, which indicates a possible causal relationship and highlights the effectiveness of this new channel. We also identified two distinctive patterns of correlations in comparison-shopping channel selection. We found that in the niche product market, participating niche shopbots has significant correlation with higher traffic rank for small online vendors. However, in mainstream product market, the correlation between participating comparison-shopping and higher traffic rank can only be identified with top shopbot when combined with the effect of the total number of static hyperlinks to the vendor.

In addition to the findings, one important contribution made by this paper is the novel way of collecting data we used to examine this new marketing channel. Instead of using a survey on small online vendors, we used objective data collected from multiple online data sources.

There are many future research opportunities in this area. A more comprehensive research similar to this one could be conducted to validate the results in other product categories. Future research can use a survey method to make a complementary study to verify this pattern and the actual strategy small online vendors used.

Another research direction is to investigate how small online vendors choose Shopbots and to identify the criteria on which that choice is based. Following the preliminary findings from this research, different strategies and decision criteria by small online vendors for mainstream and niche products should be expected. Also, it might be very interesting to explore combining comparison-shopping channel with other Web marketing channels to increase site traffic and overall revenue.

REFERENCES

Adamic, L. A., Huberman, B. A., Barabasi, A. L., Albert, R., Jeong, H., & Bianconi, G. (2000). Power-Law Distribution of the World Wide Web. *Science, 287*(5461), 2115a-.

Ariely, D. (2000). Controlling the Information Flow: Effects on Consumers, Decision Making and Preferences. *Journal of Consumer Research, 27*(2), 233-248.

Belsley, D. A., Kuh, E., & Welsch, R. E. (1980). *Regression Diagnostics*. New York, NY: John Wiley and Sons.

Brin, S., & Page, L. (1998). The Anatomy of a Large-Scale Hypertextual Web Search Engine. *WWW7/Computer Networks, 30*(1-7), 107-117.

Brown, J. R., & Goolsbee, A. (2002). Does the Internet make markets more competitive. *Journal of Political Economy, 110*(3), 481-507.

Coughlan, A. T., Anderson, E., Stern, L. W., & El-Ansary, A. I. (2001). *Marketing Channels* (6th ed.). Upper Saddle River, New Jersey: Prentice Hall.

Crowston, K. (1997). *Price Behavior In a Market With Internet Buyer's Agents*. Paper presented at the International Conference on Information Systems, Atlanta, GA.

Crowston, K., & MacInnes, I. (2001). The effects of market-enabling Internet agents on competition and prices. *Journal of Electronic Commerce Research, 2*(1), 1-22.

Doorenbos, R. B., Etzioni, O., & Weld, D. S. (1997). *A Scalable Comparison-Shopping Agent for the World Wide Web*. Paper presented at the International Conference on Autonomous Agents, Marina del Rey, California.

Gimein, M. (1999). Why won't Amazon help you compare prices? Retrieved January 5, 2005, 2005, from http://www.salon.com/tech/log/1999/08/05/amazon/

Haubl, G., & Murray, K. B. (2003). Preference Construction and Persistence in Digital Marketplaces: The Role of Electronic Recommendation Agents. *Journal of Consumer Psychology, 13*(1&2), 75-91.

Haubl, G., & Trifts, V. (2000). Consumer Decision Making in Online Shopping Environments: The Effects of Interactive Decision Aids. *Marketing Science, 19*(1), 4-21.

Hoffer, J., George, J., & Valacich, J. (2004). *Modern System Analysis and Design* (Fourth ed.). Upper Saddle River, NJ Prentice Hall.

Iyer, G., & Pazgal, A. (2003). Internet Shopping Agents: Virtual Co-Location and Competition. *Management Science, 22*(1), 85-106.

Kephart, J. O., Hanson, J. E., & Greenwald, A. R. (2000). Dynamic pricing by software agents. *Computer Networks, 32*, 731-752.

Krulwich, B. (1996). The BargainFinder Agent: Comparison Price Shopping on the Internet. In J. Williams (Ed.), *Bots, and Other Internet Beasties* (pp. 257-263). Indianapolis: Macmillan Computer Publishing.

Malone, T. W., Yates, J., & Benjamin, R. I. (1987). Electronic Markets and Electronic Hieratchies. *Communications of the ACM, 30*(6), 484-497.

Markopoulos, P. M., & Kephart, J. O. (2002). *How Valuable are Shopbots?* Paper presented at the International Conference on Autonomous Agents & Multiagent Systems (AAMAS), Bologna, Italy.

Montgomery, L. A., Hosanagar, K., Krishnan, R., & Clay, K. B. (2003). Designing a Better Shopbot. *Management Science, 50*(2), 189-206.

Plitch, P. (2002). Are Bots Legal? *Wall Street Journal, 240*(54), R13.

Russell, S., & Norvig, P. (2002). *Artificial Intelligence: A Modern Approach* (2nd ed.). Upper Saddle River, NJ Prentice Hall.

Schwartz, B. (2004). *The Paradox of Choice.* New York: HarperCollins.

Simon, H. A. (1956). Rational choice and the structure of the environment. *Psychological Review, 63*, 129-138.

Smith, M. D., & Brynjolfsson, E. (2001). Consumer Decision-Making at an Internet Shopbot. *Journal of Industrial Economics, 49*(4), 541-558.

Tan, C. H. (2003, December). *Comparison-Shopping websites: An Empirical Investigation on the Influence of Decision Aids and Information Load on Consumer Decision-Making Behavior.* Paper presented at the The 24th Annual International Conference on Information Systems (ICIS), Seattle, WA.

Tanenbaum, A. S. (2002). *Computer Networks* (Fourth ed.). Upper Saddle River, NJ Prentice Hall PTR.

White, E. (2000). E-Commerce (A Special Report): The Lessons We've Learned --- Comparison Shopping: No Comparison --- Shopping `bots' were supposed to unleash brutal price wars. Why haven't they? . *Wall Street Journal*, R.18.

White, H. (1980). A Heteroskedasticity-Consistent Covariance Matrix estimator and a Direct Test for Heteroskedasticity. *Econometrica., 48*, 817-838.

ADDITIONAL READINGS

Bailey, J. P., Faraj, S., & Yuliang, Y. (2007). The Road More Travelled: Web Traffic and Price Competition in Internet Retailing. *Electronic Markets, 17*(1), 56-67.

Brian Grow and Ben Elgin, w. M. H. (2006). Click Fraud. *Business Week*(4003), 46.

Carter, D. (1996). THE FUTURE OF Interactive MARKETING. *Harvard Business Review, 74*(6), 157-157.

Chen, F. Y., Jian, C., & Yongbo, X. (2007). Optimal Control of Selling Channels for an Online Retailer with Cost-per-Click Payments and Seasonal Products. *Production & Operations Management, 16*(3), 292-305.

Clark, D. (2000). Shopbots: help or hindrance? *IEEE Expert Intelligent Systems & Their Applications, 15*(2), 8-9.

Fitzgerald, K. (2004). Another Life for Internet Ads. *Credit Card Management, 17*(7), 64-67.

Lee, J. W., & Lee, J. K. (2006). Online advertising by the comparison challenge approach. *Electronic Commerce Research and Applications, 5*(4), 282-294.

Lisa, H., & Geraldine, C. (2003). Marketing in the Internet age: What can we learn from the past? *Management Decision, 41*(9), 944.

Lynch, J. G., & Ariely, D. (2000). Wine Online: Search Costs and Competition on Price, Quality, and Distribution. *Marketing Science, Volume 19*(1).

Mylene, M. (2006). E-Commerce; Ad Vantage: New tools help marketers figure out which campaigns are worth it -- and which aren't. *Wall Street Journal*, p. R.11.

Nelson, R. A., Cohen, R., & Rasmussen, F. R. (2007). An analysis of pricing strategy and price dispersion on the internet. *Eastern Economic Journal, 33*(1), 95-110.

Rosen, E. (2000). *The anatomy of buzz: how to create word-of-month marketing* (First Edition ed.). New York: Random House.

Saeed, K. A., Hwang, Y., & Grover, V. (2003). Investigating the Impact of Web Site Value and Advertising on Firm Performance in Electronic Commerce. *International Journal of Electronic Commerce, 7*(2), 119-141.

KEY TERMS

Channel Selection: The strategy online vendors employ to maximum their ROI on customer acquisition. For example, an online vendor could select only the most popular shopbot to list their product or select a few specialized shopbots to list their products.

Comparison-Shopping Market: The shopbot-mediated electronic commerce market consisting of online shoppers, online vendors and shopbots in which online shoppers are referred to online vendors by the comparison-shopping services.

Cost Per Click: a revenue model by comparison-shopping service providers that charge the online vendors for each customers it refers to the vendor. For example, online shoppers want to buy an iPod and searched shopping.com. Shopping.com provides a list of online vendors that offer the iPod model requested by the online shopper. The online shopper find one vendor from the list and click through to the vendor site to buy the product. The vendor paid shopping.com for this referral based on the agreed rate regardless whether the purchase is complete or not.

General Shopbots: Shopbots that provide price comparison information for products from multiple and unrelated product categories. For example, shopping.com provides price comparison for electronics, books, computers, furniture, toys, etc.

Online Marketing Channel: the way an online vendor reaching the customer. There are several ways an online vendor can reach the potential customer. They could launch a website and established a brand name like Amazon.com so customers could go to them directly. They could also list their product in popular auction sites like eBay.com or list them in comparison-shopping sites like shopping.com.

Shopbots: Web-based software agents that help online shoppers search price and related product information from multiple vendor sites.

Small Online Vendors: Online vendors without an established brand name and mainly depend on third party technology to operate their online store.

Specialized Shopbots: Shopbots that provide price comparison information for products from one or a few related categories. For example, addall.com provides price comparison for books, CDs, and DVDs.

Traffic Rank: The number of hits a website receives in a specific time period. It is an indicator for the popularity of the site.

ENDNOTES

a   Here we use Media Metrix's 200,000 minimum measurement as the benchmark for qualification as a major ecommerce website.

b   In certain circumstances, product manufacturers or service providers may place their product or service in comparison-shopping market directly. For example, lendingtree.com is the leading shopbots for personal loans and various financial institutions are loan issuers, including not only loan companies but also banks. In this research, our focus is on online retailing, thus shopbots are marketing channel for online vendors.

c   Before a shopbot could successfully identify product information from a vendor site, it needs to formulate the wrapper, and this formulation process is semi-automatic. It became un-realistic for manual intervention when a shopbot has to search hundreds of online vendors. Comparatively, current shopbots, like shopping.com, could list products from thousands of online vendors by using data feeding technology.

d   Some tricks used by established online vendors to avoid the crawling of shopbots is not listing the price of a popular product, but instead, asking the shopper to put that product in the shopping cart to see the price.

e   Small online vendors mainly partner with a major shopbot and use its engine to power their own shopping site (like Yahoo). Some choose to bid a large number of keywords from shopbots to attract customers to their site (like Amazon).

f   Some specialized shopbots we used in this research covers only textbook market, which fully qualifies the niche concept.

g   For example, the existence of the search engine optimization (SEO) industry exists solely on the purpose of maximizing the traffic for a Web site as wished by site owners.

h   Alexa has developed an installed based of millions of toolbars, one of the largest Web crawls and an infrastructure to process and serve massive amounts of data collected from its users. It represents a typical sampling of the whole Internet user group.

Chapter VIII
Comparison Shopping Behaviour in Online Environments:
The Case of Spanish E-Shoppers

Carla Ruiz Mafé
University of Valencia, Spain

Silvia Sanz Blas
University of Valencia, Spain

ABSTRACT

The aim of this chapter is to analyse antecedents of search engines use as prepurchase information tools. Firstly, there is a literature review of the factors influencing search engines use in online purchases. Then, there is an empirical analysis of a sample of 650 Spanish E-shoppers. Logistical regression is used to analyse the influence of demographics, surfing behaviour and purchase motivations on willingness to use search engines for E-shopping. Data analysis shows that experience as Internet user and as Internet shopper are negative key drivers of search engine use. Most of the utilitarian shopping motivations analyzed predict comparison shopping behaviour. Demographics are not determinant variables in the use of search engines in online purchases. This research enables companies to know the factors that potentially affect search engine use in E-shopping decisions and the importance of using search engines in their communication campaigns.

INTRODUCTION

The Internet is becoming an increasingly popular medium to facilitate prepurchase informa-tion search, choice and purchase. It encourages comparison-shopping behaviour, providing tools that shoppers can use to identify and select products.

A search engine is a web application that gathers information from the web using different strategies (crawlers or spiders) and then performs the basic retrieval task, accepting a query, comparing a query with the records in a database, and producing a retrieval set as output (Rowley, 1998, pp. 186-7).

People who are looking for information on the Internet commonly query a search engine to locate the information they seek. Search engines allow users to browse through comprehensive lists of vendors arranged by product, price and service, or to search for a vendor by name or page content, all from the convenience of a home computer (Brynjolfsson, Dick & Smith, 2004; Rowley, 2000; Teo &Yeong, 2003). Among the different comparison-shopping tools, this paper focuses on pure search engines (such as Google), because most product searching is directly through such tools.

Search engine usage in Europe is highest in the UK at 85%, followed by France (83%) and Spain (83%) and ahead of the U.S. (77%) (Nielsen/Netratings, 2007). Search engine use grew dramatically during 2006 in France (27%) and Spain (21%), again ahead of the US (8%). Google is currently the most prominent source of traffic for shopping websites in Spain, and is growing more rapidly as a source of shopping traffic than the search engine category as a whole.

Despite the increasing importance of comparison-shopping services for companies and consumers, there has been little research on their influence in the online purchase decision. Thus, while more research is being done on the way search engines work and their design (Montgomery, Hosanagar, Krishnan & Clay, 2004), the products and brands searched for (Rowley, 2000), shopbots (Brynjolfsson et al., 2004; Brynjolfsson & Smith, 2000; Smith, 2002), advantages and disadvantages of search engines and their influence on markets (Maes et al., 1999; Smith, 2002), there is still very little literature on the profile of Internet users who buy products/services using

search engines, their use motivations and the implications of online experience for search engines use as a prepurchase information tool.

This chapter aims to present an in-depth study of the factors influencing search engines use in online purchases, and specifically to:

1. Provide a holistic view of factors influencing consumer behaviour when using search engines.
2. Analyse the perceived benefits that encourage consumers to use search engines.
3. Provide empirical research on the Spanish market that analyses the influence of demographics, online experience and shopping orientations in the use of search engine information in the online purchasing process.

The chapter is structured as follows. Firstly, there is a literature review of the factors influencing use of search engines in online purchases. Then, there is an empirical analysis of a sample of 650 Spanish E-shoppers. Logistical regression is used to analyse the influence of demographics, surfing behaviour and purchase motivations on willingness to use search engines for E-shopping. Finally we report the conclusions, limitations and future research lines.

THEORETICAL FRAMEWORK: ANTECEDENTS OF SEARCH ENGINE USE

In this section we present a conceptual model for analysing the antecedents of search engine use in online purchases.

Demographics

Men and women seem to differ in their shopping orientations and online behaviour. Sociocultural pressure has made men generally more independent in their purchase decisions, while women place greater value on social relations (Cross & Madson, 1997; Citrin, Stern, Spangenberg & Clark, 2003). These schemes of interdependency influence the individual's personality and attitude towards different situations such as browsing or shopping behaviour (Markus & Oyserman, 1989; Wollin, 2003). Thus, men's purchase motivations are usually mainly utilitarian (Hofstede, 1980; Steenkamp, Hofstede & Wedel, 1999). In contrast, social motives increase women's satisfaction with shopping and encourage them to browse, find out about colours and shapes and compare prices before shopping.

Women see themselves as global information processors, assimilating all possible suggestions, while men see themselves as selective information processors, only assimilating the most interesting suggestions (Wollin, 2003). The quickest way to locate a merchant is to know the URL of the website and to enter this into a browser (Rowley, 2002). Therefore, men probably prefer to use this system, while women prefer to access detailed search engine information before shopping on a given website. As Yoon, Cropp & Cameron (2002) pointed out, women prefer to use research tools and are more likely than men to express familiarity with them.

To sum up, women like using search engines more than men because men are goal-oriented shoppers but for women, browsing is more important.

The literature review suggests that consumer needs, interests and attitudes vary with age, and the youngest consumers use the Internet from a very early age. As young people's motivations include more than just education or work, they know a lot of websites for the products which interest them (leisure, culture, entertainment, etc..) (Joines, Scherer & Scheufele, 2003).

Trocchia & Janda (2000) maintain that lack of experience with the new technologies and resistance to change are the main reasons why mature consumers do not shop by Internet. Lack of familiarity with the medium prevents mature consumers from evaluating the benefits of Internet in the prepurchase information search and means that they tend to prefer to use other information sources for their purchases such as the television, press or social interaction with friends and relations. Search engines help E-shoppers to collect product information and compare different products (Rowley, 2000). Given that search engines facilitate online shopping, they are likely to be used more by low-experienced mature consumers.

Educational level correlates positively with channel knowledge and influences online shopping behaviour (Li, Kuo & Russell, 1999; Trocchia & Janda, 2003). This statement is verified in the study by Eastman & Iyer (2004) where educational level is one of the key drivers in the willingness of mature consumers to use Internet as a shopping channel, since it influences channel knowledge. Therefore, it is likely that low-educated consumers need to use search engines to purchase online because they lack familiarity with Internet.

Online Experience

By repeated use of an activity, consumers acquire more knowledge (Alba & Hutchinson, 1987; Bettman & Park, 1980; Punj & Staelin, 1983). Therefore, Internet users who spend more time surfing the net or who access it more frequently are likely to be more familiar with what Internet can offer and will know more about using it as a shopping channel (Steckel, 2000).

Greater use and knowledge of Internet will doubtless modify shopping behaviour and response to marketing actions (Dahlen, 2002). Thus, expert users surf more quickly (Lazonder, Biemans & Wopereis, 2000), have shorter sessions and visit a reduced number of given websites (Dahlen, 2002). Many studies (Brynjolfsson et al., 2004; Furse, Punj & Stewart, 1984; Lohse, Bellman & Johnson, 2000; Newman & Staelin, 1972) suggest that the likelihood of browsing for alternative products or brands reduces as use, experience, learning, satisfaction and repeat purchase with a specific brand increase.

Consumers learn to search efficiently as their online experience increases, so there is an inverse relationship between online shopping experience and search effort (Srinivasan and Ratchford, 1991). As their experience in the channel grows, consumers perceive fewer benefits from comparing alternatives and therefore search less (Teo and Yeong, 2003).

Shopping Motivations

Shopping motivations influence search behaviour and online shopping. Convenience-oriented shoppers value convenience more than price and often prefer to pay a premium for shopping online rather than travelling to brick-and-mortar outlets. Degeratu, Rangaswamy & Wu (2000) found that high income online shoppers are not very price sensitive, as their main purchase motivation is convenience. These consumers value the chance to shop online whenever they want and do other activities at the same time (Dholakia and Uusitalo, 2002; Srinivasan, Anderson and Ponnavolu, 2002). They do not wish to negotiate with several sellers when shopping, because of the increased search effort (Brynjolfsson & Smith, 1999; Zhu, Siegel & Madnick, 2001). Search engine grouping of available alternatives avoids the inconvenience of having to find competitors' websites, therefore, convenience-oriented consumers will prefer using search engines rather than comparing a lot of websites.

Another group of consumers try and save time to improve their quality of life, and one way of doing this is to reduce shopping time (Dholakia and Uusitalo, 2002). The speed and ease of comparing products at home, may lead increasing numbers of consumers who value their free time, or consider shopping to be a monotonous domestic chore, to use search engines for online shopping.

Consumers can easily find a wide range and assortment of products and detailed informa-

tion online (Park and Kim, 2003). This is one of the success factors for online stores (Rohm and Swaminathan, 2004; Trocchia and Janda, 2003), since choice is an advantage for consumers because it increases the chances of finding a product that meets their needs. Search engines allow customers to search for product characteristics from online retailers at the click of a button. Product information is queried directly from retailers and presented in formatted comparison tables, allowing customers to evaluate it easily (Brynjolfsson et al., 2004; Rowley, 2000). In addition, by providing better quality information, search engines can increase consumer satisfaction (Peterson, Balasubramanian and Bronnenberg, 1997).

Reibstein's study (2002) shows that price is another important choice criteria used by most consumers in deciding where to shop online. It also points out that consumers guided only by this type of motivation constantly compare offers with those of competitors, changing supplier when there is the least reduction in price for the products and services they need. Peterson et al., (1997) note that if price-oriented consumers have already decided which brand they want, they search for price information on different websites, thus increasing competition between online retailers.

Alba & Hutchinson (1987) speculate that if online retailing reduces the information search costs for price information, consumers will become more price sensitive. Search engines automatically search a large number of online stores, providing consumers with nearly all offered prices for a particular product at a given point in time. Compared with the traditional sequential search process describe by Stigler (1961), search engines clearly lower the cost of acquiring price information. Therefore, price-oriented shoppers will prefer to use search engines in their online shopping (Ellison & Ellison, 2001; Montgomery et al., 2004; Smith, 2002; Smith & Brynjolfsson, 2001).

Iyer & Pazgal (2003) point out that consumers differ in loyalty to retailers and propensity to use search engines. They capture consumer behaviour through three segments: (1) "Store loyals" who will only buy from a certain retailer and do not use search engines at all. They are willing to pay a higher price for dealing with their favourite retailer. (2) "Search engines loyals" who use search engines to purchase items for the lowest price. They have no store loyalty. (3) "Partial loyals" who visit search engines but who buy at their favourite retailer as long as the price they are required to pay is not higher than the average price they can get by comparison shopping. Therefore, the greater the willingness to pay a higher price for shopping on a certain website, the lower the use of search engines for online purchases.

THE CASE OF SPANISH INTERNET SHOPPERS

After identifying the key drivers of search engines use, the second part of the chapter presents an empirical study of the Spanish market.

Internet has become a popular communication channel, due in part to its advantages for businesses and consumers, and its enormous

popularity, fast growth rate and penetration. The use of Internet in Spain began around 1997 with 1.6% penetration. According to data from the General Mass Media Study (AIMC, 2008), Internet penetration currently stands at 41.8%, far exceeding other media penetration such as newspapers, magazines and the cinema. Focusing on the evolution of online purchases, empirical research by the Red.es study (2007) shows that in 1997, B2C transactions were at 0.47 million euros rising to 2,178 million euros in 2006.

Seventy-three per cent of Spanish Internet shoppers in 2006 found information about the products or services they wanted online by using a search engine (Red.es, 2007). In Spain, search engine use is becoming the focus of on-line marketing strategies for many companies due to the growth in the number of Internet shoppers using search engines as a prepurchase information tool.

The conceptual model of comparison-shopping services use (see Figure 1) which is contrasted in the Spanish market is an outcome of the literature review presented above.

The quantitative analysis provides answers to the following research questions:

Figure 1. Conceptual model

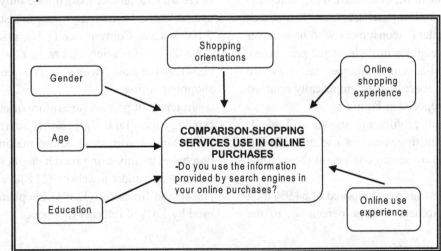

1. Who uses search engines?
2. What is the main purpose for using search engines in e-shopping?
3. How does online experience influence the use of search engines for purchasing online?

Methodology

For quantitative research we examined data from 650 personal interviews given to Internet shoppers aged 14 years and above with quota sampling based on gender and age range determined by the AECE study (2005). The field work was done from March to April 2006. A research instrument with close-ended questions was used for this study. Questionnaires were delivered to and collected from volunteer participants. A research instrument with close-ended questions was used for this study. Questionnaires were delivered to and collected from volunteer participants. A total of 730 individuals, located in Valencia, were contacted during the survey; 680 agreed to participate in this study. Among the questionnaires received, 650 (95.5%) were completed and analyzed for this study.

In the quantitative analysis we firstly tested for significant differences between the demographic and behavioural profiles of "search-engines adopters" (consumers who have used search engines in their online purchases) and "Non search engines adopters" (consumers who have never used search engines in their online purchases), using the chi-square technique. Secondly, we used logistic regression to empirically contrast the model proposed in Figure 1.

Respondent profiles are shown in Table 1. 59.5% of Spanish consumers use the information provided by search engines in their online purchases.

The total sample is composed of 64.9% men and 35.4% women. A large percentage of the sample belongs to the age segment between 25 and 44 (60.5%). In terms of educational level, highly educated individuals predominate (48.5%). A significant percentage of those interviewed (81.3%) have been using the Internet since 2002, although only 23.2% said they had shopped online before 2002.

Consumers who use search engines in their online purchases are mainly men (64.6%), aged between 25-44 years old (66.2%) and highly educated (50.9% have high university studies). The E-shopper who uses search engines when shopping is a less experienced Internet user (76.3% for more than 3 years) and shopper (16.7% over 3 years) than the E-shopper who does not use search engines.

Online experience was measured following the same criteria used in other research work (Igbaria, 1993; Igbaria, Parasuraman and Baroudi, 1996; Andarajan, Simmers and Igbaria, 2000), so length of experience was considered to be a representative item for this concept (see Table 1). Demographic variables were measured as follows: age was measured continuously, education level was measured as ordinal variable with five response intervals from 1=primary education to 5= 5 year university course.

The importance of each of the shopping motivations analyzed (convenience, price reductions, range and variety of assortment, only channel available and time saving) were measured on a 5 point scale. Convenience (3.57), price reductions (2.42) and variety and range of assortment (2.34) are the main reasons interviewees give for shopping online.

In terms of prepurchase information sources typology (see Table 3), Spanish Internet shoppers search information before making online purchases mainly using search engines (59.5%), directly on vendor's website (21.8%) and using portals and directories (12.0%). Shopbots are only used by 1.4% of Internet shoppers.

Table 1. Description of the sample

Variables		Search engine users (N = 387)	Non-users (N = 263)	Total (N = 650)	Chi-Square
Gender	Male	64.6%	73.9%	64.9%	$\chi^2 = 0.044$; p = 0.834
	Female	35.4%	26.1%	35.1%	
Age	Between 14 and 19	6.2%	14.1%	9.4%	$\chi^2 = 65.605$; p = 0.134
	Between 20 and 24	12.4%	15.2%	13.5%	
	Between 25 and 34	42.4%	31.6%	38%	
	Between 35 and 44	23.8%	20.5%	22.5%	
	Between 45 and 54	10.9%	14.4%	12.3%	
	Over 54	4.4%	4.2%	4.3%	
Education	Primary education	16%	19.2%	17.5%	$\chi^2 = 3.035$; p = 0.386
	Secondary	16.3%	16%	16.2%	
	3 year university course	16.8%	19.4%	17.8%	
	5 year university course	50.9%	44.9%	48.5%	
Online use experience	Internet users since 2005	5.8%	2.7%	3.5%	$\chi^2 = 11.027$; p = 0.035
	Shoppers since 2004	7.6%	3.4%	5.9%	
	Shoppers since 2003	5.9%	3%	4.8%	
	Shoppers since 2002	4.4%	4.6%	4.5%	
	Before 2002	76.3%	86.3%	81.3%	
Online shopping experience	Shoppers since 2005	12.9%	8.8%	10.5%	$\chi^2 = 11.757$; p = 0.019
	Shoppers since 2004	33.8%	31.3%	32.3%	
	Shoppers since 2003	25.1%	22.5%	23.5%	
	Shoppers since 2002	11.4%	9.8%	10.5%	
	Before 2002	16.7%	27.6%	23.2%	

Results

A logistical regression (N=650 Internet shoppers) was used to test the proposed model. For the regression, search engines use for purchasing online was measured on a dichotomous scale with two possible reply categories: individuals who use search engine information in their online purchases (n=387) and those who do not (N=263). Independent variables included demographics (age, gender and education), online experience (online use experience and online shopping ex-

perience) and shopping orientations (convenience, price reductions, only channel available, wide assortment, time saving) (see Table 4).

We obtained the following results (see Table 4):

- Demographics and one of the shopping orientations (only channel available) are not determinant variables in the use of search engines in online purchases.
- Most Internet purchase motivations (convenience, time saving, price reductions and

Table 2. Shopping motivations

Motivations	Search engine use in E-shopping (N =387)	Non search engine use in E-shopping (N =263)	% of total (N =650)
Price reductions	2.63	2.16	2.42
Only channel available	1.83	2.02	1.93
Variety and range of assortment	2.53	2.11	2.34
Convenience	3.58	3.57	3.57
Time saving	2.05	2.56	2.34
MEAN	2.35	2.66	2.52

Table 3. Prepurchase information sources for Spanish Internet shoppers

		(N = 650)
When you are going to shop online… Where do you search for information on the products and services that you wish to purchase?	Shopbots	1.4%
	General search engines	59.5%
	Recommendations from consumers	6.9%
	Directly on vendor's website	21.8%
	Portals/Directories	12.0%
	E-mail	3.4%
	Banners	3.8%
	Others (TV commercials, magazines, newspapers)	6.1%

variety of assortament) positively influence consumer use of search engines in online purchases.

- The greater the online shopping experience and the online use experience, the less likely it is that search engines will be used in online purchases.

The model has a very good predictive capacity: 64.9% of cases are correctly classified for a cut-off value of 0.5.

CONCLUSION

The main academic contribution of this chapter is that it provides insight into the different factors that influence search engines use in online environments from the consumer perspective. In addition, these factors are applied to the specific context of the Spanish market. In particular, this study will improve managers' understanding of consumer demographics, online use and experience and shopping orientations and their relation to willingness to use search engines in their online purchases.

Table 4. Logistic regression for predicting membership of search engine use groups

Variable	Beta Coef	Std. Error	Wald	Df	Sig.	Exp(B)
GEN	0.051	0.177	0.084	1	0.771	1.503
AGE	0.005	0.008	0.445	1	0.505	1.005
EDUCAT			3.538	4	0.472	
EDUCAT (1)	-6.672	15.629	0.182	1	0.669	0.001
EDUCAT (2)	0.533	0.491	1.181	1	0.277	1.705
EDUCAT (3)	-0.173	0.313	0.305	1	0.581	0.841
EDUCAT (4)	-0.376	0.355	1.123	1	0.289	0.686
IUSEEXP			7.472	4	0.113	
IUSEEXP (1)	-1.126	0.723	2.426	1	0.119	0.324
IUSEEXP (2)	-0.040	0.495	0.007	1	0.935	0.960
IUSEEXP (3)	-0.122	0.405	0.091	1	0.763	0.885
IUSEEXP (4)	-0.946	0.433	4.774	1	0.029	0.388
ISHOPPINGEXP			10.425	4	0.034	
ISHOPPINGEXP (1)	-0.888	0.339	6.854	1	0.009	0.412
ISHOPPINGEXP (2)	-0.675	0.252	7.161	1	0.007	0.509
ISHOPPINGEXP (3)	-0.652	0.311	4.402	1	0.036	0.521
ISHOPPINGEXP (4)	-0.607	0.249	5.954	1	0.015	0.545
CONVENIENCE	0.561	0.193	8.484	1	0.004	1.752
ONLY CHANNEL	0.247	0.278	0.790	1	0.374	1.280
VARIETY/RANGE	0.411	0.232	3.147	1	0.048	1.508
PRICE REDUCTIONS	0.400	0.207	3.740	1	0.041	1.491
TIME SAVING	0.740	0.278	7.085	1	0.008	2.095
Intercept	1.919	0.838	5.238	1	0.022	6.813

The present research has identified six factors that potentially affect search engine use in online purchases. Of the antecedents considered, price, convenience, time saving and variety seeking orientations were found to have a positive impact on search engine use, but online use experience and online shopping experience negatively influenced search engine use for online purchases. Gender, age and education have no significant influence on the use of search engines, possibly due to the uniform sample of E-shoppers.

Online experience is a key driver of search engine use. People who have been shopping online for several years use search engines less than novice E-shoppers. Moreover, shoppers with less experience of using the Web, use search engines more. This result is consistent with the results of many studies done in other countries (e.g., Brynjolfsson et al., 2004; Furse et al., 1984; Lohse et

al., 2000; Newman & Staelin, 1972) which suggest that the likelihood of browsing decreases as experience increases.

The analyses performed also show that most shopping orientations (price reductions, convenience, time saving and variety and range of assortment) are decisive factors in search engines use. The results confirm that Spanish consumers guided by financial motives when shopping, use search engines more when shopping online. They constantly compare offers with those of the competitors and change supplier to obtain even the slightest reduction in price. This has also been reported in previous studies done in other countries (Montgomery et al., 2004; Reibstein, 2002; Smith, 2002).

Our findings have evidenced that Spanish convenience and time saving-oriented shoppers use search engine information for their online purchases. They value the grouping of available alternatives in a search engine when shopping because they do not like wasting time on purchase tasks or high information search efforts. Previous research (Dudek, Mastoni and Landoni, 2007) has found that search engine speed is a high priority for users.

Search engines make it easy for consumers to collect and evaluate information on products and services offered online (Brynjolfsson, Dick & Smith, 2004; Rowley, 2002). That may be why consumers who seek variety and a wide assortment also prefer to use search engines when purchasing online.

The purchase motivation "only channel available" has no significant influence on search engines use, possibly because these consumers have no other choice but to purchase online and may prefer to shop through traditional channels when they are available.

The study results allow us to suggest a set of managerial recommendations:

- Agents involved in Internet, from service providers (ISP) to advertisers and B2C companies, should exploit the advantages of search engines to facilitate the purchasing process. We recommend they promote search systems to provide fast, easy access to information on their products and/or services. By doing so, they could attract low-intensity Internet users, and improve website visibility. Moreover, individuals will become aware that Internet is also useful for finding information to purchase online.

- Companies should try to position themselves in the main search engines using both organic and paid results, as the leading positions are the most visited. In particular, they should configure their websites so that they appear among the first, organic results. Managers who implement search-engine optimizers can heighten the retrievability of their websites. They should also contract paid results

to appear in the first positions as this would improve perception of company image and reduce mistrust, one of the main obstacles to purchase.

- Given that purchase motivations (to compare prices, characteristics of the assortment etc..), influence the use of search tools, it is important when creating the advertising campaign in search engines to select texts containing these motivations. Companies should therefore select the most appropriate search terms and try to personalise the message as far as possible.

FUTURE RESEARCH TRENDS

One limitation of the empirical study is sample uniformity, as the population was all online shoppers. Therefore, we are considering as a line of research, to propose and empirically test a general model of search engines use for application to a sample of Internet users (E-shoppers and non E-shoppers).

As previous research (Girard, Silverblatt & Korgaonkar, 2002) suggests that not all goods will be as successful on Internet, another possible line of study would be to analyse whether search engine use is influenced by the characteristics of the goods and services being marketed.

The selection and listing criteria by which a search engine presents results differ from one search engine to the next and are frequently hidden from the user. Search engines lack transparency in that they do not clarify how results are found, or how they are connected to the search terms. Moreover, minors have intentional or unwitting access to content which may be harmful for them. Another line of study would be to analyse the social responsibility of search-engine operators and their influence on the information available to a user on a selected topic.

REFERENCES

AECE (Asociación Española de Comercio Electrónico) (2005). Estudio sobre Comercio Electrónico B2C. Retrieved February 14, 2006, from http://www.aece.es.

AIMC (Asociación de Investigación de los Medios de Comunicación) (2008), Estudio General de Medios. Tercera ola 2007, Madrid. Retrieved July 2, 2008, from http://www.aimc.es.

Alba, J., & Hutchinson, J. (1987). Dimensions of Consumer Expertise. *Journal of Consumer Research, 13*(4), 411-454.

Andarajan, M., Simmers, C., & Igbaria, M. (2000). An exploratory investigation of the antecedents and impact of Internet usage: an individual perspective. *Behaviour and Information Technology, 19*(1), 69-85.

Bettman, J., & Park, W. (1980). Effects of Prior Knowledge and Experience and Phase of the Choice Process on Consumer Decision Processes: A Protocol Analysis. *Journal of Consumer Research, 7*(3), 234-248.

Brynjolfsson, E., Dick, A.A., & Smith, M.D. (2004). Search and product differentiation at an Internet Shopbot. *Working paper*, MIT Sloan School of Management, July. Cambridge, Massachusetts.

Brynjolfsson, E., & Smith, M.D. (2000). *The great equalizer?. Consumer choice behaviour at Internet shopbots* (Working paper). Massachusetts: MIT Sloan School of Management, Cambridge.

Brynjolfsson, E., & Smith, M. (1999). *Frictionless commerce? A comparison of Internet and conventional retailers* (Working paper). Massachusetts: MIT Sloan School of Management, Cambridge.

Citrin, A., Stern, D., Spangenberg, E., & Clark, M. (2003). Consumer need for tactile input. An Internet retailing challenge. *Journal of Business Research, 56*(11), 915-922.

Cross, S., & Madson, L. (1997). Models of the self: self-constructuals and gender. *Psychological Bulletin, 122*, 5-37.

Dahlen, M. (2002). Learning the web: Internet User Experience and Response to Web Marketing in Sweden. *Journal of Interactive Advertising, 3*(1). Retrieved September 10, 2004, from http://www.jiad.org/vol3/no1/dahlen/index.html.

Darian, J. (1987). In home shopping: Are there consumer segment? *Journal of Retailing, 63*(2), 163-186.

Degeratu, A., Rangaswamy, A., & Wu, J. (2000). Consumer choice behavior in online and traditional supermarkets: the effects of brand name, price and other search attributes. *International Journal of Research in Marketing, 17*(1), 55-78.

Dholakia, R., & Uusitalo, O. (2002). Switching to Electronic Stores: Consumer Characteristics and the Perception of Shopping Benefits. *International Journal of Retail & Distribution Management, 30*(10), 459-469.

Dudek, D., Mastora, A., & Landoni, M. (2007). Is Google the answer? A study into usability of search engines. *Library Review, 56*(3), 224-233.

Eastman, J., & Iyer, R. (2004). The elderly's uses and attitudes towards the Internet. *Journal of Consumer Marketing, 21*(3), 208-220.

Ellison, G., & Ellison, S. F. (2001). *Search, obfuscation and price elasticities on the Internet* (Working paper). Massachusetts: MIT Sloan School of Management, Cambridge.

Furse, D., Punj, G., & Stewart, D. (1984). A typology of individual search strategies among purchasers of new automobiles. *Journal of Consumer Research, 10*(4), 417-431.

Girard, T., Silverblatt, R., & Korgankoar, P. (2002). Influence of product class on preference for shopping on the Internet. *Journal of Computer Mediated Communications, 8*(1). Retrieved August 21,

2005, from http://www.ascusc.org/jcmc/vol8/issue1/girard.html.

Hofstede, G. (1980). *Culture's consequences: International differences in work relates values.* Newbury Park (CA): Sage Publications.

Igbaria, M. (1993). User acceptance of microcomputer technology: an empirical test. *International Journal of Management Science, 21,* 73-90.

Igbaria, M., Parasuraman, S., & Baroudi, J. (1996). A motivational model of microcomputer usage. *Journal of Management Information Systems, 13,* 127-143.

Iyer, G. A., & Pazgal, A. (2003). Internet shopping agents: Virtual co-location and competition. *Marketing Science, 22*(1), 85-106.

Joines, J., Scherer, C., & Scheufele, D. (2003). Exploring motivations for consumer Web use and their implications for E-commerce. *Journal of Consumer Marketing, 20*(2), 90-108.

Korgaonkar, P., & Wollin, L. (1999). A multivariate analysis of Web usage. *Journal of Advertising Research, 39*(2), 53-68.

Lazonder, A., Biemans, J., & Wopereis, G. (2000). Differences between novice and experienced users in searching information on the world wide web. *Journal of the American Society for Information Science, 51*(6), 576-581.

Li, H., Kuo, C., & Russell, M. (1999). The impact of perceived channel utilities, shopping orientations, and demographics on the consumer's online buying behaviour. *Journal of Computer Mediated Communications* 5(2). Retrieved March 15, 2002, from http://www.ascusc.org/jcmc/vol5/issue2/hairong.html.

Lohse, G., Bellman, S., & Johnson, E. (2000). Consumer buying behavior on the Internet: findings from panel data. *Journal of Interactive Marketing, 14*(1), 15-29.

Markus, H., & Oyserman, D. (1989). Gender and thought: the role of the self-concept. In M. Cradfort, & M. Gentry (Ed.), *Gender and thought: psychological perspectives,* (pp.100-127). New York: Springer-Verlag.

Modahl, M. (2000). *Now or never.* New York: Harper Collins.

Montgomery, A.L., Hosanagar, K., Krishnan, R., & Clay, K.B. (2004). Designing a better shopbot. *Management Science, 50*(2), 189-206.

Mulhern, F. (1997). Retail Marketing: From distribution to integration. *International Journal of Research in Marketing, 14*(2), 103-124.

Newman, J. W., & Staelin, R. (1972). Prepurchase information seeking for new cars and major household appliances. *Journal of Marketing Research, 9* (August), 249-257.

Nielsen//NetRatings (2007). Search Engine Strategies conference 2007, 13-15 February. Retrieved July 2, 2008, from http://www.searchenginesstrategies.com.

Park, C., & Kim, Y. (2003). Identifying key factors affecting consumer purchase behaviour in an online shopping context. *International Journal of Retail and Distribution Management, 31*(1), 16-29.

Peterson, R., Balasubramanian, S., & Bronnenberg, B. (1997). Exploring the implications on the Internet for consumer Marketing. *Journal of the Academy of Marketing Science, 25*(4), 329-346.

Peterson, R.A., Albaum, G., & Ridway, N.M. (1989). Consumer who buy from direct sales companies. *Journal of Retailing, 65*(3), 273-286.

Punj, G., & Staelin, R. (1983). A model of consumer information search for new automobiles. *Journal of Consumer Research, 9*(4), 336-380.

Red.es (2007). Estudio sobre Comercio Electrónico B2C. Retrieved May 14 2007, from http://www.red.es.

Reibstein, D. (2002). What attracts customers to online stores and what keeps them coming back? *Journal of the Academy of Marketing Science, 30*(4), 465-473.

Rohm, A., & Swaminathan, V. (2004). A typology of online shoppers based on shopping motivations. *Journal of Business Research, 57*(12), 748-757.

Rowley, J. (1998). *The Electronic Library.* London: Facet Publishing.

Rowley, J. (2000). Product searching with shopping bots. *Internet Research, 10*(3), 203-215.

Rowley, J. (2002). 'Window' shopping and browsing opportunities in cyberspace. *Journal of Consumer Behaviour, 1*(4), 369-378.

Sim, L., & Koi, S. (2002). Singapore's Internet shoppers and their impact on traditional shopping patterns. *Journal of Retailing and Consumer Services, 9*(2), 115-124.

Smith, M. (2002). The impact of shopbots on electronic markets. *Journal of the Academy of Marketing Science, 30*(4), 446-454.

Smith, M., & Brynjolfsson, E. (2001). Consumer decision making at an Internet shopbot: Brand still matters. *The Journal of Industrial Economics, 49*(4), 541-558.

Srinivasan, S., Anderson, R., & Ponnavolu, K. (2002). Customer loyalty in e-commerce: an exploration of its antecedents and consequences. *Journal of Retailing, 78*(1), 41-50.

Srinivasan, N., & Ratchford, B.T. (1991). An empirical test of a model of external search of automobiles. *Journal of Consumer Research, 18*, 233-242.

Steckel, J. (2000). *On-line shopping: how many will come to the party? And when they will get there?* (Working paper). New York: University of New York, Stern School of Business.

Steenkamp, J., Hofstede, G., & Wedel, M. (1999). A cross-national investigation into the individual and national antecedents of consumer innovativeness. *Journal of Marketing, 63* (April), 55-69.

Stigler, G. (1961). The economics of information. *The Journal of Political Economy, 49*(3), 213-225.

Teo, T.S.H., & Yeong, Y.D. (2003). Assesing the consumer decision process in the digital marketplace. *The International Journal of Management Science, 31*, 349-363.

Trocchia, P., & Janda, S. (2000). A phenomenological investigation of Internet usage among older individuals. *Journal of Consumer Marketing, 17*(7), 605-616.

Trocchia, P., & Janda, S. (2003). How do consumers evaluate Internet retail service quality? *Journal of Services Marketing, 17*(3), 243-253.

Wollin, L.D. (2003). Gender issues in advertising-An oversight synthesis of research: 1970-2002. *Journal of Advertising Research*, March, (pp. 111-129).

Wotruba, T., & Privoba, M. (1995). Direct selling in an emerging market economy: A comparison of central Europe with the U.S. In T. Wotruba (Ed.), *Proceedings of the International Academic Symposium on Direct Selling in Central and Eastern Europe* (pp. 87-193). Washington, DC: Direct Selling Education Foundation:

Yoon, D., Cropp, F., & Cameron, G. (2002). Building relationships with portal users: the interplay of motivation and relational factors. *Journal of Interactive Advertising, 3*(1). Retrieved July 13, 2005, from http://jiad.org/vol3/no1/yoon.

Zeithaml, V. (1988). Consumer perceptions of price, quality, and value: a means-end model and synthesis of evidence. *Journal of Marketing, 52* (January), 2-22.

Zhu, H., Siegel, M., & Madnick, S. (2001). *Information aggregation. A value–added E-service.* Paper presented at the International Conference on Technology, Policy and Innovation: Critical Infraestructures (paper 106), The Netherlands.

ADDITIONAL READING

Ariely, D. (2000). Controlling the information flow: effects on consumers, decision making and preferences. *Journal of Consumer Research, 27,* 233-248.

Athanassopoulos, A., Gounaris, S., & Stathakopoulos, V. (2001). Behavioural Responses to Customer Satisfaction: An Empirical Study. *European Journal of Marketing, 35*(5/6), 687-707.

Babin, B., & Attaway, J. (2000). Atmospheric affect as a tool for creating value and gaining share of customer. *Journal of Business Research, 49*(2), 91-99.

Babin, B., Darden, W., & Griffin, M. (1994). Work And/ Or Fun: Measuring Hedonic and Utilitarian Shopping Value. *Journal of Consumer Research, 20*(4), 644-656.

Drèze, X., & Zufryden, F., (2004). Measurement of Online visibility and its impact on Internet traffic. *Journal of Interactive Marketing, 18*(1), 20-37.

Feldman, S., & Spencer, M. (1965). The effect of personal influence in the selection of consumer services. In P. Bennett (Ed.). *Marketing and Economic Development* (pp. 440-452). Chicago: American Marketing Association.

File, K., Judd, B., & Prince, R. (1992). Interactive marketing: the influence of participation on positive word-of-mouth referrals. *The Journal of Services Marketing, 6*(4), 5-11.

Haübl, G., & Trifts, V. (2000). Consumer decision making in online shopping environments: the effect of interactive decision aids. *Marketing Science, 19*(1), 4-21.

Hoffman, D., & Novak, T. (1996). Marketing in hypermedia computer-mediated environments: conceptual foundations. *Journal of Marketing, 60,* 50-68.

Holbrook, M. (1999). Introduction to Customer Value. In Holbrook, M. (Ed.) *Costumer Value: a Framework for Analysis and Research* (pp. 1-28). New York: Routledge.

Lightner, N. J., & Eastman, C. (2002). User preference for product information in remote purchase environments. *Journal of Electronic Commerce Research, 3*(3), 174-186.

Maes, P., Guttman, R., & Moukas, A. (1999). Agents that buy and sell: transforming commerce as we know it. *Communications of the ACM, 42*(3), 81-83.

Mcguire, W. (1974). Psychological motives and communication gratifications. In: Blumler, JF. and Katz, J. (Eds.) *The uses of mass communications: current perspectives on gratification research* , (pp. 106-167), Beverly Hills (CA): Sage.

West, P., Ariely, D., Bellman, S., Bradlow, E., Huber, J., Johnson, E., Kuhn, B., Little, J., & Schkade, D. (1999). Agents to the rescue? *Marketing letters, 10,* 285-301.

Westbrook, R. (1987). Product/consumption-based affective responses and postpurchase processes. *Journal of Marketing Research, 24* (March), 258-270.

KEY TERMS

Convenience-Oriented Consumers: Consumers who value convenience value more than price reductions and often prefer to pay a premium for shopping online rather than travelling to brick-and-mortar outlets. These consumers do not wish to negotiate with several sellers when shopping, because of the increased search effort.

Hedonic Shopping Motivations: This term reflects the value found in the shopping experience itself independent of task-related activities. Hedonic motivations refer to experiential benefits and sacrifices, such as entertainment and escapism or social interaction. Individuals who focus on hedonic motivations prefer to be stimulated by internal gratifications such as emotions, entertainment and contact with other consumers rather than convenience or price reductions.

Online Shopping: Process consumers go through to purchase products or services over the Internet.

Price-Oriented Shoppers: Consumers who see price as an important cost component and compare prices between different alternatives before purchasing. Price is the most important choice criteria used by these consumers in deciding where to shop online. Price-oriented consumers constantly compare offers with those of competitors, changing the supplier when there is the least reduction in price for the products and services they need.

Search Engine: Web application that gathers information from the web using different strategies (crawlers or spiders) and then performs the basic retrieval task, accepting a query, comparing a query with the records in a database, and producing a retrieval set as output.

Search Engine Marketing: Form of Internet marketing that seeks to promote websites by increasing their visibility in search engine result pages

Utilitarian Shopping Motivations: This term reflects the task-related value of a shopping experience. In particular, they refer to time savings and the chance to avoid shopping tasks that Internet offers. Search engines allow consumers to achieve some utilitarian shopping orientation goals such as: convenience, time saving, variety seeking and price reductions.

Variety-Seekers: Consumers who like to compare among a wide range and assortment of products before purchasing. These consumers also like to find detailed information online.

Chapter IX
Service Features, Customer Convenience, and Shopping Intention in the Context of Mobile Commerce

Wen-Jang (Kenny) Jih
Middle Tennessee State University, USA

ABSTRACT

Technological advancements in Wireless communication and Internet capabilities are rapidly converging to provide an unprecedented level of convenience for online shopping. Despite much discussion regarding the unique capabilities of mobile commerce in supporting online shopping via unprecedented convenience, the relationship between mobile commerce service features and convenience perception remains an unanswered issue from both the vendor and customer points of view. Although the concept of consumer-perceived convenience has been extensively discussed in marketing and consumer behavior literature, in the context of mobile commerce, however, these discussions are subject to systematic validation with empirical data to be convincing. This study conducted a field survey to investigate how mobile commerce service features and customer perception of convenience are correlated. It also examined the effect of convenience on customers' intention of shopping via their mobile communication devices. The primary data collected in Taiwan were used in the analysis. It was found the service features and customer convenience perceptions are significantly correlated. It also showed a significant relationship between the convenience perception and shopping intention. Further, there was a positive effect of convenience perception on shopping intention. The findings may have practical implications for mobile commerce strategists by providing more understanding of the mobile commerce success factors from a consumer behavior point of view.

INTRODUCTION

The rapid advancement in the Web-enabled online shopping and wireless communications has led to the development of an emerging market for mobile e-commerce, or m-commerce. As the business impact of e-commerce can be witnessed in almost every facet of the business arena, the unique features of wireless Internet access capabilities add even more flexibility to the online shopping experience (Haskin, 1999). Web-enabled wireless devices are convenient shopping tools for they allow users to search, communicate, and purchase products and services without restriction of time and space. These convenient features are especially welcomed by today's busy customers and are promising to make e-commerce grow even further (Goi, 2008).

Wireless communications technology has received much attention in both voice and data communication markets. A marketing research firm, iSuppli, predicts that the global wireless market will increase from the $520 million of 2004 to $430 million by 2010 (Focus on Internet News and Data, 2006). Telecom Trends estimates that almost 100 million people are m-commerce users today, and their numbers are expected to double in the near future (Fitchard, 2004). Lewis (1999) predicts that, as the average cost of wireless usage drops substantially in the next several years, wireless Internet devices will outnumber wired devices. Wireless Business Forecast (2005) predicts that U. S. wireless customers will expand from the current 175 million to 200 million by 2008. Portio Research, a British research firm, estimates that a half of the world population will become mobile phone users by the year 2009 (Wu, 2006). China currently adds 3 million to 4 millions cellular phone users each month. By the end of January 2006, its cellular phone population has reached 400 million, the largest in the world (Focus on Internet News and Data, 2006). Although some of these specific forecast numbers don't match, as is typical with many other types

of forecasts, it is clear that as wireless technologies and standards for security, bandwidth and interoperability continue to advance, the impact of online shopping via wireless communication devices is bound to become a crucial issue for information system professionals as they strive to support their organizations' marketing and strategic initiatives.

Most of the existing literature on mobile commerce developments anecdotally reports on either technological advancement (e.g., Olla, et al., 2003) or business activities of technological service providers. Relatively less is reported on the feedback of m-commerce customers, however. This demand side information is essential for a healthy understanding of this technology-enabled business phenomenon. Stated differently, systematic empirical investigation into major aspects of m-commerce development to support theory building in this field is relatively limited. This problem was pointed out by Clarke (2001), who states that "Despite tremendous interest in the melioration of m-commerce, there is little, if any, research that examines how to develop a comprehensive consumer-oriented mobile e-commerce strategy (p. 134)." This situation has not been significantly improved as of today. In attempting to provide a theoretical basis for academic research, Clarke (2001) proposed four value propositions for m-commerce applications: ubiquity, convenience, localization, and personalization. Zhang, et al. (2002) also suggested three driving forces to account for m-commerce success: technology innovation, evolution of a new value chain, and active customer demand. Two related themes stand out in these studies regarding m-commerce: the importance of integrated business strategies that truly accommodate the unique features of mobile communication devices for mobile phone users and the significance of consumer-perceived convenience provided by the mobile devices.

The concept of service or product convenience as a research construct has primarily been discussed in the marketing and consumer behavior literature (for example, Berry, et al., 2002; Ng-Kruelle, et al. 2002; Gross and Sheth, 1989; Brown, 1990; Seiders, Berry, and Gresham, 2000). Although mostly conceptual and speculative in nature, the literature on the significance of convenience consistently argues for the positive impact of product and service convenience on customers' shopping and the resulted satisfaction from the use experience (Brown, 1989; Berry, Seiders, & Grewal, 2002; Litan & Rivlin, 2001). Little research has been reported, however, about the effort that empirically investigates the impact of service or product convenience on various aspects of customer behaviors, such as shopping intention. The need for research regarding the significance of convenience that is conducted in the context of m-commerce is especially important, given the unique features and appeals of wireless communication products and services. The primary purpose of this study is to help bridge this gap by investigating the perception of cellular phone users concerning the effects of m-commerce service convenience perception on the intention of shopping via the Internet-enabled cellular phone. The relationship between perception of specific cellular phone service features and convenience perception is also examined.

The remainder of the paper first briefly reviews the existing academic literature on consumer-perceived convenience as well as some distinctive characteristics of m-commerce. The literature review serves as the basis for the formulation of research hypotheses. The paper then describes the research method of the study, including questionnaire design, collection of the research data, and the statistical techniques employed to analyze the data. The results of data analysis and our interpretations as related to hypotheses testing are presented in the subsequent section. The final section summarizes the research findings, highlights the implications for practice and research, and also proposes some promising directions for future research.

LITERATURE REVIEW AND HYPOTHESES

Distinctive Characteristics of M-Commerce

Briefly, m-commerce can be defined as the use of wireless communications technologies as the primary interaction vehicle between buyers and sellers of products or services. Currently, the Web-enabled cellular phone is the most popular device used by the customers of m-commerce. Other mobile communication devices, such as laptop computers and hand-held personal digital assistants, are also used. The definition given above can be viewed as a common denominator of a number of slightly different definitions found in the literature. For example, Siau & Shen (2002) defined m-commerce transactions as those conducted via mobile devices using wireless telecommunication networks and other wired e-commerce technologies. In O'Dea's (2000) study, m-commerce was defined as an extension of e-commerce beyond the static terminal of the PC/TV to anytime, anyplace, anywhere on mobile and other wireless devices. As the wireless communication technology continues to advance along many directions (e.g., bandwidth, security, user interface, pricing strategy, etc.) (White, 2002), the substantial growth potential of m-commerce in the near future has been predicted by both practitioners (Fitchard, 2004) and academicians (Zhang, et al., 2002).

Innovative business strategies must be developed to leverage the unique features of wireless communications in order to offer unique and appealing customer value. Contrasted with the traditional, wired telecommunication networks, a wireless communication infrastructure is relatively less expensive to construct in terms of capital requirement and time frame. This cost advantage is applicable to wide-area, metropolitan-area, and local-area network installations

(White, 2004). Wireless communication devices are also more tightly tied to the service users than desktop personal computers or fixed line-based telephones. This personalization capability has allowed m-commerce companies to more closely connect customers with their major business processes, such as new product development, in the attempt to enhance customer satisfaction and loyalty (Napier, et al., 2003; Ng-Kruelle, et al., 2002). In addition, when equipped with wireless cards and Web browsing capability, user wireless devices, such as laptop computers or even cellular phones, can be used to access internal as well as external information resources with little concern of wiring for network connection.

Researchers have identified major advantages of m-commerce that can be derived from these unique features of wireless communications. For example, Wen and Gyires (2002) indicated the key ingredients of m-commerce to be portability, connectivity, usability, and ubiquity. Ng-Kruelle, et al. (2002) listed six advantages of m-commerce: ubiquity, reachability, security, convenience, localization, and personalization. Clarke (2001) pointed out four value propositions of m-commerce that set m-commerce apart from conventional e-commerce: ubiquity, localization, personalization, and convenience. Frolick and Chen (2004) indicated that m-commerce contributes to overall business operations through real time interactions with customers and immediate dissemination of decision support information to employees. Thayer (2002) emphasized the advantage of expanded contact points with customers. In explicating major differences between m-commerce and e-commerce, Zhang, Yuan, and Archer (2002) contended that "M-commerce is not simply a new distribution channel, a mobile Internet or a substitute for PCs. Rather, it is a new aspect of consumerism and a much more powerful way to communicate with customers (p. 83)." Rather than treating m-commerce merely as an extension of e-commerce, a new way of thinking has been called for in order to unleash the value of m-commerce associated with the role of mobility (Nohria and Leestma, 2001; Clarke, 2001). From a strategic perspective, the potential of m-commerce can be realized only through the development of mobile-specific business strategy (Clarke, 2001). Viewed from customers' points of view, the technical capability of mobility essentially forms the basis of convenience.

The Concept of Customer Convenience

Convenience is an important value proposition to customers in the e-commerce business. Merriam-Webster's online dictionary defines convenience as, "something (as an appliance, device, or service) conducive to comfort or ease; fitness or suitability for performing an action or fulfilling a requirement." While the first definition links to a psychological dimension and the second refers to problem solving, both definitions suggest the subjective and perceptive nature of the concept.

In business literature, convenience is typically viewed as a multidimensional construct. It first appeared in the business literature as Copeland (1923) defined convenience goods as a class of consumer products that were intensively distributed and required minimal time and physical and mental effort to purchase. Some later definitions of convenience also focused on resources such as time and effort required of the consumer in shopping for a product (Brown, 1990). Other researchers, however, expanded the concept of convenience to incorporate non-shopping activities. For example, Yale and VenKatseh (1986) identified six aspects of convenience: time utilization, accessibility, portability, appropriateness, handiness, and avoidance of unpleasantness. However, this framework was criticized for the lack of theoretical underpinning and means of measurement (Brown, 1989; Gehrt and Yale, 1993; Berry, et al., 2002). In the context of Internet-enabled commerce, the five-dimension framework of convenience proposed by Brown (1989) appears to be both inclusive and measurable: time dimension, place dimension, acquisition dimension, use dimension, and execution dimension. Some researchers even contend that convenience is the most critical benefit of the Internet. Economists Litan & Rivlin (2001), for example, suggested that "Much of the benefit from the Internet is likely to show up in improved consumer convenience and expanded choices, rather than in higher productivity and lower prices (p. 317)," as a conclusion of a team research conducted to examine the economic impact of the Internet.

The notion of convenience perception also receives much attention in the field of information systems. Studies in the technology acceptance model (TAM) (Davis, 1989; Gefen & Straub, 2000), for example, examine the impact of perceived ease-of-use on intended adoption of information technology. In a simulation study conducted to validate a theoretical explanation of the effects of perceived ease-of-use on IT adoption, Gefen & Straub (2000) distinguish between the extrinsic vs. intrinsic aspects of IT characteristics with regards to IT adoption. Citing purchasing a book through a Web site as an example, they clarify that the purchasing itself is a task extrinsic to the IT because the IT serves only as an interface of an integrated system. The entire system typically consists of many other components such as shipping and payment handling system modules. Conversely, using the same Web site to inquire about a book represents an intrinsic IT task because the Web site provides a complete application associated with the actual service. Their data support the proposition that perceived ease of use only affects intended use of tasks that are intrinsic to the IT. In light of unique characteristics of mobile commerce such as personalization and localization, however, our study adopts Brown's framework described above for the operational definition of convenience perception. The question items devised to measure the extrinsic and intrinsic characteristics of perceived ease of use in Gefen & Straub (2000) appear to indicate that

Brown's framework seems to define convenience perception in a broader sense than perceived ease of use in TAM.

In summary, the literature in consumer behavior indicates that convenience is a multi-dimensional and context-dependent perception. An empirical investigation of its impact on customers' shopping behavior must treat convenience as a composite variable and be conducted in a specific context, such as mobile commerce in the case of this research. In addition, since the perception is subjective in nature, it may be measured differently between the mobile commerce companies and their customers.

Research Hypotheses

In order to investigate of role of customer perception of convenience in the context of m-commerce, three research hypotheses are established for statistical testing. First of all, due to its subjective nature, it is assumed that the value of convenience may be affected by individual differences. In Bergada's (1990) study, consumers' perception of convenience was found to vary with their demographical characteristics as well as their shopping patterns. Specific individual characteristics that are capable of affecting convenience perception include: time inclination (Luqmani, 1994; Gagliano and Hathcote, 1994), tolerance of time pressure (Landy, et al., 1991), empathy (Aaker and Williams, 1998), and experience (Brucks, 1985; Krumer, et al., 1997). The first hypothesis is set up to explore the influence of demographical characteristics on the perceived customer convenience.

H₁: The customer perception of convenience is significantly related to m-commerce customers' demographical characteristics.

Secondly, the convenience features of m-commerce are provided by specific product/service items offered by the wireless communications service providers and the m-commerce websites. Given the subjective nature of customer convenience perception, although service providers usually strive to incorporate customer-friendly features in their offerings, all specific product/service items may not be equally associated with customers' convenience perception. The second research hypothesis is formulated to test the relationship between the product/service features and the customers' convenience perception:

H₂: M-commerce customers' convenience perceptions are significantly correlated with product/service features.

Finally, the concept of convenience has strategic and tactical implications in marketing. Brown (1989) proposed a five-dimension convenience model (time dimension, place dimension, acquisition dimension, use dimension, and execution dimension) and demonstrated its value for marketing decision analysis. Berry et al. (2002) also developed a decision model that centered on service convenience. This model identified five classes of service convenience: decision convenience, access convenience, transaction convenience, benefit convenience, and post-benefit convenience. Viewed from the life cycle perspective, each of these conveniences may contribute to customers' shopping or re-shopping decision. In an empirical study, Anderson and Srinivasan (2003) found that consumer's convenience motivation was a major factor affecting the impact of e-satisfaction on e-loyalty. As indicated by Anderson (1972), when properly integrated into marketing decisions, the concept of convenience may become a powerful enabling tool. This leads to the following research hypothesis:

H₃: M-commerce customers' shopping intention is significantly affected by their convenience perception.

RESEARCH METHODOLOGY

Collection and Analysis of Research Data

In order to investigate the effect of convenience on m-commerce customers' shopping intention, a questionnaire survey was conducted using young cellular phone users in Taiwan as the convenience sample. The questionnaire contained three sets of questions that were devised to collect primary data from the research sample about the three research constructs: the perception of Internet services offered to Internet-enabled cellular phone users, the perception of product/service convenience associated with m-commerce, and the demographical distribution of the respondents. A total of twenty-three cellular phone services were compiled from the providers' company Web pages, covering most of the popular services offered by wireless communication service providers. The development of the convenience feature perception questions was based on an expanded version of Brown's (1989) model. In addition to the original five dimensions (time, place, acquisition, use, and execution), three questions representing Web-based service are included to account for the specificity of m-commerce. Sixteen questions in total were developed to measure these five dimensions of the convenience construct. In the attempt to determine how basic demographical characteristics affected the usage of service items as well as convenience perceptions, we include three questions regarding gender, age, and usage experience in the questionnaire. Shopping intention is measured with a question that asks cellular phone users to indicate their general shopping intention via cellular phones. With the exception of demographical characteristics, the questions are not necessarily all mutually exclusive and are evaluated using the Likert scale with 1 indicating very unimportant and 5 very important.

As a pilot test, the questionnaire was administered to one hundred cellular phone users to evaluate the adequacy of the questionnaire. The reliability measures of the questionnaire evaluated by Cronbach's α values as well as the feedbacks from the questionnaire respondents were used to subsequently refine the questionnaire. According to Nunnally (1978), a data collection instrument that has a Cronbach's α higher than 0.7 is considered to be highly reliable. The evaluation of the construct validity of the questionnaire was based on Kerlinger's (1986) suggestion: The correlation coefficients between the individual question item scores and the total score were used as the construct validity measures. As shown in Table 1, the questions in all categories have Cronbach's α values higher than 0.8, and the item-total correlation coefficients are all close to 0.7 or above. The former value indicates that the questionnaire is reliable, and the latter suggests a good validity of the data collection instrument.

College students were used as the convenience sample in this study for both the pilot test and the formal survey because they represented the most active group of cellular phone users as well as m-commerce customers in Taiwan (Jih and Lee, 2004; Lin, et al. 2001). Another reason is that, although the widespread use of the cellular phone for shopping is still at the initial stage of innovation diffusion, the experience of the current college students will grow in synchronization with the maturing process of the technology itself. College students' perception of m-commerce will serve as a good reference and thereby facilitates sound business decision-making on the part of m-commerce companies. Students of a variety of majors in six colleges participated in the study. A total of 400 copies of the questionnaire were distributed, and 370 were deemed effective responses. The high response rate was achieved because

Table 1. Measuring convenience: Item-total correlation and dimension reliabilities

Convenience Dimensions	Question number	Item-Total Correlation	Cronbach's α Value
Use Dimension	1	0.56	0.8058
	2	0.66	
	3	0.62	
	4	0.66	
	5	0.48	
Time Dimension	6	0.82	0.9023
	7	0.83	
	8	0.77	
Place Dimension	9	0.70	0.8218
	10	0.70	
Shopping (Execution) Dimension	11	0.69	0.8347
	12	0.74	
	13	0.68	
Service Dimension	14	0.74	0.8805
	15	0.80	
	16	0.76	

the questionnaires were distributed in class and the students were encouraged to respond on an anonymous and voluntary basis. The effective respondents consist of 43.2% males and 56.8% females; 48.1% with ages 17-20, 41.6% with ages 21-25, and 10.3% with ages outside these typical college student age ranges.

The research hypotheses were tested using t-test, analysis of variance (ANOVA) canonical correlation analysis, and regression analysis. The difference of convenience perception between different demographical groups (H_1) was tested using t-test and ANOVA. Canonical correlation analysis was used to test the correlation relationship between specific service items and convenience factors (H_2). Regression analysis was employed to determine the impact of convenience factors on shopping intention (H_3).

RESULTS OF DATA ANALYSIS

Service and Convenience Preferences

An issue of practical concern regarding the Internet services via wireless communications and the perception of convenience features in m-commerce is how they are ranked by customer preference. Mean scores are used to provide the rankings. Among the 23 specific service items offered by most service providers, the five most welcome ones are: emergency service, short message, e-mail, medical information, and transportation acquisition service. Among the 16 convenience perception items reviewed by the cellular phone users, the five most desirable ones are: portability of user device, light weight and compactness of user device, convenience of information search, transaction or information search not limited by location, and service on demand. These responses are not surprising. Other than psychological and other non-technical reasons, these top-ranked desires reflect, to

a certain degree, the problem of crowded traffic on the densely populated island as well as the phenomenon that most people, especially the young generation, appear to be extremely busy in this fast-paced world. The services provided by the wireless communications technology and m-commerce service providers are increasingly becoming an essential part of many people's lives (www.find.org.tw/news/).

Factor Analysis of Internet Services and Convenience Perception

Before the research hypotheses were tested, factor analysis was performed to compress the number of Internet service variables from twenty-three to four (Table 2) and the number of convenience perception variables from sixteen to two (Table 3). The four latent variables that represent the observed Internet service variables and the two representing observed convenience perception were then used to test the research hypotheses. In addition, the Bartlett's sphericity test was computed to validate significant correlation between the observed variables, and the Kaiser-Meyer-Olkin (KMO) measure of sampling adequacy was obtained to further establish the adequate use of factor analysis on the data. A significantly high χ^2 value indicates significant correlation between the observed variables and a high KMO value (>= .80) indicates high shared-variance and low uniqueness in variance. Both evaluation criteria measures signify that the data are appropriate for factor analysis. Both sets of variables were analyzed using principal component analysis to extract the factors and varimax rotation to achieve a simplified factor structure.

As summarized in Table 2, the result of factor analysis produced four factors for Internet services on cellular phones: Life-Enhancement Services, Value-Added Services, Entertainment Features, and Basic Services. The accumulated variance of these four factors is 58.358% with the overall reliability 0.9162. The reliability measures of the four factors are 0.8946, 0.8357, 0.8019, and 0.5338, respectively. Nunally (1978) suggests a Cronbach's α Value 0.7 as the cutoff point for acceptable reliability. A less strict criterion for reliability evaluation is suggested by Cuieford (1965). This criterion contends that a Cronbach's α Value 0.7 or higher indicates highly reliable, that between 0.35 and 0.7 indicates acceptable, and that below 0.35 unacceptable. Due to the exploratory nature of the questions, Cuieford's criterion was adopted to accept the fourth factor, Basic Service, in our analysis. The χ^2 value from the Bartlett's test

is 4075.727 at the p value < 0.01 and the KMO measure is 0.906. Both measures suggest that the data is appropriate for factor analysis.

The result of factor analysis of convenience perception is shown is Table 3. The two factors produced are labeled Transaction Convenience and Operational Convenience. The accumulated variance extracted by these two factors is 60.935%, with the overall reliability measure 0.9401. The reliability measures for the individual factors are 0.9069 and 0.8789, respectively. These are high reliability measures even by the more strict,

Table 2. Factor analysis of Internet services for cellular phone users

Factors	Variables	Factor Loading				Cronbach's α Values
		1	2	3	4	
Life-Enhancement Services	Ticket Shopping	0.774	0.136	-0.007	0.108	0.8946
	Medical Information	0.741	0.138	0.138	0.063	
	Service Reservation	0.677	0.106	0.183	0.166	
	e-Learning Service Use	0.647	0.434	-0.003	-0.051	
	Transportation Service Acquisition	0.639	0.032	0.080	0.218	
	Employment Information	0.634	0.147	0.309	-0.130	
	Online Banking	0.621	0.161	0.176	-0.095	
	Discount Coupon	0.618	0.158	0.186	0.137	
	Transportation Information	0.614	0.243	0.250	0.056	
	Emergency Service Use	0.613	-0.145	-0.004	0.303	
	News	0.567	0.352	0.127	-0.168	
	E-mail	0.480	0.175	0.368	0.276	
Value-Added Services	Horoscope	0.034	0.834	0.299	0.107	0.8357
	Psychological Testing	0.057	0.830	0.283	0.102	
	Food Menu Information	0.443	0.627	0.145	-0.006	
	Online Shopping	0.493	0.598	0.105	0.103	
	Lottery Shopping	0.328	0.492	0.265	-0.259	
Entertainment Features	Game	0.058	0.067	0.852	0.115	0.8019
	Entertainment Information	0.239	0.200	0.752	0.010	
	Fellowship and Social Interaction	0.122	0.332	0.646	-0.111	
	E-book	0.315	0.336	0.642	-0.009	
Basic Services	Short Message	0.196	-0.085	-0.010	0.799	0.5338
	Ring Pattern Download	0.101	0.413	0.177	0.636	
Eigenvalue		8.337	2.410	1.433	1.242	
Explained Variance (%)		36.246	10.480	6.230	5.401	Overall Reliability 0.9162
Accumulated Explained Variance (%)		58.358				

Table 3. Factor analysis of convenience perception of cellular phone users

Factors	Variables	Factor Loadings		Cronbach's α Values
		1	2	
Transaction Convenience	Immediate payment for shopping	0.821	0.110	0.9069
	Individual password for shopping payment	0.802	0.141	
	Multiple means of payment for online shopping	0.722	0.182	
	localization service	0.649	0.442	
	Transaction inquiry on holidays	0.611	0.521	
	24-hour-based online Inquiry	0.596	0.540	
	Any-time Internet connection	0.588	0.316	
	Service not limited by location	0.568	0.528	
	Convenience of information search	0.547	0.541	
Operational Convenience	Portability of user device	0.009	0.830	0.8789
	Light weight and compactness of user device	0.166	0.792	
	Ease of operation	0.400	0.647	
	Reduction of information search time	0.567	0.593	
	Transaction or information search not limited by location	0.563	0.580	
	Multimedia-based communications	0.437	0.544	
	Service on demand	0.530	0.532	
Eigenvalue		8.518	1.231	Overall Reliability: 0.9401
Explained Variance		53.240%	7.695%	
Accumulated Explained Variance		60.935%		

Nunnaly's (1978) standard. The χ^2 value from the Bartlett's test is 3850.51 at $p < 0.01$. The KMO coefficient is 0.94. Both measures indicate that the data is also appropriate for factory analysis.

Results of Hypotheses Testing

In order to test the hypothesis H_1 (The perception of convenience is significantly related to m-commerce customers' demographical characteristics),

a t-test was conducted with each of the two convenience perception factors as the dependent variables and gender and age as the independent variables. T-test was also conducted with wireless Internet service factors as the dependent variable and gender and age as the independent variables to determine the effect of gender and age on the evaluation of Internet services offered to cellular phone users. The hypothesis is accepted according to the results of the analysis:

1. Females have significantly higher perception of both transaction convenience and operational convenience than males at $p < 0.05$.
2. The perception of older users of both transaction convenience and operational convenience are significantly higher than their younger counterparts at $p < 0.01$.

With regard to the effect of gender and age on the evaluation of wireless Internet services, it is found that while females have significantly higher evaluation of life-enhancement services at $p < 0.05$, males' evaluation of entertainment services are significantly higher than females at $p < 0.01$. Age is also found to be a significant factor regarding the evaluation of wireless Internet services: Older cellular phone users' evaluations are higher than their younger counterparts on life-enhancement services and lower on entertainment services, both at $p < 0.05$.

The second hypothesis, H_2: M-commerce customers' convenience perceptions are significantly correlated with product/service features, was tested using canonical correlation analysis. Two sets of canonical variates were produced as the result (Table 4 and Figure 1). The first set of canonical variates significantly relates all four service categories (life-enhancement services, value-added services, entertainment features, and basic features) with both types of convenience perception at $p < 0.01$ (canonical correlation coefficient $\rho = 0.692$). The second set of canonical variates significantly relates two service categories (value-added services and basic services) only with operational convenience at $p < 0.05$ (canonical correlation coefficient $\rho = 0.227$). According to these analysis results, those cellular phone users who favor life-enhancement services, value-added services, entertainment features, and basic features tend to place more emphasis on all types of convenience offered by m-commerce businesses. In addition, those who emphasize basic services and neglect value-added

services tend to favor the aspect of convenience associated with handling and operation of the cellular phone. These results lead to the acceptance of the second hypothesis.

The impact of convenience perception on shopping intention stated in the third hypothesis, H_3: M-commerce customers' shopping intention is significantly affected by their convenience perception, was tested using regression analysis. The results show that the type of convenience perception labeled Transaction Convenience has a significant impact on customers' intention to shop with mobile commerce companies using their cellular phones (regression coefficient = 0.497, $p < 0.01$). The fact that operational convenience does not exhibit a significant impact on shopping intention (regression coefficient = 0.172, $p = 0.139$) suggests that it may take more than just commonly available features to attract customers' attention in the mobile commerce business. The high F-value ($F = 53.920$) indicates that, in general, customers' shopping intention is significantly affected by their perception of convenience offered by mobile commerce businesses ($p < 0.01$). The third hypothesis, "M-commerce customers' shopping intention is significantly affected by their convenience perception," is accepted.

The results of hypotheses testing, stated in the alternative form, are summarized below:

H_1: The customer perception of convenience is significantly related to m-commerce customers' demographical characteristics. (Accepted)

H_2: M-commerce customers' convenience perceptions are significantly correlated with product/service features. (Accepted)

H_3: M-commerce customers' shopping intention is significantly affected by their convenience perception. (Accepted)

Table 4. Canonical analysis of relationship between convenience perceptions and service categories

Service Categories	Canonical Variates		Convenience Perceptions	Canonical Variates	
	χ_1	χ_2		η_1	η_2
Life-Enhancement Services	0.984	-0.164	Transaction Convenience	0.982	-0.189
Value-Added Services	0.597	-0.314			
Entertainment Services	0.530	0.028	Operational Convenience	0.919	0.394
Basic Services	0.479	0.801			
Percentage of Variance Extracted	46.0	19.2	Percentage of Variance Extracted	90.4	9.6
Redundancy	0.221	0.099	Redundancy	0.433	0.005
ρ^2	0.479	0.052			
Canonical Correlation	0.692	0.227			

Figure 1. Path diagram of significant relationship between service features and convenience perceptions

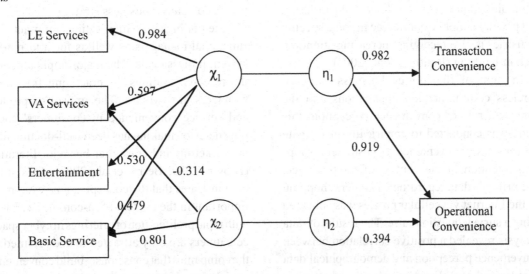

CONCLUSION

Strategic deployment of information technology requires integrating unique capabilities of technological tools with innovative customer-centered business processes. The convergence of Internet-based services and wireless communications creates technological business possibilities which, if properly harnessed, have the potential to transform a company's competitive advantage. The advancement of wireless communication technology has allowed the smooth and secure exchange of multimedia messages and data with little regard for geographical distance or time consideration. The capability to transmit voice and data over the same network connection and the convenience provided through such features as location-based service offer virtually unlimited possibilities for innovative businesses in designing product and service offerings.

When contrasted with traditional electronic commerce using desk-top personal computers, one of the most cited attractions of using mobile devices as a consumer shopping vehicle is convenience (Frolic and Chen, 2004; NG-Kruelle, et al., 2002; Seager, 2003; Siau and Shen, 2002). A subjective perception that typically varies between different people and across different contexts, convenience perception can significantly influence consumer behavior in various stages of the shopping process (Anderson, 1972; Brown, 1989; Gehrt and Yale, 1993). Along with the use of mobile communication devices for ordering and payment, mobile commerce in some specific industries is also receiving increasing attention, such m-banking (Routray, et al., 2008).

In light of the unique business value of wireless communication applications and the important role of convenience perception, this study was conducted to empirically investigate the impact of convenience on customers' shopping intention in the context of m-commerce. The primary data regarding customers shopping on the Internet via cellular phones was collected using a survey questionnaire. The results of data analysis revealed a positive correlation between convenience perception and demographical data (gender and age). Females were found to value

convenience more than males. Older m-commerce customers were found to value convenience more than their younger counterparts. A positive correlation relationship also exists between the convenience perception and the user evaluation of wireless Internet services. Those who appreciate the use of wireless communication services also tend to value the convenience of shopping in m-commerce. Most notably, the study showed that customers' intention of shopping on the Internet via their cellular phones was positively affected by their perception of convenience features offered by m-commerce businesses, wireless communication service providers, and vendors of user devices. In other words, convenience offering should be viewed as an important element in an m-commerce company's business strategy.

The findings have implications for practicing functional managers as well as for information system professionals. The major implications of the research findings for practicing functional managers are twofold. The impact of product and service convenience in consumers' shopping decision making has been well-documented in marketing and consumer behavior literature (Brown, 1989; Berry, et al., 2002). This study demonstrates that the concept can be even more important in the context of m-commerce. Faced with rapid proliferation of offerings in cyber space, consumers are only attracted to and retained by the companies that consciously build convenience into their websites and the entire customer relationship management program.

Table 5. Regression analysis of the impact of convenience perception on shopping intention

Convenience Perception	Regression Coefficient	t-value	p-value
Constant Item	0.561	2.164	0.031*
Transaction Convenience	0.497	4.540	0.000**
Operational Convenience	0.172	1.485	0.139
R^2	0.227		
F	53.920		0.000**

*: $p < 0.05$ **: $p < 0.01$

The second implication presented to practitioners by the research findings is associated with the way a convenient customer interface may be designed. Through regression analysis, the study found that, although both categories of convenience (transaction convenience and operational convenience) have significant impact on customers' shopping intention, transaction convenience appears to have more influence than operational convenience. In other words, it tends to be the transaction convenience, rather than the operational convenience, features that provide differentiating value.

Information system professionals must take into consideration the importance of consumer perceptions of the mobile commerce offerings and design a website that is both technically versatile in processing capability and convenient in its user interface. Traditionally, user-friendliness of user interface primarily requires ease of operation and ease of learning. In mobile commerce, however, integrating transaction convenience with operational convenience is essential to winning customer attention in the vast cyber business market space.

Due to several research limitations mentioned below, the findings reported herein must be interpreted and applied with due caution on the part of the reader. The use of college students in Taiwan as the source of research data may restrict the external validity of the study. The difference between college students and other age groups must be accounted for. As in many other survey research projects, this study assumes that the questionnaire respondents filled out the survey instrument seriously. In addition, the convenience perception factor in different consumption cultures may play a different kind of role in m-commerce.

The results of this study shed some light on an important characteristic of business applications of wireless communications technology – users' convenience perception. An inter-disciplinary research field, mobile commerce is still in its in-

fancy in many ways and requires more systematic inquiries to be conducted from different angles. First of all, this study operationalizes the concept of convenience based on Brown's (1989) definition of convenience. A different framework may be used to determine if a significant difference would result from different definitional frameworks of convenience. For example, the model of service convenience proposed by Berry, et al. (2002), which characterizes consumer's time and effort perceptions in terms of decision convenience, access convenience, transaction convenience, benefit convenience, and post-benefit convenience, may also be empirically validated for comparison. Secondly, as mobile communication devices are increasingly used as an avenue of advertisement, it is important to know how users perceive, through an independent research, this new mode of advertisement. Thirdly, since convenience perception usually interacts with other factors, such as service characteristics and individual differences, in affecting user perceptions, research that investigates compound effects of these relevant factors would contribute to formulation of effective business strategy for m-commerce. Another interesting and important area of research involves cross cultural comparative studies. Currently, European and Asian customers are ahead of American customers in using the cellular phone as a shopping tool. The results of this study may be validated in different cultures to allow more general conclusions to be drawn. From the technological development point of view, information system researchers may examine possible impacts of technological capabilities, such as screen display or bandwidth, on user perception of convenience and shopping intentions. The best ways in which commerce contents, such as product display or promotion messages, should be presented on the small screen for relatively impatient consumers also deserve more research. Finally, it can be expected that more industry-specific mobile commerce applications will be offered in the future to leverage the domain-specific factors for the benefit of enhanced convenience (Lin and Bi, 2008; Routray, et al., 2008).

REFERENCES

Aaker, J. L., & Williams, P. (1998). Empathy Versus Pride: The Influence of Emotional Appeals Across Cultures. *Journal of Consumer Research, 25*(December), 241-261.

Anderson, R. E., & Srinivasan, S. S. (2003). E-Satisfaction and E-Loyalty: A Contingency Framework. *Psychology & Marketing, 20*(2), 123-138.

Anderson, W. T. Jr. (1972). Convenience Orientation and Consumption Behavior. *Journal of Retailing, 48*(Fall), 49-71.

Bergadaa, M. (1990). The Role of Time in the Action of the Consumer. *Journal of Consumer Research, 17*(December), 289-302.

Berry, L. L., Seiders, K., & Grewal, D. (2002). Understanding Service Convenience. *Journal of Marketing, 66*(3), 1-17.

Brown, L. G. (1989). The Strategic and Tactical Implications of Convenience in Consumer Product Marketing. *Journal of Consumer Marketing, 6*(Summer), 13-19.

Brown, L. G. (1990). Convenience in Services Marketing. *Journal of Service Marketing, 4*(Winter), 53-59.

Brucks, M. (1985). The Effect of Product Class Knowledge on Information Search Behavior. *Journal of Consumer Research, 12*(June), 1-16.

Clark, I. III. (2001). Emerging Value Propositions for M-Commerce. *Journal of Business Strategy, 18*(2), 133-148.

Copeland, M. T. (1923). Relation of Consumers' Buying Habits to Marketing Methods. *Harvard Business Review*, April, 282-289.

Cuieford, J. P. (1965). *Fundamental Statistics in Psychology and Education, 4th Edition.* New York: McGraw Hill.

Davis, F. D. (1989). Perceived Usefulness, Perceived Ease of Use and User Acceptance of Information Technology. *MIS Quarterly, 13*(3), 319-339.

Fitchard, K. (2004). The Two M's of Commerce. *Telephony, 245*(8). P.26.

Focus on Internet News and Data. (2006). Retrieved on 03/17/2006 from http://www.find.org.tw/find/home.aspx?page=news&id=4185.

Focus on Internet News and Data. (2006). Retrieved on 03/01/2006 from http://www.find.org.tw/find/home.aspx?page=news&cal&p=1.

Frolick, M. N., & Chen, L. (2004). Assessing M-Commerce Opportunities. *Information Systems Management, 21*(2), 53-61.

Gagliano, K., & Hathcote, B. J. (1994). Customer Expectations and Perceptions of Service Quality in Retail Apparel Specialty Stores. *Journal of Services Marketing, 8*(1), 60-69.

Gefen, D., & Straub, D. (2000). *The Relative Importance of Perceived Ease of Use in IS Adoption: A Study of E-Commerce Adoption.* Retrieved from http://jais.isworld.org/articles/1-8/article.htm.

Gehrt, K. C., & Yale, L. J. (1993). The Dimensionality of the Convenience Phenomenon: A Qualitative Reexamination. *Journal of Business and Psychology, 8*(2), 163-180.

Goi, C. L. (2008). Review of the Implementation of Mobile Commerce in Malaysia. *Journal of Internet Banking and Commerce, 13*(2), 1-11.

Gross, B. L., & Sheth, J. N. (1989). Time-Oriented Advertising: A Content Analysis of *United States Magazine Advertising*, 1890-1988. *Journal of Marketing, 53*(October), 76-83.

Haskin, D. (1999). *Analysts: Smart phones to lead e-commerce explosion.* All-NetDevices. Retrieved from http://www.allnetdevices.com/news/9911/991103ecomm/991101ecomm.html.

Jih, W. J., & Lee, S. F. (2004). Relationship between Online Shoppers' Motivation and Life Style Indicators. *Journal of Computer Information Systems, XLIV*(2), 65-73.

Kerlinger, F. N. (1986). *Foundations of Behavioral Research.* 3rd Edition, New York McGraw-Hill.

Kumar, P., Kalwani, M. U., & Dada, M. (1997). The Impact of Waiting Time Guarantees on Consumer Waiting Experiences. *Marketing Science, 16*(4), 295-314.

Landy, P. J., Rastegary, H., Thayer, J., & Colvin, C. (1991). Time Urgency: The Construct and Its Measurement. *Journal of Applied Psychology, 76*(5), 644-657.

Lewis, T. (1999). Ubiner: The ubiquitous Internet will be wireless. *IEEE Computer, 32*(10), 56-63.

Lin, C. E., & Bi, L. Y. (2008). A Model Electronic Toll Collection for E-Commerce Applications. *Journal of Theoretical and Applied Electronic Commerce Research, 3*(2), 111-129.

Lin, S., Chen, Y. J, & Lin, T. T. (2001). A Study of College Students' Usage of and Satisfaction with Mobile Phones – The Cases of Taipei University and Chiao-Tung University. *Seventh Internet Conference – Taiwan.* Tanet.net.

Litan, R., & Rivlin, A. M. (2001). Project the Economic Impact of the Internet. *The American Economic Review, 91*(2), 313-317.

Luqmani, M., Yavas, U., & Quraeshi, Z. A. (1994). A Convenience-Oriented Approach to Country Segmentation: Implications for Global Marketing Strategies. *Journal of Consumer Marketing, 11*(4), 29-40.

Napier, H. A, Judd, P. J., Rivers, O. N., & Adams, A. (2003). *E-Business Technologies.* Boston, Massachusetts: Course Technology.

Ng-Kruelle, G., Swatman, P. A., Rebme, D. S., & Hampe, J. F. (2002). The Price of Convenience: Privacy and Mobile Commerce. *Quarterly Journal of Electronic Commerce, 3*(3), 273-285.

Nohria, N., & Leestma, M. (2001) A Moving Target: The Mobile-Commerce Customer. *Sloan Management Review, 42*(3), 104-115.

Nunnally, J. (1978). *Psychometric Theory.* New York: McGraw-Hill.

O'Dea, F. (2000). Mobile-Commerce – Trend in Wireless Interactions. *Anderson Consulting Report.*

Olla, P., Atkinson, C., & Gandceha, R. (2003). Wireless Systems Development Methodologies: An Analysis of Practice Using Actor Network Theory. *Journal of Computer Information Systems, XXXXIV*(1), 102-119.

Routray, S., Sherry, A. M., & Reddy, B. V. R. (2208). Wireless ATM: A Technological Framework to m-Banking. *Journal of Internet Banking and Commerce 13*(1), 1-11.

Seager, A. (2003). M-Commerce: An Integrated Approach. *Telecommunications International, 37*(2), 36-38.

Seiders, K., & Berry, L. L. (1998). Service Fairness: What It Is and Why It Matters. *Academy Management Executive, 12*(2), 8-21.

Siau, K., & Shen, Z. (2002). Mobile Commerce Applications in Supply Chain Management. *Journal of Internet Commerce, 1*(3), 3-14.

Solomon, M. R. (1986). The Missing Link: Surrogate Consumers in the Marketing Chain. *Journal of Marketing, 50*(October), 208-218.

Thayer, G. (2002a). M-Commerce: Long Trek to the Promised Land. *Pen Computing 9*(45), 17.

Wen, H. J., & Gyires, T. (2002). The Impact of Wireless Application Protocol (WAP) on M-Commerce Security. *Journal of Internet Commerce,* (3), 15-27.

White, C. (2004) *Data Communiations and Computer Networks* (3rd ed.). Boston, Massachusetts: Course Technology.

Whitt, W. (1999). Improving Service by Informing Customers about Anticipated Delays. *Management Science, 45*(2), 192-207.

Wireless Business Forecast. (2005). Wireless in the Driver's Seat. *Wireless Business Forecast, 13*(4), Feb. 24, 1.

Wu, C. H. (2006). *Portio Research: Half of World Population will be Pan-Pacific Mobile Phone Users in Ten Years.* Retrieved from http://www.find.org.tw/find/home.aspx?page=news&id=4117 .

Yale, L., & VenKatseh, A. (1986). Toward the Construct of Convenience in Consumer Research. *Advances in Consumer Research, 13*, 403-408.

Zhang, J. J., Yuan, Y., & Archer, N. (2002). Driving Forces for M-Commerce. *Journal of Internet Commerce, 1*(3), 81-106.

KEY TERMS

M-Commerce: Using mobile communication devices and the Internet to complete business transactions.

M-Commerce Service Features: Specific services provided by mobile commerce vendors. Examples include order placement, payment, security and privacy measures, inquiry, etc.

M-Commerce Customer Perception of Convenience: The ease of access to and use of the services offered by m-commerce service providers.

Chapter X
How Good is Your Shopping Agent?
Users' Perception Regarding Shopping Agents' Service Quality

Călin Gurău
GSCM – Montpellier Business School, France

ABSTRACT

The use of online shopping agents has increased dramatically in the last 10 years, as a result of e-commerce development. Despite the importance of these online applications, very few studies attempted to identify and analyse the main factors that influence the users' perception regarding the service quality of online shopping agents, and consequently, the elements that determine the users' choice of online shopping agents. The present study attempts to fill this literature gap, identifying on the basis of primary data analysis, the various circumstantial or personal factors that can determine the choice of a specific searching strategy and shopping agent.

INTRODUCTION

The rapid development of the Internet in the last 10 years has had a profound impact on traditional marketing paradigms and practices (see Table 1), because of three specific and co-existent characteristics that differentiate it from any other communication channel:

- **Interactivity:** The Internet offers multiple possibilities of interactive communication, acting not only as an interface, but also as a communication agent, allowing a direct interaction between individuals and software applications;
- **Transparency:** The information published online can be accessed and viewed by any

Internet user, unless this information is password protected;

- **Memory:** The web is not only a channel for transmitting information, but also for storing information – in other words, the information published on the web remains in the memory of the network until it is erased.

E-commerce has created new opportunities for both companies and customers. On one hand, the sellers had access to a larger market, without limitations of space or time; on the other hand, the customers had the possibility to choose the desired goods from a much larger offer than that available on the physical, traditional market. However, despite the increased choice, the sheer amount of information available on the Internet has introduced new challenges for companies and buyers. In the information-rich online environment, the firms must increase the distinctiveness of their offer, in order to make it visible to the targeted

market segments. The buyers also have particular problems: although they might know exactly the technical specifications and the type of the desired product, how can they quickly identify the best offer in terms of quality-price? In many cases the amount and the variety of information available to customers create a situation of information overload (Aggarval, & Vaidyanathan, 2003).

Specific online applications have been created to solve this problem: search engines and intelligent agents. The use of these applications raises important questions related to their quality and **reliability**. The present study attempts to investigate the users' perceptions about the quality of shopping agents, answering to the following research questions:

1. What are the characteristics that define the quality of shopping agents in users' mind?
2. Are there any differences determined by the customer profile in the usage of shopping agents?

Table 1. The new marketing paradigm shift determined by the Internet. Source: Kiani (1998)

From	To	Sources
One-to-Many communication model	Many-to-Many communication model	Hoffman and Novak (1996)
Mass Marketing Marketing	Individualised	Martin (1996)
Monologue	Dialogue	Blattberg and Deighton (1996)
Branding	Communication	Martin (1996)
Supply-side thinking	Demand-side thinking	Rayport and Sviokla (1995)
Megabrand	Diversity	Martin (1996)
Centralised market	Decentralised market	Blattberg et al. (1994)
Customer as a target	Customer as a partner	McKenna (1995)
Segmentations	Communities	Armstrong and Hagel III (1996)

3.   What are the transaction-related factors that influence the perceived quality of shopping agents?

After a brief literature review on the role and usage of shopping agents, the research methodology applied to collect secondary and primary data is presented. The main results obtained through data analysis are then discussed, in direct relation with the research questions defined above. The future trends in the development of online shopping agents are also analysed and the chapter ends with a summary of the main findings and with propositions for further research.

BACKGROUND

Shopping agents can be defined as specialised software applications which help users to search specific types of products or services offered online, and to collect additional information about these offers. After the user enters a query into the shopping agent, the software visits various e-shops or online merchant sites, collecting information about the product or service demanded (Rowley, 2002). The search is usually done on the basis of keywords or product categories, which are listed on the shopping agent's web page (Rowley, 2000a).

The use of **shopping agents** is determining significant changes in e-commerce strategies and operations, both from the part of companies as well from the part of customers. The capacity of shopping agents to search various web sites, to extract and to display specific information for the online customer modifies the conditions of online competition among vendors. The use of shopping agents to search for the lowest possible price offer increases the pressure for vendors to reduce the selling price, aligning it to the smallest existing level (Iyer, & Pazgal, 2003). However, several studies showed that the differences in online prices remain significant (Iyer, & Pazgal, 2003;

Sen, King, & Shaw, 2006). This can be explained by the choice of some vendors to focus on quality and personalisation rather than low price, in order to increase the loyalty of their customers. Other online vendors decide to restrict the access of shopping agents to their offers (Iyer, & Pazgal, 2003; Kerstetter, 1999) in order to reduce the visibility of their price levels.

On the other hand, the services offered by **shopping agents** to online customers significantly reduce the time and effort required to search and compare online information. Some authors have developed mathematical models that attempt to predict the **shopping behaviour** of online customers when using shopping agents (Iyer, & Pazgal, 2003; Sen et al., 2006). However, in most cases, they defined consumers' **shopping behaviour** in relation to their price orientation and to the level of their loyalty towards a particular brand or vendor (Iyer, & Pazgal, 2003)

If we consider the classical model of the consumer **decision-making process** (Brassington, & Pettitt, 1997; Engel, Blackwell, & Miniard, 1990; Rowley, 2000), the online **shopping agents** represent supporting tools for information search (allowing the customer to search for specific information about the products and/or services offered online), and information evaluation (permitting a direct and immediate comparison of various online commercial offers). On the other hand, the support provided in these two stages of the **decision-making process** will directly influence the purchasing decision made by the customer in terms of product, price, product characteristics and vendor. Finally, **shopping agents** can also be used in the post-purchase evaluation stage, when the buyer can continue to consult the information provided by online shopping agents in order to evaluate the value of the acquisition in comparison with other online offers (see Figure 1).

A somehow different model of consumer behaviour is presented by Guttman, Moukas and Maes (1998), which comprises six successive stages: (1) need identification, (2) product

Figure 1. The consumer decision-making process and the use of shopping agents

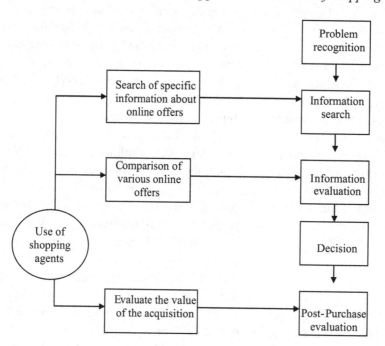

brokering, (3) merchant brokering, (4) negotiation, (5) purchase and delivery, and (6) service and evaluation. Their analysis indicates that online shopping agents are particularly useful for the stages of product brokering, merchant brokering, and, sometimes, negotiation.

Rowley (200b) presents the stages of product/service search using a shopping agent (see Figure 2). The process is sequential and logical, but does not provide any clues regarding the attitudes/behaviour of consumers during the search process. In terms of e-marketing, the factors that influence consumers' perceptions about the quality of shopping agents will determine the choice and use of a specific shopping agent, and finally, the level of satisfaction.

It is also logical to consider various elements that can influence the use of shopping agents and the satisfaction derived from their services. Sproule and Archer (2000) indicate a series of factors that determine a change in the type of information accessed by users and in their searching strategies, such as the purchasing situation (new versus frequent purchase) and the level of perceived risk (high versus low risk). Cooke, Sujan, Sujan and Weitz (2002) indicate that the online search strategy will be different for familiar and for unfamiliar products, focusing in their paper on the online marketing of unfamiliar products. Despite these studies, it is obvious that the range of factors that can influence the use of online shopping agents and the users' level of satisfaction is much bigger. The present study attempts to fill this literature gap, identifying, on the basis of primary data analysis, the various circumstantial or personal factors that can determine the choice of a specific search strategy and shopping agent.

The theories of **e-service quality** are based on the traditional **SERVQUAL** model (Parasuraman, Zeithaml, & Berry, 1988). This model is based

Figure 2. Stages in product search using a shopping bot (Rowley, 200b, p. 205)

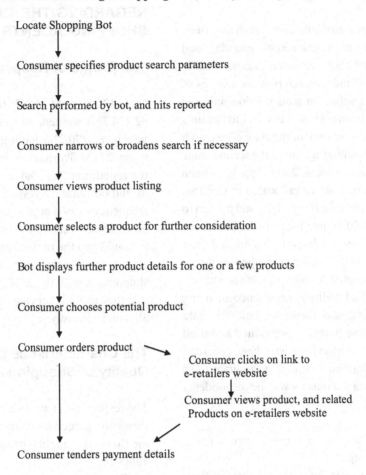

Locate Shopping Bot

Consumer specifies product search parameters

Search performed by bot, and hits reported

Consumer narrows or broadens search if necessary

Consumer views product listing

Consumer selects a product for further consideration

Bot displays further product details for one or a few products

Consumer chooses potential product

Consumer orders product

Consumer clicks on link to e-retailers website

Consumer views product, and related Products on e-retailers website

Consumer tenders payment details

on extensive research conducted by Parasuraman, Zeithaml, & Berry (1985 and 1988), who have initially defined ten determinants of service quality: tangibles, reliability, responsiveness, competency, courtesy, communication, credibility, security, access, and understanding the customer. Using factor analysis, these dimensions were later reduced to five features: tangibles, reliability, responsiveness, assurance and empathy.

The specific characteristics of the Internet have required a significant adaptation of these quality dimensions to online services. Zeithaml,

Parasuraman and Malhotra (2001 and 2002) have identified a series of **e-service quality** dimensions: reliability, responsibility, access, flexibility, ease of navigation, efficiency, assurance/trust, security, price knowledge, site aesthetics and customisation/personalisation, developing on their basis an **e-SERVQUAL** model.

However, these elements can be applied mainly for retail web-site, which have a higher level of complexity than shopping agents.

RESEARCH METHODOLOGY

In order to answer to the three research questions presented in the Introduction, both secondary and primary data have been accessed and analysed. In the first stage of the research process a series of texts published online, in academic journals and in books have been reviewed in order to obtain a comprehensive overview of the state of research in the area of shopping agents. In the second stage of data collection process, 200 people have been approached in Internet cafes located in London, Southampton and Edinburgh, UK, and invited to participate in a 20 minute face-to-face interview, regarding their use of shopping agents and their perception about the quality of shopping agents. 146 people accepted to take part in the survey, but only 121 had a direct experience of using shopping agents, and therefore, only the data provided by these people was retained and used for analysis. The interviews have been recorded and then transcribed in order to facilitate their analysis. During the interviews, the respondents were asked to:

- Describe their general experience in using shopping agents;
- Provide a series of elements that, in their opinion, determines the users' perception about the quality of shopping agents;
- Discuss the elements that could influence the users' perceptions about the quality of shopping agents;
- Indicate their usual searching strategy and the type of shopping agent they prefer.

Data about the profile of respondents was also collected, such as: gender, age, frequency of Internet usage, frequency of e-shopping and frequency of shopping agents' usage.

The transcribed interviews were than manually analysed, the identified patters of answers being codified and introduced into the SPSS software for frequency and cross-tabulation analysis.

USERS' PERCEPTIONS REGARDING THE QUALITY OF SHOPPING AGENTS

The Profile of Respondents

From 121 respondents, 79 (65.3%) were men and 42 (34.7%) women. Most of respondents were young, 85 (70.2%) having between 18 and 25 years, 27 (22.3%) having between 26 and 40, and the remaining 9 (7.5%) of respondents between 41 and 60 years. 66 respondents reported a high frequency of e-shopping (at least once a week), 38 indicated a medium frequency (at least once a month) and the remaining 17 a low e-shopping frequency (less than once a month). In terms of shopping agents' usage, 42 respondents indicate that they use this service regularly, 67 occasionally, and 12 rarely.

The Characteristics that Define the Quality of Shopping Agents

The respondents have indicated during the interviews the perceived characteristics that define, for them, the quality of **shopping agents** (see Table 2).

The capacity of the **shopping agent** to find the lower price offer is considered important by 81% of respondents. These are probably the 'bargain-oriented shoppers', which use the Internet primarily for the opportunity to find competitive price offers. Ease of interaction is outlined by 80.2% of respondents as an important quality dimension of shopping agents. This characteristic is a rather complex concept which includes: the **reliability** and the **functionality** of shopping agent website, the ease of navigation within the site, the clarity of various information/indications provided on the website, the tools available (search, select from a list, order the results in relation to various headings). 76.8% evaluate as important the precision of the shopping agent, defined as its capacity to find the required product. 70.2% of respondents expect to receive additional information about the offer and/or about the vendor, either in the form of short reports, or as links, that can then be explored by the user. Finally, 58.7% of respondents like the shopping agents that, beside the online offers, provide also access to product rankings or product reports written by previous customers. This service requires the existence of a specific software function which has to be actively implemented by the shopping agent.

The Differences Determined by the Customer Profile in the Perception of Shopping Agents' Quality

Considering the relative and subjective nature of perceiving e-services quality, it can be expected that the characteristics defining the quality of online **shopping agents** will vary in relation to the personal profile of respondents. In order to identify this variation, the four elements which have been selected to define the profile of the respondents in this study: (1) gender, (2) age, (3) frequency of e-shopping and (4) frequency of shopping agents' usage, have been cross-tabulated with the quality characteristics indicated by respondents.

The results presented in Table 3 indicate the influence of respondents' gender on the perceived quality characteristics of online **shopping agents**. Male respondents seem to consider more than the female respondents that the precision of the shop-

ping agent (in terms of finding the right product and the lower price), represents an important quality element. On the other hand, a larger proportion of women respondents indicated as important quality dimensions the provision of additional information about the offer and/or vendor (92.5%), the ease of interaction (97.5%) and the access to previous clients' ranking and/or recommendations. These variations can be explained by the differences in the shopping behaviour of men and women. Men seem to be more focused on the efficiency of the search process, while women like to have access to additional data in order to make a more informed choice.

The age of respondents is also determining a variation in the respondents' perception of the defined quality characteristics. The younger respondents are focused on the precision of shopping agents (both in terms of price and specific product), while the older respondents appreciate positively the capacity of the search engine to provide additional information and the ease of interaction. An interesting trend is the progression (or regression) of percentages from one group age to another. The regression is significant in what concerns the capacity to find the lower price offer (from 91.8% to respondents aged between 18 and 25 years old, to 22.2% of respondents aged between 41 to 60 years old). Similarly, the progression of percentages is important for the capacity of the shopping agent to provide additional information about the product and/or vendor, the ease

Table 2. Characteristics that define the quality of shopping agents

Quality element	Number	Frequencies
Capacity to find the lower price offer (C1)	98	81
Additional information about the offer and/or vendor (C2)	85	70.2
Capacity to find the required product C(3)	93	76.8
Ease of interaction C(4)	97	80.2
Previous clients' ranking and/or recommendations C(5)	71	58.7

Table 3. Cross-tabulation between the perceived quality elements and the gender of respondents

Quality element/ Gender	Male		Female		Total
	N	%	N	%	
Capacity to find the lower price offer (C1)	66	83.5	32	76.2	98
Additional information about the offer and/or vendor (C2)	46	58.2	39	92.8	85
Capacity to find the required product C(3)	68	86.1	25	59.5	93
Ease of interaction C(4)	56	70.9	41	97.6	97
Previous clients' ranking and/or recommendations C(5)	37	46.8	34	80.9	71
Total	79	100	42	100	

Table 4. Cross-tabulation between the perceived quality elements and the age of respondents

Quality element/ Age	18-25		26-40		41-60		Total
	N	%	N	%	N	%	
Capacity to find the lower price offer (C1)	78	91.8	18	66.7	2	22.2	98
Additional information about the offer and/or vendor (C2)	50	58.8	26	96.3	9	100	85
Capacity to find the required product C(3)	74	87	13	48.1	6	66.7	93
Ease of interaction C(4)	49	57.6	27	100	9	100	97
Previous clients' ranking and/or recommendations C(5)	41	48.2	22	81.5	8	88.9	71
Total	85	100	27	100	9	100	

Table 5. Cross-tabulation between the perceived quality elements and the frequency of e-shopping reported by respondents

Quality element/ E-shopping frequency	High		Medium		Low		Total
	N	%	N	%	N	%	
Capacity to find the lower price offer (C1)	64	97	25	65.8	9	52.9	98
Additional information about the offer and/or vendor (C2)	41	62.1	27	71	17	100	85
Capacity to find the required product C(3)	53	80.3	24	63.1	16	94.1	93
Ease of interaction C(4)	55	83.3	35	92.1	17	100	97
Previous clients' ranking and/or recommendations C(5)	38	57.6	18	47.4	15	88.2	71
Total	66	100	38	100	17	100	

of interaction and the access to previous clients' rankings and recommendations. These results can be explained by the need of older users to easily interact with the software application, and to compare in more detail the various offers selected by the shopping agent.

The frequent online shoppers seem to appreciate particularly the capacity of the shopping agent to find the lower price offer (97% of respondents from this category indicated this quality dimension as important). On the other hand, the people that are using less frequently the online market are interested in rich information and ease of interaction (all the respondents defined as less frequent shoppers indicated this element as important), but also in the capacity of the shopping agent to identify properly the required product (94.1% of respondents from this category considered this important). These results are logical, considering that the less frequent shoppers associate online transactions with high levels of risk, and therefore require precise and extensive information about the offer and the vendor. However, additional research it is necessary to provide an unambiguous interpretation of the data presented in Table 5.

The trends identified in relation to the e-shopping frequency are similar with the results based on the frequency of shopping agent usage (see Table 6). This might indicate that frequent e-shoppers are also using frequently online shopping agents, projecting in their responses their specific behavioural profile. However, this is not entirely true, because the frequent users of online shopping agents represent only 63.6% of the respondents that have indicated a frequent e-shopping behaviour. Again, more research is necessary to understand why some frequent shoppers are not also frequent users of online shopping agents. A possible explanation is their preference to shop mostly from known and trusted online vendor, which eliminates the need for shopping agent services.

The Transaction Factors Influencing the Perceived Quality of Shopping Agents

The relative importance of quality dimensions is different in relation to various transaction-related elements. The respondents indicated that the most important transaction elements influencing the perceived quality of shopping agents are: level of selling price, familiarity of with the product, familiarity with the vendor, length of product use, and the time available for decision and purchas-

ing. The results displayed in Table 3 present the evaluation of respondents regarding the influence of various transaction factors on the shopping agents' quality dimensions. The two figures displayed near each of the five quality characteristics represent the number and respectively, the percentage of respondents who considered the characteristic as important in that particular transaction circumstance.

In a situation of a high selling price the capacity of the **shopping agent** to identify the lower price offer is considered important by the majority of respondents. High percentages are also provided for the capacity of the shopping agent to select the required product, to provide additional information about offer and/or vendor, as well as for the rankings and comments of previous customers. These results can be explained by the high transaction risk that is associated with a high product price. Gradually, as the price level becomes medium and low, the need for additional information becomes less important. The need for a precise selection of the lower price offer and of the required products is lower when the price is small, but the percentage of respondents that consider these factors as important still remains relatively high. The proportion of people that indicated the ease of interaction as important remains quite stable in all three price situations.

As expected, a low familiarity of the customer with the product determines a high demand for information related to the offer, vendor and previous customers' experience. Inversely, the shoppers that are familiar with the product indicate a low importance of additional information, focusing their needs on the capacity of the shopping agent to precisely identify the best price offer and a specific product.

When the product acquired online will be used a long time, the respondents consider as particularly important the capacity to obtain rich information about the product, vendor and previous customers' experience. This tendency is determined by the risk associated with the transac-

Table 6. Cross-tabulation between the perceived quality elements and the frequency of shopping agents usage reported by respondents

Quality element/ Shopping agents usage	Regularly N	Regularly %	Occasionally N	Occasionally %	Rarely N	Rarely %	Total
Capacity to find the lower price offer (C1)	40	95.2	51	76.1	7	58.3	98
Additional information about the offer and/or vendor (C2)	36	85.7	38 56.7		11	91.7	85
Capacity to find the required product C(3)	35	83.3	46	68.6	12	100	93
Ease of interaction C(4)	23	54.8	62	92.5	12	100	97
Previous clients' ranking and/or recommendations C(5)	28	66.7	32	47.8	11	91.7	71
Total	42	100	67	100	12	100	

Table 7. The influence of various transaction elements on users' perception of quality characteristics of shopping agents

	High level	Medium level	Low level
Selling price	C1 - 116 - 95.9% C2 - 105 - 86.8% C3 - 98 - 80.9% C4 - 83 - 68.6% C5 - 107 - 88.4%	C1 - 107 - 88.4% C2 - 102 - 84.3% C3 - 97 - 80.2% C4 - 80 - 66.1% C5 - 85 - 70.2%	C1 - 72 - 59.5% C2 - 35 - 28.9% C3 - 81 - 66.9% C4 - 79 - 65.3% C5 - 42 - 34.7%
Familiarity with product	C1 - 105 - 86.8% C2 - 27 - 22.3% C3 - 101 - 83.5% C4 - 79 - 65.3% C5 - 11 - 9.1%	C1 - 94 - 77.7% C2 - 71 - 58.7% C3 - 108 - 89.2% C4 - 91 - 75.2% C5 - 84 - 69.4%	C1 - 101 - 83.5% C2 - 121 - 100% C3 - 119 - 98.3% C4 - 97 - 80.2% C5 - 118 - 97.5%
Familiarity with vendor	C1 - 59 - 48.8% C2 - 25 - 20.7% C3 - 63 - 52.1% C4 - 89 - 73.5% C5 - 14 - 11.6%	C1 - 71 - 58.7% C2 - 66 - 54.5% C3 - 81 - 66.9% C4 - 87 - 71.9% C5 - 79 - 65.3%	C1 - 76 - 62.8% C2 - 109 - 90.1% C3 - 87 - 71.9% C4 - 89 - 73.5% C5 - 113 - 93.4%
Length of product use	C1 - 82 - 67.8% C2 - 118 - 97.5% C3 - 96 - 79.3% C4 - 86 - 71.1% C5 - 105 - 86.8%	C1 - 83 - 68.6% C2 - 74 - 61.1% C3 - 91 - 75.2% C4 - 104 - 85.9% C5 - 82 - 67.8%	C1 - 89 - 73.5% C2 - 48 - 39.7% C3 - 77 - 63.6% C4 - 89 - 73.5% C5 - 35 - 28.9%
Time available	C1 - 75 - 61.9% C2 - 34 - 28.1% C3 - 42 - 34.7% C4 - 69 - 57% C5 - 21 - 17.3%	C1 - 79 - 65.3% C2 - 86 - 71.1% C3 - 54 - 44.6% C4 - 101 - 83.5% C5 - 48 - 39.7%	C1 - 115 - 95% C2 - 104 - 85.9% C3 - 121 - 100% C4 - 119 - 98.3% C5 - 113 - 93.4%

tion, taking into account that, usually, the products with a long life-time are also relatively expensive. However, the other quality characteristics are also considered important by a large proportion of respondents, the profile of results being quite similar with the data provided in the case of expensive products. This similarity is also preserved in the evolution of percentages for products with a medium lifetime and for products with a short lifetime. Interestingly, in this last situation, the shopper is specifically interested in the capacity of the shopping agent to provide the best price offer, indicating that the shopping decision might be determined by the level of price.

The answers provided are particularly interesting when the shopper has a very short time to find the desired product and to conduct the transaction. In this case, all the five quality dimensions are indicated as highly important by a very large proportion of respondents. The percentages are decreasing progressively when the customer has more time to conclude the transaction, which creates better conditions for a thorough information search and comparison of various available offers.

FUTURE TRENDS

Although the **functionality** of **shopping agents** has continuously evolved in the last 10 years, there is still significant scope for their further improvement and development (Rowley, 2000b). Maes, Guttman and Moukas (1999) suggest four functions that can be included in the shopping agents' range of services:

- automatically build models (profiles) of shoppers;
- recommend products to shoppers;
- negotiate on behalf of shoppers;
- personalise the **shopping experience**.

Some of these predictions are already a reality. A specific category of shopping agents, the recommendation agents, have the capacity to memorise the interaction history with a specific shopper, providing recommendations for new, sometimes even unsolicited products, based of the shopper's pattern of preferences. For example, the shopping agents that are active on the Amazon. com website may recommend to shoppers CD offers with music that matches their reading preferences. The technology used in these situations

is based on shopping agents with the capacity to memorise, learn, and identify a specific pattern of consumption. The value of the service provided to the user is thus increased, enhancing the **shopping experience** and the level of customer satisfaction. However, one problem related with these learning shopping agents is their capacity to collect information about the shopping profile of particular customers, information that can be sold, transmitted to, and used without the consent of the shopper, by other vendors or market research companies. A solution to this privacy threat is the development of personal shopping agents that can be eventually created, trained and used (with the help of specific online applications) by individual shoppers. These agents may incorporate not only the capacity to search for specific online offers, on the basis of the specifications provided by the user, but also functions such as negotiation and buying.

CONCLUSION

Despite the increased importance of **shopping agents** for the development of online consumer markets and transactions, the existing literature has not yet considered the specific quality characteristics of shopping agents, as they are perceived by users, in relation to their personal profile and the specific circumstances of various transactions. This study has adopted an exploratory approach, attempting to provide an insight into the way in which users perceive, use and evaluate online shopping agents.

The study has a number of limitations, determined by its exploratory approach. The sample of respondents is relatively small, and the data provided was analysed at a general level. The focus of this project was more to understand what are the perceived quality dimensions of the online shopping agents, and what are the factors that influence this perception (personal and transactional), rather than finding out why the respondents are perceiving a specific quality dimensions of e-shopping agents. This empirical problem requires further research, in which the statistical analysis of quantitative data has to be complemented by a qualitative approach. This approach can provide a better understanding of the way in which online customers interact with shopping agents.

REFERENCES

Aggarwal, P., & Vaidyanathan, R. (2003). The perceived effectiveness of virtual shopping agents for search vs. experience goods. *Advances in Consumer Research, 30*, 347-348.

Armstrong, A., & Hagel, J. III. (1996). The real value of online communities. *Harvard Business Review, 74*(3), 134–141.

Blattberg, R. C., & Deighton, J. (1996). Manage Marketing by the Customer Equity Test. *Harvard Business Review*, 74(4), 136-144.

Blattberg, R. C., Glazer, R., & Little, J.D.C. (eds.) (1994). Introduction. *The Marketing Information Revolution, 1*. Boston: Harvard Business School Press.

Brassington, F., & Petitt, S. (1997). *Principles of Marketing*. London: Pitman Publishing.

Engel, J. F., Blackwell, R. D., & Miniard, P. W. (1990). *Consumer Behaviour*. Hinsdale: Dryden.

Cooke, A. D. J., Sujan, H., Sujan, M., & Weitz, B.A. (2002). Marketing the Unfamiliar: The Role of Context and Item-Specific Information in Electronic Agent Recommendations. *Journal of Marketing Research, 39*(4), 488-497.

Guttman, R. H., Moukas, A. G., & Maes, P. (1998). Agents as Mediators in Electronic Commerce. *International Journal of Electronic Markets, 8*(1), 22-27.

Guttman, R.H., Moukas, A., & Maes, P. (1999). Agent-mediated Electronic Commerce: A Survey, *Knowledge Engineering Review, 13*(2), 147-159.

Hoffman, D. L., & Novak, T. P. (1996). Marketing in Hypermedia Computer-Mediated Environments: Conceptual Foundations. *Journal of Marketing, 80*(4), 50-68.

Iyer, G., & Pazgal, A. (2003). Internet Shopping Agents: Virtual Co-Location and Competition. *Marketing Science, 22*(1), pp. 85-106.

Kerstetter, J. (1999). New generation of shopping 'bots swarms in. *ZFDnet.co.uk*. Retrieved June 2007, from http://news.zdnet.co.uk/internet/0,1000000097,2073092,00.htm.

Kiani, R. G. (1998). Marketing opportunities in the digital world. *Internet Research: Networking Applications and Policy*, 8(2), 185-194.

Maes, P., Guttman, R., & Moukas, A. (1999). Agents that buy and sell: transforming commerce as we know it. *Communications of the ACM, 42*(3), 81-91.

Martin, J. (1996). *Cybercorp: The New Business Revolution*. New York: AMACOM.

McKenna, R. (1995). Real-Time Marketing. *Harvard Business Review, 73*(4), 87-96.

Parasuraman, A., Zeithaml, V. A., & Berry, L. L. (1985). A Conceptual Model of Service Quality and Its Implications for Future Research. *Journal of Marketing, 49*(4), 41-50.

Parasuraman, A., Zeithaml, V. A, & Berry, L. L. (1988). SERVQUAL: a multiple-item scale for measuring consumer perceptions of quality. *Journal of Retailing, 64*(1), 12-40.

Rayport, J. F., & Sviokla, J. J. (1995). Exploiting the Virtual Value Chain. *Harvard Business Review, 73*(6), 75-85.

Rowley, J. (2000a). Product search in e-shopping: a review and research propositions. *Journal of Consumer Marketing, 17*(1), 20-35.

Rowley, J. (2000b). Product searching with shopping bots, *Internet Research: Eletronic Networking Applications and Policy, 10*(3), 203-214.

Rowley, J. (2002). 'Window' shopping and browsing opportunities in cyberspace. *Journal of Consumer Behaviour, 1*(4), 369-378.

Sen, R., King, R. C., & Shaw, M. J. (2006). Buyers' Choice of Online Search Strategy and Its Managerial Implications. *Journal of Management Information Systems, 23*(1), 211-238.

Sproule, S., & Archer, N. (2000). A buyer behaviour framework for the development and design of software agents in e-commerce. *Internet Research: Electronic Networking Applications and Policy, 10*(5), 396-405.

Zeithaml, V. A., Parasuraman, A., & Malhotra, A. (2001). A conceptual framework for understanding e-service quality: implications for future research and managerial practice. *MSI Working Paper Series*, No 00-115, Cambridge MA, 1-49.

Zeithaml, V. A., Parasuraman, A., & Malhotra, A. (2002). Service quality delivery through Web sites: a critical review of extant knowledge. *Journal of the Academy of Marketing Science, 30*(4), 362-375.

ADDITIONAL READINGS

Dignum, F., & Siera, C. (Eds.) (2001). *Agent Mediated Electronic Commerce: The European AgentLink Perspective.* London: Springer.

Fasli, M. (2007). *Agent Technology For E-Commerce.* Chichester: Wiley & Sons.

Gay, R., Charlesworth, A., & Esen, R. (2007). *Online Marketing: A Customer-Led Approach.* Oxford: Oxford University Press.

Henderson-Sellers, B., & Giorgini, P. (2005). *Agent-oriented Methodologies.* Hershey: IDEA Group Publishing.

Lain, L.C., Chen, Z., & Ichalkaranje, N. (Eds.) (2002). *Intelligent Agents and Their Applications.* Heidelberg: Physica-Verlag.

Liu, J., & Ye, Y. (Eds.) (2001). *E-Commerce Agents: Marketplace Solutions, Security Issues, and Supply and Demand.* London: Springer.

Padgham, L., & Winikoff, M. (2004). *Developing Intelligent Agent Systems: A Practical Guide.* Chichester: Wiley & Sons.

Pal, N., & Rangaswamy, A. (2006). *The Power of One: Gaining Business Value from Personalization Technologies.* Penn State University: eBRC Press.

Rahman, S.M., & Bignall, R.J. (2001). *Internet Commerce and Software Agents: Cases, Technologies and Opportunities.* Hershey: IDEA Group Publishing.

Shaw, M., Blanning, R., & Strader, T. (Eds.) (2000). *Handbook on Electronic Commerce.* London: Springer.

KEY TERMS

Bargain-Oriented Shoppers: Buyers that search for the best existing offers, attempting to maximise the rapport between quality and price for the product/services they buy.

E-Commerce: The process of buying and selling goods and/or services using the Internet.

Individualised Marketing: A marketing strategy in which the firm adapts its commercial and promotional activities to the specific characteristics of individual customers.

Mass Marketing: A marketing strategy in which the firm attempts to attract one or more large customer segments with a standardised offer or products/services.

Megabrand: A brand of products and or services that is widely known, recognised and bought by consumers, generating a large and constant amount of revenues.

SERVQUAL: A theoretical model developed by Zeithaml, Parasuraman and Berry which can be used to evaluate service quality.

Shopping Agent: Specialised software application that can be interactively used by customers to search for and compare Stores, Products/Services or Prices, on the basis of specific selection criteria.

Chapter XI
Multi–Channel Retailing and Customer Satisfaction

Patricia T. Warrington
Texas Christian University, USA

Adam Hagen
Purdue University, USA

Richard Feinberg
Purdue University, USA

ABSTRACT

Customer satisfaction/dissatisfaction can occur at/after the store, on the telephone, on the internet, after a catalog purchase. Customer satisfaction leads to repurchase/loyalty. Customer dissatisfaction leads to lower repurchase/loyalty. However, no research has looked at how satisfaction/dissatisfaction (S/D) in one channel affects the repurchase/loyalty in the same or different channels and the same/different stores. While S/D will increase/decrease the S/D in the same channel it does not always affect S/D in other channels the same way. In addition, S/D in a channel in one retailer may affect S/D in that same channel but in a different retailer.

INTRODUCTION

Retail success has really never been a secret. Michael Porter defined the secrets very clearly (but few have listened well ...except maybe WalMart*and Disney). According to Porter (1985)

a retailer can have unique products and services. A retailer can have the lowest prices. A retailer can provide a differentiated and/or interesting experience. Now, today, whatever the foundation the retailer chooses for success, they must be where the customer wants when they want it...anytime, anywhere, any place, anyhow (Feinberg, Trotter, & Anton, 2000).

The problem with unique products and services is that there really is no such thing as uniqueness because so much is so easily copied. The problem with low price is that although the business captures large market share that market share does not mean profitability unless your cost structure is lower than the competition (like WalMart*). (Few people realize that WalMart*'s success is not that they have "everyone's grandparent" greeting you as you walk in but because they sell merchandise (what the customer wants) before they have to pay for it and have a super efficient and effective distribution system (which means a very low cost structure and lower prices to the consumer while still making money). Today, success is defined by a multichannel presence. Customers want seamless multi-channel access (Chu & Pike, 2002; Close, 2002; Johnson, 2004; Pastore, 2000; Thompson, 2003). The reason is quite simple – retailers must be where shoppers want them, when they want them...anytime, anywhere, and in multiple formats (Feinberg, Trotter, & Anton, 2000). If customers want to shop from a store, retailers must have a physical location; if customers want to shop over the telephone, retailers must be available by phone; if customers want to shop over the Internet, retailers must be accessible online. And, in the future, if customers want to shop via a wireless device, retailers must be available by wireless. Multi-channel access is considered one of the top ten trends for all businesses in the next decade (Ernst & Young, 2003; Feinberg & Trotter, 2003; Levy & Weitz, 2003). Indeed, surveys show that consumers not only want multi-channel access, they expect it (Burke, 2000; Johnson, 2004).

Electronic customer relationship management (eCRM) has the potential to enable retailers to better meet the needs of their customers across retail formats and, at the same time, maximize the strategic benefits of a multi-channel strategy. By effectively using modern information technology,

retailers are able to offer shoppers the advantages of a one-to-one relationship yet reap the profit savings that accrue from mass-market operating efficiencies (Chen & Chen, 2004). Customer retention lies at the heart of eCRM. As such, eCRM is increasingly viewed as vital to building and maintaining customer loyalty.

The research on eCRM has been very conceptual in nature outlining research agendas and possible strategic models of the nature and scope of eCRM (e.g., Parasuraman & Zinkham, 2002; Varadarajan & Yadav, 2002). The most recent review of the eCRM literature suggests that we really know three things about eCRM (Zeithaml, Parasuraman and Malhotra, 2002).

1. eCRM is multidimensional and each study examines a "favorite" attribute it finds to be important. But, as yet, we do not know if ease of use, privacy, site design, or any of a variety of attributes is determinant of some eCRM outcome.
2. Consumers really care about eCRM after negative online shopping or service experiences. Consumers seem less concerned with eCRM issues following routine web interactions.
3. While there is anecdotal evidence to suggest e-satisfaction to be important for purchase, repurchase and loyalty, the evidence is simply not empirical and/or strong.

In reading Zeithaml, Parasuraman, and Malhotra's review of the eCRM literature, it appears that eCRM is seen as an independent issue from other points (channels) of satisfaction. This may actually simplify a more complex process that is going on. eCRM is part of a broader issue of customer satisfaction. What happens in the "e" channel, what happens in the store channel, and what happens in any other channel has an effect within the channel it occurs and in the retailer's other channels.

Satisfaction is a key determinant of retail customer loyalty (Cronin, Brady, & Hult, 2000). To date, the extant research is relatively silent regarding the effect of shopping satisfaction (or dissatisfaction) on consumers' channel choices. Our research involves two questions:

1. What is the effect of a shopping experience with a retailer in one particular channel with future channel shopping intentions? What is the likelihood of purchase from a retailer in the same or different channel following a positive or negative shopping experience?
2. What is the effect of service failure (customer dissatisfaction) and possible recovery in a multichannel retail environment? What is the likelihood of repurchase from the same or different channels given service failure and recovery in one channel of purchase?

CUSTOMER SATISFACTION AND MULTI-CHANNEL RETAILING

Multi-channel access allows retailers to reach a greater market and to leverage their skills and assets to increase sales and profits. It allows a single organization to overcome the limitations of any single channel. The goal of retailing is to attract consumers, keep consumers, and increase "wallet share," and a multi-channel presence increases the probability of all three (Chu and Pike, 2002).

One can construct an argument for the importance of multi-channel retailing for retail success by noticing that most of retail sales on the Internet are done by multi-channel retailers (Johnson, 2004). Research on multi-channel retailing has focused on the factors that drive channel choice (e.g., Burke, 2000; Chu & Pike, 2002; Inman, Shankar, & Ferraro 2004; Wu, Mahajan, & Balasubramanian, 2003) and the nature of the multi-channel shopping experience generally (Burke, 2000). As reported by Chu

and Pike (2002), the National Retail Federation's Shop.org found that 78% of online shoppers also made a purchase at the retailer's physical store and 45% bought merchandise from the retailer's catalog. The same study reported that 23% of catalog shoppers also shopped at the retailer's Internet site (e.g., Eddie Bauer catalog shopper also purchased at eddiebauer.com). Only 6% of store shoppers purchased from the retailer's online site. However, slightly more than half of catalog shoppers and 75% of store shoppers search for pre-purchase information online.

Unfortunately, research has neglected the complex relationship between shopping experiences and future shopping behavior in a multi-channel environment. The complexity of the relationship between store-based, catalog, and online shopping extends beyond the mere description of what people are doing inter- and intra-channel. It encompasses the relationship between encounters in one channel and subsequent decisions to shop in the same or another channel. Is a good experience in one channel equivalent to a good experience in another channel as it relates to future channel choice? Indeed a recent study showed very clearly that there are tradeoffs that consumers make between channels and these tradeoffs are not equal; a positive/negative experience differs in value depending on the channel and the resulting choices differ as well (Keen, Wetzels, de Ruyter, & Feinberg, 2004).

Substantial research supports the premise that satisfaction/dissatisfaction of customer experience in a store has a direct impact on the probability of revisit to the store (e.g., Feinberg, 2001; Fornell, Johnson, Anderson, Cha, & Bryant, 1996; Loveman, 1998; Rust & Zahorik, 1993; Rust, Zeithaml, & Lemon, 2000). Satisfaction is generally viewed as the foundation for any marketing relationship (e.g., Morgan & Hunt 1994; Selnes, 1998). Research on e-retailing has been founded on the same premise with the same general finding: customer satisfaction is related to return visits to a website (Balasubramanian, Konana, & Menon

2003; Freed, 2003; Reibstein, 2002; Zeithaml, Parasuraman, & Malholtra, 2002). The belief in customer satisfaction as the "prime directive" of the retail-consumer relationships is further supported by the extensive range of popular books on the subject (e.g., Blanchard & Bowles, 1993; Sewell & Brown, 2002). If customer satisfaction is important for decisions in one channel alone, there is likely to be some relationship between the satisfaction in one channel and future channel decisions. Multi-channel retailers will benefit from understanding the nuances of these effects and be better able to successfully implement and fine-tune eCRM strategies.

PURDUE STUDIES

Over the past three years we have conducted a series of experimental studies where we control the outcome and experience in a particular channel and watch behavior and test attitudes in the same and other channels. Here is what we have learned:

Q1- What is the effect of a shopping experience with a retailer in one particular channel with future channel shopping intentions?

Positive retail encounters influence the likelihood that consumers will revisit and possibly buy again from a retailer on future shopping trips (Cronin, Brady, & Hult, 2000). Thus, satisfied shoppers are likely to shop again from a given retailer in the same channel (i.e., store, catalog, or Internet). In other words, a positive experience with Retailer A in a particular channel (e.g., store) will have an impact on a subsequent decision to patronize Retailer A in that same channel.

We have also found that a favorable shopping experience with a retailer in a particular channel is likely to increase the possibility of shopping with the retailer across all channels. Brand recognition and the value associated with the retailer in one channel is transferred to the retailer in all channels in the same manner that positive beliefs about a core brand favorably influence consumers' evaluations of the brand's extensions (e.g., Randall, Ulrich & Reibstein, 1998). This effect occurs as a result of a categorization process whereby feelings and beliefs are transferred by association to other stimuli that are similar. For example, a consumer's positive experience with a multi-channel retailer in the store channel leads to the belief that the consumer will have a positive shopping experience at the retailer's website or from the retailer's catalog. Negative experiences should lead to lower probability in the same way; that is, a negative shopping experience at the retailer's store lowers the probability of shopping at the retailer's Internet site or from their catalog.

Consumer's preference for e-retailing is increasing in popularity. Increased broadband access has driven an increase in e-shopping. There are still consumers who have not "e-shopped". But do it one time you do it a second time. The growth of e-retailing is based on new first time doers and increasing multiple time shoppers. It is logical to assume a satisfying shopping experience in a given channel will influence preference for that channel in the future. A positive shopping experience online is likely to build a consumer's confidence in shopping online, which, in turn, enhances the likelihood of shopping online in the future. Similarly, a positive catalog shopping experience is likely to reinforce a consumer's decision to shop and purchase from catalogs in the future. Alternatively, a negative shopping experience in a given channel is likely to have an unfavorable impact on the probability of shopping in the channel in the future.

Whereas subjects' responses across channels were similar for positive experiences, future purchase intentions for negative shopping experiences varied. We found that that channels are not neutral vessels of experience but differ in important ways. Internet shoppers were significantly more likely to patronize another channel (with the same retailer) than were store shoppers or catalog shoppers following a dissatisfactory experience. Intuitively, this seems reasonable as Internet shoppers are usually store shoppers as well, but store shoppers are not always Internet shoppers. In other words, when a consumer's Internet shopping encounter is less than satisfactory, the person is likely to attribute some of the negative experience to the channel. For a store shopper, the negative encounter will weaken the likelihood the person will consider shopping with the retailer online or through a catalog. Thus, channel characteristics play a role in how a negative encounter influences a shopper's future shopping intentions.

Dissatisfied catalog shoppers were equally as likely as satisfied catalog shoppers to consider making a future purchase from a catalog retailer in the future. The effect of a negative catalog shopping encounter seems to have very little effect on the decision to shop in the future from catalog retailers. A negative shopping encounter significantly increased the likelihood that a store shopper would purchase from a competing store retailer. Interestingly, the effect was reversed for the Internet shoppers. A negative shopping encounter significantly decreased the likelihood that an Internet shopper would purchase from a competing Internet retailer. In other words, satisfied Internet shoppers were more likely than dissatisfied Internet shoppers to express a willingness to purchase from a competing Internet retailer. Thus, satisfied Internet shoppers will return to the channel again but not the retailer. In essence, all Internet retailers benefit from positive Internet experiences. On the other hand, dissatisfied Internet shoppers will not only choose another retailer, but they will also choose another channel. This could mean that repeat purchase behavior, and even customer loyalty, is more difficult to sustain in the Internet channel as compared to other retail channels. Further research is needed to more thoroughly investigate these interpretations.

We replicated the study using a Dutch sample of consumers. There were significant European/American differences and these are important. The differences by sample group suggest that there are differing retail experiences across cultures and these differences affect consumer behavior. The lack of consistency in the findings here suggests that cross cultural studies need to be very careful in explaining and generalizing their findings. European studies need to be sensitive to the fact that their results might differ from US results and vice versa. Internet/Store/Catalog shopping in the US differs from Europe and these differences may result in consumer behavior that differs for the same stimulus environment.

Q2- What is the effect of service failure (customer dissatisfaction) and possible recovery in a multi-channel retail environment?

In a perfect world, retailers would always meet or exceed the expectations of their customers. Customers would always be able to find the product they want, at the price they want to pay, in the channel they wish to transact in, without encountering any problems regarding out of stock items, poor treatment by the retailer, or dissatisfactory purchases. Many retailers have implemented customer relationship management strategies in an attempt to satisfy consumers in all of their encounters with the retailer and to effectively manage their operations (Chan, 2005; Feinberg et al, 2002). Unfortunately the reality exists that breakdowns will occur between the retailer and the customer due to uncertainties and complexities that arise within the relationships between suppliers, the retail structure, technological mediums, and front line employees' interactions with consumers.

These breakdowns are referred to as service failures and occur any time that a customer perceives a discrepancy between their expectations and their perceptions of the experience (Gronroos, 1988; Parasuraman, Zeithaml, and Berry,

1985). Bitner, Booms, and Tetreault's (1990) defined three broad groups of service failures (employee response to service delivery system failures, employee response to customer needs and requests, and unprompted and unsolicited employee actions), fifteen specific subgroups were identified. Policy failures, slow or unavailable service, system pricing, packaging errors, out of stock items, product defects, hold disasters, and bad information comprise failures attributed to employee response to service delivery system/ product errors. Employee response to customer needs and requests was broken into two subgroups, order and request and admitted customer error. Being mischarged, accusations of shoplifting, embarrassments, and attention failures comprised the final group of failures stemming from unsolicited employee actions (Kelley, Hoffman, and Davis, 1993).

Despite the fact that service failures will inevitably occur, the retailer has the option of implementing means to deal with the situation in an attempt to satisfy the customer. Any action taken by the retailer to rectify the situation and restore customer satisfaction is referred to as service recovery (Gronroos, 1988). Some typical forms of recovering from failure that have been found to lead to satisfaction include offering discounts, manager/other employee intervention, correction of the initial problem plus additional compensation, apology, refund, product replacement, and correction such as locating misplaced merchandise or making immediate repairs. Other retailer responses to failure that have been found unacceptable include failure escalation, store credit, unsatisfactory correction such as faulty repairs, and the "non-recovery" strategy of doing nothing to remedy the situation (Kelley, Hoffman, and Davis, 1993). Unfortunately a "one size fits all" method of recovering from failure does not exist as a customer's dissatisfaction with the failure and subsequent satisfaction or dissatisfaction with the recovery lie in his/her perceptions of equity in the process and outcome.

Numerous studies have examined the antecedents of satisfaction with recovery and the effects of a customer's satisfaction with recovery efforts on their subsequent likelihood of repeat patronage or future actions against the retailer (Bansal et al, 2004; Burnham et al, 2003; Moshe, 2003; Stauss, 2002; Aron, 2001 Andreassen, 2000; Hoffman and Kelley, 2000; Tax and Brown, 1998; Tax et al, 1998; Blodgett et al, 1997). Some differences in satisfaction and repeat purchasing result from the type of failure the retailer is recovering from. Stauss (2002) found that recovery from outcome failures significantly increased customer satisfaction with the handling of the complaint, but process recoveries lead to increased repurchase behavior.

Other studies have focused on the customer's perceptions of equity in the resolution of failure rather than specifically at the type of failure that has occurred. A recurring theme in this stream of research has been that the exact failure and type of recovery are inconsequential as compared to the perceived equity that arises from the failure/recovery incidents from the consumer's standpoint. Andreassen (2000) found that equitable recovery leads to customer satisfaction with the recovery effort regardless of the initial negative affect that the consumer holds after the initial failure incident. They key to satisfactory recovery efforts is for the retailer to provide a solution that restores equity to the relationship. The recovery tactic must be perceived as at least as great as the cost of the failure.

Furthermore, a customer may view the recovery efforts along differing dimensions of justice in the resolution of the failure. Satisfaction with the recovery effort is based in the perceived justice from the ending outcome the customer receives (such as the product), the means in which the retailer overcomes the recovery (the processes employed in the recovery attempt), as well as the interactions that occur between the customer and the retailer throughout the process (interpersonal communication). These dimensions have been defined as distributive, procedural, and inter-actional justice (Tax et al, 1998). The retailer's response must meet the customer's expectations along each dimension to adequately recover from failure. This fact reinforces the notion that there is no single solution to failure and that retailers must adapt strategies to deal with customers on an individual basis as those customers may view the same failure differently or put more value on a particular dimension or take a holistic view across dimensions (Hoffman and Kelley, 2000; Kelley, Hoffman, and Davis, 1993).

The implementation of recovery has various effects on the retailer. Not only does successful recovery lead to satisfied customers and customer retention (Bansal et al, 2004; Burnham et al, 2003; Moshe, 2003; Blodgett et al, 1997; Kelley, Hoffman, and Davis, 1993), but it also has an impact on the profitably of the individual customer involved with the failure incident as well as other customers. In some cases, a customer becomes more profitable to the retailer after a failure has been addressed properly. Satisfactory recovery leads to customer loyalty and also sparks positive word of mouth in which the customer aids in bringing new customers to the retail establishment (Moshe, 2003; Tax and Brown, 1998). Failing to recover has a reciprocal effect. When the recovery attempt does not meet the consumer's standards of procedural justice, customer dissatisfaction, defection, and negative word of mouth transpire (Bansal et al, 2004; Moshe, 2003; Blodgett et al, 1997). A lack of satisfactory recovery efforts from failure may also lead to the extreme of consumer grudgeholding wherein the customer views the failure as a flashpoint that if not properly resolved may lead not only to defection or negative word of mouth but also to more extreme forms of retaliation against the retailer such as threats or legal action (Aron, 2001).

One could conceive of the relationship between service failure recovery and channel as a problem of balance. Heider's (1958) balance theory has been used to illuminate relationships or attitudes consisting of more than two individuals, entities, or attitude objects. The relational paths between objects may represent direct associations from relationships or from similarities and differences between attitude objects. In any context, individuals strive to exist in a balanced state. Similar to the equitable state wherein inputs equal outputs in equity theory, balance theory proposes that individuals must have harmonious sentiments between multiple players.

Under the assumptions of balance theory, various relationships may from triads from which balance is desired (See Figures 1 and 2). Typically, a positive relationship is denoted as +, and a negative relationship is denoted as -. When observing a triad, the product of multiplying the positive or negative paths will result in a balanced (+) state or an unbalanced state (-). Individuals who find themselves in an unbalanced state are expected to change their attitudes, actions, or relations to maintain a positive balance and avoid cognitive dissonance. A simplistic example follows in which you have three individuals: James, Jon, and Nick. If Nick likes Jon (Nick to Jon path is positive), and Jon dislikes James (Jon to James path is negative), then Nick will also dislike James (Nick to James path is negative). Using the previous example, if Nick likes Jon, and Jon dislikes James, but Nick still has a positive or liking relationship with James, an unbalanced (negative product) of the relational paths occurs. In this case it is expected that the tensions of the relationships will cause a change to occur which will restore a balanced state.

In the retail setting, two competing retailers should appear opposed to each other in the customer's mind (a negative relational path). For balance to uphold, the customer should only feel positive attitudes towards one of the retailers and a negative attitude toward the other. In the case that the relational inputs change due to some incident (as is with inequity in equity theory),

Figure 1. The relationship between service failure recovery and consumer behavior with service recovery

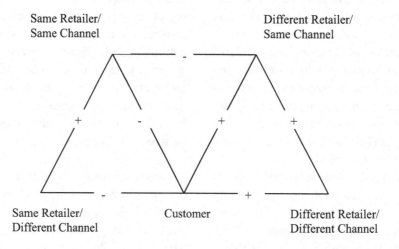

Figure 2. The relationship between service failure recovery and consumer behavior without service recovery

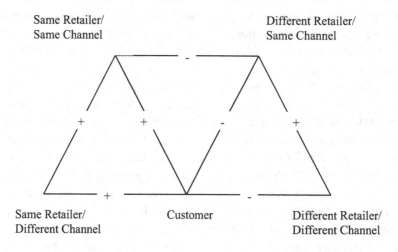

the other relational paths must change in accordance. In a similar matter, attitudes towards other divisions of a particular retailer can also be examined with balance. A retailer's website, catalog, and physical store should be linked by a positive association, and the customer should try to preserve balance in his/her attitudes to the segments of the retailer.

After encountering service failure, a customer's repeat purchase intentions with the same retailer in the same channel was higher for those who received service recovery than those who did not. After encountering service failure, a customer's purchase intentions with a different retailer in the same channel was higher for those who did not receive service recovery than those who did. After encountering service failure, a customer's purchase intentions with the same retailer in a different channel will be higher for those who received service recovery than those who did not. After encountering service failure, a customer's purchase intentions with a different retailer in a different channel will be higher for those who did not receive service recovery than those who did.

CONCLUSION

If retailers are not offering shoppers multiple channel options now it is expected that pressure will increase for all retailers to do so in the future. The findings of our studies suggest that above all else channel satisfaction/dissatisfaction is a significant issue – but not in an equal way. For some channels satisfaction/dissatisfaction has a greater or lesser impact. In addition channels are not all equal. Independent of satisfaction and dissatisfaction the likelihood of switching channels and switching retailer's differs across the three channels studied.

Here are the major lessons learned from these studies:

1. A positive experience is the prime directive for any retailer hoping to keep a consumer loyal to any particular channel.
2. A positive experience in the Internet channel may actually increase the likelihood of trying the Internet channel of another retailer. This may have significant implications for e-retailing. Clearly the goal of e-retailing is to move store and catalog customers to "e". Yet in doing so a retailer may dig their own

grave by also making it likely the consumer will try another Internet retailer also. If their experience at that site is more positive than the original retail site the unintended side effect of moving a consumer to "your" site is destroyed.
3. The current study shows the importance of service recovery following failure in a multi-channel environment and how the effects extend beyond an individual retailer's channel offerings to those of its competitors. Failing to recover when a customer's expectations are not met is crucial for a retailer's future business in both the channel in which failure occurred as well as in other channels offered by the retailer. Doing nothing to resolve a failure results in failing to make future sales with the customer and sparks the flame of customer defection to competitors.
4. One of these questions lies in the interaction of recovery attempts and the channel of encounter on the likelihood of purchasing from a different retailer in the same channel. Defection to a competitor seems evident when failure is experienced in a physical store in the case that no recovery response is offered. However, our results show that if the same situation occurs within a non-physical channel, a negative relationship exists between the failure and the likelihood to purchase from a different retailer in the same channel.
5. Failure without recovery leads to channel abandonment regardless of the failing party. Retailers should strive to separate their channel contact points from those of their competitors to avoid this potentially dangerous and unprofitable situation. Channel defection for catalog and internet sales after failure also raises questions of customization and personal contact. Perhaps if means were taken to ensure the same personalization of response that a customer would experience in a physical store with face to face

employees, experiences in these intangible channels may come to resemble those in the tangible world.

There are a number of multi-channel opportunities for retailers. Retailers can leverage strong brand value by adding channels. For example, Internet only retailers can establish brand equity by opening physical stores or merging with an existing store-based retailer (e.g., Sears's acquisition of Lands' End). Multi-channel retailing leverages advertising and marketing expenses as well as distribution and supplier networks. Benefits of a multi-channel strategy to store-based retailers include access to expanded demographic and psychographic segments, opportunity to drive cross channel traffic, and the ability to use existing stores for distribution and return of merchandise purchased offline. And, as this study shows, multi-channel retailing leverages customer satisfaction. Customer satisfaction in one channel transfers to other channels. Successful multi-channel retailing is contingent on understanding the variation in consumer responses that positive/negative shopping experiences produce in different channels and different cultures. Channel-specific eCRM strategies that take into account these variations should contribute positively to improved customer service and operational efficiencies.

Multi-channel retailing will clearly be a growth industry for retailing if for no other reason than multi-channel consumers spend more. Promotions and incentives will need to be multi-channel. Customer service as well as operational systems and processes will need be integrated and customized for each channel. The customer's interaction with a retailer's brand should be seamless across all channels. More research is clearly needed better understand how the customer's experience in one channel affects the behavioral responses toward other channels.

This research shows that the assumption that eCRM is equivalent to CRM in non-Internet chan-

nels is not complete. Too many studies appear to be focused on the examination of the antecedents and composition of eCRM and not its consequences both within and across retail channels. In effect, eCRM has the potential to create positive benefits for the multi-channel retailer in the form of positive affect (i.e., customer satisfaction) across all the retailer's channels as well as positive affect for the channel in general.

REFERENCES

Andreassen, T. W. (2000). Antecedents to satisfaction with service recovery. *European Journal of Marketing, 34(1/2), 156-175.*

Aron, D. (2001). Consumer grudgeholding: Toward a conceptual model and research agenda. *Journal of Consumer Satisfaction, Dissatisfaction, and Complaining Behavior, 14,* 108-119.

Balasubramanian, S., Konana, P., & Menon, N. (2003). Customer satisfaction in virtual environments: A study of online trading. *Management Science, 49,* 871-889

Bansal, H. S., McDougall, G. H. G., Dikalli, S. S., & Sedatole, K. L. (2004). Relating e-satisfaction to behavioral outcomes: An empirical study. *Journal of Services Marketing, 18*(4), 290-302.

Berman, B., & Thelen, S. (2004). A guide to developing and managing a well-integrated multi-channel retail strategy. *International Journal of Retail & Distribution Management,* 32(3), 1147-156.

Bitner, M. J., Booms, B. H., & Tetreault, M. S. (1990). The service encounter: Diagnosing favorable and unfavorable incidents. *Journal of Marketing, 54*(1), 71-84.

Blanchard, K., & Bowles, S. (1993). *Raving fans: A revolutionary approach to customer service.* NY: William Morrow.

Blodgett, J. G., Hill, D. J., & Tax, S. S. (1997). The effects of distributive, procedural, and interactional justice on postcomplaint behavior. *Journal of Retailing, 73*(2), 185-210.

Burke, R. (2000). *Creating the ideal shopping experience: What consumers want in the physical and virtual store.* NY: KPMG. Available at www.kelley.iu.edu/retail/research/iukpmg00b.pdf

Chan, C. O. (2005). Toward a unified view of customer relationship management. *Journal of American Academy of Businmess, 6*(1), 32-38.

Chen, Q., & Chen, H. (2004). Exploring the success factors of eCRM strategies in practice. *Database Marketing & Customer Service Strategy Management, 11*, 333-343.

Chu, J., & Pike, T. (2002). *Integrated multichannel retailing (IMCR): A roadmap to the future.* IBM Institute for Business Value. Available at http://www-1.ibm.com/services/strategy/e_strategy/integrated_multi_channel.html

Close, W. (2002). CRM at work: Eight Characteristics of CRM Winners. *Defying the Limits, 3*, 66-68.

Cronin, Jr., J., Brady, M, & Hult, G. (2000). Assessing the effects of quality, value, and customer satisfaction on consumer behavioral intentions in service environments. *Journal of Retailing, 76*, 93-218.

Ernst & Young (2003). Global Online Retailing. http://www.ey.com/GLOBAL

Feinberg, R. (2001). Customer service and service quality. In G. Salvendy (Ed.). *Handbook of Industrial Engineering.* NY: John Wiley and Sons, Inc., (pp. 651-664).

Feinberg, R.A., Kadam, R., Hokama, L., & Kim, I. (2002). The state of electronic customer relationship management in retailing. *International Journal of Retail & Distribution Management, 30*(10), 470-481.

Feinberg, R., Trotter, M., & Anton, J. (2000). At any time- From anywhere- In any form. *Defying the Limits: 1*, 296- 304.

Feinberg, R., & Trotter, M. (2003). The customer access evolution: Leveraging touch points for customer acquisition, retention, and wallet share. *Defying the Limits, 2*, 30-35.

Fornell, C., Johnson, M. D., Anderson, E. W., Cha, J., & Bryant, B. E. (1996). The American Customer Satisfaction Index: nature, purpose, and findings, *Journal of Marketing, 60*, 7-18.

Freed, L. (2003). *The insiders view of e-retailing 2003.* www.foreseereults.com

Gronroos, C. (1988). Service quality: The six criteria of good perceived service. *Review of Business, 9*(3), 10-13.

Hoffman, K. D., & Kelley, S. W. (2000). Perceived justice needs and recovery evaluation: A contingency approach. *European Journal of Marketing, 34*(3/4), 418-432.

Inman, J., Shankar, V., & Ferraro, R. (2004). The roles of channel-category associations and geodemographics in channel patronage. *Journal of Marketing, 68*, 51-71.

Johnson, C. (2004). The growth of multichannel retailing: A Forrester document prepared for: National Governor's Association and the National Conference of State Legislatures. Available at www.nga.org/cda/files/0407MULTICHANNEL.PDF

Keen, C., Wetzels, M., de Ruyter, K., & Feinberg, R. (2004). E-tailers versus retailers: Which factors determine consumer preferences. *Journal of Business Research, 57*, 685-695

Kelley, S. W., Hoffman, K. D., & Davis, M. A. (1993). A typology of retail failures and recoveries. *Journal of Retailing, 69*(4), 429-452.

Levy, M., & Weitz, B. (2003). *Retail Management,* 5th edition . NY: McGraw Hill

Loveman, G. (1998). Employee satisfaction, customer loyalty, and financial performance: an empirical examination of the service project chain in retail banking. *Journal of Service Research, 1*, 18-31.

Morgan, R., & Hunt, S., (1994). The commitment-trust theory of relationship marketing. *Journal of Marketing, 58*, 20-38.

Moshe, D. (2003). Have you heard the word? The effect of word of mouth on perceived justice, satisfaction and repurchase intentions following complaint handling. *Journal of Consumer Satisfaction, Dissatisfaction, and Complaining Behavior, 16*, 67-80.

Pastore, M. (2000). *Future of E-tail lies with multichannel retailers.* http://cyberatlas.internet.com/markets/retailing/article/0,1323,6061_417411,00.html

Parasuraman, A., Zeithaml, V. A., & Berry, L. L. (1985). A conceptual model of service quality and its implications for future research. *Journal of Marketing, 49*(4), 41-50.

Parasuraman, A., & Zinkham, G. (2002). Marketing and serving customers through the internet: An overview and research agenda. *Journal of the Academy of Marketing Science, 30*, 286-295.

Porter, M. E. (1985). *The Competitive Advantage: Creating and Sustaining Superior Performance.* N.Y.: Free Press,

Randall, T., Ulrich, K., & Reibstein, D. (1998). Brand equity and vertical product line extension. *Marketing Science, 12*, 356-379.

Reibstein, D. (2002). What attracts customers to online stores and what keeps them coming back. *Journal of the Academy of Marketing Science, 30*, 465-473.

Rust, R., & Zahorik, A., (1993). Customer satisfaction, customer retention, and market share. *Journal of Retailing, 69*, 193-215.

Rust, R., Zeithaml, V., & Lemon, K. (2000). *Driving customer equity: How customer lifetime value is reshaping corporate strategy.* NY: Free Press.

Selnes, F. (1998). Antecedents and consequences of trust and satisfaction on buyer-seller relationships. *European Journal of Marketing, 3*, 305-322.

Sewell, C., & Brown, P. (2002) *Customers for life: How to turn that one buyer into a customer for life.* NY: Doubleday.

Stauss, B. (2002). The dimensions of complaint satisfaction: Process and outcome, complaint satisfaction versus cold fact and warm act complaint satisfaction. *Managing Service Quality, 12*(3), 173-183.

Tax, S. S., & Brown, S. W. (1998). Recovering and learning from service failure. *Sloan Management Review, 40*(1), 75-88.

Tax, S. S., Brown, S. W., & Chandrashekaran, M. (1998). Customer evaluations of service complaint experiences: Implications for relationship marketing. *Journal of Marketing, 6292*, 60-76.

Thompson, B. (2003). Multi-Channel service: Boosting customer value and loyalty. *RightNow Technologies. Available* for download at http://www.rightnow.com/resource/crm-whitepapers.html

Varadarajan, R., & Yadav, M. (2002). Marketing strategy and the Internet: An organizing framework. *Journal of the Academy of Marketing Science, 30*, 296-312.

Wu, F., Mahajan, V., & Balasubramanian, Sridhar (2003). An analysis of e-business adoption and its impact on business performance. *Journal of the Academy of marketing Science, 31*, 425-447.

Zeithaml, V., Parasuraman, A., & Malholtra, A. (2002). Service quality delivery through web sites: A critical review of extant knowledge.

Journal of the Academy of Marketing Sciences,
30, 362-375.

KEY TERMS

Balance Theory (http://en.wikipedia.org/wiki/Balance_theory): First proposed by Fritz Heider (http://en.wikipedia.org/wiki/Fritz_Heider) to explain and describes the relationships between people and objects/other people. Heider proposed that positive and negative feeling/beliefs/relationships must be in psychological balance.

Customer Satisfaction/Dissatisfaction (http://en.wikipedia.org/wiki/Customer_satisfaction): is a measure of how satisfied a customer is with your products and services. Customer satisfaction/dissatisfaction is a predictor of the degree to which customer will remain loyal, repurchase products and services, and tell others (see also netpromoter) (http://www.netpromoter.com)

eCRM—Electronic Customer Relationship Management: eCRM (http://en.wikipedia.org/wiki/ECRM) is the use of the information technologies and the Internet to manage relationships with the customer. Examples of e-CRM include frequently asked questions (FAQ's) ,

chat, e-mail, mobile, sales force management, customer database.

E-Retailing (www.internetretailer.com): a storefront on the Internet (also known as Internet retailing). An e-retailer can be part of a chain of retail stores (e.g., Walmart* has 3500+ stores as well as a website) or the only access a consumer has to your business.

Multichannel: Multichannel retailing/marketing is the use of different marketing channels to reach a customer. A multichannel retailer (http://www.mckinsey.com/practices/retail/knowledge/knowledge_multichannel.asp) might have stores, catalogs, an Internet site, kiosks, direct mail, e-mail access for the customer.

Service Failure: the failure of a business to meet the expectations of a customer.

Service Recovery: the identification of points of customer pain and be willing to address these issues to achieve customer satisfaction. The ability to recover after a service failure is important because customers are more loyal if a company has addressed a failure than if they never address the failure or never had the failure at all. (http://www.amazon.com/Knock-Your-Socks-Service-Recovery/dp/081447084X)

Chapter XII
Evolution of Web–Based Shopping Systems:
Characteristics and Strategies

Changsu Kim
Yeungnam University, Korea

Robert D. Galliers
Bentley College, USA, & London School of Economics, UK

Kyung Hoon Yang
University of Wisconsin–La Crosse, USA

Jaekyung Kim
University of Nebraska–Lincoln, USA

ABSTRACT

This article offers a theoretical analysis of evolutionary processes in WBSS strategies. For that purpose, we propose a research model that shows strategy patterns. Based upon the model, we identified several types of strategies. In our research model, WBSS are classified into four types: (1) general-direct-sales (GDS); (2) general-intermediary-sales (GIS); (3) specialized-direct-sales (SDS); and (4) specialized-intermediary-sales (SIS). On the basis of these four categories of WBSS, we analyze the characteristics of WBSS and suggest five evolution strategies for WBSS, which have implications for both theory and practice. Amazon.com's strategic movements, such as product line expansion through alliance and acquisition, provide an exemplary case of the evolution of WBSS strategy. We expect that this research will serve as a guide for Internet businesses and as a catalyst for new research agendas relevant to Web-based shopping and electronic commerce.

INTRODUCTION

E-commerce has been actively diffused on the basis of advanced Internet technologies, enlarging its sphere of utilization and the scale of the global electronic market, radically (Feeny, 2001; Looney & Chatterjee, 2002). The most well-known Internet business models are the so-called dot-coms, which have adopted several types of WBSS applications (Kim & Galliers, 2004, 2006; Porter, 2001). Dot-coms are located around the world and are pursuing a variety of opportunities as global marketers, interacting with global customers and businesses through the Internet (Howcroft, 2001; Rifkin & Kurtzman, 2002; Worthington & Boyes, 2001). However, early in 2000, many dot-com companies collapsed. The lesson learned is that making money on the Internet is still not easy, which makes it necessary to create new ways of doing business (Gulati & Garino, 2000; Holzwarth, Janiszewski, & Neumann, 2006; Paper, Pedersen, & Mulbery, 2003). Even though many dot-com companies have disappeared and competition is getting severe, the diffusion of Web-based shopping businesses is continuous, increasing in both the number of customers and the volume of business (Kim, Galliers, & Yang, 2005).

The aim of this paper is to address what WBSS must do to survive and prosper continuously. We insist that the appropriate evolution strategy can be one of the most critical factors. To verify our premise, we classify four types of WBSS models, analyze the characteristics of each WBSS model, and attempt to address the evolutionary path of each WBSS strategy. We show the case of Amazon.com's evolutionary path as an example to demonstrate our theory. Thus, we expect this study to serve as a useful guide for researchers to build theoretical e-commerce models and for practitioners to make plans for their Internet businesses.

LITERATURE REVIEW

Web-Based Shopping in E-Commerce

According to Arlitt, Krishnamurthy, and Rolia (2001), Web-based shopping aims to personalize online shopping to provide global interactive business, customer convenience, and global market efficiency, which implies that Web-based shopping belongs to the business-to-consumer (B2C) e-commerce business model. As of yet, there is no agreed upon terminology for Web-based shopping (Van Slyke, Comunale, & Belanger, 2002). There are, however, many terms in use, which include Internet mall, virtual mall, cyber mall, electronic mall, virtual storefront, online storefront, online store, online shopping mall, electronic shopping mall, Internet shopping mall, electronic shopping systems, cyber mall systems, and WBSS. Generally, WBSS are described as Internet-based shopping systems for selling and buying products, information, and services; and they are classified by transaction patterns (Arlitt et al., 2001), which include e-tailers such as the virtual merchant; clicks and bricks; manufacturer direct; and the market creator. Therefore, we limit the scope of this research to B2C e-commerce.

Web-Based Shopping Systems

WBSS have been researched from two viewpoints: business and technical. Studies focusing on the business aspects explored the phenomenon of Internet business through Web sites, online stores, and virtual markets as a limited concept of WBSS (Heijden, 2003; Nour & Fadlalla, 2000). Spiller and Lohse (1998) identified five different types of Internet retail stores: (1) super stores, (2) promotional store fronts, (3) plain sales stores, (4) one page stores, and (5) product listings. These are classified by size, type of services, and interface quality. However, this classification system does not consider the technical aspects of the Internet.

Nour and Fadlalla (2000) also classified Internet-based virtual markets according to two principal categories: product type and delivery mode. They identified four distinct Internet-based virtual markets: (1) electronic publishing and software, (2) electronic tele-services, (3) digitally enabled merchandising, and (4) digitally enabled services. However, this is a broad conceptual model for virtual markets rather than a model of WBSS. This research, therefore, seems somewhat limited in explaining the taxonomy and the evolution of WBSS. Torkzadeh and Dhillon (2002) measured factors that influence the success of Internet commerce. They suggested that the relative strength of shopping convenience and ecological issues are fundamental objectives. Recently, Heijden (2003) investigated an extension of the technology acceptance model (TAM) to explain the individual acceptance and usage of a Dutch generic portal Web site.

Several studies explored the technical aspects of WBSS, including scalability, network traffic, architecture, and virtual reality. Arlitt et al. (2001)

investigated the issues affecting the performance and scalability of WBSS. They found that personalization and robots can have a significant impact on scalability. Their study was one of the first to adopt the terminology of WBSS. Choi, Choi, Park, and Kim (1998) examined the issue of reducing the volume of network traffic in the cyber mall system. They also suggested that the basic architecture of the cyber mall system consists of four major technical components: (1) the cyber mall creator, (2) the cyber mall server, (3) the cyber mall player, and (4) the WWW server. They argued that the increasing demands for virtual reality are placing excessive strain on the current network volume. Yet, earlier research by Baty and Lee (1995) proposed a functional architecture of electronic shopping systems to promote comparison and contrast between product differentiations. Table 1 summarizes the previous research.

To summarize, most studies focused on a limited view of WBSS and considered WBSS only as a static system, ignoring WBSS as an evolving system in dealing with environmental and organizational change. To understand the general characteristics of WBSS, it is necessary to consider them as dynamic systems that evolve

Table 1. Summary of previous research related to WBSS

Dimension	Author(s)	Research Domain	Insight and Analysis
Business aspect	Heijden (2003)	Web sites	Investigates an extension of TAM to explain the individual acceptance and usage of Web sites
	Torkzadeh and Dhillon (2002)	Internet commerce	Measures factors that influence the success of Internet commerce
	Nour and Fadlalla (2000)	E-tailer, Internet-based virtual market	Classifies a broad conceptual model for Internet-based virtual markets rather than a model of WBSS
	Spiller and Lohse (1998)	Internet retail store	Identifies five different Internet retail stores, which overlap with each online store group
Technical aspect	Arlitt et al. (2001)	Web-based shopping system	Examines the issues affecting the performance and scalability of WBSS
	Choi et al. (1998)	Cyber mall system, portal	Investigates the issue of reducing the volume of network traffic in the cyber mall system
	Baty and Lee (1995)	Electronic shopping system	Provides architecture of electronic shopping systems to promote comparison and contrast between product differentiations

corresponding to changes encountered. The strategic and evolutionary paths of WBSS can provide information that has been neglected in previous WBSS studies. Therefore, this research attempts to develop a WBSS classification model and provide strategic planning recommendations for each type of WBSS.

METHODOLOGY

For the methodology of this research, we did a two-stage research approach: conceptual analysis and the use of a focus group. In the conceptual analysis, we developed the theoretical research model and verified the model using the focus group.

Conceptual Analysis

According to Piercy and Cravens (1995), marketing planning should integrate the type of product and the approach to generating sales as the key enterprise process. As a global business medium, it would appear helpful to classify various types of WBSS applications, therefore, by product type and sales type. As a business channel, WBSS supports two sales types between the seller and the customer. One is direct sales, in which the WBSS is directly responsible for the guarantee of quality and delivery of products or services (Ranchhod & Gurau, 1999). In the other type, indirect sales, the WBSS relays business transactions between the manufacturer, merchant, distributor, and consumer (Kim et al., 2005).

Many dot-com companies such as Amazon.com and Dell are directly responsible for the products sold on their WBSS, while still many others such as eBay.com, in the role of intermediary, is indirectly responsible for sales products. Therefore, we infer that the sales types of WBSS are classified into two types: direct sales and indirect sales, as seen in Figure 1.

Another distinguishing factor of a WBSS is the type of product being sold. There are vertical products and horizontal products. Vertical industry product and unified group image products are two types of vertical products. Vertical industry products are defined as the products that have a vertical relationship in an industry, such as auto parts, tires, and automobile accessories. Unified group image products are defined as products that can create synergy effects even though they belong to different industries.[1] Examples of unified group image products are movies and movie-related toys; beer and baby diapers; and ski and golf equipment.[2] In contrast to these vertical products, horizontal products are defined as two or more industrial products that are not unified into a group. This type of sales attracts customers by the variety of products.

In order to gain meaningful insight into classifying different product types sold by WBSS, this study explores the products sold by some well-known dot-com companies. For example, Dell.com and Amazon.com sell products directly to global customers without any intermediaries. Dell.com handles only a vertically related product line of computers and computer accessories, and Amazon.com carries unified group image products that have synergy effects with books, such as CDs and software. In this paper, these kinds of product lines will be referred to as vertical products. On the other hand, Walmart.com carries a variety of products that do not have any related synergy effects. Therefore, these are referred to as horizontal products. From the aforementioned facts, we are able to infer that the product types sold on WBSS are divided into two groups: vertical product and horizontal product, as outlined in Table 2.

On the basis of the product and the sales type of WBSS, a classification model of WBSS can be developed (Table 3). In the model, the vertical axis displays the product type and the horizontal axis displays the sales type. This research thereby

Figure 1. The sales type of WBSS

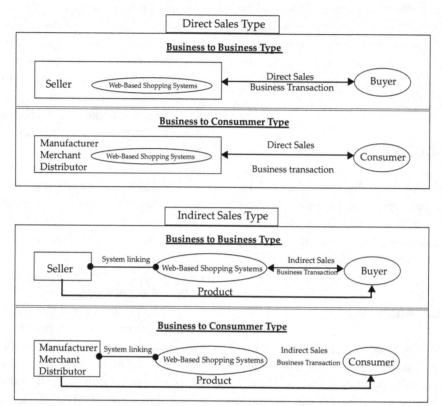

Table 2. Product type of WBSS

Type	Definition	Examples
Vertical product	Vertical industry product	Computer, computer accessories, and computer software
	Unified group image product	Beer and baby diapers in convenience stores, and ski and golf equipment
Horizontal product	More than two industrial products and products that are not unified into a group	Department store products

proposes a model that classifies WBSS into the following types: (1) SDS, (2) GDS, (3) SIS, and (4) GIS. However, not all WBSS conform to these four types: Hybrids are possible, for example. Nonetheless, this model serves primarily as a basic model of WBSS for analytical purposes. Characteristics of each type of WBSS, with exemplary cases and their strategic evolutionary paths, are introduced in detail in the fourth and fifth, respectively.

Table 3. Classification model of WBSS

Classification Model of WBSS		Sales Type of WBSS	
		Direct sales	Indirect sales
Product type	Vertical	Specialized-direct sales	Specialized-intermediary sales
	Horizontal	General-direct sales	General- intermediary sales

Use of Focus Group

To verify the types of WBSS and to gain useful insight related to the strategic evolutionary path, we organized a focus group. Members of the group were chosen according to expertise and experience on the recommendation of one of the authors, who is a professor at the London School of Economics. The group consisted of 11 experts who worked in London-area, dot-com companies as CEOs, CIOs, administrators, system developers, and Web masters. Focus groups usually fare better when conducted with relatively homogeneous strangers. However, since the concept of WBSS should be considered from several aspects, the group consists of diversified members. Before the focus group meeting, we e-mailed the participants the documents that explained the major objectives of the meeting and the questions about the classification of WBSS, the evolutionary paths, and the correspondence between strategies and evolutionary paths. In the meeting, we presented our model, which consisted of the classification of the WBSS and the evolutionary strategies for each type. After that, we discussed these topics in an informal brainstorming procedure. The experts shared their opinions and made suggestions for our research model. The recorded session continued for a duration of 3 hours. After the meeting, we analyzed the discussions and comments and summarized the contents of the meeting. We visited the experts individually seven times in total to obtain clearer information.

The comments we obtained can be summarized as follows: It is logically possible for a WBSS to switch from a horizontal to a vertical product type. However, on a realistic basis, this switching can be regarded as a failing of the Web-based shopping business. This is because customers are already accustomed to horizontal products, so they may have a negative image when the company suddenly reduces the type of products sold to a vertical product. In this case, as experts suggested, dot-com companies would do better to maintain the WBSS as it is, or close the site and then make a new WBSS for vertical product sales. Furthermore, it is not realistic to shift from indirect sales to direct sales because of the greater difficulty guaranteeing the quality and delivery for the sales product.

CHARACTERISTICS OF THE FOUR TYPES OF WBSS

We analyzed the characteristics of the four categories of WBSS based on eight analysis domains: (1) seller/WBSS relationship, (2) number of sellers in WBSS, (3) product type, (4) responsibility of guarantee for the product sold, (5) comparable firms, (6) e-commerce strength, and (7) recommended strategy (Looney & Chatterjee, 2002; Molenaar, 2002; Piercy & Cravens, 1995). These domains explain the reasons for such classifications of WBSS.

First, the relationship between the seller and the WBSS is examined. For example, some sellers are owners of the WBSS, or lessees or brokers within the WBSS (Looney & Chatterjee, 2002). Our second focus is on the number of sellers

(Piercy & Cravens, 1995), the third on product type, and the fourth on responsibility of guarantee for the product sold (Molenaar, 2002). For the fifth, based on these four analyses, an appropriate WBSS type is suggested. Next, we illustrate the strength of the four types of WBSS (Looney & Chatterjee, 2002). Finally, an attempt is made to analyze the strategic paths each WBSS follows, in accordance with the strategic options suggested by Rackoff, Wiseman, and Ullrich (1985). In their theory of strategic thrusts, five major competitive moves (defensive or offensive) are introduced: (1) differentiation, (2) low cost, (3) innovation, (4) growth, and (5) alliance.

While this theory is based on Porter's (1980) competitive strategy model, Rackoff et al. (1985) expanded the original generic strategies with two additional strategies: growth and alliance. They also addressed the strategic use of IS to uncover opportunities related to supplier, customer, and competitor. Since a WBSS is an IS that can be strategically utilized to deliver more value to customers and suppliers and to achieve a competitive advantage over competitors, we believe the theory of strategic thrusts can explain the strategic paths of WBSS properly. According to the analysis domains defined previously, detailed characteristics of the four types of WBSS are investigated (with four dot-com company cases).

General-Direct Sales (GDS)

The GDS type is applicable to direct sales and horizontal products. This type uses the WBSS to sell many products that are identical to those of an actual department store. Examples of GDS are Buy.com and Overstock.com. In this type, the owner of the WBSS is the only seller, selling several kinds of products to multiple buyers in the world. The GDS type is therefore directly responsible for the guarantee of the product sold. The strength of the GDS type is that it provides a cyber warehouse that needs less initial investment expense and fewer staffing requirements in com-

parison to actual department stores. Therefore, the GDS type cannot only make high profits due to a reduction in maintenance and other costs, but it can also solve traffic and parking problems, because customers do not need to leave their home to go shopping.

WBSS of this type are in keen competition with each other. Therefore, a differentiation strategy would be well-matched with a GDS type to gain a competitive advantage through differentiation of service or products, in comparison to other competitor WBSS. Detailed explanations follow.

Example 1: Overstock.com

Overstock.com is an online closeout store selling excess inventory through the Internet including bed-and-bath goods; home decor; kitchenware; watches; jewelry; electronics and computers; sporting goods; and apparel and designer accessories, among other products. Overstock.com offers manufacturers, distributors, and other retailers an alternative sales channel for liquidating their inventory. Overstock.com is a GDS WBSS because it sells general merchandise to the customers.

Example 2: Buy.com

Buy.com is a cyber department store, which means that it does not have any physical shops and it sells several kinds of products that are identical to those of an actual department store. The product prices in this category are cheap because goods can be sold directly to the customer without a salesperson, and intermediaries such as suppliers can be cut out. In doing so, Buy.com can reduce the transaction costs of selling products. In addition, Buy.com provides one-to-one marketing based on customer management databases that store information to analyze customers' needs and preferences. Moreover, it carries out differentiation strategies such as a "Bill Me Later" payment option, quick delivery, membership management, and a variety of other services such as BuyMagazine. "Bill Me Later" is a payment option that provides customers with the flexibility to purchase without using their credit card.

General-Intermediary Sales (GIS)

The general-intermediary type of WBSS is suitable for indirect sales and horizontal products. This type includes many shops such as book stores, computer shops, gift shops, wine stores, and sports stores. There are many sellers dealing in several types of products for a variety of customers in the GIS type of WBSS. These sellers are lessees within the GIS. Thus, the GIS itself has an indirect responsibility for products sold because individual sellers within the GIS are directly responsible for the products. This type of WBSS provides a strategic opportunity to small and medium-sized enterprises (SMEs), which are faced with a shortage of funds, human resources, and technical expertise in comparison to larger companies. This is because this type of WBSS allows relatively easy and low-cost entry of SMEs into Web-based shopping business areas. The strength of the GIS type of WBSS is that it provides various cyber malls that customers can choose from according to their needs and preferences. This kind of selective buying can serve as a major attraction to customers, as compared to other types of WBSS. Other types of WBSS cannot establish the variety of shops nor provide the range of products that the GIS type can, due to limited capability such as systems management, operating costs, and human resources. Therefore, GIS has a competitive advantage over other types of WBSS, through its ability to provide a diversity of products, high quality service, and many kinds of shops. Thus, the most suitable strategy for the GIS would appear to be a growth strategy. WBSS in these categories include Yahoo! Shopping, Amazon. com, and Pricegrabber.com. Yahoo! Shopping and Amazon.com lease cyber store space under the WBSS to many individual stores. Therefore,

these WBSS have multiple sellers who directly sell a variety of products. They can be regarded as online marketplace providers, which create space for sellers and buyers to gather sellers and buyers. Pricegrabber.com is explained next as a type of GIS WBSS.

Example 1: PriceGrabber.com

PriceGrabber.com is a leading e-commerce company that helps businesses participate in WBSS. Based on its full suite of e-commerce solutions, PriceGrabber.com claims that it helps customers and merchants safely and easily compare prices and allows them to buy and sell merchandise online. The PriceGrabber.com WBSS provides millions of products and services from more than 40,000 merchants. Customers can rapidly and efficiently search the variety of products by comparative shopping functions on the PriceGrabber.com WBSS. It not only supports technology and outsourcing services to retailers, manufacturers, and other businesses, but also launches and manages the WBSS on their behalf. Shoppers can purchase desired products and services from merchants located around the world. The major strategic option of PriceGrabber.com focuses on the global community. By pursuing strategic alliances and partnerships in other regions of the world, PriceGrabber.com is hoping to accelerate its goal of becoming a pre-eminent Internet business service provider worldwide.

Example 2: Yahoo! Shopping

Yahoo! Shopping is another example of a GIS WBSS. It is a cyber mall with many lessees that handle a variety of products. Products offered by individual stores are tied to the Yahoo search engine, and reviews compiled by its massive user base are also listed. Consumers on Yahoo! Shopping can visit a retailer's store site directly or through the search result of the Yahoo search engine. The Yahoo! Shopping WBSS takes care of billings and charges commissions on the purchases made through the retailers, who then ship the goods to the consumers.

Specialized-Direct Sales (SDS)

The SDS type is a specialized WBSS dealing with direct sales and vertical products. The seller is identical to the owner of the SDS WBSS. Thus, the seller is a single seller as well as an owner of the SDS type of WBSS. As a result, the SDS itself bears direct responsibility for the product sold. This type of WBSS provides opportunities for global businesses to manufacturing companies and smaller shops, which have limited capital and business resources. For example, manufacturing companies can sell products directly to the customer without any intermediary. Also, this WBSS type can help smaller shops compete with giant corporations because physical size is not an important factor in determining market strength. The strength of the SDS type lies in its ability to provide a specialized cyber shop. Organizations that have limited resources can efficiently focus their capabilities on selling a specialized vertical product. The initial stage of Dell.com is a major example of this type of application. The SDS type needs to concentrate on a cost strategy since it is necessary to maintain lower prices for specialized products in comparison to prices listed on WBSS that sell various kinds of products. Through the lowered cost of selling products, this kind of WBSS will have a competitive advantage against general types of WBSS. Other examples in this category are online financial institutions such as PayPal.com, esurance.com, and Egg-online.co.uk. They provide specialized products in direct sale mode through the Internet. They can provide financing at a lower cost. This is the strength of these WBSS. Detailed examples of SDS are presented next.

Example 1: Dell.com

Dell.com is one of the best examples of the specialized direct sales type of WBSS. Dell.com sells computer equipment directly to its customers on the WBSS. Dell.com sold more than $50 million in PC products per day through its WBSS (Dell Computer Timeline, 2004). The company expects to handle half of all its business, ranging from customer inquiries to orders and follow-up services, through the SDS type of WBSS. The advantages of the Dell.com model are claimed to include near-zero inventory; less risk of obsolescence; more customized state-of-the-art products; and a favorable cash flow (Bharati & Chaudhury, 2004; Kraemer, Dedrick, & Yamashiro, 2000).

Example 2: PayPal.com

PayPal provides an online money transaction service to individuals and businesses. Buyers can tie any of their existing banking services (e.g., credit card, debit card, or bank account) into their PayPal account and pay for their purchases from online stores. On the other hand, PayPal allows sellers to accept credit cards, debit cards, and bank account payments from buyers in exchange for the transaction fee. PayPal also provides about 5% average yield rate for their account balances, which is higher than the usual bank deposit. As characteristics of SDS WBSS, this unique middleman service for individual or business online transactions is the specialization of PayPal, which has direct control of its service.

Specialized-Intermediary Sales (SIS)

This type of WBSS sells vertical products indirectly. The SIS type of WBSS can be thought of as a basic level of a virtual organization that links people, assets, and ideas to create and distribute products and service (Sadeh & Lee, 2003). This is because buyers and sellers can negotiate and trade products, services, and information in real time, based on a SIS shopping architecture. As seen in the case of Fastparts.com, there are many sellers selling vertical products, within SIS. These sellers take on the role of a broker. Thus, the SIS type itself has an indirect responsibility for the product sold, because individual sellers within the SIS type of WBSS are directly responsible for the product guarantee. The SIS architecture offers a significant opportunity for auction markets, in particular, and acts as an intermediary between seller and buyer. Therefore, the SIS type needs to be kept up-to-date to provide the most recent data on products and services because companies may want to access the latest information related to their market. The strength of the SIS type of WBSS is that it plays the role of a cyber agent that is able to support business-to-business e-commerce. Its role as cyber agent between businesses is a basic form of virtual organization because the key attribute of a virtual organization is strategic alliances or partnering (Introna, 2001). The successful evolution of this type of WBSS will depend on alliances and tight coordination with various WBSS. Therefore, an alliance strategy is well matched with this type of WBSS in order to gain a competitive advantage because firms can negotiate directly with each other and trade products and services with other types of WBSS. Examples in these categories include online travel agency Web sites such as Orbitz.com, Expedia. com, and Travelocity.com. These WBSS mediate airline and hotel reservation sales. Multiple sellers are involved, and products and services are sold indirectly. Since many sellers are involved in the WBSS, auction is the more suitable form, and it is usually aligned with airline and hotel companies. Fastparts.com is another example of a SIS WBSS. Detailed explanations follow.

Example 1: Expedia.com

Through its WBSS, Expedia.com provides direct access to a broad selection of travel industry companies offering products and services that include airline tickets, hotel reservations, car rental, and cruises. Working with a number of internationally recognized airline, hotel, cruise, and rental car brands, Expedia.com provides reservation services. This makes Expedia a specialized intermediary in the WBSS travel industry.

Example 2: Fastparts.com

Fastparts.com provides an Internet-based trading exchange and marketplace for the electronics manufacturing and assembly industry. Fastparts. com has sold $140 billion in electronic parts and hundreds of millions of dollars in manufacturing equipment. In addition, FastParts.com periodically offers various inventories to sell its members' products on Internet auctions. Auctions are pre-announced to all members, and bidding is generally open for 2 or 3 days. Though anyone can use the FastParts.com to access information on parts, price, and availability, the actual bidding, buying, or selling of parts requires membership. There is no charge to become a member. All members must agree to abide by the FastParts. com operating rules and protocols.

In this section, we have analyzed the major characteristics of the four types of WBSS, utilizing appropriate examples from practice. As a result of this analysis, specific characteristics are synthesized in Table 4.

As shown in Table 4, the four kinds of WBSS have different characteristics, each having its own strengths and weaknesses as an enabler of new business. As such, the development of new business processes, strategic planning, and system architectures should be necessary for success. The characteristics of the four categories of WBSS provide insight for researchers investigating Web-based shopping business and potentially helpful guidelines for practitioners seeking ways to gain sustainable advantages over their e-business competitors.

EVOLUTIONARY PATHS OF WBSS AS STRATEGIC PLANNING

Review of Evolutionary Path

Organizations such as dot-com companies need to continuously improve the functionality of their WBSS in order to survive and progress in the Web-based shopping business world (Pinker, Seidmann, & Foster, 2002; Rifkin & Kurtzman, 2002). Therefore, these organizations must consider multiple strategies to find the best ways to expand.

Based on our observations of evolutionary paths of WBSS, we can suggest a model of strategic planning for WBSS to provide useful guidelines for practitioners and for academic research. While it appears unprofitable to shift from horizontal to vertical products or from indirect to direct sales type, a shift from vertical to horizontal products or from direct to indirect sales type can be a successful evolutionary path for WBSS.

The theory of strategic thrusts (Rackoff et al., 1985) provides an explanation for the success of these evolutionary paths. There are five strategic thrusts proposed in this theory: (1) differentia-

tion, (2) low cost, (3) innovation, (4) growth, and (5) alliance.

Among the five strategic thrusts, growth, and alliance are the most useful in explaining evolutionary paths of WBSS. When a WBSS evolves from dealing with vertical product types to horizontal product types (SDS → GDS or SIS → GIS), the evolutionary path can be seen as a growth strategy through which the WBSS achieves a competitive advantage by volume or geographical expansion, backward or forward integration, or product-line or entry diversification. On the other hand, when a WBSS evolves from selling products directly to selling products indirectly (SDS → SIS or GDS → GIS), this path can be seen as an alliance strategy through which a WBSS achieves competitive advantage by forging marketing agreements, forming joint ventures, or making acquisitions of other WBSS.

While growth and alliance strategies can be viewed as the major thrusts, differentiation, cost, and innovation strategies can be achieved in the context of the growth and alliance strategy thrusts. For example, a WBSS may expand its product type to differentiate itself from other WBSS. Amazon.com started as bookstore WBSS and expanded its product lines to toys and other goods (SDS→GDS)

Table 4. A taxonomy of WBSS

Analysis Domain	Types of WBSS			
	GDS	GIS	SDS	SIS
Seller	Owner	Lessee	Host	Brokerage
Seller number	Single	Multiple	Single	Multiple
Product type	Horizontal	Horizontal	Vertical	Vertical
Guarantee of product sold	Direct	Indirect	Direct	Indirect
Comparable firm	Department store	Small and medium enterprise	Shop manufacture	Auction
Strength	Cyber warehouse	Cyber malls	Cyber shop	Cyber agent
Strategy type	Differentiation	Growth	Cost	Alliance
Similar business model	Catalog-merchant	Portal, Virtual-merchant	Merchant-direct	Service provider, community provider
Example	Buy.com	Yahoo! Shopping	Dell.com	Expedia.com

sold directly and indirectly through alliances. Amazon.com achieved cost leadership because it utilized an existing infrastructure to handle additional product types (cost). It also allows a customer to buy many types of products without leaving the WBSS, making it a one-stop shopping place. This convenience of broad selection differentiates Amazon.com from Barnsandnoble. com, an SDS WBSS (differentiation). When both product and sales types change (SDS → GIS), we need an innovation strategy to support rapid change of the WBSS structure caused by product and sale type expansions (Innovation).

As seen in Figure 2, we suggest five evolutionary paths of strategy planning for WBSS: (1) from SDS to GDS, (2) from SDS to SIS, (3) from SDS to GIS, (4) from GDS to GIS, and (5) from SIS to GIS. A detailed explanation of each path follows.

Evolutionary Path from SDS to GDS

This evolutionary path implies that the organization expands its vertical product type into horizontal products. The case of Amazon.com is one of the best examples. Initially, Amazon.com sold vertical products—books. Subsequently, it has diversified its range to include products such as CDs, software, and the like. This strategy option can reduce the initial risk of WBSS investment. This is because organizations can initially build the SDS type of WBSS based on a vertical product type and then easily expand the product type into a horizontal product type. Therefore, this may be an effective strategy for small- to medium-sized firms.

Evolutionary Path from SDS to SIS

This strategic option is suitable for special businesses of small to medium size. For example, in the case of flower selling, no one shop can cover an entire country. In a situation like this, the owner of the WBSS constructs a countrywide chain

for flower selling and entrusts a district flower shop with the delivery and guarantee of quality for the sales product. However, before shops can be admitted into the partnership, they must be carefully reviewed by the company managing the WBSS. This process can directly affect the reliance of the customer on this type of WBSS. Major businesses suitable for this type of strategic planning are furniture, clothes, real estate, books, tourist bureaus, stationary, computers, and software. Through this strategic planning, businesses of small to medium size can strengthen national or global business power. However, this strategic option might need considerable investment and time for advertising and publicizing to establish a critical mass-scale WBSS.

Evolutionary Path from SDS to GIS

Though the starting point is the same as the previous strategy, the strategic direction is different. SDS shifts from a vertical cyber shop to a horizontal cyber mall, as well as from vertical to horizontal product types. In the final stage of this shift, an organization rents out shops in the cyber mall to businesses that want to provide products or services via a WBSS. Throughout this process, organizations can shift from the SDS type to the GIS type of WBSS. This approach can be well matched with venture businesses (e.g., finding new business models related to e-commerce). This is because venture businesses initially implement the SDS type of WBSS, consisting of a vertical product such as software or CDs. After this, they increase the number of cyber shops and products for sale. However, not all venture businesses can adopt this strategy because of the risk associated with the heavy investment required.

Evolutionary Path from GDS to GIS

The GDS type of WBSS is similar to an actual department store. Similarly, it is difficult to supply all the products a customer may wish to purchase.

Figure 2. Strategic planning of WBSS

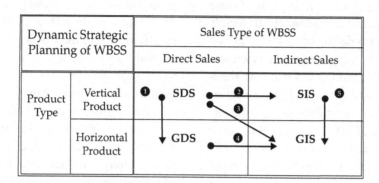

Therefore, it is an effective strategy to entrust the selling of certain products to other specialized sellers. Based on this strategy, organizations can concentrate their core competence on best-selling products, carrying out the sales of other products through other vendors within its WBSS. Through this process, a GDS type can shift to a GIS type, which has various cyber shops and sells horizontal products. It is essential, however, that the quality of products or services supplied by these other sellers is strictly maintained by this kind of GIS.

Evolutionary Path from SIS to GIS

Organizations can carry out the SIS to GIS evolutionary path more easily than others because they can simply add product types for sale within the same WBSS. At this time, it is a better approach to add a product type that is closely related to the current product type of SIS. Based on this strategy, organizations can aim at arriving at a similar level as Amazon.com, which is one example of the GIS type. With regards to its responsibility for products sold, an IT/telecommunication company carrying out Web-based shopping business on its WBSS seems to be best suited for this strategic approach. This is because this sort of company can easily switch from vertical to horizontal product types.

EXEMPLARY CASE OF STRATEGY: AMAZON.COM

Founded as an online bookstore in July 1995, Amazon.com is one of the most prominent Internet retailers. Amazon.com has expanded its product lines to include music; electronics; health and beauty products; kitchen and housewares; tools; toys; videos; and services such as auctions, 1-Click ordering, and zShops (Filson & Willimson, 2001).

There are two reasons for focusing on Amazon.com in this study. One is that Amazon.com is an excellent example of a WBSS starting as a SDS type and expanding to other types of WBSS in our taxonomy. The other is that Amazon.com has announced its major strategic movements (e.g., strategic alliances and acquisitions) publicly on its Web page. Thus, it is possible to follow its strategic planning clearly, as shown in Figure 2.

Amazon.com has expanded its product line through a series of alliances, which exemplifies the alliance strategic thrust (Rackoff et al., 1985), and through the acquisitions of providers of a variety of products, which exemplifies the growth strategic thrust (Rackoff et al., 1985). Acquisitions usually require the removal of redundant operations and functionalities, while alliances usually keep the partners' business operations and entities. Examining Amazon.com's strategic movements, we analyze its strategic planning of WBSS in this section.[3]

Evolutionary Path from SDS to GDS

This evolutionary path implies that the WBSS expands its sales of vertical products type to sales of horizontal products. The case of Amazon.com is one of the best examples. Initially Amazon.com sold vertical products—books. Subsequently, it has diversified its range to include products such as CDs, and software. This strategy option can reduce the initial risk of WBSS investment. This is because organizations can initially build the SDS type of WBSS based on a vertical product type, and then can easily expand the product type into a horizontal group.

Evolutionary Path from SDS to SIS

In April 2001, Amazon.com announced its alliance with Borders Group, one of the largest book superstores, to provide the e-commerce platform needed to re-launch Borders.com as a co-branded Web site. This is one of the most significant strategic movements of Amazon.com for the evolution from SDS to SIS because Borders.com deals with the same product types as Amazon.com and the products of Borders.com are not sold directly through Amazon.com.

Other examples for this strategic path include Amazon.com's expansion to similar products such as audio books and electronic books.[4] Through the alliance with Audible.com on May, 2000, Amazon.com, expanded its spoken audio content and had more than 4,700 audio books and speeches, lectures, and other audible materials (e.g., audio files for newspaper articles). This alliance gives Amazon.com a variety of book-related products while Audible.com has a better platform for audio service.

It also launched an electronic bookstore through the strategic alliance with Microsoft in August, 2000. Microsoft provides a customized Amazon.com version of Microsoft Reader, giving consumers the ability to purchase and download eBook titles directly from Amazon.com. (www. microsoft.com/presspass/ press/2000/Aug00/ AmazonPR.mspx, 2000)

Evolutionary Path from SDS to GIS

This type of strategic movement was achieved through alliances with or acquisition of other WBSSs. For Amanzon.com, these alliances brought more variety of product types, which means more potential customers with different buying needs. For other alliance partners, alliances brought powerful and proven marketing channels because the name value and recognition of Amazon.com is strong and people on the Internet visit Amazon.com frequently. These visitors have more chances to find products through Amazon. com than on the individual alliance partner's WBSS.

One of the early efforts on the path from SDS to GIS was the fulfillment agreement with Toys "R" Us in August, 2000 and Target store alliance in September, 2001. Later, Amazon. com continued the path along with its alliance with Drugstore.com in October, 2005 and the acquisition of Shopbop.com in February, 2006. For smaller merchants, Amazon launched zShops' e-commerce platform in 1999 to allow individual sellers to open their own shops under the roof of Amazon.com. These are Amazon's efforts to provide a one-stop, online shopping experience by expanding special direct sales to general indirect sales. Other major movements of Amazon.com are its alliance with Toysrus.com in August, 2000, to create a co-branded toy and video games store, its alliance with Ofoto in October, 2000 to provide information, products, and service for cameras and photos, and its alliances with AT&T, Sprint PCS, and Voicestream Wireless in November, 2000 for wireless phones and service.

Evolutionary Path from GDS to GIS

After becoming a GDS WBSS with direct sales of horizontal products such as books, pharmaceutical products, and pet products, Amazon.com expanded its product line by allowing other WBSSs to join its platform to sell the same type of products. This represented indirect sales of similar horizontal products already sold by Amazon.com. In this case, Amazon.com becomes an e-marketplace where many products are sold from many sellers in one single market place. Not only does Amazon.com allow Borders.com to sell books, CDs, and movies, it also allows virtually all categories of products (Table 5) to be sold through numerous WBSS, off-line retailers and even individuals.

Products are sold and shipped through these varying sources. The only part of the transaction that Amazon.com is involved in is information listing and payment on which a commission for each transaction is based.

DISCUSSION AND CONCLUSION

WBSS are spreading very rapidly across national boundaries. From groceries stores to department stores, from SMEs to large firms, and from young organizations to well-established organizations, a growing number of companies are taking advantage of WBSS by selling products, services, and information. WBSS not only increase the ability of organizations to trade with customers, but they also offer firms a new opportunity to reach millions of consumers worldwide. WBSS also have the potential to radically change the way businesses interact with their customers. However, many WBSS are disappearing from the Internet, so organizations are struggling to find new strategies in order to survive in the world of e-commerce (Arlitt et al., 2001; Lumpkin, Droege, & Dess, 2002; Van Slyke & Belanger, 2004). In order to provide meaningful guidelines for such a situation, we have presented a taxonomy of four types of WBSS. On the basis of four types of WBSS, this study presents five evolutionary paths for strategic planning: (1) from SDS to GDS, (2) from SDS to SIS, (3) from SDS to GIS, (4) from GDS to GIS, and (5) from SIS to GIS. As a consequence of the discussion so far, Table 6 presents the characteristics of the five types of strategic planning.

As seen in Table 6, each of the five evolutionary paths has its associated strengths and weaknesses, which require shrewd consideration by potential adopters before practical application. Although we believe that the WBSS strategic planning presented in this paper is a fundamental concept, evolutionary paths of each taxonomy category

Table 5. Strategic path of Amazon.com (SCCI, 2006)

Amazon.com WBSS Product Line Expansion		Strategic Planning of Amazon.com WBSS	
Date	Event	Type of WBSS	Strategic Path
1995 July	Amazon.com sells first book	SDS	
1999 July	Opens consumer electronics, and toys & games stores	SDS, GDS	Expanding to GDS (SDS → GDS)
1999 Sept.	Launches zShops	SDS,GDS, GIS	Expanding to GIS (SDS → GIS, GDS → GIS)
2000 Aug.	Announces Toys "R" Us alliance	SDS, GDS, GIS, SIS	Expanding to SIS (SDS →SIS)

Table 6. Overall strategic planning of WBSS

Types of Strategic Planning	Strategic Approach	Strength	Suitable Firm	Customer	Supplier	Competitors
SDS ⇨ GDS	• Vertical product ⇨ Horizontal product	• Lower initial investment & risk	• SME • Shop	Extend the scope of core customers' purchase	Diversify the suppliers	Growth, Differentiation, Cost
SDS ⇨ SIS	• Direct sales ⇨ Indirect sales	• Partnership	• Specialized small- medium size business	Focus on existing customers	Focus on existing suppliers or just extend the scope a little	Alliance, Cost, Differentiation
SDS ⇨ GIS	• Direct sales ⇨ Indirect sales • Vertical product ⇨ Horizontal product	• WBSS provider	• Venture business	Resources needed for customers and suppliers strategies	Need resources both customers and suppliers strategies	Innovation
GDS ⇨ GIS	• Direct sales ⇨ Indirect sales	• Global intermediary	• IT/telecommunications company	Use current customer strategies	Emphasize the supplier and supply chain management	Alliance, Cost, Differentiation
SIS ⇨ GIS	• Vertical product ⇨ Horizontal product	•Strengthening core competence	• Department store	Extend the scope of core customers' purchase	Similar to strategy SDS ⇨ SIS Diversify the suppliers	Growth, Differentiation, Cost

could prove useful in advancing WBSS, in providing guidelines into new business opportunities, and in providing academic insights for further WBSS research. Their practical application seems to depend on organizational circumstances, considering the whole organizational capability to determine the most appropriate option. The discussion in this paper is an on-going study of how we can extend and apply the concept of WBSS strategic planning. The model of WBSS strategic planning suggested in this paper can be a useful guideline for organizations seeking the best way to advance their WBSS, for achieving continuous competitive advantages, and surviving in a global e-commerce environment.

The limited number of analyzed cases may be a weakness of this paper. However we are hopeful that this paper will provide researchers and practitioners with both a detailed understanding of WBSS and a theoretical base for further research of Web-based shopping businesses and e-commerce.

ACKNOWLEDGMENT

The authors thank the associate editor and four anonymous referees for their comments on earlier drafts of the paper. Their comments and suggestions were helpful in improving the quality of the paper. All errors are those of the authors.

REFERENCES

Arlitt, M., Krishnamurthy, D., & Rolia, J. (2001). Characterizing the scalability of a large Web-based shopping system. *ACM Transactions on Internet Technology, 1*(1), 44-69.

Baty, J. B., & Lee, R. M. (1995). InterShop: Enhancing the vendor/customer dialectic in electronic shopping. *Journal of Management Information Systems, 11*(4), 9-31.

Bharati, P., & Chaudhury, A. (2004). Using choiceboards to create business value. *Communications of the ACM, 47*(12), 77-81.

Choi, J. D., Choi, J. S., Park, C., & Kim, D. (1998). A cell-based shared virtual world management mechanism in the cyber mall system. *Computer Networks and ISDN Systems, 30,* 1865-1874.

Dell Computer Timeline. (2004). *Processor, 26*(2), 7. Retrieved April 2, 2007, from http://www.processor.com/articles//P2602/24p02/24p02timeline.pdf.

Feeny, D. (2001). Making business sense of the e-opportunity. *Sloan Management Review, 42*(2), 41-51.

Filson, D., & Willimson, K. (2001). The impact of e-commerce strategies on firm value: Lessons from Amazon.com. Working paper.

Gulati, R., & Garino, J. (2000). Get the right mix of bricks & clicks. *Harvard Business Review, 78*(3), 107-114.

Heijden, H. (2003). Factors influencing the usage of Websites: The case of a generic portal in the Netherlands. *Information & Management, 40,* 541-549.

Holzwarth, M., Janiszewski, C., & Neumann, M. M. (2006). The influence of avatars on online consumer shopping behavior. *Journal of Marketing, 70*(4), 19-36.

Howcroft, D. (2001). After the goldrush: Deconstructing the myths of the dot.com market. *Journal of Information Technology, 16*(4), 195-204.

Introna, L. (2001). Defining the virtual organization. In S. Barnes & B. Hunt (Eds.), *E-commerce & v-business* (pp. 143-152). Oxford: Butterworth-Heinemann.

Kim, C., & Galliers, R. D. (2004). Deriving a diffusion framework and research agenda for Web based shopping systems. *Journal of Electronic Commerce Research, 5*(3), 199-215.

Kim, C., & Galliers, R. D. (2006). The development and application of a configuration model of Web-based shopping systems. *International Journal of Electronic Business, 4*(1), 1-17.

Kim, C., Galliers, R. D., & Yang, K. H. (2005). Comparison of Web-based shopping systems in the UK and Korea. *International Journal of Global Information Technology Management, 8*(4), 49-66.

Kraemer, K. L., Dedrick, J., & Yamashiro, S. (2000). Refining and extending the business model with information technology: Dell computer corporation. *Information Society, 16*(1), 5-21.

Looney, C. A., & Chatterjee, D. (2002). Web-enabled transformation of the brokerage industry. *Communication of the ACM, 45*(8), 75-81.

Lumpkin, G. T., Droege, S. B., & Dess, G. G. (2002). E-commerce strategies: Achieving sustainable competitive advantage and avoiding pitfalls. *Organizational Dynamics, 30*(4), 325-340.

Molenaar, C. (2002). *The future of marketing: Practical strategies for marketers in the post-Internet age.* London: Financial Times Prentice Hall.

Nour, M. A., & Fadlalla, A. (2000). A framework for Web marketing strategies: The e-commerce revolution. *Information Systems Management, 17*(22), 41-50.

Paper, D., Pedersen, E., & Mulbery, K. (2003). An e-commerce process model: Perspectives from e-commerce entrepreneurs. *Journal of Electronic Commerce in Organizations, 1*(3), 28-47.

Piercy, N. F., & Cravens, D. W. (1995). The network paradigm and the marketing organization. *European Journal of Marketing, 29*(3), 7-34.

Pinker, E. J., Seidmann, A., & Foster, R. C. (2002). Strategies for transitioning "old economy" firms to e-business. *Communications of the ACM, 45*(5), 77-83.

Porter, M. E. (1980). *Competitive strategy.* New York: The Free Press.

Porter, M. E. (2001). Strategy and the Internet. *Harvard Business Review, 79*(3), 63-76.

Rackoff, N., Wiseman, C., & Ullrich, W. (1985). Information systems for competitive advantage: Implementation of a planning process. *MIS Quarterly, 9*(4), 285-294.

Ranchhod, A., & Gurau, C. (1999). Internet-enabled distribution strategies. *Journal of Information Technology, 14*(4), 333-346.

Rifkin, G., & Kurtzman, J. (2002). Is your e-business plan radical enough? *Sloan Management Review, 43*(3), 91-95.

Sadeh, N. M., & Lee, J. K. (2003). Advances in B2B e-commerce and e-supply chain management. *Journal of Organizational Computing & Electronic Commerce, 13*(3/4), 163-165.

SCCI. (2006). *Amazon timeline history Q3 2006.* Retrieved April 2, 2007, from http://media.corporate-ir.net/media_files/irol/17/176060/TimelineHistoryQ32006.pdf.

Spiller, P., & Lohse, G. L. (1998). A classification of Internet retail stores. *International Journal of Electronic Commerce, 2*(2), 29-56.

Torkzadeh, G., & Dhillon, G. (2002). Measuring factors that influence the success of Internet commerce. *Information Systems Research, 13*(2), 187-204.

Van Slyke, C., & Belanger, F. (2004). Factors influencing the adoption of Web-based shopping: The impact of trust. *Database for Advances in Information Systems, 35*(2), 32- 49.

Van Slyke, C., Comunale, C. L., & Belanger, F. (2002). Gender differences in perceptions of Web-based shopping. *Communications of the ACM, 45*(7), 82-86.

Worthington, S. L. S., & Boyes, W. (2001). *E-business in manufacturing: Putting the Internet to work in the industrial enterprises.* Research Triangle Park, NC: Instrumentation, Systems and Automation Society.

ENDNOTES

[1] These can be considered complementary goods

[2] These are classical examples of products that have been found to have synergy effects.

[3] Since Amazon.com started as SDS, the SIS→GIS evolutionary path is not applicable.

[4] These product expansions might be viewed as SDS to GIS path if we regard audio books or electronic books as separate types of product from different industries. Due to the expansion that occurred through the alliance, this is labeled as an evolutionary path from direct sales to indirect sales.

This work was previously published in the Journal of Electronic Commerce in Organizations, edited by M. Khosrow-Pour, Volume 5, Issue 4, pp. 70-87, copyright 2007 by IGI Publishing (an imprint of IGI Global).

Chapter XIII
Exogenous and Endogenous Antecedents of Online Shopping in a Multichannel Environment:
Evidence from a Catalog Retailer in the German-Speaking World

Maria Madlberger
Vienna University of Economics and Business Administration, Austria

ABSTRACT

Multichannel retailing can offer a wide range of synergies for retailers when their distribution channels accommodate consumers' preferences and buying behaviors. Among the large number of retail types, mail-order companies are well-suited to benefit from electronic commerce. Not only can they use their infrastructure and experience with direct selling, but they also seek to use the Internet to attract new target groups in order to increase their typically small, narrow customer bases. Currently, we do not know enough about the antecedents of channel choices, especially in the mail-order sector. This article addresses this issue and draws special attention to exogenous (i.e., independent of the retailer) factors that influence online shopping behavior. These variables include perceived convenience and perceived security of online shopping in general and consumers' attitudes toward the catalog as the existing distribution channel. One endogenous factor—attitude toward the online shop—is assumed to influence buying behavior at the online shop. In order to examine relationships between the catalog and the online shop, 2,363 consumers who were familiar with both distribution channels of a mail-order company were surveyed online. The structural equation model developed reveals that attitudes toward the printed catalog most strongly influence attitudes toward the online shop. Further, the analysis showed that antecedents of buying behavior at the online shop are moderated by gender. Shopping behaviors of men are influenced by their attitudes toward the catalog, while shopping behaviors of women are determined by their attitudes toward the online shop.

INTRODUCTION

Successful online retailers such as Amazon or eBay have become symbols of profitable e-commerce activities. However, pure Internet players generated only 31% of total Internet sales in 2003, whereas multichannel retailers (i.e., retailers that use online and off-line distribution channels simultaneously) accounted for 52% of Internet sales (Grosso, McPherson & Shi, 2004). One of the most well-known examples is the case of Tesco. com, one of the most successful electronic food retailers in the world (Madlberger, 2004). Tesco integrates its online distribution channel very strongly with its stores (Dawson, 2001). Also, other retailers such as Sears, Gap, and Land's End demonstrate that synergies can be exploited when one organization has different distribution channels. Consequently, it is not surprising that today's e-commerce landscape (apart from a few exceptions) is largely dominated by multichannel retailers (Haeberle, 2003).

Studies on success factors in e-commerce have identified several synergies that facilitate online retailing for multichannel players. Retailers with a network of physical stores can achieve synergies in the form of lower costs, differentiation through value-added services, improved trust, and the possibility of extending product markets when they go online (Steinfield, Bouwman, & Adelaar, 2002). In addition, multichannel retailers can spread their risks among several channels, which strengthens their financial standing.

Among traditional types of retailers, mail-order companies are in the best position to capitalize on synergies. These retailers, in fact, are considered well-suited for online business. This is also why most mail-order companies began to develop electronic marketing channels quite early in order to complement their catalog-based channels. For example, the apparel retailer Land's End launched its online shop as early as 1995 (Alptekinoglu & Tang, 2005). In addition, the target groups of many mail-order companies are stable but nondynamic and limited in size, which forces them to target new customer segments. The Internet could provide them with the opportunity to attract new customer segments and to benefit from various synergies.

However, these synergies can only be turned into competitive advantages and financial gains if electronic retailers successfully respond to consumer needs. Hence, in addition to the analysis of potential synergy effects for multichannel retailers, consumer behavior has to be taken into account. Besides the analysis of antecedents of online shopping, the distinction between influencing factors that are exogenous to the online shop and those that are endogenous (Monsuwé, Dellaert, & deRuyter, 2004) is critical. In order to gain insights into the antecedents of consumers' channel choices, we have formulated the following two research questions:

- Which exogenous factors influence consumers' attitudes toward a mail-order company's online shop as an endogenous factor?
- To what extent do their attitudes toward the online shop as an endogenous factor influence their buying behavior at that particular shop?

In order to answer these key questions, we have developed a structural equation model based on the Theory of Reasoned Action as well as on findings from the literature on distribution channel choice. In particular, we address the role of exogenous factors (Monsuwé et al., 2004). In order to test this model, we have conducted an empirical survey in cooperation with a mail-order company.

The article is organized as follows. First, we provide the theoretical basis of the research questions and discuss the literature used for the development of the model. The subsequent section focuses on the development of the model and explains the constructs before the research design is outlined and the results of the structural equation model are presented. Ultimately, the results are discussed and conclusions are drawn from the findings.

MULTICHANNEL RETAILING AND MAIL-ORDER RETAILING

Channels of distribution are a key research area in the context of retailing, marketing, and e-commerce (Coughlan, Anderson, Stern, & El-Ansary, 2001). Since the emergence of electronic commerce, research on consumers' channel choices has gained in attention and recognition from academia. Early research focused on channel choices between direct and retail-store-based channels (Alba et al., 1997; Balasubramanian, 1998; Fain, 1994). With the increasing relevance of e-commerce and Web-based distribution channels, more research on channel choice was conducted (Alptekinoglu & Tang, 2005; Balabanis & Reynolds, 2001; Berman & Thelen, 2004; Coelho, Easingwood, & Coelho, 2003; Kaufman-Scarborough & Lindquist, 2002; Wallace, Giese, & Johnson, 2004).

Electronic commerce is regarded as "an important catalyst for the recent proliferation of distribution-sales channels in retailing" (Alpteki-noglu & Tang, 2005, p. 802), as it enables retailers to increase sales (Gabrielsson, Kirpalani, & Luostarinen, 2002). Companies often have multiple channels because they add channels incrementally in order to expand their businesses (Moriarty & Moran, 1990). Multichannel strategies are extremely complex and require a thorough examination of intraorganizational and environmental conditions. Distribution channels can behave in an undulating manner when they contract or expand, which may cause limitations to multichannel retailing in some industries. Companies may face the risk of disintermediating important parts of the value chain by driving out intermediaries that add value. Another risk that is especially relevant for suppliers is channel pressure from strong retailers for which the new multichannel retailers become additional competitors. Conversely, new channel-extending intermediaries also can act as new competitors to existing companies (Gallaugher, 2002).

The retail sector comprises a large number of store types (Berman & Evans, 2001) that differ in their range of goods, price levels, and store-related or Web-site-related particularities. The largest differences exist between non-store-based retailers, which do business through direct selling channels, and store-based retailers. Grosso et al. (2004) provide a categorization framework of online retailers, distinguishing between online retailers with physical stores and those without physical outlets.

Retailers without physical stores are not a new phenomenon. They not only have a long history but also come in a variety of forms. Besides the classic catalog mail-order business, there are party plan businesses and television-based shopping channels. Direct selling has its roots in the U.S., where it originally resulted from the logistical needs to reach consumers in remote areas that did not have an adequate commercial infrastructure (Burton, 2000). Meanwhile, direct selling in Europe has gained in popularity, because many mail-order companies sell on credit and, therefore, offer clear advantages over most physical stores.

Following Grosso et al.'s (2004) framework, mail-order companies are classified as online retailers without physical stores. Compared with other types of retailing, a mail-order business is most similar to electronic commerce. The main tasks that the catalog fulfills are shifted to a Web site. Any processes that are related to ordering and distribution are equivalent to online and mail-order retailing. As mail-order companies are largely experienced with direct selling and possess an appropriate infrastructure for physical distribution, they are likely to have competitive advantages in online shopping also vis-à-vis store-based retailers. From a logistics perspective, mail-order companies that run a Web shop are likely to have ship-to-one logistics, whereas store-based retailers usually opt for pallet-shipping logistics. As a consequence, the investment necessary to build up and maintain the online channel is much lower from a logistics perspective. For example, JCPenny.com reached profitability within its first year, while the online store of Wal-Mart, the world's largest store-based retailer, is still in the red.

When mail-order companies go online, they can exploit a number of synergies, such as a wider range of goods, a higher degree of service personalization, and enhanced opportunities for price variances, such as temporary price reductions or discounts, all of which cannot be obtained that easily in the catalog business alone. Synergies that are beneficial to store-based multichannel retailers (e.g., cross-channel promotional opportunities, enhanced consumer confidence or the opportunity to tap new customer segments) (Madlberger, 2006) are available to mail-order companies, as well. Among the strategic alternatives proposed by Grosso et al. (2004), mail-order companies operating online should turn out to be efficiency machines that generate large sales volumes. However, as many classic mail-order companies typically attract only a small consumer segment, they belong, rather, to niche leaders.

An important issue for a multichannel retailer is consumers' channel choices. For a retailer, it is crucial not only to obtain knowledge about costs and benefits associated with different channels but also to develop an optimized channel architecture. Multichannel retailers should try to lure customers to the optimal channel instead of waiting for them to choose one (Myers, Pickersgill, & Van Metre, 2004). Schoenbachler and Gordon (2002) have developed a framework for analyzing potential antecedents of channel choice. They propose a research model that includes perceived risk, prior direct marketing experiences, motivation to buy from a channel, product category, and Web-site design. Further, previous research has identified the main motivating factors for traditional catalog shopping (Eastlick & Feinberg, 1999). Functional motivations (Sheth, 1983) include convenience (Eastlick & Feinberg, 1999; Jasper & Lan, 1992), range of goods (Reynolds, 1974), unique merchandise offerings (Januz, 1983), and a favorable price level (Korgaonkar, 1984). Arguing that nonfunctional motives for catalog shopping are also relevant, Eastlick and Feinberg (1999) discuss perceptions by the store clientele, promotions, and reputation of the mail-order company.

MODEL DEVELOPMENT

This survey focuses on channel-specific antecedents of buying behavior of a multichannel retailer's online shop. Previous studies on online shopping behavior have examined them in various contexts, focusing on the factors influencing online shopping behavior. For example, Gupta, Su, and Walter (2004) developed and tested an economic model that identifies channel characteristics and consumer risk profiles as antecedents. Also, the fit between information formats and shopping tasks influences shopping behavior on the Internet (Hong, Thong & Tam, 2004). A key issue that has been discussed exhaustively in the literature is the role of trust in online shopping (Bhattacherjee, 2002; Reichheld & Schefter, 2000; Suh & Han, 2003).

A considerable body of previous research on online shopping behavior has drawn on the technology acceptance model (Davis, 1989). For example, Gefen, Karahanna, and Straub (2003), Gefen (2000), and Lederer, Maupin, Sena, and Zhuang (2000) investigated TAM-based factors that influence online buying behavior. Pavlou (2003) added perceived risk to the model and regarded trust as a key independent variable. By taking into account perceived usefulness and perceived ease of use of a firm's online shop, TAM is related to factors that can be controlled by the retailer at least to some extent.

TAM is believed to be appropriate for explaining the acceptance of specific corporate information technologies (Monsuwé et al., 2004), but is criticized for neglecting factors that go beyond the attributes of this special technology application (Moon & Kim, 2001). For this reason, Monsuwé et al. (2004) call for the consideration of exogenous variables in analyses of online shopping behavior. Exogenous factors are independent of a retailer's online shop and cannot be influenced by it. Similarly, Jarvenpaa and Todd (1997) point to the importance of investigating the relationship between perceived characteristics of Web shopping in general and user intentions. Although Monsuwé et al. (2004) recommend using these variables chiefly for investigations of online shopping in general, there is evidence that suggests that exogenous factors should be taken into account, as well, when analyzing the acceptance of a particular firm's online shop.

A literature review by Chang, Cheung, and Lai (2005) shows that previous research has focused on three antecedents of online shopping: (1) perceived characteristics of the Web as a sales channel; (2) Web site and product characteristics; and (3) consumer characteristics. Several researchers have investigated how people's perceptions of Web characteristics in general influence their percep-

tions of an online shop. McKnight, Choudhury, and Kacmar (2002b) found that the risks associated with the Web negatively influence consumers' willingness to share personal information and their intention to purchase. Similarly, Burroughs and Sabherwal's (2002) work has revealed a significant influence of Internet security on purchasing behavior on an online store.

We are heeding Monsuwé et al.'s (2004) call for integrating exogenous factors into the research design. As suggested by them, relevant exogenous factors that can influence online shopping behavior are consumer traits, situational factors, product characteristics, previous online shopping experiences, and trust in online shopping. Since the research model used in this article is an initial investigation of the impact of exogenous factors, we focus on those variables that emerge from the literature review as likely to be relevant. Therefore, we look at constructs related to previous online shopping experiences and trust in online shopping as consumers' perceptions of the attractiveness of online purchasing in general. As gender turned out to be a relevant sociodemographic factor, we investigated whether the suggested dependencies vary between men and women. The analysis does not account for situational factors, since this requires respondents to recall individual purchasing transactions. Also, product characteristics are not included in the model, because the participating mail-order company sells products in a large number of categories with considerably different characteristics.

Previous online shopping experiences may be influenced by a variety of impressions, including, for example, product information, delivery terms, services offered, privacy, and visual appeal (Burke, 2002). Among these factors, perceived convenience and perceived security have turned out to be important factors in online shopping from the consumers' point of view (Ibbotson & Fahy, 2004). These factors are independent of a particular Web site's characteristics and, therefore, are not controllable by a single retailer. For this reason, we analyze perceived convenience and perceived security of online shopping as antecedents of consumers' attitudes toward an online shop. Previous research on online shopping also has revealed that attitudes toward one distribution channel influence attitudes toward another distribution channel (Balabanis & Reynolds, 2001; Kaufman-Scarborogh & Lindquist, 2002). Also, this factor is exogenous to the online shop but not exogenous to the retailer. Hence, we add attitudes toward the catalog as another exogenous antecedent of attitudes toward the online shop.

The endogenous factor (i.e., the factor that is related directly to the online shop) is measured by using the construct attitude toward the online shop. Attitudes toward a particular technology are a key element of TAM, which regards this construct as a factor influencing people's intentions to adopt a particular technology. As the focus of the study is on the importance of exogenous factors, we did not include the antecedents of attitudes toward the online shop (e.g., perceived usefulness, perceived ease of use).

The dependent variable is shopping behavior at the retailer's online shop. Unlike the TAM, we did not include intention to buy in the model but decided to look directly at actual behavior. We

did this for two reasons. First, there is a strong relationship between the intention to display a particular behavior and the behavior itself, as previous research on the Theory of Reasoned Action (TRA) (Ajzen & Fishbein, 1980) and the Theory of Planned Behavior (TPB) (Ajzen, 1991) has shown. Second, the analysis focuses on consumers who are related closely to the retailer, and so their intentions to buy can be expected to be very high.

Shopping behavior has many facets. For commercial firms, parts of shopping behavior that directly influence monetary success are of special relevance. In addition, spending money is the ultimate and most consequent way of interacting with any kind of shop. Hence, shopping behavior in the research model is related to spending at the online shop.

So far, there has been no empirical evidence that attitudes toward a mail-order company's printed catalog influence shopping behavior at the same retailer's online shop. The survey addresses this issue and investigates the influence of attitudes toward the catalog on shopping behavior at the online shop. On the basis of these considerations, we derive the research model summarized in Figure 1. In the following, the individual constructs and the related hypotheses are discussed.

Figure 1. Research model

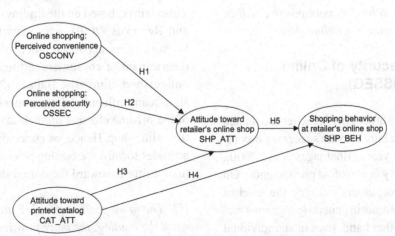

Perceived Convenience of Online Shopping (OSCONV)

Like traditional mail-order retailers, online shops argue that perceived convenience is one of the major advantages of direct selling compared with store-based shopping. Proponents of this argument hold that this convenience results from time savings. With consumers being faced with increasing time constraints, they benefit from saving time that would otherwise be spent driving to a store and back (Bhatnagar, Misra, & Rao, 2000). On the other hand, delays caused by long page loading times can negatively impact their evaluation of a Web site (Dellaert & Kahn, 1999). Perceived convenience consists of several dimensions that can be characterized by their occurrence during the transaction phases. These include access and search convenience (Seiders, Berry, & Gresham, 2000) and time and place convenience (Kaufman-Scarborough & Lindquist, 2000). The latter denotes that there is no need to leave the present location in order to visit a shop. Also, a study by Torkzadeh and Dhillon (2002) reveals that perceived convenience is a key determinant of online shopping behavior. Based on these findings, we can conclude that perceived convenience of online shopping as an exogenous factor has a positive effect on attitudes toward the online shop.

H1: The more convenient consumers perceive online shopping to be, the more positive will be their attitudes toward the online shop.

Perceived Security of Online Shopping (OSSEC)

Consumers' fears of security breaches and related risks have been a hurdle to the success of e-commerce for many years (Bhatnagar et al., 2000). Perceived security is a twofold phenomenon. On the one hand, consumers evaluate the level of security of the Internet in general (exogenous factor), but on the other hand, trust in an individual

vendor can influence buying behavior (Lee & Turban, 2001) as an endogenous factor. The second issue has been investigated in different contexts (Doney & Cannon, 1997; Hoffman, Novak, & Peralta, 1999; Jarvenpaa, Tractinsky, & Vitale, 2000; McKnight, Choudhury, & Kacmar, 2002a; Suh & Han, 2003). Previous research has found strong interrelations between trust and perceived security (Edwards, 2004; Lee & Turban, 2001). Yousafzai, Pallister, and Foxall (2003) argue that perceived security is an antecedent of trust. As the focus of this research is on exogenous variables characterized by perceived attributes of online shopping, the construct of perceived security rather than trust is used.

H2: The more secure consumers perceive online shopping to be, the more positive will be their attitudes toward the online shop.

Attitude Toward the Catalog (CAT_ATT)

As the retailer's online shop is the virtual counterpart of the catalog-based distribution channel, an image transfer from the existing channel to the Web-based channel could take place, thus influencing attitudes toward the online shop. Consumers do not regard the Internet as an independent world separate from other shopping channels (Kaufman-Scarborogh & Lindquist, 2002). This claim is based on the findings by Balabanis and Reynolds (2001), who identified the store network of an apparel retailer as an important determinant of consumers' attitudes toward an online shop. Similarly, Hansen (2005) found a significant influence of consumers' perceptions of the off-line channel on their attitudes toward the online shop. Hence, we conclude that people's attitudes toward the catalog positively influence their attitudes toward the online shop.

H3: The more positive people's attitudes are toward the catalog, the more positive will be their attitudes toward the online shop.

We also assume that their attitudes toward the printed catalog as the complementary distribution channel directly influence shopping behaviors at the online shop. Ahn, Ryu, and Han (2004) investigated the influence of off-line features such as delivery and customer service on the perceived usefulness of an online shop. However, a direct relationship between attitude toward one distribution channel and buying behavior at another channel has not been investigated yet, although there are indications that this relationship might be relevant. Customers who are familiar with the printed catalog but are not experienced in using the Web site may decide to shop online, irrespective of their attitudes toward the online shop. In addition, the existing distribution channel (i.e., the printed catalog) might be more prominent in the consumers' minds than the relatively new online shop. Hence, we assume that the more positive consumers' attitudes are toward the printed catalog, the more intensively they will buy from the online shop.

H4: The more positive consumers' attitudes are toward the catalog, the more they will spend at the online shop.

Attitude Toward the Online Shop (SHP_ATT)

Attitude toward the online shop is the only endogenous factor influencing shopping behavior in the model. Yang and Lester (2004) and Lepkowska-White (2004) have empirically demonstrated that online buyers have a more positive attitude toward online shopping than nonbuyers. According to the Theory of Reasoned Action (Ajzen & Fishbein, 1980) and Ajzen's (1991) Theory of Planned Behavior, attitudes have a considerable impact on behavior (Churchill & Iacobucci, 2002). Therefore, we hypothesize that consumers' attitudes toward the online shop positively influence shopping behavior.

H5: The more positive consumers' attitudes are toward the online shop, the more they will spend at the online shop.

H3, H4, and H5 imply that consumers' attitudes toward the online shop can be assumed to directly influence shopping behavior as well as to mediate the influence of attitudes toward the catalog on shopping behavior. Hence, the model includes a mediational triangle with partial mediation (Venkatraman, 1989), as proposed in the models specified by Taylór and Todd (1995) and Pflughoeft, Ramamurthy, Soofi, Yasai-Ardekani, and Zahedi (2003).

RESEARCH METHODOLOGY

The consumer survey was carried out in cooperation with a major mail-order company in the German-speaking part of Europe and took place in the context of a master thesis under the author's supervision (Hummel, 2005). The cooperating company (henceforth, the retailer) had been doing catalog business successfully for many years before it established an online shop in the mid-1990s. The retailer issues a printed catalog twice a year with a volume of approximately 1,300 pages. In addition, several special catalogs are available. Describing the retailer by means of Coelho and Easingwood's (2003) framework, we can say that the investigated shop is linked closely to its traditional distribution channel. The online shop is wholly owned by the retailer and is highly integrated. The retailer exclusively uses these two channels. The online shop comprises almost the same range of goods as the catalog and charges the same prices. Like the printed catalog, the online shop is divided into several product groups. The retailer offers a wide range of goods, including the following product categories: apparel (ladies' wear, men's wear, children's wear, sportswear), furniture, consumer electronics, jewelry, sports and leisure, gardening, home improvement, cosmetics, toys, baby products, and car accessories.

All these categories are sold via the catalog and the online shop. The retailer uses the same logos and product photos online and in the printed catalog, and has chosen a Web site design similar to the catalog design. Since the two channels are rather similar and do not target different consumer groups, they are classified as a monolithic channel system (Cespedes & Corey, 1990).

The online survey was conducted among the recipients of the retailer's newsletter in a period of one month in October and November, 2004. A total of 35,000 subscribers of the retailer's free newsletter were contacted via e-mail and directed to the questionnaire. It was not necessary to be a customer of the company in order to receive the newsletter, but users had to register to be able to subscribe to the newsletter. Recipients were informed regularly via e-mail about the retailer's promotions and special offers. Respondents were unable to access the questionnaire more than once. As an incentive for participation, a weekend trip was given away as a prize.

Before the survey was carried out, the questionnaire was revised by the retailer's marketing manager and two marketing assistants as well as by the IT manager and two employees in the IT department. Next, the questionnaire was pretested by asking 12 undergraduate students to fill it out online. The questionnaire was not changed considerably after the pretest. Only

minor adjustments in wording were necessary to ensure that the items would be interpreted correctly. Furthermore, a question concerning specific features of the online shop was removed, since it was not directly related to the model. This question also was eliminated in order to reduce the questionnaire's length. Finally, a status bar on each page indicated the completion progress of the questionnaire.

A total of 4,433 respondents answered the questionnaire, which corresponds to a response rate of 12.7%. Out of these, 2,070 incomplete questionnaires were eliminated, since they could not be used for model testing, which resulted in a sample of 2,363 completed questionnaires to be used for the analysis. A description of the sample's sociodemographic attributes is displayed in Table 1.

As Table 1 shows, the sample contains a high proportion of female respondents, which can be put down to the similar gender distribution of the retailer's customers and its newsletter recipients. To some extent, the age structure of the sample also reflects the structure of the retailer's customers. However, the extremely small proportion of young users among the respondents (less than 1%) is striking for two reasons. First, the vast majority of young people under the age of 20 use the Internet regularly in the country where the study was conducted (Integral, 2006). Second, young people usually are more likely to participate in surveys than older persons. Both facts increase the prob-

Table 1. Sample demographics (n=2,363)

Gender		Age	
Male	34.2%	Younger than 20 years	.9%
Female	64.7%	20–29 years	16.4%
Education		30–39 years	32.2%
Primary school	5.2%	40–49 years	29.6%
Apprenticeship/vocational school	41.4%	50–59 years	16.2%
Secondary school	18.4%	60 years and older	4.7%
High school	24.7%		
University	10.3%		

ability that this age group would participate in a survey. However, the age breakdown suggests differently, which can be explained by the structure of customers and prospective buyers of the mail-order company involved in the survey. Like many other mail-order companies, this retailer also has relatively few young customers. The educational level of the respondents is less biased. Although university graduates are a bit overrepresented, the educational structure is representative of the population of Internet users.

The respondents are very familiar with the Internet and online shopping. 53.7% have used the Internet for more than four years, and 75.3% are online daily. The most popular purposes of Internet usage are information gathering (65.2% strongly agreed), banking (50.2%), and communicating (42.4%). 24.7% strongly agreed that they used the Internet for shopping purposes, while only 14.7% disagreed or strongly disagreed with this statement. Most respondents are also frequent online shoppers. 49.6% bought more than 10 times online last year, and 30.3% bought online five to 10 times.

SCALE DEVELOPMENT

In order to test the research hypotheses already discussed, a set of scales has been developed for measuring the constructs, either derived from the literature or developed from scratch. The scales for perceived convenience were adapted mainly from

Yang and Lester (2004), who investigated attitudes toward online shopping among online shoppers and nonshoppers. The perceived security items are derived from Hoffmann, Novak, and Peralta's (1999) study on consumer perceptions of online shopping and Miyazaki and Fernandez's (2001) research on privacy and security risks in online shopping. Attitudes toward the online shop were measured using and adapting the scales developed by Kim and Stoel (2004), who identified dimensions of Web-site quality and satisfaction. The scales pertaining to attitudes toward the online shop were derived from Gehrt and Yan (2004) and Dholakia, Zhao, and Dholakia (2005). The former investigated factors influencing consumers' choices among online, catalog, and store channels, while the latter focused on channel choices between online shops and catalogs, taking into account catalog-specific aspects. Finally, online shopping behavior was measured using two items that capture the average frequency of buying from the online shop and the average amount of money spent there. All individual items and their sources are displayed in Table 3.

For item measurement, a 5-point Likert-type scale was used. It ranged from 1 (=strongly agree) to 5 (=strongly disagree). The constructs were the result of an exploratory factor analysis. In Table 2, the number of items used for each construct and the corresponding Cronbach alpha values are presented.

Carrying out an exploratory factor analysis, we developed the constructs using formative items.

Table 2. Reliabilities of constructs

Construct	Number of Items	Cronbach Alpha
OSCONV (perceived convenience of online shopping)	6	.863
OSSEC (perceived security of online shopping), reverse coded	6	.831
SHP_ATT (attitude toward the online shop)	5	.851
CAT_ATT (attitude toward the printed catalog)	5	.819
SHP_BEH (shopping behavior at the online shop)	2	.614

Table 3. Factor loadings of the individual items

	Perceived Convenience of Online Shopping (OSCONV)	Perceived Security of Online Shopping (OSSEC)	Attitude Toward the Online Shop (SHP_ATT)	Attitude Toward the Printed Catalog (CAT_ATT)	Online Shopping Behavior (SHP_BEH)	Source of Items
Online shopping 24 hours a day	.817					Yang & Lester (2004)
Product and price comparison	.726					Yang & Lester (2004)
Shopping independent of location	.772					Yang & Lester (2004)
Time saving	.688					Yang & Lester (2004)
Convenient because of home delivery	.653					new
No time pressure	.812					new
Access to personal and payment data*		.653				Miyazaki & Fernandez (2001)
Security problems during payment*		.702				new
Data misuse for advertising purposes*		.776				Hoffman, Novak, & Peralta (1999)
Trustworthiness of online shops		.676				new
Misuse of personal data*		.853				Hoffman, Novak, & Peralta (1999)
Sharing of sensitive data with third parties*		.748				Hoffman, Novak, & Peralta (1999)
Quick loading of shop			.763			Kim & Stoel (2004)
Good image quality of shop			.790			new
User-friendliness of shop			.741			Kim & Stoel (2004)
Visually appealing design of shop			.736			Kim & Stoel (2004)
Up-to-date pages of shop			.644			new
Good design of catalog				.580		new
Easy and quick ordering from catalog				.697		Gehrt & Yan (2004)
Easy calculation of shopping amount				.676		new
Easy handling of returns				.746		Dholakia, Zhao, & Dholakia (2005)
Confidential treatment of personal data				.726		Gehrt & Yan (2004)
Frequency of buying at online shop					.823	new
Average annual spending at online shop					.849	new
Eigenvalue	6.446	3.293	2.183	1.387	1.184	
Variance explained	.153	.137	.136	.117	.061	

* *reverse coded*

Prior to this analysis, we ran the Kaiser-Meyer-Olkin test, which resulted in a value of .902 (above the recommended value of .90). Hence, the data are considered appropriate for factor analysis. Subsequently, we applied the main component analysis with Varimax rotation. Only factors with Eigenvalues >1 were used, which left us with five factors. The total explained variance is 60.39%. Table 3 shows the items and their sources, the constructs, and their factor loadings.

STUDY RESULTS

In order to analyze the antecedents of shopping behavior at the retailer's online shop, we calculated a structural equation model (SEM) using AMOS 5 (Arbuckle, 1999). Only fully completed questionnaires were used for the analysis.

Table 4 shows the standardized regression weights and their levels of significance obtained by the SEM. It indicates that all hypotheses, except for H2, are accepted. The asterisks denote the level of significance (see bottom of Table 4). All paths are significant at least at a .05 level. Since the regression weight of H2, however, is close to zero, this hypothesis is rejected.

H1 assumed an influence of perceived convenience of online shopping (OS_CONV) on attitudes toward the online shop (SHP_ATT). This hypothesis is supported, given the standardized regression coefficient of .198 with p < .001.

H2 stated that attitudes toward the online shop (SHP_ATT) are influenced by perceived security of online shopping (OSSEC). The coefficient of -.049 is highly significant, but as this relationship is very weak, we reject H2. The next relationship investigated, posited by H3, pertains to the influence of attitudes toward the printed catalog (CAT_ATT) on attitudes toward the online shop (SHP_ATT). Here, the standardized regression coefficient amounts to .676 and is highly significant, as well (p < .001). This value, in fact, is the highest in the whole model. H4 also is supported by the model with a coefficient of .118 and a p of <.01. Finally, a relatively weak but still significant relationship is revealed by H5, which assumed that attitudes toward the online shop (SHP_ATT) influence buying behavior (SHP_BEH). The SEM procedure yields a standardized regression coefficient of .095 and a p level of .013.

In order to evaluate how well the model represents the real structure of the data, a series of fit indices is calculated using AMOS 5. In the following, those indices that have proved to be appropriate indicators in previous research are presented in Table 5, together with the values recommended in the academic literature (Anderson & Gerbing, 1984; Bentler, 1990; Brown & Cudek, 1993; Byrne, 2001; Hair, Anderson, Tatham, & Black, 1995). Table 5 also provides a short description of the fit measures. Being sensitive to large data sets, the Chi-square statistic is not used as an index of fit in this survey (Kline, 1998).

Table 4. Results of the structural equation model

Hypothesis	Path	Regression Weights	Significance	Hypothesis Accepted/Rejected
H1	OSCONV –> SHP_ATT	.198	***	accepted
H2	OSSEC –> SHP_ATT	-.049	**	rejected
H3	CAT_ATT –> SHP_ATT	.676	***	accepted
H4	CAT_ATT –> SHP_BEH	.118	**	accepted
H5	SHP_ATT –> SHP_BEH	.095	*	accepted
*** p < .001, ** p < .01, * p < .05, n.s. not significant				

Table 5. Fit indices of the hypothesized model

Goodness of Fit Measure	Explanation	Recommended Value	Calculated Value
GFI	Goodness of fit index: compares the hypothesized model with no model at all and, therefore, is a measure of overall degree of fit	.90 (Gefen et al., 2003)	.933
AGFI	Adjusted goodness of fit index: adjusted for the number of degrees of freedom	.80 (Gefen et al., 2003)	.919
RMSEA	Root mean square error of approximation: tests how well the model would fit the population covariance matrix with unknown but optimally chosen parameter values	.08 (Brown & Cudek, 1993)	.055
Tucker-Lewis	Tucker-Lewis or non-normed fit index (NNFI): comparative index between the hypothesized and the null model with a measure of parsimony	.90 (Hair et al., 1995)	.913
NFI	Normed fit index: in contrast to the Tucker-Lewis index, the NFI compares the hypothesized model with the null model	.90 (Hair et al., 1995)	.911
CFI	Compared fit index: compares the hypothesized model with the independent model	.90 (Myerscough, 2002)	.921

Table 6. Regression weights and hypotheses testing for the male sample

Male Respondents (n=809)				
Hypothesis	Path	Standardized Regression Weights	Significance	Hypothesis Accepted/ Rejected
H1	OSCONV –> SHP_ATT	.201	***	accepted
H2	OSSEC –> SHP_ATT	-.015	n.s.	rejected
H3	CAT_ATT –> SHP_ATT	.549	***	accepted
H4	CAT_ATT –> SHP_BEH	.213	***	accepted
H5	SHP_ATT –> SHP_BEH	.053	n.s.	rejected
*** p < .001, ** p < .01, * p < .05, n.s. not significant				

As Table 5 shows, GFI, AGFI, and RMSEA comply with the recommended values. Also, the baseline comparisons of the Tucker-Lewis index, the NFI, and the CFI exceed the .9 level. As a whole, the fit indices suggest a good fit of the model to the data.

In a next step, the influence of gender on the hypothesized model was analyzed. For this purpose, a multigroup analysis was performed (Byrne, 2001). The results are summarized in Table 6 for male respondents and in Table 7 for female respondents. The total number of male and female respondents is lower than the total

sample size, as 26 respondents did not indicate their gender and, thus, were excluded from the gender-specific analysis.

As shown in Tables 6 and 7, tests of Hypotheses 1, 2, and 3 yield results consistent with the overall analysis. Women's attitudes toward the catalog influence their attitudes toward the online shop more strongly than those of men (regression weight of .725 compared with .549). Among women, attitudes toward the online shop also are influenced by perceived security to a higher extent. However, since the regression weight of .072 is still rather small, Hypothesis 2 is not accepted.

Table 7. Regression weights and hypotheses testing for the female sample

Female Respondents (n=1,528)				
Hypothesis	**Path**	**Standardized Regression Weights**	**Significance**	**Hypothesis Accepted/Rejected**
H1	OSCONV –> SHP_ATT	.197	***	accepted
H2	OSSEC –> SHP_ATT	-.072	***	rejected
H3	CAT_ATT –> SHP_ATT	.725	***	accepted
H4	CAT_ATT –> SHP_BEH	.038	n.s.	rejected
H5	SHP_ATT –> SHP_BEH	.120	**	accepted
*** p < .001, ** p < .01, * p < .05, n.s. not significant				

Concerning Hypotheses 4 and 5, significant differences between men and women can be observed. Hypothesis 4 is accepted for the male sample but rejected for the female sample. Hence, among men, online shopping behavior is influenced by their attitudes toward the catalog but not by their attitudes toward the online shop. Conversely, Hypothesis 5 is rejected for the male sample but accepted for the female sample, suggesting that the opposite is true for women. Their online shopping behavior is influenced by their attitudes toward the online shop but not by their attitudes toward the catalog. This difference also explains the weaker significance level of Hypotheses 4 and 5 in the analysis of the whole sample.

DISCUSSION

The study investigated exogenous and endogenous antecedents of online shopping behavior of a multichannel retailer. As the results show, the most important factor influencing consumers' attitudes toward an online shop is their attitudes toward the catalog, which is a variable exogenous to the online shop. This result strengthens the assumption that image transfer effects are key determinants of consumers' attitudes toward an online sales channel. For an electronic retailer, this means that online and off-line distribution channels marketed under the same brand name should

not be separated from each other. This result is consistent with the findings from several empirical studies (Balabanis & Reynolds, 2001; Kaufman-Scarborough & Lindquist, 2002), reporting that there are close links among distribution channels of a company. Since Internet buyers have a strong tendency to switch channels (Dholakia et al., 2005), brands can serve as anchors for retailers by building online loyalty and preventing customer switching (Chen & Hitt, 2002).

Among the other exogenous variables, perceived convenience of e-commerce has a significant influence on consumers' attitudes toward the online shop. Hence, consumers' general perceptions of the Internet as a shopping channel can have an impact on attitudes toward an individual online retailer. Consumers who regard online shopping as convenient have more favorable attitudes toward the online shop. Since a large proportion of the consumers surveyed are also catalog shoppers, we conclude that convenience is an important factor for them. Convenience of online shopping thus can lead to more favorable attitudes toward the multichannel retailer's online shop among catalog shoppers and, eventually, toward online shopping.

Perceived security of online shopping does not seem to have any noteworthy effects on attitudes toward the online shop, with the relationship in the female sample being slightly stronger than that for the male sample. People who believe that online shopping is secure do not view the shop more positively. This result is consistent with the findings by Salisbury, Pearson, Pearson, & Miller (2001), who showed that perceived Web security does not influence consumers' intention to buy online. Also, the TAM-based research model by McCloskey (2004) reveals no significant impact of security concerns on buying behavior.

Notably, the antecedents of buying behavior at the retailer's online shop differ significantly for the two genders. This suggests that gender moderates the relationships between attitudes toward the catalog, attitudes toward the online shop, and buying behavior at the online shop. In the mediational triangle of the model, the paths resulting from the regression weights of men and women differ substantially. Gender differences in online shopping have been examined in numerous empirical studies such as Hansen (2005), Chang and Samuel (2004), and Rodgers and Harris (2003), all of which reveal that gender significantly influences various aspects of online shopping and related antecedents. Also, Eastlick and Feinberg (1994) have investigated differences between the two genders in the context of catalog shopping.

The present study reveals that men's attitudes toward the catalog are an important antecedent of purchasing behavior at the online shop, suggesting that attitudes become influential across channels among men. One explanation for this may be existing buying habits; for example, when consumers select products from the catalog and order them online. As Cheung and Limayem (2005) point out, habits are an important determinant of usage intentions. Catalog shoppers are used to the printed catalog and may regard it as the retailer's main distribution channel. However, this is only a speculative assumption that requires additional empirical evidence and cannot be confirmed by this study. The buying behavior of women, however, is determined by their attitudes toward the online shop rather than toward the catalog. Further research is needed in order to investigate the differences in buying patterns of men and women.

The results have several managerial implications for retailers: First, the study supports the notion that multichannel retailers can exploit synergies from their different distribution channels (Madlberger, 2006). If a positive attitude toward the printed catalog leads to a positive attitude toward the online shop, this fact is important for a mail-order company in a heterogeneous and complex online shopping environment. Even if a direct influence of attitudes toward the catalog on online buying behavior is observed only for men, attitudes toward the catalog also are indirectly relevant for women. The results imply, however, that marketing activities should be adapted to male and female target groups. Male customers of the retailer facilitating the survey mainly order electronics and men's wear but also ladies' wear and linens, whereas women order ladies' wear, linens, men's wear and children's wear most frequently. Also, sportswear and home textiles are ordered by female consumers, in particular. Hence, for product categories that are chiefly of interest to men, an online catalog retailer should focus on creating positive attitudes toward the catalog. For categories that are targeted mainly at women, positive attitudes toward the online shop should be the goal. For both genders, perceived convenience of Internet shopping is relevant. Therefore, a retailer not only needs to offer a high level of convenience but also should depend on consumers' general perceived convenience of Internet shopping. Consumers who have had bad experiences in this context might transfer these impressions to the online shop.

The model demonstrates that an online distribution channel strongly depends on the catalog business. As attitudes toward the printed catalog exert direct and indirect influences on online buying behaviors, the majority of online customers are committed to the existing distribution channel. This appears to be a critical issue when mail-order companies want to attract new target groups, since attitudes toward the catalog seem to be a kind of gateway to the online shop. The retailer cannot rely on the possibility of the online shop attracting new consumers. In view of a very stable but narrow customer base with a small proportion of young and well-educated people, the Internet would be an interesting supplement to the traditional catalog business. However, the findings of this study suggest that it will be hard for mail-order companies to expand their customer bases and to change the sociodemographic structure of their customers.

CONCLUSION AND LIMITATIONS

The results of this study have confirmed that an existing distribution channel has an influence on buying behavior at a retailer's online shop. This study is a first step toward understanding channel choices, particularly in the context of mail-order companies. It has several limitations that provide interesting avenues for future research in order to gain deeper insights into this topical issue in e-commerce.

Limitations of this study are twofold and pertain to both the proposed model and the survey method. First, the proposed model is a very simplistic one, given the high complexity of multichannel retailing. Some important variables have been left out that might play a key role in understanding consumer behavior in multichannel retailing.

Within the proposed model and its endogenous variable, antecedents of attitudes toward the online shop should be addressed in future studies. Research on TAM in an online shopping context is an appropriate point of departure for this area and justifies the application of perceived usefulness and perceived ease of use. Additionally, factors that have turned out to be relevant for online shopping in prior research, such as trust in the retailer or the design of the online shop (Ahn et al., 2004), should be addressed. Also, the mediating effect of attitude toward the online shop could be investigated more closely.

A key point that needs further attention is research on the reasons for the different antecedents of online buying behaviors between men and women. Special attention should be paid to buying processes and buying patterns across channels. Habits might play a major role in this context and might moderate relationships, as well (Cheung & Limayem, 2005).

In the context of exogenous variables, attitude toward the catalog is a key influencing factor. Therefore, antecedents of this variable should be investigated, as well. A starting point could be the research by Duffy (2004) and Gehrt and Yan (2004). Attitudes and perceived characteristics of Internet shopping in general might differ considerably between experienced and inexperienced online shoppers, thus moderating the relationship between exogenous and endogenous variables. In addition, other exogenous variables, such as the perceived value of individualization or general online shopping patterns, could be investigated. Finally, additional sociodemographic attributes could be included in the investigation.

Concerning the research methodology and the sample, it has to be stressed that the study was conducted in cooperation with one specific mail-order company, which limits the generalizability of the results. The respondents to the questionnaire were consumers who had subscribed to the retailer's newsletter and, therefore, had a certain relationship with the company. As most of the respondents also were customers, we do not gain insights into how other target groups behave and how the retailer could attract new customers. The study is restricted to the target group of one particular retailer, which limits the generalizability of the model to other retailers' customers, although most mail-order companies in the German-speaking world are faced with similar conditions and, thus, may draw conclusions from the previous results. In order to obtain results that are more representative, the study should be replicated among a less-specific group of consumers.

ACKNOWLEDGMENTS

We thank the cooperating mail-order company that wants to be kept anonymous for participation and support of the survey. The management's engagement in the survey was essential for carrying out the investigation. The author is also very grateful to Michael Hummel, undergraduate student at the Vienna University of Economics and Business Administration. He assisted in preparing the questionnaire and collected data under the author's supervision.

REFERENCES

Ahn, T., Ryu, S., & Han, I. (2004). The impact of the online and offline features on the user acceptance of Internet shopping malls. *Electronic Commerce Research and Applications, 3*(4), 405–420.

Ajzen, I. (1991). The theory of planned behavior. *Organizational Behavior & Human Decision Processes, 50*(2), 179–211.

Ajzen, I., & Fishbein, M. (1980). *Understanding attitudes and predicting social behavior.* Englewood Cliffs, NJ: Prentice Hall.

Alba, J., Lynch, J, Weitz, B., Janiszewski, C., Lutz, R., Sawyer, A., et al. (1997). Interactive home shopping: Consumer, retailer, and manufacturer incentives to participate in electronic marketplaces. *Journal of Marketing, 61*(3), 38–53.

Alptekinoglu, A., & Tang, C.S. (2005). A model for analyzing multi-channel distribution systems. *European Journal of Operational Research, 163*(3), 802–824.

Anderson, J.C., & Gerbing, D.W. (1984). The effect of sampling error on convergence, improper solutions, and goodness-of-fit indices for maximum likelihood confirmatory factor analysis. *Psychometrika, 49*(2), 155–173.

Arbuckle, J.L. (1999). *Amos user's guide, version 4.0.* Chicago, IL: Smallwaters Cooperation.

Balabanis, G., & Reynolds, N.L. (2001). Consumer attitudes towards multi-channel retailer's Web sites: The role of involvement, brand attitude, Internet knowledge, and visit duration. *Journal of Business Strategies, 18*(2), 105–131.

Balasubramanian, S. (1998). Mail versus mall: A strategic analysis of competition between direct marketers and conventional retailers. *Marketing Science, 17*(3), 181–195.

Bentler, P.M. (1990). Comparative fit indexes in structural models. *Psychological Bulletin, 107*(2), 238–246.

Berman, B., & Evans, J.R. (2001). *Retail management—A strategic approach.* Upper Saddle River, NJ: Prentice-Hall.

Berman, B., & Thelen, S. (2004). A guide to developing and managing a well-integrated multi-channel retail strategy. *International Journal of Retail & Distribution Management, 32*(2/3), 147–156.

Bhatnagar, A., Misra, S., & Rao, H. R. (2000). On risk, convenience, and Internet shopping behaviour. *Communications of the ACM, 43*(11), 98-105.

Bhattacherjee, A. (2002). Individual trust in online firms: Scale development and initial tests. *Journal of Management Information Systems, 19*(1), 211–242.

Brown, M.W., & Cudeck R. (1993). Alternative ways of assessing model fit. In K.A. Bollen, & S. Long (Eds.), *Testing structural equation models* (pp. 136–162). Newbury Park, CA: Sage Publications.

Burke, R.R. (2002). Technology and the customer interface: What consumers want in the physical world and virtual store. *Journal of the Academy of Marketing Science, 30*(4), 411–432.

Burroughs, R.E., & Sabherwal, R. (2002). Determinants of retail electronic purchasing: A multi-period investigation. *Journal of Information System Operation Research, 40*(1), 35–56.

Burton, D. (2000). Postmodernism, social relations and remote shopping. *European Journal of Marketing, 36*(7/8), 792–810.

Byrne, B.M. (2001). *Structural equation modeling with AMOS*. Mathwah, NJ: Lawrence Erlbaum Associates.

Cespedes, F.V., & Corey, E.R. (1990). Managing multiple channels. *Business Horizons, 33*(3), 67–77.

Chang, J., & Samuel, N. (2004). Internet shopper demographics and buying behavior in Australia. *Journal of the Academy of Business, 5*(1/2), 171–176.

Chang, M.K., Cheung, W., & Lai, V.S. (2005). Literature derived reference models for the adoption of online shopping. *Information & Management, 42*(4), 543–559.

Chen, P.-Y., & Hitt, L.M. (2002). Measuring switching costs and the determinants of customer retention in Internet-enabled businesses: A study of the online brokerage industry. *Information Systems Research, 13*(3), 255–274.

Cheung, M.K., & Limayem, M. (2005). The role of habit and the changing nature of the relationship between intention and usage. In *Proceedings of the 13th European Conference of Information Systems*, Regensburg, Germany.

Churchill, G.A.J., & Iacobucci, D. (2002). *Marketing research: Methodological foundations*. Mason, OH: South-Western Publishing.

Coelho, F., & Easingwood, C. (2003). Multiple channel structures in financial services: A framework. *Journal of Financial Services Marketing, 8*(1), 22-34.

Coelho, F., Easingwood, C., & Coelho, A. (2003). Exploratory evidence of channel performance in single vs. multiple channel strategies. *International Journal of Retail and Distribution Management, 31*(11/12), 561-573.

Coughlan, A.T., Anderson, E., Stern, L.W., & El-Ansary, A.I. (2001). *Marketing channels*. Upper Saddle River, NJ: Prentice Hall.

Davis, F.D. (1989). Perceived usefulness, perceived ease of use, and user acceptance of information technology. *MIS Quarterly, 13*(3), 317–340.

Dawson, M. (2001). Land in Sicht. *Lebensmittelzeitung Spezial E-Business, 1*, 60–61.

Dellaert, B.G.C., & Kahn, B.E. (1999). How tolerable is delay? Consumer's evaluation of Internet Web sites after waiting. *Journal of Interactive Marketing, 13*(1), 41–54.

Dholakia, R.R., Zhao, M., & Dholakia, N. (2005). Multichannel retailing: A case study of early experiences. *Journal of Interactive Marketing, 19*(2), 63–74.

Doney, P.M., & Cannon, J.P. (1997). An examination of the nature of trust in the buyer-seller relationship. *Journal of Marketing, 61*(2), 35–51.

Duffy, D.L. (2004). Using online retailing as a springboard for catalog marketing. *Journal of Consumer Marketing, 21*(3), 221–225.

Eastlick, M.A., & Feinberg, R.A. (1994). Gender differences in mail-catalog patronage motives. *Journal of Direct Marketing, 8*(2), 37–44.

Eastlick, M.A., & Feinberg, R.A. (1999). Shopping motives for mail catalog shopping. *Journal of Business Research, 45*(3), 281–290.

Edwards, L. (2004) Reconstructing consumer privacy protection on-line: A modest proposal. *International Review of Law Computers, 18*(3), 313–344.

Fain, D. (1994). *Consumers navigating channels: Behavior motivations for direct vs. retail.* Unpublished manuscript, New York University, New York.

Gabrielsson, M., Kirpalani, V.H.M., & Luostarinen, R. (2002). Multiple channel strategies in the European personal computer industry. *Journal of International Marketing, 10*(3), 73–95.

Gallaugher, J.M. (2002). E-commerce and the undulating distribution channel. *Communications of the ACM, 45*(7), 89–95.

Gefen, D. (2000). E-commerce: The role of familiarity and trust. *Omega: The International Journal of Management Science, 28*(6), 725–737.

Gefen, D., Karahanna, E., & Straub, D.W. (2003). Trust and TAM in online shopping: An integrated model. *MIS Quarterly, 27*(1), 51–90.

Gehrt, K.C., & Yan, R.-N. (2004). Situational, consumer, and retailer factors affecting Internet, catalog, and store shopping. *International Journal of Retail and Distribution Management, 32*(1), 5–18.

Grosso, C., McPherson, J., & Shi, C. (2004). Retailing: What's working online. *McKinsey Quarterly, 2005*(3), 18–20.

Gupta, A., Su, B., & Walter, Z. (2004). Risk profile and consumer shopping behavior in electronic and traditional channels. *Decision Support Systems, 38*(3), 347–367.

Haeberle, M. (2003). On-line retailing scores big. *Chain Store Age, 79*(7), 48.

Hair, J., Anderson, R.E., Tatham, R.L., & Black, W.C. (1995). *Multivariate data analysis with readings.* Englewood Cliffs, NJ: Prentice-Hall.

Hansen, T. (2005). Understanding consumer online grocery behavior: Results from a Swedish study. *Journal of Euromarketing, 14*(3), 31–58.

Hoffman, D.L., Novak, T.P., & Peralta, M. (1999). Building consumer trust online. *Communications of the ACM, 42*(4), 80–85.

Hong, W., Thong, J.Y.L., & Tam, K.Y. (2004). The effects of information format and shopping task on consumers' online shopping behavior: A cognitive fit perspective. *Journal of Management Information Systems, 21*(3), 149–184.

Hummel, M. (2005). *E-commerce—Eine Sonderform des Versandhandels?* Master's thesis, Vienna University of Economics and Business Administration, Vienna.

Ibbotson, P., & Fahy, M. (2004). The impact of e-commerce on small Irish firms. *International Journal of Services Technology & Management, 5*(4), 317–331.

Integral. (2006). Austrian Internet Monitor Internet-Entwicklung 3. *Quartal 2005.* Retrieved February 22, 2006, from http://www.integral. co.at/dImages/AIM-C_3.%20Quartal2005.pdf

Januz, L.R. (1983). It's helpful to know who is purchasing through the mail. *Marketing News, 17*, 4.

Jarvenpaa, S.L., & Todd P.A. (1997). Consumer reactions to electronic shopping on the World Wide Web. *International Journal of Electronic Commerce, 1*(2), 59–88.

Jarvenpaa, S.L., Tractinsky, N., & Vitale, M. (2000). Consumer trust in an Internet store. *Information Technology and Management, 1*, 45–71.

Jasper, C.R., & Lan, P.-N.R. (1992). Apparel catalog patronage: Demographic, lifestyle and motivational factors. *Psychology and Marketing, 9*(4), 275–296.

Kaufman-Scarborough, C., & Lindquist, J.D. (2002). E-shopping in a multiple channel environment. *Journal of Consumer Marketing, 19*(4/5), 333–350.

Kim, S., & Stoel, L. (2004). Apparel retailers: Website quality dimensions and satisfaction. *Journal of Retailing and Consumer Services, 11*(2), 109–117.

Kline, R.B. (1998). *Principles and practice of structural equation modeling.* New York: Guilford.

Korgaonkar, P.K. (1984). Consumer shopping orientations, non-store retailers, and consumers' patronage intentions: A multivariate investigation. *Journal of the Academy of Marketing Science, 12*(1), 11–22.

Lederer, A.L., Maupin, D.J., Sena, M.P., & Zhuang, Y. (2000). The technology acceptance model and the World Wide Web. *Decision Support Systems, 29*(3), 269–282.

Lee, M.K.O., & Turban, E. (2001). A trust model for consumer Internet shopping. *International Journal of Electronic Commerce, 6*(1), 75–91.

Lepkowska-White, E. (2004). Online store perceptions: How to turn browsers into buyers? *Journal of Marketing Theory & Practice, 12*(3), 36–47.

Madlberger, M. (2004). *Electronic retailing.* Wiesbaden, Germany: Deutscher Universitaets-verlag.

Madlberger, M. (2006). Multi-channel retailing in B2C e-commerce. In M. Khosrow-Pour (Ed.), *Encyclopedia of e-commerce, e-government, and mobile commerce.* Hershey, PA: Idea Group Reference.

McCloskey, D. (2004). Evaluating electronic commerce acceptance with the technology acceptance model. *Journal of Computer Information Systems, 44*(2), 49–57.

McKnight, D.H., Choudhury, V., & Kacmar, C. (2002a). Developing and validating trust measures for e-commerce: An integrative typology. *Information Systems Research, 13*(3), 334–359.

McKnight, D.H., Choudhury, V., & Kacmar, C. (2002b). The impact of initial consumer trust on intentions to transact with a Web site: A trust building model. *Journal of Strategic Information Systems, 11*(3-4), 297–323.

Miyazaki, A.D., & Fernandez, A. (2001). Consumer perceptions of privacy and security risks for online shopping. *The Journal of Consumer Affairs, 35*(1), 27–44.

Monsuwé, T.P.Y., Dellaert, B.G.C., & deRuyter, K. (2004). What drives consumers to shop online? A literature review. *International Journal of Service Industry Management, 15*(1), 102–121.

Moon, J.W., & Kim, Y.-G. (2001). Extending the TAM for a World-Wide-Web context. *Information & Management, 38*(4), 217–230.

Moriarty, R., & Moran, U. (1990). Managing hybrid marketing systems. *Harvard Business Review, 68*(6), 146–155.

Myers, J.B., Pickersgill, A.D., & Van Metre, E.S. (2004). Steering customers to the right channels. *McKinsey Quarterly, 2004*(4), 36–47.

Myerscough, M.A. (2002, August). Information systems quality assessment: Replicating Kettinger and Lee's USIF/SERVQUAL combination. In *Proceedings of the 8th Americas Conference on Information Systems,* Dallas, Texas, USA (pp. 1104–1115).

Pavlou, P.A. (2003). Consumer acceptance of electronic commerce: Integrating trust and risk with the technology acceptance model. *International Journal of Electronic Commerce, 7*(3), 101–134.

Pflughoeft, K.A., Ramamurthy, K., Soofi, E.S., Yasai-Ardekani, M., & Zahedi, F. (2003). Multiple conceptualizations of small business Web use and benefit. *Decision Sciences, 34*(3), 467–512.

Reichheld, F., & Schefter, P. (2000). E-loyalty: Your secret weapon on the Web. *Harvard Business Review, 78*(4), 105–113.

Reynolds, F.D. (1974). An analysis of catalog buying behavior. *Journal of Marketing, 38*(3), 47–51.

Rodgers, S., & Harris, M.A. (2003). Gender and e-commerce: An exploratory study. *Journal of Advertising Research, 43*(3), 322–329.

Salisbury, W.D., Pearson, R.A., Pearson, A.W., & Miller, D.W. (2001). Perceived security and World Wide Web purchase intention. *Industrial Management & Data Systems, 101*(3/4), 165-176.

Schoenbachler, D.D., & Gordon, G.L. (2002). Multi-channel shopping: Understanding what drives channel choice. *The Journal of Consumer Marketing, 19*(1), 42–53.

Seiders, K., Berry, L.L., & Gresham, L.G. (2000). Attention, retailers! How convenient is your convenience strategy? *Sloan Management Review, 41*(3), 79–89.

Sheth, J.N. (1983). An integrative theory of patronage preference and behavior. In W.R. Darden, & R.F. Lusch (Eds.), *Patronage behavior and retail management* (pp. 9–28). New York: Elsevier Science Publishing.

Steinfield, C., Bouwman, H., & Adelaar, T. (2002). The dynamics of click-and-mortar electronic commerce: Opportunities and management strategies. *International Journal of Electronic Commerce, 7*(1), 93–119.

Suh, B., & Han, I. (2003). The impact of customer trust and perception of security control on the acceptance of electronic commerce. *International Journal of Electronic Commerce, 7*(3), 135–162.

Taylor, S., & Todd, P.A. (1995). Understanding information technology usage: A test of competing models. *Information Systems Research, 6*(2), 144–176.

Torkzadeh, G., & Dhillon, G. (2002). Measuring factors that influence the success of Internet commerce. *Information Systems Research, 13*(2), 187–204.

Venkatraman, N. (1989). The concept of fit in strategy research: Toward verbal and statistical correspondence. *Academy of Management Review, 14*(3), 423–444.

Wallace, D.W., Giese, J.L., & Johnson, J.L. (2004). Customer retailer loyalty in the context of multiple channel strategies. *Journal of Retailing, 80*(4), 249–263.

Yang, B., & Lester, D. (2004). Attitudes toward buying online. *Cyber Psychology & Behavior, 7*(1), 85–91.

Yousafzai, S.Y., Pallister, J.G., & Foxall, G.R. (2003). A proposed model of e-trust for electronic banking. *Technovation, 23*(11), 847–860.

This work was previously published in the Journal of Electronic Commerce in Organizations, edited by M. Khosrow-Pour, Volume 4, Issue 4, pp. 29-51, copyright 2006 by IGI Publishing (an imprint of IGI Global).

Chapter XIV
Examining Online Purchase Intentions in B2C E-Commerce:
Testing an Integrated Model

C. Ranganathan
University of Illinois at Chicago, USA

Sanjeev Jha
University of Illinois at Chicago, USA

ABSTRACT

Research on online shopping has taken three broad and divergent approaches viz, human-computer interaction, behavioral, and consumerist approaches to examine online consumer behavior. Assimilating these three approaches, this study proposes an integrated model of online shopping behavior, with four major antecedents influencing online purchase intent: Web site quality, customer concerns in online shopping, self-efficacy, and past online shopping experience. These antecedents were modeled as second-order constructs with subsuming first-order constituent factors. The model was tested using data from a questionnaire survey of 214 online shoppers. Statistical analyses using structural equation modeling was used to validate the model, and identify the relative importance of the key antecedents to online purchase intent. Past online shopping experience was found to have the strongest association with online purchase intent, followed by customer concerns, Web site quality, and computer self efficacy. The findings and their implications are discussed.

INTRODUCTION

Internet and Web technologies have fundamentally changed the way businesses interacted, transacted and communicated with consumers. As a business medium, the Internet is unique in permitting firms to create interactive online environments that allow consumers to gather and evaluate information, assess purchase options, and directly buy products at their own convenience. Web-based retailing has become a global phenomenon with steady increase in online sales across the globe. The growth in online shopping has been motivated by several reasons—convenience, ease, pricing, comparative analysis, wider selection of products and services, and so forth.

Although online shopping has been on the rise, the challenges associated with Web-based retailing have also increased. First, the growing numbers of traditional merchants and pureplay Internet firms have greatly intensified online competition. With blurring geographical boundaries and reduced barriers to entry, the digital marketplace has become crowded with a large number of players. Second, while the online customer acquisition costs have increased significantly, the switching costs of online consumers have diminished exponentially. Third, despite the growing popularity of online shopping, several factors such as fear of fraud, security concerns, lack of trust have dissuaded consumers to purchase online (Gefen, Karahanna, & Straub, 2003; Kiely, 1997). Several studies have documented the problems associated with attracting and retaining online consumers. For instance, Vatanasombut, Stylianou, and Igbaria (2004) deliberated on the difficulty of retaining online customers and proffered strategies to keep novice and sophisticated users happy and loyal. Chen and Hitt (2002) suggested developing strategies to raise customer switching costs in order to deter them from moving to other Web sites.

Rise in online shopping has generated a growing body of research on online consumer behavior. This research can be grouped into those adopting a technological perspective and others with a marketing perspective. Scholars embracing a technological perspective have focused on technical elements such as Web-site navigation and design (Everard & Galletta, 2005; Liu & Arnett, 2000; Spiller & Lohse, 1997), software tools and technological aids (Heijden, Verha-

gen, & Creemers, 2003; Salaun & Flores, 2001; Wan, 2000). Researchers adopting a marketing perspective have focused their attention on the decision making process (Gefen, 2000; McKnight, Choudhury, & Kacmar, 2002a), and the marketing elements such as pricing, promotion, branding, reputation and customer attitude (Bart, Shankar, Sultan, & Urban, 2005; Chu, Choi, & Song, 2005; Iwaarden, Wiele, Ball, & Millen, 2004; Urban, Sultan, & Qualls, 2000). These research developments notwithstanding, several significant gaps still remain unaddressed. First, these divergent approaches seem to portray only a partial, yet unclear picture of online consumer behavior. While prior studies have helped identify key issues, lack of an integrated focus has marred the broader applicability of the findings. Second, while past research has identified several technological, behavioral and individual factors as important in influencing online consumer behavior, it is not clear if these factors have a differential impact (i.e., a more clear understanding is required if any of the factors explain or predict online shopping behavior more than the others). Third, a large number of studies have used student samples (Gefen, 2000; Mauldin & Arunachalam, 2002; McKnight, Choudhury, & Kacmar, 2002a, 2002b; Pavlou, 2003), thus raising questions on the generalizability of the findings to a large online consumer community.

In this article, we seek to extend our current knowledge on online shopping behavior in the following ways. Our primary research objective is to combine the key technological, behavioral, and consumer-related constructs identified in prior literature and propose an integrated model of online consumer behavior. Our study directly responds to the research calls to provide an integrated perspective on online consumer behavior (Bart et al., 2005; Heijden, 2003). Further, we test our integrated model using a sample of actual online consumers with prior experience in purchasing goods and services online. We pool together the key technological and behavioral factors and empirically examine the relative importance of these constructs in predicting online purchase intention of consumers.

LITERATURE REVIEW

An analysis of extant literature on online shopping reveals three distinct orientations underlying these studies; viz, Human–Computer Interaction (HCI), behavioral, and consumerist orientations. These three streams have also been identified by Chang, Cheung, and Lai (2005), who reviewed over 45 empirical studies of online consumer behavior. We summarize the essence of these approaches and propose an integrated model that encompasses key elements from all the three streams of research.

HCI research is primarily concerned with design and implementation of user interfaces that are easy to learn, efficient, and pleasant to use. Scholars embracing a HCI orientation have investigated Web-site related characteristics that potentially influence online consumer behavior. These researchers emphasize factors such as information content (Ranganathan & Ganapathy, 2002); visual attractiveness of the Web site (Heijden, 2003); quality of information provided (Salaun & Flores, 2001); ease of navigation, time taken for information search (Evarard & Galletta, 2005; Spiller & Lohse, 1997; Tarafdar & Zhang, 2005); and the overall design of the Web site (Flavin, Guinaliu, & Gurrea, 2006; Huizingh, 2000; G. Lee & Lin, 2005; Zviran, Glezer, & Avni, 2006). This stream of research places technological factors to be at the forefront of factors influencing online consumer shopping behavior.

The second group of scholars has taken a behavioral approach, wherein they have investigated the factors influencing customer concerns in online shopping (CCOS). While a few studies have focused on the trust elements influencing online shopping (Gefen & Straub, 2004; Kaufaris & Hampton-Sosa, 2004; Schlosser, White, &

Lloyd, 2006), others have investigated the factors that inhibit or encourage online shopping (Burroughs & Sabherwal, 2002; Brynjolfsson & Smith, 2000). These researchers argue that the primary requirement for the online shopping is a sense of trust between consumers and online merchants (Eastlick, Lotz, & Warrington, 2006; Jarvenpaa, Tractinsky, & Vitale, 2000; Urban et al., 2000). Since the transactions take place in a virtual market and customers do not physically interact with sellers, it is important that customers exude confidence in sellers and are ready to part with personal information to them.

The third group has focused on consumer characteristics and their influence on online shopping behavior. The basic notion underlying this stream is that individual characteristics such as the demographics, personality, and profiles play a larger role in determining the online shopping behavior (De Wulf, Schillewaert, Muylle, & Rangrajan, 2006; Liao & Cheung, 2001; Zhang, Prybutok, & Koh, 2006). Extending the traditional marketing theories, this group argues for consumer characteristics to be dominant in influencing their intention to engage in online purchases. These studies have focused on the variables like technology friendliness of customers and their comfort level in online shopping (Heijden, 2003; Mauldin & Arunachalam, 2002; Pavlou, 2003; Shih, 2004). A few researchers have also looked into the effect of past online shopping experience on future online buying behavior of consumers (Pavlou, 2003; Yoh, Damhorst, Sapp, & Laczniak 2003).

These three broad streams of research place emphasis on divergent technological, attitudinal, and consumer-related elements to provide insights into how these factors affect online shopping behavior. However, our central thesis is that integrating and combining these divergent yet complementary approaches could provide a richer perspective. Online consumer behavior is a multidimensional concept that requires an integrated examination of key elements from all the three research streams (Bart et al., 2005; Heijden, 2003). Integrating insights from these multiple streams, we identify Web-site quality (HCI factor), customer concerns in online shopping (behavioral approach), computer self-efficacy, and past online experience (consumerist variables) to be the key potential predictors of online purchase behavior. Our focus is on examining key variables rather than proposing a comprehensive model with a full set of factors. The conceptual framework for our research is depicted in Figure.1. Our primary research goals are to

a. Empirically examine the association between Web-site quality, customer concerns in online shopping, computer self-efficacy, and past online experience with online purchase intention of consumers;
b. Investigate the relative importance of each of these factors in order to prioritize their significance in predicting online purchase behavior.

Development of Hypotheses

In this section we discuss development of our research model and various hypotheses. To this end, we review pertinent literature from IS, e-commerce, and marketing disciplines to present the operationalization of our research constructs, and the rationale for our hypotheses. The research model is presented in Figure 2 and sources of variables are presented in Table 1.

Web Site Quality

Given that a Web site is the dominant medium of interaction between merchants and consumers in online shopping, it is imperative that the quality of the Web site is given adequate importance. Past research on Web quality can be classified into four complementary approaches (Ethier, Hadaya, Talbot, & Cadieux, in press). The first approach focused on the functional features of the site. Under this approach, scholars examined the content, style, presentation, navigation and other features of the Web site (Tarafdar & Zhang, 2005). The second approach drew upon the technology acceptance model to view Web quality as an overarching construct that included elements such as information quality, systems quality, and service quality. The third approach emphasized the fundamental service that the business-to-consumer (B2C) Web site provided. Here, Web

Figure 1. Conceptual framework

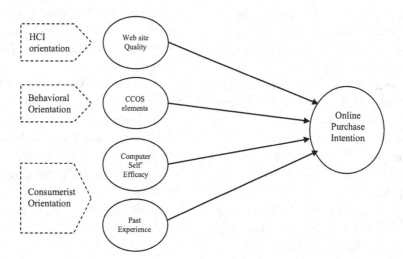

Table 1. Constructs, key variables, and references

Web site quality	
Web-site Content	De Wulf et al. 2006; Huizingh, 2000; Liu and Arnett, 2000; Ranganathan and Ganapathy, 2002; Salaun and Flores, 2001; Spiller and Lohse, 1997
Web-site Design	De Wulf et al. 2006; Heijden, 2003; Huizingh, 2000; Liu and Arnett, 2000; Lohse and Spiller, 1999; Maudlin and Arunachalam, 2002; Ranganathan and Ganapathy, 2002; Spiller and Lohse, 1997; Wan, 2000
Customer Concerns in Online Shopping	
Privacy	Belanger, 2002; Dinev and Hart, 2005–2006; Eastlick et al., 2006; Ranganathan and Ganapathy, 2002; Schlosser et al 2006; Suh and Han, 2003; Vijayasarathy, 2004
Security	Belanger, 2002; Burroughs and Sabherwal, 2002; Koufaris and Hampton-Sosa, 2004; Liao and Cheung, 2001; Ranganathan and Ganapathy, 2002; Scholsser et al., 2006, Vijayasarathy, 2004
Product Delivery & Returns	Bart et al., 2005; Pechtl, 2003; Ranganathan and Ganapathy, 2002; Vijayasarathy, 2004
Computer Self Efficacy	
IT Attitude	Bellman et al., 1999; Liao and Cheung, 2001; Maudlin and Arunachalam, 2002
IT Skills	Burroughs and Sabherwal, 2002; Liao and Cheung, 2001; Maudlin and Arunachalam, 2002; Vijayasarathy, 2004
Past Online Shopping Experience	Bart et al. 2005; Pavlou, 2003; Yoh et al., 2003

quality was assessed with subdimensions like reliability, responsiveness, assurance, empathy, and tangibility. The fourth approach viewed Web quality through the lens of the consumer attitudes and perceptions (Aladwani & Palvia, 2002). Extending these approaches, scholars have also proposed multiple instruments for assessing Web quality (e.g., WEBQUAL [Loiacono, Watson, & Goodhue, 2002]; SiteQual [Webb & Webb, 2004]; SERVQUAL [Iwaarden & Wiele, 2003], etc.) that try and incorporate dimensions from one or more of these approaches.

A review of past research on Web site quality reveals little consensus on what constitutes this construct. Multiple terms such as *Web quality, Web site quality, service quality, site usability,* and so forth, have been used to denote different dimensions of Web site quality. Earlier studies adopted a dominant HCI perspective focusing on the quality of the medium through which online commerce was conducted between businesses and consumers. As more behavioral and consumerist studies emerged, multiple lenses were used to

assess Web site quality, thus leading to varied terminology and mixed empirical findings. However, there is a broad agreement that quality of a B2C Web site is a multidimensional and a more complex construct (Ethier et al. in press).

In this study, we conceptualize Web site quality as primarily reflecting the content and design functionalities of a B2C site. From a HCI lens, Web site quality simply represents the quality of the online medium, rather than the services or transactions rendered through the Web site. Our approach is consistent with Tarafdar and Zhang (2005), who took a HCI-orientation to view Web-site usability as reflecting the quality of a B2C Web site.

Within the HCI research stream, Web site quality has been fundamentally assessed using two factors: Web site content and Web site design. Huizingh (2000) stressed on the importance of distinguishing content and design while discussing Web site quality. Ranganathan and Ganapathy (2002) defined content as the information, features or services offered in the Web site

Figure 2. Research model

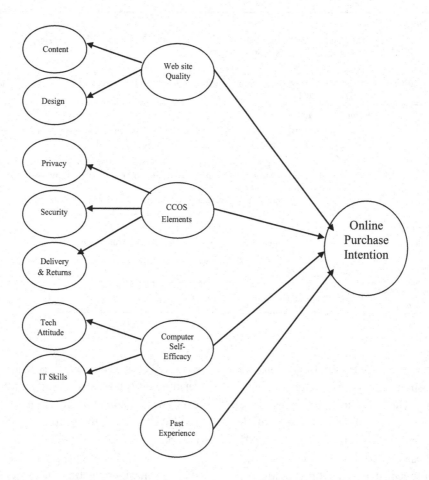

and design as the way by which the contents are presented to customers. Spiller and Lohse (1997) reported interface quality as one of the three key qualities on which online stores differed. Everard and Galletta (2005) found that errors, poor style, and incompleteness of information in Web sites negatively impacted online buying intentions. Wan (2000) offered a framework of Web-site design to promote customer values. Based on a study of 271 students, Mauldin & Arunachalam (2002) found strong association between Web site design and intention to purchase online. Using a fairly large sample of online consumers, Heijden (2003) found visual attractiveness of Web sites to significantly influence online consumers. Lee and Lin (2005) surveyed 297 online consumers to find a significant association between Web site design, consumer satisfaction and online purchase intentions. Zviran, Glezer, & Avni (2006) further confirmed the linkage between Web site design and customer satisfaction. Lepkowska-White (2004) found that online buyers and online browsers differed significantly in their evaluation of B2C sites. Online browsers viewed sites more negatively than buyers on various parameters such as site enjoyment, speed of downloads, personalization of information, relevance of information, ease of navigation, and so forth. Flavin et al. (2006) found Web usability (assessed in terms of Web site structure, simplicity, ease of navigation, speed, etc.) to influence buyer satisfaction and loyalty. All these studies point to the importance of content and design elements in Web sites.

Since a Web site forms the primary medium of communication and interaction between merchants and consumers, the quality of the Web site, in terms of the way its contents are structured and the way the Web channel is designed, has the potential to influence the purchase behavior of online consumers. Therefore,

H1: Web site quality will be positively associated with online purchase intent.

Customer Concerns in Online Shopping (CCOS)

The very mechanism of online shopping mandates that customers have faith in Internet sellers. Despite low barriers to entry and almost negligible search costs, not all online firms are successful. Online shoppers have a variety of concerns and they shop where they feel most comfortable doing so. Gefen (2000) conducted a questionnaire survey of 217 students to find that familiarity with Internet vendors and their processes influenced respondents' intention to transact with them. Lee and Turban's (2001) study of Internet shopping emphasized the importance of online merchant's integrity. Online firms that address customers' concerns gain customers confidence and loyalty. Chu et al. (2005) found brand and reputation of online merchants to be significant in determining consumer purchase intentions. Torkzadeh and Dhillon (2002), in a two-phase survey, found trust in online sellers to be one of the major factors influencing the success of the Internet commerce. In other words, although technologically possible, competitors are not a click away and it is important therefore to understand the components of concerns that dissuade customers from shopping online.

Customer concern in online shopping is primarily composed of three important factors: security, privacy of personal information, and assurance of delivery (Suh & Han, 2003). Belanger, Hiller, and Smith (2002) found online shoppers to provide personal information based on their perceptions of trustworthiness of Web merchants. Ranganathan and Ganapathy (2002) empirically validated privacy and security to be significant determinants of online shopping behavior. Vijayasarathy (2004) reported similar results on privacy and security. Koufaris and Hampton-Sosa (2004) also found security control in an online store to significantly affect consumer concerns in purchasing online. Examining online privacy issues, Dinev and Hart (2005–2006) found a strong negative relationship between privacy concerns and consumer intent to conduct online transactions. Eastlick et al. (2006) found strong negative association between privacy concerns and online purchase intentions, with privacy concerns directly and indirectly affecting purchase intent through online trust. Bart et al. (2005) and Schlosser et al. (2006) also found security and privacy concerns to influence online trust that ultimately determined consumer purchase intention. Apart from security and privacy of a Web site, assurances on delivery and returns also form a critical component of consumer concerns. Pechtl (2003) found convenience of a delivery service to have positive influence on the adoption of online shopping. Bart et al. (2005) also found order fulfillment to be a key determinant of online trust and purchase intentions. Based on the previous research findings we believe that customer concerns in terms of security, privacy, delivery and returns in an online store will have a negative influence on the online purchase intentions of customers. Therefore,

H2: Customer concerns in online shopping will be negatively associated with online purchase intent.

Computer Self-Efficacy

Computer self-efficacy reflects the belief in one's capabilities to execute computer-oriented actions to produce desired goal attainments. Individuals with little confidence in using the Internet, dissatisfaction with their Internet skills or uncomfortable using the Web have weak self-efficacy beliefs. Computer self-efficacy influences individual decisions about technology usage, the amount of effort and persistence put forth during obstacles faced, and the overall behavior towards the technology. The linkage between computer self efficacy and IT use has been empirically verified (Compeau & Higgins, 1995).

Computer self-efficacy is a byproduct of the consumer's attitude towards information technology (IT) and the extent of IT skills and knowledge possessed by the consumer. Scholars have argued that an individual's disposition and comfort level towards a specific technology influences the extent of technology usage. Some studies have specifically focused on Internet-specific self-efficacy though the broader construct of computer self-efficacy covers Web related efficacy as well (Hsu & Chiu, 2004). Researchers have identified technology attitude (Maudlin & Arrunachalam, 2002) and skill levels (Vijayasarathy, 2004) to be critical determinants of an individual's disposition towards a specific technology. Moreover, the extent of IT skills especially those related to Internet has been found to augment intentions to conduct online transactions (Dinev & Hart, 2005-2006). Based on the previous research studies we hypothesize computer self-efficacy to have a positive influence on the online purchase intentions of customers. Therefore,

H3: Computer self-efficacy will be positively associated with online purchase intent.

Past Online Shopping Experience

Based on a survey, Yoh et al. (2003) reported customers' prior Internet experience to be a strong determinant of their online shopping behavior. Pavlou (2003) validated that consumers' satisfaction with past online shopping resulted in building trust in the Web merchant, which in turn influenced further online transactions. Based on the above studies we propose that past Web shopping experience will have a strong influence on the online purchase intentions of customers. Therefore,

H4: Past Web shopping experience will be positively associated with online purchase intent.

The complete research model, showing key constructs, operational variables, and hypothesized relationships is shown in Figure 2.

METHODOLOGY

Survey Questionnaire

We identified operational measures for all of our constructs from extant literature. These operational measures were summarized into various items and a survey instrument was created. This questionnaire requested the respondents to rate the level of their agreement with the items in relation to their online shopping experience. The respondents rated each item on a scale of 1 to 7, where 1 represented *strongly disagree*, and 7 represented *strongly agree*. In addition to the above items, we also collected demographic data from the respondents. This included questions regarding their experience in using the Internet, extent and frequency of the Internet usage for different activities, how many purchases they made in last 6 months, and also the amount they spent in shopping online during this period.

The respondents also answered four questions about their online shopping intention. These questions dealt with their likelihood, willingness, likely frequency, and the probability of their making their online purchase. The first three questions were to be answered on a 7-point scale, with 1 equal to *very low* and 7 equal to *very high* probability. The last question was also to be answered on a 7-point scale, with 1 equal to *no chance* of buying to 7 equal to *certain chance* of buying.

After doing a pilot study, we conducted a survey in Illinois over a period of two weeks. Respondents were sought in public places like malls, computer shops, and electronics stores. A total of 409 individuals were administered the survey. Since our intention was to assess the on-line purchase behavior of consumers, only those individuals with recent prior online shopping experience had to be included as subjects for our study. Out of 409 responses, only 214 individuals had made online purchases in the past 6 months and, therefore, only these responses were considered for analysis.

Sample

We had a diverse sample, with 57% male and 43% female respondents. Nearly 60% of the sample was in the 21 to 30 years of age group. More than 80% of the respondents had more than 1 year of experience in Internet surfing. Over 20% of the respondents in our sample made six or more online

purchases in last 6 months. More than 50% of the respondents had spent over US$ 100 in online shopping in the last 6 months. The profile of the respondents suggests that the respondents were considerably exposed to the Internet and online shopping. Table 2 provides some details of the respondents' profile.

DATA ANALYSIS

Validity and Reliability Assessment

Construct validity is the degree to which a measurement scale represents and acts like the concept being measured. In order to assess convergent and discriminant validities, the 29 items used to measure 8 research variables were subjected to principle component analysis. The analysis resulted in eight factors, with cumulative 75.85% of variance. Two items were dropped, one from delivery and the other from security, due to poor loadings. The detailed factor loadings are presented in Table 3.

Further, we did reliability analysis using Cronbach's coefficient alpha, to ensure that the

Table 2. Profile of respondents (N = 214)

Experience in Internet surfing	
< 3 months	5 (2.3%)
Between 3 and 6 months	8 (3.7%)
Between 6 and 12 months	11 (5.1%)
Between 1 and 2 years	15 (7%)
Between 2 and 3 years	46 (21.5%)
Between 3 and 5 years	85 (39.7%)
> 5 years	44 (20.6%)
Amount spent in online shopping in last 6 months	
< US$ 10	13 (6.1%)
Between US$ 10 and 25	17 (7.9%)
Between US$ 25 and 50	33 (15.4%)
Between US $ 50 and 100	29 (13.6%)
Between US$ 100 and 250	53 (24.8%)
Between US$ 250 and 500	31 (14.5%)
Between US$ 500 and 1000	22 (10.3%)
> US$ 1000	13 (6.1%)

items for each of the factors were internally related. The value of the Cronbach's coefficient alpha for seven of the eight variables was much higher than the recommended 0.60 (Table 3). Alpha value for "Delivery & Returns" variable was 0.52. However, we continued with this variable, because this came out as one of the factors with high loadings in our principal component analysis.

Structural Equation Model Analysis

Consistent with our conceptualization, Web site quality, CCOS, and computer self-efficacy were modeled as second order constructs. Web site quality was assessed using two constructs: *Content* and *Design*. For assessing CCOS elements, we used three factors, namely, *Privacy, Security,* and *Delivery & Returns*. Computer self-efficacy was composed of two constructs: *Attitude* towards information technology and *IT Skills*. Past online shopping experience was modeled as a first order construct.

Rather than directly measuring some of our key constructs, our modeling approach involved constructing Web site quality, CCOS and computer self efficacy as second order constructs. We believe Web site quality, CCOS, and computer self-efficacy are latent constructs that are best captured using some of the key dimensions underlying them. This rationale guided us to model them as second order constructs. We assessed these three constructs based on their constituent first order latent constructs.

Structural equation modeling (SEM) using AMOS was used to test and analyze our hypotheses. According to Hair, Anderson, Tatham, & Black (2004), SEM provides an appropriate method of dealing with multiple relationships simultaneously while providing statistical efficiency. SEM evaluates the given model using goodness-of-fit measures to evaluate the model fit and model parsimony. The evaluation of the overall fit of the model is done according to the goodness-of-fit index (GFI), the adjusted goodness-of-fit index (AGFI). The comparative fit index (CFI) and the root-mean-square error of approximation (RMSEA) are also used to assess the model fit. The details of the overall model fit indices along with the recommended values are presented in Table 4. The results of our analysis are shown in Figure 3. Except the GFI, all other indices are as per the recommended value. GFI value of 0.833 suggests a moderate fit of our model to the data collected.

While the overall model was supported (χ^2 / df = 1.64, p < 0.01), the good-of-fit as assessed by GFI and AGFI indicated a moderate fit. However, the CFI and RMSEA scores indicate a good overall fit of the model. These figures provide support for our effort in integrating constructs from HCI, behavioral and consumerist streams of research on online shopping.

Based on the standardized path coefficients shown in Figure 3, all of our hypotheses were supported. Of the key constructs affecting online shopping behavior, past experience with online shopping had a relatively larger association with online purchase intentions as is evident from the high co-efficient (0.518, $p < 0.01$). The next high coefficient was for CCOS as assessed by security, privacy and delivery and return assurances (-0.443, $p < 0.01$). Web site quality was also found to be strongly, and positively associated with online purchase intent (0.35, $p < 0.01$), though its influence was relatively lower than those of CCOS and past online shopping experience. Our results also indicate computer self-efficacy to be a significant predictor of online purchase intent (0.153, $p < 0.05$), though the magnitude of its association (assessed by the standardized path coefficient) with online shopping intent is lower than those of other three constructs.

In summary, SEM analysis showed that past online shopping experience had the most dominant effect on online purchase intention, which was followed by CCOS, Web site quality, and computer self-efficacy. The analysis also successfully dem-

Table 3. Validity and reliability analysis

	Loadings	Cronbach's Alpha
Web site quality		
Content	0.81	
Information to compare across alternatives	0.82	
Provide decision-making aids (like calculator, comparison charts, calendar, etc.)	0.84	0.88
Complete information about the firms, products and services	0.82	
Opportunities to communicate and interact with the company		
Design		
Easy to navigate for information	0.85	
Consume less time for finding the information I am looking for	0.88	0.89
Visual presentations enhance the information provided	0.85	
Customer Concerns in Online Shopping		
Privacy	0.80	
Concerned about the Web-sites that gather my personal information	0.70	
Don't prefer to shop from sites that ask for my personal information.	0.85	0.88
Think twice before giving personal information online	0.77	
It's important to know how the personal information collected will be used		
Security		
Secure modes of transactions.	0.74	
Order products on line, but prefer making payments offline	0.79	
Prefer to have an individual account with a logon-id and password.	0.81	0.87
General concern about security of transaction	0.68	
Delivery & Returns		
Delivery concern deter me from purchasing online	0.81	0.52
Concerns about returning the product	0.71	
Computer Self Efficacy		
Tech Attitude		
Technologies such as internet have made me more productive	0.73	
Technologies like internet make it easy to keep in touch with friends and family	0.78	0.83
Technologies like internet have made my life easy and comfortable	0.73	
IT Skills		
Quite comfortable using computers	0.85	
Quite comfortable surfing the Internet	0.86	
Spend considerable time on Internet	0.81	0.91
Consider myself computer and net-savvy	0.82	
Past Online Shopping Experience	0.90	
Rate your satisfaction with recent online purchases	0.91	0.93
Rate your experience with recent online purchases	0.89	
Compare your experience in on-line purchasing with retail purchasing		

onstrated the validity of our proposed integrated model and the efficacy of the multidimensional perspective of online shopping.

DISCUSSION

As Internet technologies continue to proliferate retail and marketing transactions, firms must devise appropriate response mechanisms to assimilate these technologies. Fundamental to such response is a good understanding of online consumer behavior. To address this important research issue, we developed a framework integrating diverse orientations for examining online consumer behavior. Our research had two related goals: (a) to combine the HCI, behavioral and consumerist approaches to propose an integrated model, and (b) to empirically assess the relative importance of the different antecedents on online purchase

Table 4. SEM results

	Score	Recommended Value
Chi-Square	680.104	
p value	0.000	> 0.05
Degrees of freedom	414	
Chi-Square/ Degrees of freedom	1.643	< 3.00
Goodness-of-fit index (GFI)	0.833	> 0.90
Adjusted goodness-of-fit index (AGFI)	0.800	> 0.80
Root mean square error of approximation (RMSEA)	0.055	< 0.10
Comparative fit index (CFI)	0.946	> 0.90

Figure 3. Results of SEM analysis

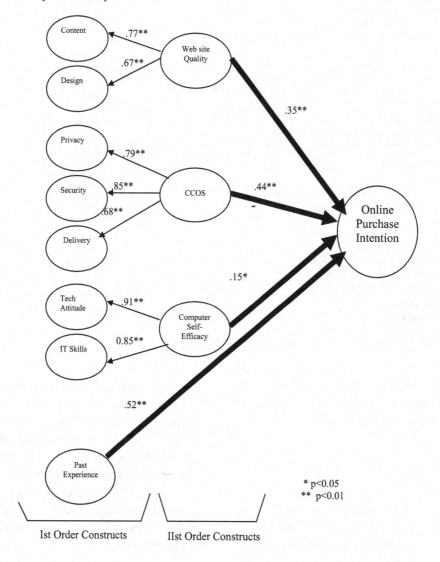

behavior. Our results highlight the significance of the key predictors, their relative importance and demonstrate the potency of our integrated framework.

We proposed and tested a framework with Web site quality, CCOS, computer self-efficacy, and past online shopping experience as potential antecedents to online purchase intentions. Our results support all of our hypotheses, thus providing evidence for positive association of all these constructs.

Our results reveal a strong negative association between CCOS and online purchase intentions. Although previous studies have studied and operationalized CCOS, the main approach has been to capture trust as a behavioral-attitudinal construct. To obtain contextually meaningful operational items, we captured CCOS through subconstructs; viz, privacy, security, and delivery. These subconstructs emphasize the importance of reducing CCOS through both online and offline mechanisms. By effectively integrating security, privacy and offline delivery and returns, companies can enhance consumer trust, thereby increasing the online purchase intentions. Our findings validate and confirm previous findings on the importance of addressing consumer concerns in online marketing environments (Gefen, 2003; Gefen et al., 2004). As Urban et al. (2000) note, "For the Internet, trust-based marketing is the key to success. Companies can use the Internet to provide customers with a secure, private and calming experience."

We assessed Web site quality through its content and design related aspects, and found site quality to be strongly associated with purchase intentions of customers. Though content and design are basic components of a Web site, the nature of content and the design, and the way in which these two are built can have a major impact on customer perceptions. To enhance Web site quality, online merchants need to provide customers with accurate, up-to-date and complete information on their business, products and services. The Web

sites also need to have easy-to-use and smooth navigation that makes searching, comparing, and shopping a pleasure.

While customer concerns and Web site quality could be directly controlled and manipulated by firms trying to engage in B2C e-commerce, computer self-efficacy, and online shopping experience reflect consumer-related variables that are tied to specific consumers. Our study revealed strong positive influence of both self efficacy and past online experience of consumers. Our results also reveal relative influence of both controllable and noncontrollable constructs on online shopping. Research studies have revealed changing attitudes of consumers towards the Internet, with growing use of broadband and Internet connectivity in homes. Consumers have developed more experience with Web over time, though concerns of Internet fraud and privacy violations have not yet been fully addressed.

CONCLUSION

This article makes three main contributions to the research on online shopping. First, we reconcile three different orientations in the literature on online consumer behavior. Extant research typically adopts a single orientation—HCI, behavioral, or consumerist, and rarely integrates all the three facets to assess their overall impact on online purchase intentions. We show that an integrated model provides richer insights rather than relying solely on singular orientations. Only when the three orientations are examined in a composite manner can the effects of these facets be properly assessed. We believe our study nicely complements and extends earlier research, by providing a more holistic and comprehensive picture of key factors affecting online consumer behavior.

Second, we help identify the relative importance of key predictors of online purchase intentions. While some of the factors such as Web site quality and customer concern related factors could be manipulated by online merchants, other factors such as self-efficacy are amenable to change by consumers. Our analysis reveals past online shopping experience to have stronger association with online purchase intent than all the other factors. CCOS factors and Web site quality emerged as the second and third most significant predictors of online purchase intent. Computer self-efficacy had the lowest, yet, significant positive association. Third, the insights from this research are based on responses provided by consumers who have been actively shopping online. Rather than using proxy respondents such as students, we used actual online consumers to test and validate our model.

Our study throws several important implications for online merchants and practitioners. According to our results, past experience in online shopping seems to be a strong determinant of online purchase intention. Therefore, it becomes important for online merchants to carefully plan and execute their online strategies. It is important to plan a rollout of a complete B2C e-commerce strategy rather than trying incremental, ad hoc initiatives to moving online. Moreover, positive online purchase experience seems to cultivate customer loyalty in terms of repeat and multiple purchases. Therefore, rather than experimenting with online sales, it becomes important for online merchants to "get it right" if they are serious about their B2C e-commerce efforts. Treating Internet as a lucrative and additional business channel, merchants need to concentrate on improving their online effectiveness.

Our findings also reinforce the importance of CCOS as a cornerstone of effective online strategy. For mitigating CCOS, companies need to work on allaying consumer concerns on security, privacy, delivery and returns. CCOS is an intangible, yet, powerful factor that could decide the fortunes of online sellers. Every effort must be made by merchants to build mechanisms for building and sustaining consumer trust.

Web merchants need to continuously work on the content and design elements of their Web sites, as they seem to form the building blocks of Web site quality that ultimately influences the purchase intentions of online shoppers. Currency and frequent updates of Web sites, providing pertinent up-to-date information, presented in a user-friendly and customer-centered design is likely to attract and retain a significant portion of online buyers.

Our study also has several limitations that must be kept in mind while interpreting the results. The first limitation pertains to the variables that were included from the three research streams. The variables included in our model were key variables identified from literature—nevertheless, they do not form a comprehensive list of variables affecting online consumer behavior. Recent studies have tried to identify and examine additional variables (e.g., Bart et al., 2005), and future researchers could examine online consumer behavior with a larger set of variables drawn from the three research streams. Moreover, our dataset is relatively small as compared to some of the recent studies that have examined several hundreds of consumers. Other limitations pertain to the measures we used. We relied on simpler measures rather than using lengthy instruments such as SiteQual and WebQual. It should also be noted that our measures were screened and examined for reliability and validity. We also did not test any interaction effects and this is another fruitful avenue for extending the research on this topic.

Though early research studies on online shopping had adopted a specific orientation (HCI, behavioral and consumerist) towards examining online consumer behavior, extant researchers have acknowledged the complementarity among these three research streams. Our study integrates key variables from all the three streams, thus providing a more holistic understanding of online shopping behavior. It should also be emphasized that the variables from different streams could interact with each other, thus exerting a combined influence on the consumer purchase intentions. For instance, computer self-efficacy could allay consumer concerns in online shopping and also help consumers overcome any problems with Web design and usability. Similarly, favorable past online experience could dispel security and privacy concerns and this experience could help consumers overcome any difficulties in Web site navigation and usage. Future researchers could model such interactions to enrich and extend our knowledge on online shopping behavior. In conclusion, our study proposed a more holistic model integrating HCI, behavioral and consumerist approaches to understand online shopping. We developed, tested and validated a pragmatic multidimensional model that Web merchants could adopt to attract and retain online shoppers.

REFERENCES

Aladwani, A. M., & Palvia, P. (2002). Developing and validating an instrument for measuring user-perceived Web quality. *Information & Management, 39*, 467-476.

Bart, Y., Shankar, V., Sultan, F., & Urban, G. L. (2005). Are the drivers and role of online trust the same for all Web sites and consumers? A large-scale exploratory empirical study. *Journal of Marketing, 69*(4), 133-152.

Belanger, F., Hiller, J. S., & Smith, W. J. (2002). Trustworthiness in e-commerce: The role of privacy, security, and site attributes. *Journal of Strategic Information Systems, 11*, 245-270.

Bellman, S., Lohse, G., & Eric, J. (1999). Predictors of online buying behavior. *Communications of the ACM, 42*(12), 32-38.

Brynjolfsson, E., & Smith, M. D. (2000). Frictionless commerce? A comparison of Internet and conventional retailers. *Management Science, 46*(4), 563-585.

Burroughs, R. E., & Sabherwal, R. (2002). Determinants of retail electronic purchasing: A multi-period investigation. *INFOR, 40*(1),.

Chang, M. K., Cheung, W., & Lai,V. S. (2005). Literature derived reference models for the adoption of online shopping. *Information & Management, 42*(4), 543-559.

Chen, P. Y., & Hitt, L. M. (2002). Measuring switching costs and the determinants of customer retention in Internet-enabled businesses: A study of the online brokerage industry. *Information Systems Research, 13*(3), 255-274.

Chu, W., Choi, B., & Song, M. R. (2005). The role of on-line retailer brand and infomediary reputation in increasing consumer purchase intention. *International Journal of Electronic Commerce, 9*(3) 115-127.

Compeau, E. R., & Higgins, C. A. (1995). Computer self-efficacy: Development of a measure and initial test. *MIS Quarterly, 19*(2), 189-211.

De Wulf, K., Schillewaert, N., Muylle, S., & Rangarajan, D. (2006). The role of pleasure in Web site success. *Information & Management, 43*(4), 434-446.

Dinev, T., & Hart, P. (2005–2006). Internet privacy concerns and social awareness as determinants of intention to transact. *International Journal of Electronic Commerce, 10*(2), 7-29.

Eastlick, M., Lotz, S. L., & Warrington, P. (2006). Understanding online B-to-C relationships: An integrated model of privacy concerns, trust, and commitment. *Journal of Business Research, 59*(8), 877-886.

Ethier, J., Hadaya, P., Talbot, J., & Cadieux, J. (in press). B2C Web site quality and emotions during online shopping episodes: An empirical study. *Information & Management.*

Everard, A., & Galletta, D. F. (2005). How presentation flaws affect perceived site quality, trust, and intention to purchase from an online store. *Journal of Management Information Systems, 22*(3), 55-95.

Flavin, C., Guinaliu, M., & Gurrea, R. (2006). The role played by perceived usability, satisfaction, and consumer trust on Web site loyalty. *Information & Management, 43*(1), 1-14.

Gefen, D. (2000). E-commerce: The role of familiarity and trust. *Omega, 28*(6), 725-737.

Gefen, D., Karahanna, E., & Straub, D. W. (2003). Trust and TAM in online shopping: An integrated model. *MIS Quarterly, 27*(1), 51–90.

Gefen, D., & Straub, D. W. (2004). Consumer trust in B2C e-commerce and the importance of social presence: Experiments in e-products and e-services. *Omega, 32*(6), 407-425.

Hair, J. F., Anderson, R. E., Tatham, R. L., & Black, W. C. (1998). *Multivariate data analysis* (5th ed). Upper Saddle River, NJ: Prentice Hall.

Heijden, H. V. D. (2003). Factors Influencing the usage of Websites: The case of a generic portal in the Netherlands. *Information & Management, 40*(6), 541-549.

Heijden, H. V. D., Verhagen, T., & Creemers, M. (2003). Understanding online purchase intentions: Contributions from technology and trust perspectives. *European Journal of Information Systems, 12*(1), 41-49.

Hsu, M., & Chiu, C. (2004). Internet self-efficacy and electronic service acceptance. *Decision Support Systems, 38*(3), 369-381.

Huizingh, E. (2000). The content and design of Web sites: An empirical study. *Information & Management, 37*(3), 123-134.

Iwaarden, J. V., & Wiele, T. V. D. (2003). Applying SERVQUAL to Web sites: An exploratory study. *International Journal of Quality, 20*(8), 919-935.

Iwaarden, J. V., Wiele, T. V. D., Ball, L., & Millen, R. (2004). Perceptions about the quality of Websites: A survey amongst students at Northeastern University and Erasmus University. *Information & Management, 41*(8), 947–959.

Jarvenpaa, S. L., Tractinsky, N., & Vitale, M. (2000). Consumer trust in an Internet store. *Information Technology and Management, 1*(2), 45-71.

Kiely, T. (1997). The Internet: Fear and shopping in cyberspace. *Harvard Business Review, 75*(4), 13-14.

Koufaris, M., & Hampton-Sosa, W. (2004). The development of initial trust in an online company by new customers. *Information & Management, 41*(3), 377-397.

Lee, G., & Lin, H. (2005). Customer perceptions of e-service quality in online shopping. *International Journal of Retail & Distribution Management, 33*(2), 161-176.

Lee, M., & Turban, E. A. (2001). Trust model for consumer Internet shopping. *International Journal of Electronic Commerce, 6*(1), 75-91.

Lepkowska-White, E. (2004). Online store perceptions: How to turn browsers into buyers. *Journal of Marketing Theory and Practice, 12*(3), 36-48.

Liao, Z., & Cheung, T. (2001). Internet-based e-shopping and consumer attitudes: An empirical study. *Information & Management, 38*(5), 299-306.

Liu, C., & Arnett, K. P. (2000). Exploring the factors associated with Web site success in the context of e-commerce. *Information & Management, 38*(1), 23-33.

Lohse, G. L., & Spiller, P. (1999). Internet retail store design: How the user interface influences traffic and sales. *Journal of Computer Mediated Communication, 5*(2). Retrieved from www.ascusc.org/jcmc/vol5/issue2/

Loiacono, E., Watson, R., & Goodhue, D. (2002). WebQual: A Web site quality instrument. *American marketing association. Winter Marketing Educators' Conference, Austin, TX,* 432-438.

Mauldin, E., & Arunachalam, V. (2002). An experimental examination of alternative forms of Web assurance for business-to-consumer e-commerce. *Journal of Information Systems, 16,* 33-54.

McKnight, H. D., Choudhury, V., & Kacmar, C. (2002a). Developing and validating trust measures for e-commerce: An integrative typology. *Information Systems Research, 13*(3), 334-359.

McKnight, H. D., Choudhury, V., & Kacmar, C. (2002b). The impact of initial consumer trust on intentions to transact with a Web site: A trust building model. *Journal of Strategic Information Systems, 11,* 297-323.

Pavlou, P. A. (2003). Consumer acceptance of electronic commerce integrating trust and risk with the technology acceptance model. *International Journal of Electronic Commerce, 7*(3), 101-134.

Pechtl, H. (2003). Adoption of online shopping by German grocery shoppers. *The International Review of Retail, Distribution and Consumer Research, 13*(2), 145-159.

Ranganathan, C., & Ganapathy, S. (2002). Key dimensions of business-to-consumer Web sites. *Information & Management, 39*(6), 457-465.

Salaun, Y., & Flores, K. (2001). Information quality: Meeting the needs of the consumer. *International Journal of Information Management, 21,* 21-37.

Schlosser, A. E., White, T. B., & Lloyd, S. M. (2006). Converting Web site visitors into buyers: How Web site investment increases consumer trusting beliefs and online purchase intentions. *Journal of Marketing, 70*(2), 133-148.

Shih, H. P. (2004). An empirical study on predicting user acceptance of e-shopping on the Web. *Information & Management, 41*(3), 351-368.

Spiller, P., & Lohse, G. L. (1997). A classification of Internet retail stores. *International Journal of Electronic Commerce, 2*(2), 29-56.

Suh, B., & Han, I. (2003). The impact of customer trust and perception of security control on the acceptance of electronic commerce. *International Journal of Electronic Commerce, 7*(3), 135-161.

Tarafdar, M., & Zhang, J. (2005). Analyzing the influence of Web site design parameters on Web site usability. *Information Resources Management Journal, 18*(4), 62-80.

Torkzadeh, G., & Dhillon, G. (2002). Measuring factors that influence the success of Internet commerce. *Information Systems Research, 13*(2), 187-207.

Urban, G. L., Sultan, F., & Qualls, W. J. (2000). Placing trust at the center of your Internet strategy. *Sloan Management Review, 42*(1), 39-48.

Vatanasombut, B., Stylianou, A.C., & Igbaria, M. (2004). How to retain online customers. *Communications of the ACM, 47*(6), 64-70.

Vijayasarathy, L. R. (2004). Predicting consumer intentions to use on-line shopping: The case for an augmented technology acceptance model. *Information & Management, 41*(6), 747-762.

Wan, H. A. (2000). Opportunities to enhance a commercial Website. *Information & Management, 38*(1), 15-21.

Webb, H. W., & Webb, L. A. (2004). SiteQual: An integrated measure of Web site quality. *Journal of Enterprise Information Management, 17*(6), 430-440.

Yoh, E., Damhorst, M. L., Sapp, S., & Laczniak, R. (2003). Consumer adoption of the Internet: The case of apparel shopping. *Psychology & Marketing, 20*(12), 1095–1118.

Zhang, X., Prybutok, V. R., & Koh, C. E. (2006). The role of impulsiveness in TAM-based online purchasing behavior. *Information Resources Management Journal, 19*(2), 54-68.

Zviran, M., Glezer, C., & Avni, I. (2006). User satisfaction from commercial Web sites: The effect of design and use. *Information & Management, 43*(2), 157-178.

This work was previously published in the Information Resources Management Journal, edited by M. Khosrow-Pour, Volume 20, Issue 4, pp. 48-64, copyright 2007 by IGI Publishing (an imprint of IGI Global).

Chapter XV
An Exploratory Study of Consumer Adoption of Online Shopping:
Mediating Effect of Online Purchase Intention

Songpol Kulviwat
Hofstra University, USA

Ramendra Thakur
Utah Valley State College, USA

Chiquan Guo
The University of Texas–Pan American, USA

ABSTRACT

An exploratory study was conducted to investigate consumer adoption of online purchase using a survey data set. Based upon the theory of innovation and self-efficacy theory, risk aversion, online proficiency, shopping convenience, and product choice variety were proposed to influence consumer intention to shop online, which, in turn, affects online purchases. Results of regression analyses revealed that all but shopping convenience were significant predictors of consumer intention to purchase online. In addition, consumer intention directly determines consumer purchases online. Finally, consumer intention to purchase online mediates the relationship of risk aversion, shopping convenience, and product choice variety to online shopping. Research and managerial implications of the findings were discussed.

INTRODUCTION

Internet as a medium of business transaction has gained in importance in spite of the dot-com bubble burst we witnessed at the end of the century. Jupiter forecasts that online retail sales will surge to a new level, reaching $117 billion in 2008, representing 5% of total retail sales in the U.S. (Gonsalves, 2004). Although the trend of online shopping continues and shows no sign of slowdown, Internet retailing is far from reaching its full potential; only about 3% of Internet users actually make an online purchase (Betts, 2001), a particularly low percentage that must be improved in order to usher in the new era of e-commerce.

The purpose of this study is to explore the factors influencing consumer adoption of innovation in the case of online shopping. The research question is among all Internet users who are likely to make a commercial transaction through the Internet, a topic of importance and yet under-researched. In the past, many Internet firms provided free services or services for a nominal fee, a business model that turned out to be fragile and unsustainable, one of the reasons the dot.com bubble burst (Guo, 2002). As millions of consumers enjoyed the free ride that Internet technology had to offer, the challenge facing online businesses was and always has been to distinguish valuable consumers from those cheap riders who take full advantage of amenities that new technology provides, such as free e-mail and networking, but who are not willing to spend money or symbolically consume in the online community. This task is critical to company success, as e-businesses learned the lesson the hard way that they cannot treat every customer or potential customer the same, simply because not all consumers are created equal.

The organization of this article is as follows: a literature review is conducted to develop research hypotheses that are tested, followed subsequently by methodology and results analysis.

Limitations and implications of the results are also discussed.

LITERATURE REVIEW

Theoretical Foundations of Consumer Adoption of Innovation

Consumer adoption of innovation has received considerable attention among consumer researchers and is used most frequently to determine any diffusion of innovations. Classic studies from innovation literature argue that innovation adoption is related to the attributes of the innovation as perceived by potential adopters (Rogers, 1995; Rogers & Rogers, 2003; Rogers & Shoemaker, 1971). Any innovation can be described along the following five characteristics: relative advantage, compatibility, complexity, trialability (costs), and observability (communicability). Moreover, recent studies specifically have integrated technology acceptance model (TAM) with consumer adoption of online shopping (Koufaris, 2002; Gefen, Karahanna, & Straub, 2003). TAM consists of perceived usefulness and ease of use and is a well-known theory of technology acceptance.

Consistent with perceived usefulness in TAM, an innovation's relative advantage is defined as "the degree to which an innovation is perceived as being better than the idea it supersedes" (Rogers, 1995, p. 213). In their meta-analysis, Tornatzky and Klein (1982) found relative advantage to be positively related to adoption. Shopping convenience and product choice variety can be considered as relative advantage and perceived usefulness, as literature suggests that these two are of primary concerns in order for consumers to accept the Internet as a shopping medium (Bellman & Lohse, 1999). Further, the belief related to perceived usefulness influences consumers' intentions to shop online (Gefen, Karahanna, & Straub, 2003).

Rogers (1995) defines compatibility of an innovation as the "degree to which an innovation is perceived as being consistent with the existing values, past experiences, and needs of the potential adopter" (p. 223). Research found that compatibility facilitates innovation adoption (Damanpour, 1991). As consumers are concerned with transaction security and information privacy issues associated with online shopping (Novak, Hoffman, & Yung, 2000), risk aversion is a useful construct to tap the risk differential between online shopping and off-line shopping, which is the compatibility gap between existing lifestyle (e.g., brick-and-mortar shopping) and new behavior (online shopping). Furthermore, the issue of trust has become an even more significant reason whether consumers will shop online (Hoffman, Novak, & Peralta, 1999).

Contrasted to perceived ease of use, complexity is the degree to which the new innovation is perceived as difficult to use. Resulting from individual differences, online shopping is still perceived as difficult to comprehend for some groups of consumers. As such, self-efficacy theory becomes relevant to the discussion. Self-efficacy refers to the individual's belief about his or her capability and motivation to execute and to perform the course of action required to produce a given accomplishment or outcome (Bandura, 1977). It concerns not only the skills one has but also the judgments of what one can do with whatever skills one possesses, which mainly reflects an individual's self-confidence in his or her ability to perform a task. Online shopping proficiency is an individual's perceived skills and knowledge in consummating an online transaction. Consisting of online experience, knowledge, and education, online proficiency could facilitate any online search and other online activities (Kulviwat, Guo, & Engchanil, 2004). Thus, online proficiency is proposed as one of the four factors influencing consumers' decisions to shop online.

While trialability is the degree to which the innovation can be experimented with prior to

confirmation, observability is the degree to which the innovation is visible to others. Trialability and observability are not very relevant in this present context, given that the Internet is widely and easily accessed nowadays, so its cost seems less important. Also, most companies provide a trial period and result guarantee in order to provide peace of mind to consumers and to attract consumers. This contention is consistent with the innovation literature that the first three attributes are considered the most significant in affecting innovation adoption (Moore & Benbasat, 1991; Tornatzky & Klein, 1982). Next, we discuss how the four determinants affect consumer innovativeness in terms of online shopping.

Risk Aversion

Internet adoption by U.S. households is a fairly rapid process compared to television. Within a short period of six years or so from 1994 to 2000, more than half of households had access to the Internet. It took more than double that amount of time for the same percentage of households to embrace color TV (Angwin, 2001). The number of consumers with Internet access is not small, but the problem facing e-businesses is that the conversion rate, the percentage of online users that actually make an online purchase, is low (Betts, 2001). If we can find determining factors separating Internet users who are likely to shop online from those who are not likely to or never will participate in commercial exchanges over the Internet, e-businesses will be better able to devise marketing programs to attract and induce target consumers to spend online.

In an interesting project, researchers used a sample of one person to study online shopping behavior (Levy, 2001). After carefully examining marketing professor Bruce Weinberg's Internet shopping diary (Weinberg, 2000), Professor Brunel pointed out that consumers must have special incentives before switching to online shopping from a brick-and-mortar environment, because there are burdens as well as benefits with online shopping (Weinberg, 2001).

In the business literature, hygiene factors are an important concept in human resource management (Jansen, van der Velde, & Telting, 2001). Hygiene factors are those fundamental rights that employees desire in a workplace, such as fairness and job security. With unsatisfactory hygiene factors, workers will be very unhappy in their organization. On the other hand, employees will not be motivated to work extra hard, even if those hygiene factors are all taken care of, because they are deemed as basic working conditions (Levinson et al., 1962). There may exist hygiene factors in the context of online shopping (Zhang & von Dran, 2000). Burdens of online shopping could serve as a hygiene factor. As widely discussed in the literature, privacy and security issues are a major concern relating to online shopping (Caudill & Murphy, 2000; Miyazaki & Fernandez, 2001). Annihilation of privacy and security issues may not make everyone shop online, but an outstanding problem in that regard surely will discourage consumers from shopping through the Internet. In fact, 53% of consumers would shop online if more secure payment options were made available (Rheault, 2004). This is consistent with White and Truly's (1989) assertion that risk perceptions are negatively related with willingness to buy. Further, prior research has shown that as perceived risk of online purchase decreases, consumers' intentions to purchase online increase (Garbarino & Strahilevitz, 2004). Thus, we propose the following hypothesis:

H1: Risk aversion is negatively related to adoption intention of online shopping.

Online Proficiency

Derived from self-efficacy theory, online proficiency refers to the judgment of one's ability to shop online. Individuals with high online proficiency tend to perceive online shopping

as easy to use (opposite of complexity). Before jumping into shopping online, consumers must have a working knowledge of the computer and the Internet. In other words, online experience is a prerequisite to online shopping. Although most consumers are receptive to new technology, the digital divide separates people into two classes: the haves and the have-nots. Unfortunately, this adversely affects the expansion of e-commerce (Williamson, 2001). Some parental concerns, such as sexually explicit and violent material on the Web and conversing with strangers in the chatroom, further constrict the potential use of the Internet among youth (Devi, 2001). Even young adults have genuine fears toward the Internet (Grant & Waite, 2003).

Not only must fear be removed among people toward the Internet, but positive online experience is also necessary before consumers will feel comfortable enough to shop online. Online proficiency is posited to influence behavioral intentions to shop online. Several empirical studies confirm this contention. For instance, Agarwal and Karahanna (2000) found that perceived ease of use of an information technology influences behavioral intention to use the information technology. Moreover, Novak, Hoffman, and Yung (2000) suggested that online experience may be related to online intention to shopping. In fact, Koyuncu and Lien (2003) found that people with more online experience are more likely to order over the Internet, especially when they are in a more private and secure environment such as home. Since online proficiency is derived from online experience, we propose the following:

H2: Online proficiency is positively related to adoption intention of online shopping.

Shopping Convenience

Shopping convenience for online customers means time savings and ease of Internet use for shopping purpose (Seiders et al., 2000). Bhatnagar et al. (2000) suggested that the likelihood of online purchasing increase as the consumer's perception of Internet shopping convenience develops. Evidence indicates that consumers who value convenience are more likely to buy on the Web, while those who prefer experiencing products are less likely to buy online (Li et al., 1999).

To enhance consumers' online adoption intentions, a company should try to give its customers a memorable experience; as a result, customers will be more willing to buy on the Web. A company can provide a memorable experience to its customers by managing the customer's touch point (Zemke & Connelan, 2001). A touch point is anywhere a customer comes in contact with the company's Web, including ads, links, search capabilities, and other processes. A company should consider customer touch points as moments of truth. Each is an opportunity for the customer to make positive or negative judgments about the company. When customers have positive experience and find shopping online convenience, then it is more likely that they will be willing to adopt that medium for shopping.

Since Internet shopping can be viewed as an innovation (Mahajan & Wind, 1989; Peterson et al., 1997), a similar shopping channel such as catalog shopping may affect consumers' willingness to engage in online shopping, because they resemble each other in some ways (Dickerson & Gentry, 1983; Taylor, 1977). Taylor (1977) found a positive relationship between usage of a product class or service and adoption of its related products. Thus, prior knowledge of the products or services in a class may lead to an increased ability to detect superior new products in that category and, hence, to contribute to the probability of adoption.

Despite the fact that myriad people today have access to the Internet for various functions (Peterson, 1997), a small percentage of these individuals actually utilizes this medium for electronic commerce (Schiesel, 1997). Hirschman (1980) provides a potential explanation for this phenomenon,

suggesting that to transform vicarious adopters to actual purchasers of the innovation, actualized innovativeness or consumer creativity may need to be present. Thus, a person who has had a good experience in the past with catalog shopping (e.g., convenience) will be more willing to try a similar shopping avenue: online shopping.

H3: Shopping convenience is positively related to adoption intention of online shopping.

Product Choice Variety

As the Internet connects personal computers around the global, it creates a perfect platform for informational exchanges between people who otherwise are dispersed geographically. People disseminate, share, and retrieve information through the Web at their fingertips. As technology trims down the search cost to a minimum (Peterson & Merino, 2003), it encourages consumers to search for more information about a variety of products. Furthermore, search engines and comparison-shopping sites customize product information to consumers' unique needs and likings (Hoffman & Novak, 1996), giving consumers the ownership over the information. This maneuverability in combination with sheer volume of information dramatically increases information search scope and depth and enhances product choices for consumers. Compared to off-line shopping, the Internet offers not only a wide variety of information, but it also offers varying choices of brands and product types (Lynch & Ariely, 2000). Rohm and Swaminathan (2004) recently found that variety-seeking behavior is an important factor for online shopping motive. Thus, this is likely to be a significant motive to influence consumer adoption intention to shop online.

H4: Product choice variety is positively related to adoption intention of online shopping.

Online Purchase

Consistent with technology acceptance model (TAM) and theory of planned behavior (TPB), behavioral intention long has been recognized as a positive and direct determinant of behavior. Several empirical studies have confirmed that behavioral intention plays an important substantive role in predicting behavior. For instance, in a meta-analysis of the behavioral intention to behavior, Sheppard, Hartwick, and Warshaw (1988) found strong support for using intentions to predict behavior. Taylor and Todd (1995) found strong support in testing TAM, TPB, and the decomposed TPB that the path from behavioral intention to behavior was significant in all models. Given the previous studies, we propose the following:

H5: Adoption intention of online shopping is positively related to online purchase.

Moreover, behavioral intention also has been proposed as an important mediator in the relationships between behavior and other innovation attributes. While beliefs-intention-behavior relationships in TAM have been studied extensively in the context of information systems, relatively little studies have focused on the hypothesized mediating role of intention in the context of online purchase. The extant literature of TAM to address this mediation effect has shown that the results are inconclusive. The current study attempts to address the inconclusive results of mediation of adoption intention in the context of online shopping.

H6: Adoption intention fully mediates the influence of selected innovation attributes on online purchase.

A FRAMEWORK OF CONSUMER ADOPTION OF ONLINE SHOPPING

Based on the innovation theory and self-efficacy theory as well as extensive literature review, the research model is derived and proposed. All constructs are hypothesized to have direct and positive relationships (except risk aversion to have

Figure 1. Research model

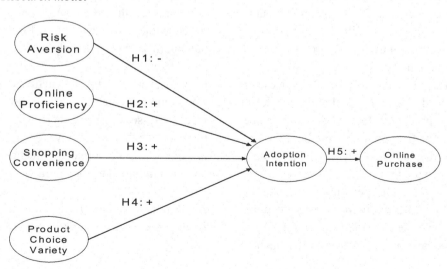

a direct and negative relationship) with adoption intention of online shopping. In turn, adoption intention has a direct and positive effect on online purchase. Figure 1 illustrates the research model that was derived from factor analyses, which we attempted to test.

METHODOLOGY

For model testing, measured items first were created to tap the major constructs. The instruments were pretested with 20 students. Once the questionnaire was finalized, data were collected from business major students in a Midwestern university. One hundred questionnaires were distributed and collected, out of which 15 questionnaires could not be used due to missing or incomplete data. Hence, the usable sample size for this study was 85. Table 1 gives the descriptive statistics on their demographics. We subjected the data to an exploratory factor analysis. Five factors emerged, and their measured items are reported in Table 2. The reliabilities for adoption intention, online purchase, risk aversion, online proficiency, shopping convenience, and product choice variety are 0.72, 0.76, 0.80, 0.73, 0.73, and 0.64, respectively. Researchers suggest Cronbach alpha of .70 for confirmatory research and .60 for exploratory research as acceptable (Fornell & Larcker, 1981; Hair et al., 1998). Thus, all constructs can be considered reliable. Correlations among five constructs are shown in Table 3.

Confirmatory factor analysis using EQS was performed to test the construct validity: convergent and discriminant validity. Table 4 shows loadings and average variance extracted (AVE) for all four unobserved constructs in the measurement model. The loadings and AVE of the constructs higher than .7 and .5, respectively, are considered good (Bentler, 1990; Hair et al., 1998). The results illustrate that all of the constructs under investigation surpass the acceptable level showing good convergent validity. Discriminant

validity is presented in Table 5. To achieve the discriminant validity, the square root of the average variance extracted in diagonal elements of the matrix should be greater than corresponding off-diagonal elements (correlation among constructs). It confirms that all of the off-diagonal values are less than the diagonal values that show support for discriminant validity.

Diagonal elements (bold) are the square root of the average variance extracted between the constructs and their measures. Off-diagonal elements are the correlations among constructs. For discriminant validity, diagonal elements should be larger than off-diagonal elements.

DATA ANALYSES AND RESULTS

Although structural equation modeling (SEM) has substantial advantages over traditional statistical techniques (e.g., multiple regression), it is recommended that the sample size be 150 or more (Anderson & Gerbing, 1988; Hair et al., 1998). Due to well below the recommended size for SEM, a multiple regression model is used for testing the hypotheses. All but one predictor are highly significant in explaining the adoption intention of online shopping (Figure 2). While online proficiency (standardized $\beta = .30$, $p < .01$) and product choice variety ($\beta = .36$, $p < .01$) are positively related to adoption intention of online shopping, risk aversion ($\beta = -.23$, $p < .05$) is negatively related to the adoption intention of online shopping, as hypothesized. Thus, hypotheses 1, 2, and 4 are supported. However, shopping convenience ($\beta = .05$, n.s.) is not related to adoption intention of online shopping, offering no support for hypothesis 3. Adoption intention of online shopping is shown to have a direct and positive effect on online purchase ($\beta = .23$, $p < .05$), thus confirming hypothesis 5. The regression results are presented in Table 6. Low VIF indicates that multicollinearity was not a problem.

Table 1. Respondent demographics

Characteristics	Percentage of All Respondents (n)
Gender	
Male	51% (n = 43)
Female	49% (n = 42)
Age	
≤ 24	66% (n = 56)
25 - 34	19% (n = 16)
35 - 44	12% (n = 10)
45 - 54	2% (n = 2)
55+	1% (n = 1)
Household Income	
< $6,999	64% (n = 54)
$10,000 to $29,999	25% (n = 21)
$30,000 to $49,999	7% (n = 6)
$50,000 to $74,999	2% (n = 2)
$75,000+	2% (n = 2)
Work Experience	
None	27% (n=23)
Less than 1 year	15% (n=13)
1-5 years	35% (n=29)
6-10 years	9% (n=8)
10+	14% (n=12)
Ethnicity	
Caucasian	60% (n=51)
African American	15% (n=13)
Asian	20% (n=17)
Hispanic	2% (n=2)
Others	2% (n=2)

To test the mediation effect in hypothesis 6, multiple regression is employed. Following Baron and Kenny (1986), the dependent variable (online purchase) is regressed on the independent variables (risk aversion, online proficiency, shopping convenience, and product choice variety). As posited, adoption intention mediated the relationships of risk aversion ($\beta = -.02$, n.s.), shopping convenience ($\beta = .07$, n.s.), and product choice variety ($\beta = .06$, n.s.). However, only online proficiency showed a direct effect on online purchase ($\beta = .31$, $p < .05$). Thus, hypothesis 6 is partially supported.

IMPLICATIONS AND LIMITATIONS

Previous research has examined the predictors of online purchase intentions (Boyle & Ruppel, 2004; Brown, Pope, & Voges, 2003; Kim & Kim, 2004)

Table 2. Measurement items and reliabilities

Constructs/Indicators	Reliability (α)
Adoption Intention	**0.72**
• Willingness to experiment with online shopping.	
• How interested are you in shopping online?	
Online Shopping	**0.76**
• How frequently do you purchase online?	
• Approximately how many items have you purchased online in last 6 months?	
• How often do you make purchases from Web-based vendors?	
Risk Aversion	**0.80**
• Providing credit card information online is one of the most important reasons I do not buy online.	
• Online shopping is risky.	
Online Proficiency	**0.73**
• I am proficient in using the Internet for purchasing.	
• Online shopping would be easy for me.	
Shopping Convenience	**0.73**
• Online shopping would allow me to do my shopping more quickly.	
• People shop online because it simplifies finding desired products.	
• I go online shopping, as it minimizes the hassles of shopping.	
Product Choice Variety	**0.64**
• Online shopping would allow me to get better price/choice when shopping.	
• Online shopping would allow me to have better item selection in my shopping.	
• People shop online to get a broad choice of products.	

Table 3. Correlations of six constructs

		DV1	INT1	RISK1	PROF1	CONV1	VARI1
Pearson Correlation	**DV1**	1.000	.322	-.064	.327	.204	.025
	INT1	.322	1.000	-.458	.584	.389	.543
	RISK1	-.064	-.458	1.000	-.495	-.286	-.181
	PROF1	.327	.584	-.495	1.000	.478	.415
	CONV1	.204	.389	-.286	.478	1.000	.360
	VARI1	.025	.543	-.181	.415	.360	1.000

DV1: Online Purchase; INT1: Adoption Intention; RISK1: Risk Aversion; PROF1: Online Proficiency; CONV1: Shopping Convenience; VARI1: Product Choice Variety

and determinants of online shopping behavior, such as amount and frequency (Corner et al., 2005). In other words, both purchase intentions and actual shopping behavior have been treated as dependent variables in various studies. Our research is different in that we incorporated adoption intention of online shopping as the mediating variable through which risk aversion, online proficiency, and product choice variety affect online shopping behavior. Our approach is similar in spirit as Kulviwat, Guo, and Engchanil (2004), who proposed a model of online information search where motivation is the mediating variable through which various factors such as perceived risk affect online search.

Table 4. CFA results for measurement model

Construct	Factor Loading	Variance Extracted
RISK1 – Item 1	.95	.70
Item 2	.70	
PROF1 – Item 1	.67	.62
Item 2	.89	
CONV1 – Item 1	.70	.50
Item 2	.54	
Item 3	.84	
VARI1– Item 1	.41	.45
Item 2	.93	
Item 3	.54	

Risk1 = Risk Aversion; Prof1 = Online Proficiency; Conv1 = Shopping Convenience; Vari1 = Product Choice Variety

Table 5. Discriminant validity matrix

Construct	RISK1	PROF1	CONV1	VARI1
RISK1	**.84**	-.49	-.28	-.18
PROF1	-.49	**.79**	.47	.41
CONV1	-.28	.47	**.71**	.36
VARI1	-.18	.41	.36	**.67**

Risk1 = Risk Aversion; Prof1 = Online Proficiency; Conv1 = Shopping Convenience; Vari1 = Product Choice Variety

Table 6. Coefficients

Model		Unstandardized Coefficients		Standardized Coefficients	t	Sig.	Collinearity Statistics	
		B	Std. Error	Beta			Tolerance	VIF
1	(Constant)	.794	.627		1.267	.209		
	RISK1	-.185	.073	-.231	-2.519	.014	.750	1.333
	PROF1	.295	.104	.296	2.832	.006	.579	1.727
	CONV1	6.638E-02	.119	.052	.558	.578	.736	1.359
	VARI1	.518	.129	.360	4.026	.000	.792	1.262
	INT	.806	.376	.233	2.147	.035	.745	1.122

Dependent Variable: DV = Adoption Intention of Online Shopping
Independent Variables: Risk1 = Risk Aversion; Prof1 = Online Proficiency; Conv1 = Shopping Convenience; Vari1 = Product Choice Variety; INT = Adoption Intention
(Note: Adjusted R square is .47 or 47%)

Results indicate that purchase intentions and online shopping are distinctive constructs, and including both in a model sheds more light on the consumer online purchase decision-making process. For example, risk aversion and product choice variety may not have a direct effect on online shopping behavior, but their effects on consumer online purchase decision making cannot be underestimated, because they influence purchase intentions, which, in turn, affect online purchase. People who expressed their intentions to shop online are more likely to do so than those who had no such intentions. That is, people talk the talk and also walk the walk. Thus, our research provides hints as to how to separate serious online shoppers from cheap riders who

Figure 2. Model result

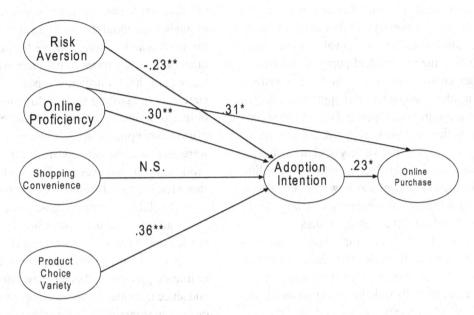

Significance at **<0.01 level; *<0.05 level; N.S. = non-significance

are having fun in the virtual community without throwing their money online or paying their dues, so to speak. One simple way to find out to which category online visitors belong is to ask them whether they would be interested in shopping online. Internet use proficiency, variety-seeking opportunity online, and reduced risk perceptions will cultivate consumer interests to shop online, which ultimately will lead to online shopping.

The results of this study have implications for both practitioners and researchers. As risk aversion is negatively related to consumer adoption intention of online shopping, it supports the notion that risk aversion is a hygiene factor. E-commerce firms must do more to beef up privacy and security measures in order to remove this major obstacle to online commerce expansion (Credit Management, 2004; FTC, 2000). One way to reduce the perceptions of risk is that e-marketers may make online shopping a multiple-stage process. Intermediate

steps are offered to familiarize customers with the online shopping environment. Perhaps incentives or protective measures could be provided to induce customers to conduct pre-purchase activities, such as online search by providing possible falsification of personal information or optional search without soliciting privacy information. For instance, on its Web site, American Airlines offers a secured information search (required login, thus personal information) as well as a non-secured information search, where no login is needed, nor is personal information collected. Another alternative is that online stores may reduce risk associated with purchase by ensuring tight control of possible losses that might result from security breach. In fact, some companies such as American Express offer disposable credit card numbers to alleviate anxiety for online shopping (Hancock, 2000).

Results also indicate that shopping convenience, one of the most often-touted benefits of Internet shopping, is not enough to attract consumers to shop online. Perhaps this is due to the fact that the subjects used in the study were college students, who may not value convenience as much as the non-student population. Instead, product choice variety should be emphasized more in advertising Internet shopping advantages vis-à-vis traditional shopping. This finding is consistent with recent work (Rohm & Swaminathan, 2004), indicating that variety-seeking behavior of consumers is a significant factor in the online environment. The question, however, remains on how much Internet product choice variety should be improved subject to future studies.

Further, results show that superior technological online skills enable individuals to utilize Internet shopping more extensively compared to those who generally lack the skills that could lead them not to be receptive to innovations. This assertion is consistent with Roger (1995), who states that those who are more capable of understanding and handling technology can generalize the results of an innovation to its full scale use and likely reap its full benefits. Individuals with superior technological skills have the ability to mobilize efforts to learn the innovation and, thus, are more likely to induce adoption intention and actual behavior. Since online experience is a prerequisite to online shopping, consumers must develop a certain level of skills so that online proficiency can be established. Positive online experience and minimum online proficiency are the springboards for online shopping. As such, e-businesses may want to provide free training courses in order to improve consumers' literacy with computers, before they throw money on a promotional scheme to attract online purchasing.

Although there are many studies in consumer adoption for off-line behavior, this study explores the determinants of consumer adoption in the case of online shopping. Thus, a number of interesting issues have surfaced from this study that could be considered for future research. Future research could identify additional variables and examine their influence on consumer online shopping.

In this study, we employed convenient sample of students. It must be acknowledged that this might be a potential shortcoming of this research. Future research might replicate the study using other sampling frames to compare whether the results still hold. Further, we used respondents' statements regarding their willingness to shop online as the measurement of consumer adoption of online shopping. Also, only two measured items were used to tap on some constructs such as online proficiency and risk aversion. The number of items should be increased to enhance construct reliability and validity in future research studies.

In addition, future research also should be carried out to see what other items could be used to tap the adoption intention construct. Since online shopping is a relatively new phenomenon, and since not much has been done specifically in online environment literature that measures consumer intention or willingness to shop online, this provides plenty of research opportunities to see if more than two items, as presented in this study, could be better used to measure this construct.

Another area of research opportunity could be how to reduce customers' feelings of risk in online environment. Since in an online environment, customers cannot get the feeling of touch, it creates a feeling of risk in their minds. In the present study, risk was measured using a two-item scale, because those two items are considered to be the most important factors that create more insecurity in customers' minds and prevent them from using a Web site. However, future studies should be carried out to see how customers feeling if risk could be minimized.

CONCLUSION

Drawing upon the innovation theory, this study examined the antecedents of consumer adoption of online shopping. The results indicate that risk aversion, online proficiency, and product choice variety are important determinants of consumer adoption intention of online shopping, whereas shopping convenience is not an important predictor of consumers' intentions to shop online. We used consumers' intentions to shop online as the mediating variable through which risk aversion, online proficiency, and product choice variety affect online purchase. The use of a mediating variable in the model is revealing in that only online proficiency has a direct impact on both intentions and actual online shopping behavior. Risk aversion and product choice variety only indirectly affect shopping behavior through intentions. As e-companies continue to look for the viable business model, they have come to a consensus that businesses must provide superior customer value in their product or service offerings so that consumers are willing to pay for products and services online and not just be a free rider (Grewal et al., 2003). Our study provides insights into what separates free riders, mere Internet users, from those who are serious about making online purchases or treating the Internet as a legitimate marketplace. As e-commerce becomes a way of life, more research on the topic is warranted.

REFERENCES

Anderson, J., & Gerbing, D. (1988). Structural equation modeling in practice: A review and recommended two-step approach. *Psychological Bulletin, 103*(3), 411-423.

Andrews, P. (2003). Christmas clicking. *U.S. News & World Report, 135*(21), 42.

Angwin, J. (2001, July 16). Consumer adoption rate slows in replay of TV's history; bad news for online firms. *Wall Street Journal*, p. B1.

Bandura, A. (1977). Self-efficacy: Toward a unifying theory of behavioral change. *Psychological Review, 84*(2), 191-215.

Baron, R. M., & Kenny, D. A. (1986, December). The moderator-mediator variable distinction in social psychological research: Conceptual,

strategic, and statistical considerations. *Journal of Personality and Social Psychology, 51*(6), 1173-82.

Bellman, S., & Lohse, G. (1999). Predictors of online buying behavior. *Communications of the ACM, 42*(12), 32-39.

Bentler, P. M. (1990). Comparative fit indices in structural models. *Psychological Bulletin, 107*(2), 238-246.

Betts, M. (2001). Turning browsers into buyers. *Sloan Management Review, 42*(2), 8-9.

Bhatnagar, A, Misra, S., & Rao, R. (2000). On risk, convenience, and Internet shopping behavior. *Communications of the ACM, 43*(11), 98-105.

Boyle, R., & Ruppel, C. (2004, February 27-28). Online purchase intent: The effect of personal innovativeness, perceived risk, and computer self-efficacy. In R. Papp (Ed.), *Proceedings of the Seventh Annual Conference of the Southern Association for Information Systems* (pp. 131-137).

Brown, M., Pope, N., & Voges, D. (2003), Buying or browsing? An exploration of shopping orientation and online purchase intention. *European Journal of Marketing, 37*(11/12), 1666-1684.

Brynjolfsson, E., & Smith, M. D. (2000). Frictionless commerce? A comparison of Internet and conventional retailers. *Management Science, 46*(4), 563-585.

Caudill, E. M., & Murphy, P. E. (2000, Spring). Consumer online privacy: Legal and ethical issues. *Journal of Public Policy & Marketing, 19*, 7-19.

Corner, J. L., Thompson, F., Dillon, S., & Doolin, B. (2005). Perceived risk, the Internet shopping experience and online purchasing behavior: A New Zealand perspective. *Journal of Global Information Management, 13*(2), 66-86.

Csikszentmihalyi, M. (1990). *Flow: The psychology of optimal experience*. New York: Harper and Row.

Damanpour, F. (1991). Organizational innovation: A meta-analysis of effects of determinants and moderators. *Academy of Management Journal, 34*(3), 555-590.

Devi, C. (2001, December 6). Guidelines to ensure safe Internet use. *New Straits Times*, p. 6.

Dickerson, M. D., & Gentry, J. W. (1983, September). Characteristics of adopters and non-adopters of home computers. *Journal of Consumer Research, 10*, 225-235.

Federal Trade Commission. (2000). *Privacy online: Fair information practices in the electronic marketplace* (Report to Congress). Retrieved from http://www.ftc.gov/privacy/index.html

Forman, A. M., & Sriram, V. (1991). The depersonalization of retailing: Its impact on the "lonely" consumer. *Journal of Retailing, 67*(2), 226-243.

Fornell, C., & Larcker, D. (1981). Evaluating structural equation models with unobservable variables and measurement error. *Journal of Marketing Research, 18*(3), 39-50.

Garbarino, E., & Strahilevitz, M. (2004). Gender differences in the perceived risk of buying online and the effects of receiving a site recommendation. *Journal of Business Research, 57*(7), 768-775.

Gefen, D., Karahanna, E., & Straub, D. W. (2003). Trust and TAM in online shopping: An integrated model. *MIS Quarterly, 27*(1), 51-90.

Gonsalves, A. (2004, January 26). Online retail sales to climb. *InformationWeek, 973*, 16.

Grant, I. C., & Waite, K. (2003). Following the yellow brick road — Young adults' experiences of the information superhighway. *Qualitative Market Research: An International Journal, 6*(1), 48-57.

Grewal, D, Gopalkrishnana, R., Iyer, R. K., & Sharma, A. (2003). The Internet and the price-value-loyalty. *Journal of Business Research, 56*(5), 391-398.

Guo, C. (2002, March/April). Competing in high growth markets: The case of e-commerce. *Business Horizons, 45*, 77-83.

Hair, J. F., Anderson, R. E., Tatham, R. L., & Black, W. C. (1998). *Multivariate data analysis with readings* (5th ed.). Englewood Cliffs, NJ: Prentice-Hall.

Hancock, B. (2000). American Express creates disposable credit card numbers. *Computers & Security, 19*(7), 571-572.

Hirschman, E. C. (1980, December). Innovativeness, novelty seeking, and consumer creativity. *Journal of Consumer Research, 7*, 283-295.

Hoffman, D. L., & Novak, T. P. (1996). Marketing in hypermedia computer-mediated environments: Conceptual foundations. *Journal of Marketing, 60*(3), 50-68.

Hoffman, D. L., Novak, T. P., & Peralta, M. (1999). Building consumer trust online. *Communications of the ACM, 42*(4), 80-86.

Jansen, P. G. W., van der Velde, M. E. G., & Telting, I. A. (2001). The effectiveness of human resource practices on advancing men's and women's ranks. *Journal of Management Development, 20*(4), 318-331.

Jarvenpaa, S. L., & Todd, P. A. (1997a). Is there a future for retailing on Internet? In R. A. Peterson (Ed.), *Electronic marketing and consumer* (pp. 139-154). Thousand Oaks, CA: Sage.

Jarvenpaa, S. L., & Todd, P. A. (1997b). Consumer reactions to electronic shopping on the World Wide Web. *International Journal of Electronic Commerce, 1*(2), 59-88.

Kim, E. Y., & Kim, Y.-K. (2004), Predicting online purchase intentions for clothing products. *European Journal of Marketing, 38*(7), 883-897.

Koufaris, M. (2002). Applying the technology acceptance model and flow theory to online consumer behavior. *Information Systems Research, 13*(2), 205-212.

Koyuncu, C., & Lien, D. (2003). E-commerce and consumer's purchasing behavior. *Applied Economics, 35*(6), 721-726.

Kulviwat, S., Guo, C., & Engchanil, N. (2004). Determinants of online information search: A critical review and assessment. *Internet Research: Electronic Networking Applications and Policy, 14*(3), 245-253.

Lee, H. G. (1998, January). Do electronic market-places lower the price of goods? *Communication of ACM, 41*, 73.

Levinson, H., Price, C. R., Munden, K. J., Mandl, H. J., & Solley, C. M. (1962). *Men, management, and mental health*. Cambridge, MA: Harvard University Press.

Levy, S. J. (2001). The psychology of an online shopping pioneer. *Advances in Consumer Research, 28*(1), 222-226.

Li, K., Kuo, C., & Russel, M. (1999). The impact of perceived channel utilities, shopping orientations, and demographics on the consumer's online buying behavior. *Journal of Computer Mediated Communication, 5*(2), 1-23.

Lynch, J., & Ariely, D. (2000, Winter). Wine online: Search costs affect competition on price, quality, and distribution. *Marketing Science, 19*, 83-103.

Mahajan, V., & Wind, J. (1989, August). Market discontinuities and strategic planning: A research agenda. *Technological Forecasting and Social Change, 36*, 185-99.

Midgley, D. F., & Dowling, G. R. (1978). Innovativeness: The concept and its measurement. *Journal of Consumer Research, 4*, 229-242.

Miyazaki, A. D., & Fernandez, A. (2001). Consumer perceptions of privacy and security risks for online shopping. *Journal of Consumer Affairs, 35*(1), 27-44.

Moore, G., & Benbasat, I. (1991). Development of an instrument to measure the perceptions of adopting an information technology innovation. *Information Systems Research, 2*(3), 192-223.

Novak, T., Hoffman, D. L., & Yung, Y. (2000). Measuring the customer experience in online environments: A structural modeling approach. *Marketing Science, 19*(1), 22-42.

Online shopping still causes anxiety. (2004, January). *Credit Management*, 12.

Peterson, R., & Merino, M. (2003). Consumer information search behavior and the Internet. *Psychology & Marketing, 20*(2), 99-122.

Peterson, R., Balasubramanian, S. A., & Bronnenberg, B. J. (1997). Exploring the implications of the Internet for consumer marketing. *Journal of the Academy of Marketing Science, 25*(4), 329-346.

Quelch, J. A., & Klein, L. R. (1996, February). The Internet and international marketing. *Sloan Management Review, 37*, 60-75.

Rheault, M. (2004). The Kiplinger monitor. *Kiplinger's Personal Finance, 58*(2), 22.

Rohm, A., & Swaminathan, V. (2004). A typology of online shoppers based on shopping motivations. *Journal of Business Research, 57*(7), 748-757.

Rogers, E. M. (1995). *Diffusion of innovations* (4th edition). New York: The Free Press.

Rogers, E. M., & Rogers, E. (2003). *Diffusion of innovations* (5th edition). New York: The Free Press.

Rogers, E. M., & Shoemaker, F. F. (1971). *Communication of innovations: A cross-cultural approach*. New York: The Free Press.

Schiesel, S. (1997, January 2). Payoff still elusive on Internet gold rush. *The New York Times*, p. C17.

Seiders, K., Berry, L. L., & Gresham, L. G. (2000). Attention, retailers! How convenient is your convenience strategy? *Sloan Management Review, 41*(3), 79-89.

Sheppard, B., Hartwick, J., & Warshaw, P. (1988). The theory of reasoned action: A meta-analysis of past research with recommendations for modifications and future research. *Journal of Consumer Research, 15*(3), 325-344.

Singh, I. (2000, March/April). Cost transparency: The net's real threat to prices and brands. *Harvard Business Review, 78*, 3.

Taylor, J. W. (1977). A striking characteristic of innovators. *Journal of Marketing Research, 14*(1), 104-107.

Taylor, S., & Todd, P. (1995). Understanding information technology usage: A test of competing models. *Information Systems Research, 6*(2), 144-176.

Tornatzky, L. G., & Klein, R. J. (1982). Innovation characteristics and innovation adoption-implementation: A metaanalysis of findings.

IEEE Transactions on Engineering Management, 29(1), 28-45.

Trevino, L. K., & Webster, J. (1992). Flow in computer-mediated communication: Electronic mail and voice mail evaluation and impacts. *Communication Research, 19*(5), 539-573.

Weinberg, B. D. (2000). *24/7 Internet Shopping Diary*. Retrieved from http://www.internetshopping 247.com

Weinberg, B. D. (2001). The three faces of e-commerce: Insight into online consumer behavior through the interpretation of an Internet consumer's experiences. *Advances in Consumer Research, 28*(1), 218-221.

Williamson, R. (2001). Creating a better brighter smarter Internet. *Interactive Week, 8*(39), 26-29.

Zhang, P., & von Dran, G. M. (2000). Satisfiers and dissatisfiers: A two-factor model for Website design and evaluation. *Journal of the American Society for Information Science, 51*(14), 1253-1268.

This work was previously published in the International Journal of E-Business Research, edited by I. Lee, Volume 2, Issue 2, pp. 68-82, copyright 2006 by IGI Publishing (an imprint of IGI Global).

Chapter XVI
Can Web Seals Work Wonders for Small E-Vendors in the Online Trading Environment?
A Theoretical Approach

Xiaorui Hu
Saint Louis University, USA

Yuhong Wu
William Paterson University, USA

ABSTRACT

Trust is a major issue in e-markets. It is an even more prominent issue when online shoppers trade with small, less-established e-vendors. Empirical studies on Web seals show that small e-vendors could promote consumers' trust and increase Web sales by displaying Web seals of approval. This article takes a theoretical approach to examine online trading when seals are used in e-markets. We establish an online shopper's decision-making model to reveal the online shopper's decision-making criteria. Criteria include when to trade with a well-established e-vendor and when to trade with a small, less-established e-vendor, with or without a Web seal. Based on our analysis of the research results, we reveal the price effect, the seal effect, the reputation effect, and their impact on a shopper's decision-making process. Meanwhile, a social welfare analysis is conducted to further demonstrate the positive impact of Web seals on small, less-established e-vendors.

INTRODUCTION

The Internet and World Wide Web have emerged as powerful media for communication and merchandise distribution. Cyberspace retailers are prospering and are now a potential threat to traditional retailers (Sanderson, 2000). Retail e-commerce sales have experienced fast and stable growth; these sales reached $110 billion in 2006, up 30% from 2005 and almost 100% from 2003. Meanwhile, e-commerce as a percentage of total sales has also steadily increased from 0.9% in 2000 to 2.8% in 2006 (U.S. Census Bureau, 2007).

Rapid growth in electronic commerce is largely due to its inherent advantages as a medium. Internet shopping has the merits of convenience (such as 24-hour availability, no travel cost, and an easy global reach), the ability to quickly and cost-effectively search product and service information, and the ability to obtain competitive prices through comparison among various e-retailers (Kau, Tang, & Ghose, 2003; Peterson, Balasubramanian, & Bronnenberg, 1997; Wolfinbarger & Gilly, 2001).

Although Internet sales are booming, many people still perceive the risks associated with online trading to be high. Consumers' inability to inspect online products and merchants results in uncertainty about product quality and distrust of e-vendors (Bhatnagar, Mishra, & Rao, 2000; Van den Poel & Leunis, 1999). In addition, consumers are concerned about privacy and security issues associated with online shopping, because their personal identification information and other important data (such as credit card numbers) could be inappropriately handled or even misused (Bhimani, 1996; Ford & Baum, 1997; Griffin, Ladd, & Whitehead, 1997; Miyazaki & Fernandez, 2001). Some recent statistics reveal how serious these issues have become. According to Internet Fraud Watch (2005) the National Consumers League (NCL) received 12,315 complaints in 2005, compared to 10,794 in 2004. In 2005, the average loss per complaint was $1,917, and double that in 2004 ($894 average loss per complaint). Meanwhile, the Internet Crime Complaint Center (IC3, 2007) received its millionth complaint on June 11, 2007. Since beginning operation in May 2000, IC3 has referred 461,096 criminal complaints to federal, state, and local law enforcement agencies around the country for further investigation. The total dollar loss from all these referred cases is estimated to be $647.1 million (see http://www.ic3.gov).

Consumers enjoy the convenience, price advantage, and other benefits of online shopping, but they want to be protected from Internet fraud and other malicious activities. Online shoppers are advised to do business only with those with whom they have had favorable experiences. When consumers become interested in trading with less-established e-vendors, they are advised to thoroughly research these e-vendors. Recommendations include checking with state or local consumer protection agencies or the Better Business Bureau and reviewing other customers' feedback about a specific vendor (Internet Fraud Watch, 2007; U.S. Department of Justice, 2007). Given that most consumers are reluctant to spend the time and effort to perform thorough background checks on small online businesses, risk-averse consumers generally will conduct business only with well-established e-vendors (Lasica, 1999). This implies that companies with an established reputation either offline (e.g., Wal-Mart, Sears) or online (e.g., eBay.com, Amazon.com) enjoy a competitive advantage in e-markets.

One might wonder whether these small, less-established e-vendors could find methods to attract online shoppers and eventually prosper in e-markets. As a matter of fact, it is the active participation of small entrepreneurs in e-markets that fosters competition, which benefits consumers with lower prices, more choices, and better services.

Recently, the use of third-party Web seals (also called Internet seals of approval) as trust-enhancing mechanisms has attracted attention from both practitioners and academic researchers. These seals attempt to address consumers' various concerns—such as information privacy, transaction security, and complete/accurate transactions—about online shopping (Cook & Luo, 2003; Kimery & McCord, 2006). A few Internet seals are becoming well known in e-markets, such as Trust*e*, VeriSign, WebTrust, Good Housekeeping, and BBB*OnLine*. The seal issuer charges e-vendors for enrollment, with fees ranging from free to thousands of dollars. Meanwhile, an e-vendor will be examined by the seal issuer for conformity to the seal issuer's standards and principles. A qualified e-vendor earns the right to display these seals on its Web site. When a seal is clicked, a detailed disclosure of the principles ensured by the seal issuer is displayed to online shoppers.

By voluntarily placing itself under the scrutiny of a third party, a small, less-established e-vendor communicates to online shoppers that it runs a trustworthy business. If trust can be promoted through display of such Web seals, a small e-vendor will have a fair chance to compete with well-established names in e-markets.

The academic community has started to explore the impact of Web seals in promoting consumers' trust and increasing Web sales (Hu, Lin, & Zhang, 2002; Kovar, Burke, & Kovar, 2000; Noteberg, Christaanse, & Wallage, 2003). However, more research in this area is needed. Prior studies on Web seals were conducted from an empirical perspective. The literature lacks a theoretical analysis of how Web seals as trust-enhancing tools affect consumers' shopping decisions. The current research aims to fill this gap.

The first objective of this article is to explore the conditions under which small, less-established e-vendors can persuade online shoppers to purchase from them rather than from a highly reputable, well-known e-vendor. We establish a decision-making model for risk-neutral and rational online shoppers and derive a set of shoppers' decision-making criteria about whether and when to trade with a less-established e-vendor than with a well-established one. Furthermore, we analyze the effect of a Web seal in helping an e-vendor win consumer trust. Based on this analysis, we demonstrate the conditions under which the price effect, the seal effect, and the reputation effect play major roles in a shopper's decision about vendor selection.

The second objective of the article is to present evidence on how much social welfare a Web seal can produce. A social welfare analysis is conducted to reveal the positive social impact associated with the participation of less-established e-vendors and the introduction of Web seals in e-markets. The results of this article provide insights for small and less-established e-vendors on gaining competitive advantages and prospering in e-markets; the results will also help social planners advance e-commerce to its true potential.

The rest of the article is organized as follows. We first provide a literature review and background on third-party Web seals. Then, we develop a decision-making model for an online shopper. The model indicates that a shopper's decision is subject to a set of criteria, including price advantage of a less-established e-vendor over a well-established e-vendor, a shopper's reservation value, proportion of honest to strategic e-vendors in e-markets, the degree of cheating from a strategic trader, and the "safeguard" effect of a Web seal in preventing a strategic e-vendor from cheating. We study how seals used as trust-enhancing tools affect a shopper's decision and thus change the structure of e-markets. We later analyze how the participation of small, less-established e-vendors and the adoption of Web seals in e-markets increase social welfare. We conclude with an analysis of our research results and offer suggestions for future research.

LITERATURE REVIEW

As the Internet's popularity as a distribution medium increases, the issue of Web trust has attracted the attention of many people. Trust is widely regarded as critical to consumer's adoption of e-commerce (e.g., Gefen, 2002; Gefen, Karahanna, & Straub, 2003; Jarvenpaa, Tractinsky, & Vitale, 2000; McKnight, Choudhury, & Kacmar, 2002; Stewart, 2003; Yoon, 2002). McKnight et al. (2002) define trust as a multidimensional construct with two interrelated components—trusting beliefs and trusting intentions. They find that trusting intentions and trusting beliefs significantly affect consumers' behavioral intentions. Jarvenpaa et al. (2000) find that trust affects consumer's attitude and willingness to purchase from an online store. Gefen (2002), Gefen et al. (2003), and Stewart (2003) also suggest that consumers' trust toward an e-vendor plays an important role in determining their online purchasing intentions. Yoon (2002) presents a model for the antecedents and consequences of consumer trust in online purchase decision making. The research results confirm that Web site trust, along with Web-site satisfaction and Web-site awareness, influences consumers' online purchase intentions.

Various studies also explore the antecedents to online trust and provide recommendations to e-vendors on how to promote online trust. Jarvenpaa et al. (2000) find that size and reputation of an Internet-based store significantly impact consumer's perceived trust in the store. Yoon (2002) proposes that Web-site trust was impacted by site properties, including image-related variables such as company awareness and company reputation. In addition, Web site trust is also driven by such personal traits as familiarity with and prior satisfaction with e-commerce. Metzger (2006) also suggests that vendor reputation is important in influencing consumers' trust. Lee and Turban (2001) propose that consumer trust in Internet shopping is influenced by such factors as trustworthiness of the Internet merchant, trustworthiness of the Internet as a shopping medium, and infrastructural/contextual factors (e.g., security, third-party certification). Urban, Sultan, and Qualls (2000) believe that to build Web-site trust, e-vendors should maximize such trust-building cues as third-party seals of approval, security technology, and/or security/privacy policies, provide unbiased and complete information, use virtual advisor technology, and fulfill expectations.

Third-party seals of approval have a fairly long history. Such approval certifies that the product or service bearing the seal meets the requirement of the seal-granting organization, and use of a seal aims to give consumers some assurance from a third party as to the quality and/or other important features of a product. For example, the Good Housekeeping seal assures buyers that if the product bearing the seal proves to be defective within two years of purchase, Good Housekeeping will replace the product or refund the purchase price. Institutions that grant seals and certifications can be independent testing companies, professional organizations, and/or government agencies. Seals of approval work to raise consumers' confidence in a particular product and are believed to significantly influence consumers' choice behavior (Parkinson, 2002).

A third-party seal is a cue that signals information to consumers (Wang, Beatty, & Foxx, 2004). In e-markets, because the true type (honest or strategic) of the e-vendor is unknown to the consumer, the e-vendor can use a seal to signal its honesty. Such a signaling process works through the seal issuer. The seal issuer, which has more information about the e-vendor than shoppers do, extends its own reputation to the e-vendor and takes on potential risk if the e-vendor is dishonest. The seal issuer generally will examine the seller and/or the product that bears the seal. In return, the seller is charged a fee. Shoppers who have little information about the seller tend to believe that a seller/product that bears a seal is trustworthy.

For example, WebTrust is an assurance service jointly developed by the American Institute of Certified Public Accountants (AICPA) and the Canadian Institute of Chartered Accountants (CICA). Any site displaying a WebTrust seal is guaranteed to have (1) been examined by a trained and licensed public accounting firm; (2) disclosed its business practices; (3) been audited to prove the site actually follows those practices;

(4) met international Trust Services Standards; and (5) an audit report, which is based on one or more Trust Services Principles, linked to the seal (see http://www.cpaWebtrust.org/seal_info.htm). An e-vendor displaying a WebTrust seal thus signals to consumers that it pursues a high standard of business practices. Indeed, one may argue that because there is little regulation in e-markets, the potential need for Web seals is huge. Signaling can be powerful, but it is also important that the targeted market and consumers adequately understand and trust the signals for them to play their role in assuring consumer trust (Kimery & McCord, 2006; Odom, Kumar, & Saunders, 2002).

Some academic research, although still limited, specifically focuses on third-party-assured Web seals and how such seals help e-vendors build consumers' trust toward the site and attract consumers. Kovar et al. (2000) find that consumers' intent to purchase online is positively related to (1) their degree of attention to the WebTrust seal, (2) their exposure to WebTrust advertising, and (3) their knowledge of CPAs. Hu et al. (2003) find that some Web seals, such as BBB*OnLine* and AOL Certified Merchant Guarantee seals, do promote consumers' willingness to buy from an e-vendor that displays such seal(s). Noteberg et al. (2003) discover that third-party assurance significantly increases consumers' likelihood of purchasing from an e-vendor and also reduces consumers' concerns about privacy and transaction integrity, concerns that might inhibit purchases. Odom et al. (2002) also find that Web seals influence consumers' online purchasing decisions. They suggest a relationship between consumers' ability to recognize a brand of Web seal and the seal's ability to influence consumers' online purchasing decisions. Nikitkov (2006) examines the use of seals on the eBay auction site, where buyers act with their own money and also have time to study the site. The results confirm that the presence of a seal on the seller's Web page does impact actual consumer purchasing behavior in

both auction and posted-price contexts. Wakefield and Whitten (2006) further the study on Web seals by examining the role played by third-party organization (TPO) credibility on Internet users' attitude toward Web sites. Their finding suggests that TPO credibility reduces consumers' perception of purchasing risk and increases their trusting attitude toward an e-vendor.

The literature enriches our understanding about the important role of online trust and empirically confirms that third-party Web seals help promote consumers' trust and increase their purchase intention from sites that display such seals. However, there is no comprehensive theoretical analysis of how the use of Web seals changes the structure of e-markets and how their use increases the competitiveness of the e-markets by altering the decisions and strategies of both online shoppers and e-vendors. The current study attempts to fill this research gap. The results of this study show how small, less-established e-vendors, by promoting trust through the adoption of Web seals, can compete with well-established e-vendors and gain market share from peers that do not deploy a trust-promoting seal. Therefore, the research shows that competitive markets can be established; these markets not only grant online shoppers more consumer surplus, but also promote a more secure online shopping environment, which benefits society as a whole.

ONLINE SHOPPERS' DECISION-MAKING MODEL

Basic Model Set-Up

In this model, we assume two types of e-vendors in e-markets: the high reputation type (HH-type) and the low reputation type (L-type). HH-type e-vendors are those with well-established reputations that trade honestly and that are trusted by online shoppers. Examples of HH-type e-vendors include Walmart.com, Dell.com, and Amazon.

com. L-type e-vendors are those that have less-established reputations. Examples include new and small market entrants. Among L-type e-vendors, we assume two sub-types: honest (denoted as LH) and strategic (denoted as LS). LH-type e-vendors are honest, have higher moral standards, and are committed to fair business practices. They do not intentionally deceive their customers for illegal profits (in this article, we ignore the case of misrepresentation, i.e., unintentional mishandling from HH- or LH-type e-vendors). LS-type e-vendors intend to deceive online customers in order to reap higher illegal profits. However, LS-type e-vendors might not cheat on every trade if certain mechanisms are in place to restrain them from cheating.

We make several assumptions before presenting the decision-making model:

1. Shoppers are rational and risk neutral. They set their goals to maximize the expected trading surplus/utility. We further assume that utility is linear.

2. The identities of HH-type e-vendors are common knowledge among online shoppers. However, among low reputation e-vendors, shoppers cannot differentiate between LH-type and LS-type. Only L-type e-vendor knows its true type.

3. Due to the differences in reputation, both LH- and LS-type e-vendors offer lower prices than HH-type e-vendors. This price advantage serves as an incentive for online shoppers to do business with the low reputation e-vendors.

4. Both LH- and LS-type e-vendors offer the same price. Although some LS-type e-vendors might use significantly lower prices to attract shoppers, we ignore that case in this article.

5. Due to various factors such as price advantage, convenience, and information availability, shopping at a physical store is assumed to be less desirable in this model.

Therefore, we ignore the option of shopping at a local brick-and-mortar store. Readers can assume that the utility of shopping at a local retail store is lower than the expected utility a consumer can achieve online.

6. Shoppers can purchase a product from either a high reputation or a low reputation e-vendor. That is, product availability is not an issue and cannot be used as a competitive advantage.

Part of the decision-making process for shoppers is evaluating the expected payoff between taking the price advantage and bearing potentially higher risk (i.e., shopping from L-type e-vendors) and taking the reputation advantage and paying a higher price (i.e., shopping from HH-type e-vendors).

We use HH-type e-vendors as a benchmark. The price an HH-type e-vendor offers is denoted as P_H, and the price an L-type e-vendor offers is denoted as P_L. We assume $P_H > P_L$, although in special cases, HH-type e-vendors might offer cheaper prices than L-type e-vendors. The reservation value of a shopper for the underlying merchandise is denoted as V. The risks associated with HH- and LH-type e-vendors are normalized as zero due to their honesty. However, there are risks associated with trading with LS-type e-vendors. The decision tree of a shopper is shown in Figure 1.

Meanwhile, we assume in e-markets among the low reputation e-vendors, α portion of them are of the honest type (LH), whereas $1-\alpha$ portion of them are of the strategic type (LS). The parameter α is within the range of [0, 1], and its value is determined by nature. In addition, we assume that shoppers, although not knowing the true type of each individual L-type e-vendor, have a perception of the approximate value of α. That perception can be formed from watching news, reading general reports about Internet safety, sharing thoughts in different forums, and similar methods.

Figure 1. The decision tree for an online shopper (before seal is introduced)

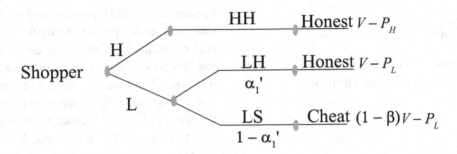

Decision Criteria

Scenario I: Before a Seal Is Introduced to E-Markets

First, we discuss the scenario in which no seal exists in e-markets. The expected utility for a shopper under the benchmark case (i.e., trading with a high-reputation e-vendor) is the difference between the shopper's valuation of the underlying product or service and the price a shopper pays. It is represented as follows: $EU(HH) = V - P_H$.

When trading with an L-type e-vendor, a shopper cannot differentiate between LH-type and LS-type. If a shopper meets an LH-type e-vendor, the expected utility for the shopper is represented as follows: $EU(HH) = V - P_L$, as the shopper gets reservation value of the merchandise and pays the low price of P_L.

However, if a shopper encounters an LS-type e-vendor, he or she might be deceived and receive only partial reservation value, $(1 - \beta)V$, where $\beta \in [0, 1]$. We call β the cheating portion. Thus, the expected utility for the shopper is represented as follows: $EU(LS) = (1 - \beta)V - P_L$. The worst case is that the shopper receives nothing from the e-vendor (i.e., when β equals one) and realizes an expected utility of $-P_L$.

Meanwhile, in e-markets, though the real portion α cannot be known to shoppers, they can have an expectation of α. In this article, we denote the shoppers' perception of the value α as α', which can be viewed as the shoppers' perceived risk factor (Cunningham, 1967), and we know that shoppers make decisions based on their perception of risk.

We first explore the conditions under which a shopper is willing to purchase from a low reputation e-vendor rather than from a high reputation e-vendor. As an L-type e-vendor can only lower its price to compete with HH-type e-vendors, we focus on finding the threshold for that price.

Proposition 1: *When*

$$\alpha' > 1 - \frac{P_H - P_L}{\beta V},$$

shoppers will purchase from an L-type e-vendor rather than from an HH-type e-vendor.

Proof: *We compare the expected payoff of trading with L-type e-vendors, EU(L), and the expected payoff of the benchmark case, EU(HH),*

$$EU(L) - EU(HH) =$$
$$\alpha'(V - P_L) + (1 - \alpha')[(1 - \beta)V - P_L] - (V - P_H) = (P_H - P_L) - (1 - \alpha')\beta V$$

257

When the above condition is greater than zero, we have the following condition:

$$(1-\alpha') < \frac{(P_H - P_L)}{\beta V}.$$

Several observations are found in this proposition. First, the relative price advantage

$$\frac{(P_H - P_L)}{V}$$

is the key factor that draws shoppers to L-type e-vendors. If an L-type e-vendor can offer a price lower than $P_H - (1 - \alpha')\beta V$, it will win shoppers from the HH-type e-vendors. Second, the higher the proportion of honest e-vendors α' among low reputation e-vendors, the more comfortable a shopper feels trading with an L-type e-vendor; thus, the higher the threshold price P_L can be. Third, the lower the expected cheating portion β is, the more likely a shopper will engage in a trade with an L-type e-vendor.

Scenario II: When a Seal is Introduced to E-Markets

Before the introduction of Web assurance seals in e-markets, less-established e-vendors could mainly win customers by reducing their product prices. The price factor was the only thing they could manipulate. Meanwhile, they were subject to the uncontrollable factors of the general perception of e-markets, such as the shoppers' perception of α' and β.

When a third party aims to ensure the trustworthiness of an e-vendor and regulates the e-vendor to abide by fair business practices, the decision-making process for online shoppers changes. Studies have shown that when shoppers are shopping online, they tend to pay attention to the various assurance seals the vendor presents on the Web site. In this study, we focus on this type of shopper, who voluntarily seeks assurance on the e-vendor's Web site and responds to that assurance if it is presented.

E-vendors who earn the right to display a well-trusted seal voluntarily agree to (1) abide by certain rules and (2) put themselves under the scrutiny of an independent third party. Therefore, such e-vendors are signaling to online shoppers that they are serious and honest merchants. As the true type of an e-vendor (honest or strategic) is unknown to shoppers, signaling can be a powerful tool for an LH-type e-vendor to convey its true type to shoppers. Previous research has proven this to be true (Kimery & McCord, 2006; Odom et al., 2002).

In this model, we assume that HH-type e-vendors are not interested in any seal. This assumption is reasonable. HH-type e-vendors have a high reputation and are believed by consumers to be trustworthy. When HH-type e-vendors do want to address consumers' concerns over an online transaction, they can post their policy on their Web sites (i.e., provide self-claimed assurance) rather than resort to a third party. For example, Walmart. com has assurance on information privacy and transaction security. Wal-Mart guarantees that it does not sell customers' personal information to any third parties under any circumstances. It also assures customers that it uses secure sockets layer (SSL) technology to encrypt and encode sensitive information before information is sent over the Internet (www.walmart.com). Wal-Mart already has a high enough reputation that its guarantees/claims are well trusted by online shoppers. Noteberg et al. (2003) empirically confirm that for unknown e-vendors, consumers' purchase intention increases significantly when there is third-party assurance (as opposed to self-claimed assurance), whereas for known e-vendors, whether the assurance is self-claimed or from a third party makes no significant difference to consumers.

For low reputation e-vendors, as they are less established and generally unknown to online shoppers, Web seals can provide an opportunity to establish their online reputations. Both LH- and LS-type e-vendors may consider adopting a seal. LH-type e-vendors may consider employing a seal to indicate its true type. However, some LS-type e-vendors may adopt a seal for other reasons. Motivations for seal adoption are complicated for LS-type e-vendors. Some are aiming to improve their reputation and obtain normal profits for a while; some are trying to establish reputations for future cheating actions; and others might intend to effectively deceive the shoppers and gain illegal profits for the short run. Although the various motivations of seal adoption from LS-type e-vendors are beyond the scope of the article, we can model the general actions derived from these motivations in a decision tree. The decision tree for a shopper is shown in Figure 2.

We assume that when an LS-type e-vendor employs no seal (i.e., it is not under the scrutiny of a third party), it will cheat. Then a shopper trading with this LS-type e-vendor might receive only partial reservation value, $1 - \beta V$, and pay the price P_L. Thus, the shopper's expected utility is $(1 - \beta)V - P_L$, the same as that in Scenario I. When LS-type e-vendors employ a seal, we assume among them θ portion will act honestly, and the other $1 - \theta$ portion will cheat, where θ is within the range of $[0, 1]$. There are two main

reasons for LS-type e-vendors to act honestly when they adopt a seal. One is that the scrutiny of the seal issuer induces them to act honestly, and the other is that they want to use the seal as a trust-promoting tool to earn solid reputations in e-markets. When an LS-type e-vendor acts honestly, a shopper's payoff is $V - P_L$; otherwise, the payoff is $(1 - \beta)V - P_L$.

We assume that in e-markets, the δ portion of the low reputation e-vendors employs a seal, while the other $1 - \delta$ portion does not. Consumers can observe whether an e-vendor adopts a seal or not when visiting its Web site, although consumers do not know whether the specific e-vendor they are trading with is honest or strategic. An LS-type e-vendor might cheat even with a seal on its Web site, while an LH-type e-vendor will not cheat even without a seal on its Web site.

A shopper must make several decisions: (1) whether he or she should trade with a low reputation e-vendor and (2) when he or she trades with a low reputation vendor, whether he or she should trade with one that adopts a seal or one that does not.

Figure 2. Decision tree for an online shopper (with a seal case)

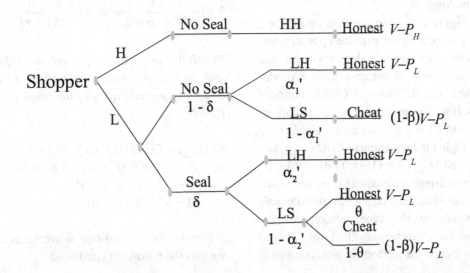

Because seal adoption can be observed by online shoppers before they make their purchase decisions, we analyze the expected utility of online shoppers under two distinct cases: trading with an L-type e-vendor with a seal on its Web site and trading with one that does not display a seal.

The expected utility of trading with an L-type e-vendor with a seal is denoted as $EU(L_{Seal})$ and with an L-type e-vendor without a seal as $EU(L_{NoSeal})$. The payoffs are shown below:

$$EU(L_{NoSeal}) = \alpha_1'(V - P_L) + (1 - \alpha_1')[(1-\beta)V - P_L]$$

$$EU(L_{Seal}) = \alpha_2'(V - P_L) + (1 - \alpha_2')\{\theta(V - P_L) + (1 - \theta)[(1-\beta)V - P_L]\}$$

In the following sections of the article, we propose to use the same parameter α' for both α_1' and α_2'. Readers might argue that α_1' and α_2' are different because they belong to two distinct groups: seal-adopting group and no-seal group. However, we have little information to project whether the percentage of the moral trader α_1' should be higher or lower in the seal-adopting group than in the no-seal group. Therefore, we use the same parameter to derive possible intuitions for the model. Meanwhile, we encourage readers to apply their own perception of α_1' and α_2' to evaluate their utility and to guide their decision making.

From Figure 2, we can see that, on average, shoppers can gain higher expected payoff when trading with an L-type e-vendor with a seal than one without a seal. When an L-type e-vendor adopts a seal, the likelihood of it acting honestly increases. If we compare the expected payoffs of $EU(L_{Seal})$ and $EU(L_{NoSeal})$, we find that $EU(L_{Seal})$ is always higher than or equal to $EU(L_{NoSeal})$ (i.e., $EU(L_{Seal}) - EU(L_{NoSeal}) = (1 - \alpha')\beta\theta V \geq 0$).

The above expression is equal to zero only when α' equals 1, or when θ or β equals 0. When α' equals one, or β equals zero, all L-type e-vendors are of the honest type. E-markets are only filled with LH-type e-vendors; thus, a seal's effect for promoting trust

diminishes. When θ equals 0, LS-type e-vendors will always cheat, whether they employ a seal or not. In such cases, a seal has absolutely no power to confine (i.e., positively impact) a strategic e-vendor's cheating behavior. Thus, the trustworthiness of a seal is significantly reduced. Consequently, no rational shopper would pay attention to a Web seal.

Those are the two extreme cases. In reality, quite neither case is quite possible. In all other cases, a seal has effect and the expected payoff of trading with an e-vendor adopting a seal is always higher than the expected payoff of trading with an e-vendor without a seal. This is useful information for LH-type e-vendors who are attempting to adopt a seal. Empirical analyses also confirm this theoretical result (e.g., Kovar et al., 2000; Noteberg et al., 2003).

Our key questions then are with the help of a trusted third party, whether a low reputation e-vendor can win business over HH-type e-vendor if it offers a lower price and employs a Web seal, and whether this price threshold can be somewhat higher than that in Scenario I.

Proposition 2: *When the following condition holds, shoppers will purchase from a low reputation e-vendor with a seal rather than from a high reputation e-vendor.*

$$\theta > 1 - \frac{P_H - P_L}{\beta V(1-\alpha')} \quad \text{or} \quad \alpha' > 1 - \frac{P_H - P_L}{\beta V(1-\theta)}.$$

Proof: *We compare the expected payoff of trading with an L-type e-vendor with a seal, $EU(L_{Seal})$, and the expected payoff of the benchmark case $EU(HH)$.*

$$EU(L_{Seal}) - EU(HH) = \alpha'(V - P_L) + (1 - \alpha')\{\theta(V - P_L) + (1 - \theta)[(1 - \beta)V - P_L]\} - (V - P_H) = (P_H - P_L) - (1 - \alpha')(1-\beta)(1 - \theta)V$$

When the above condition is greater than zero, we find the following condition:

$$(1 - \alpha') \beta (1 - \theta) < \frac{(P_H - P_L)}{V}.$$

All the parameters in the equation contribute to the balance of this condition and jointly impact a shopper's decision. Several observations are found. First, when all other parameters are fixed, as the relative price advantage between the high and low reputation type

$$\frac{(P_H - P_L)}{V}$$

is enlarged, the above condition will be easily satisfied, and shoppers will be drawn to the low reputation e-vendor with a seal and enjoy the price advantage. Second, compared to the price threshold in Proposition 1, we find that the required price for an L-type e-vendor to win shoppers over in Scenario II is indeed higher than that in Scenario I. This demonstrates that with the help of Web seals, an L-type e-vendors can compete more efficiently with HH-type e-vendors, and earn a higher profit margin. Finally, as any of the parameters α', $(1 - \beta)$, and θ increase, shoppers are more likely to trade with a low reputation e-vendor. When α' increases, it indicates that in e-markets more low reputation e-vendors are of the honest type. Therefore, shoppers' perceived risks for e-markets are reduced, and they are more willing to trade with an L-type e-vendor with a seal. Similarly, θ indicates the percentage of the strategic type e-vendors that trade honestly when a seal is adopted. Therefore, when θ increases, a shopper's perceived risk decreases, and his or her willingness to purchase from an L-type e-vendor increases. In the same fashion, β reflects potential loss per trade; when the potential loss is reduced, a shopper's gain per trade increases, and his or her interest in trading with an L-type e-vendor increases.

We further explore the question of whether a seal can create a price premium for an e-vendor.

Proposition 3: *A seal can create a price premium for an L-type e-vendor with a seal, and the price premium can be up to* $(1 - \alpha')\beta\theta V$.

Proof: *We set the expected payoffs of* $EU(L_{Seal})$ *and* $EU(L_{NoSeal})$ *to be equal and found how much more a vendor with a seal can charge online shoppers without losing them to lower price competitors without a seal. We denoted the price premium as K.*

$$EU(L_{Seal}) - EU(L_{NoSeal}) = 0$$
$$\alpha'(V - P_L - K) + (1 - \alpha')\{\theta(V - P_L - K) + (1 - \theta)[(1 - \beta) V - P_L - K]\} = \alpha'(V - P_L) + (1 - \alpha')[(1 - \beta) V - P_L]$$

Thus, $K = (1 - \alpha') \beta\theta V$ *holds.*

Therefore, as long as the price premium is between the range of $[0, (1 - \alpha') \beta\theta V]$, shoppers are more likely to purchase from an e-vendor with a seal than one without a seal. The seal premium can help the seal adopter offset some of the cost associated with the seal and gain competitive advantage. The issues of how a vendor decides the level of premium are reserved for future research. In the following discussion, we apply the same low price rule to L-type e-vendors both with and without a seal.

Price Effect, Seal Effect, and Reputation Effect

To demonstrate the dynamics of these propositions and shoppers' decision-making criteria, we draw Figures 3, 4, and 5 to show the range of various parameters and the criteria for a shopper's decision making.

In Figure 3, Range I indicates that when a shopper perceives that the proportion of honest e-vendors (α') among the low reputation types is relatively low, which is within the range of

$$[0, 1 - \frac{(P_H - P_L)}{\beta V (1 - \theta)}],$$

the shopper will surely (100% likelihood) purchase from a high reputation e-vendor even given that the low reputation e-vendor provides a price advantage and may display a seal on its Web site. We call Range I the reputation effect range. When the e-markets are perceived to be risky, and the price advantages are not significant enough, the reputation effect prevails.

However, a shopper's decision starts to change when the perceived honesty level among low reputation e-vendors is enhanced. Specifically, this is the range where the perceived α' is within the range of

$$[1-\frac{(P_H-P_L)}{\beta V(1-\theta)}, 1-\frac{(P_H-P_L)}{\beta V}].$$

Now, shoppers are drawn to the low reputation e-vendors that display a seal on their Web site (Range II) and will purchase from them rather than from an HH-type e-vendor. We call

Range II the seal effect range. A seal signals to the shoppers that the e-vendor might be honest; as a seal does induce an extra θ portion of LS-type e-vendor to trade honestly, the perceived risk decreases in doing business with such a seal-bearing vendor. Online shoppers therefore are attracted to purchase from a low reputation vendor with a seal.

Range III implies that when the expected percentage of LH-type e-vendors is higher than

$$1-\frac{(P_H-P_L)}{\beta V},$$

the shoppers would even prefer to purchase from low reputation e-vendors that adopt no seal than from the HH-type e-vendors. Range III combines the effects of price advantage and a safer online environment, which draw shoppers to L-type e-vendors. We call this range the combined effect range.

Figure 3. Shopper's decision making w.r.t α'

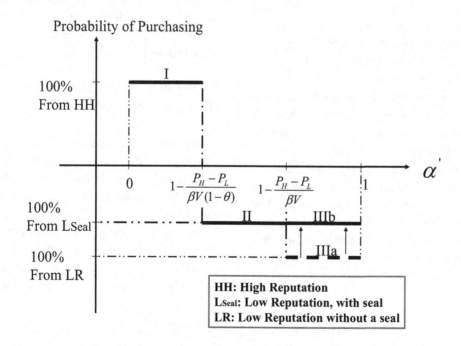

Figure 4. Shoppers' decision making w.r.t ε'

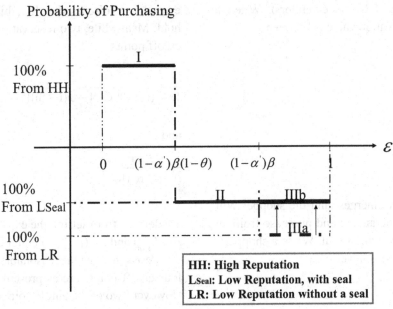

However, prior discussion indicates that, on average, shoppers are better off purchasing from an L-type e-vendor with a seal than from an L-type e-vendor without a seal. Therefore, if a shopper can choose between L-type e-vendors with or without a seal, they will definitely choose to trade with one that adopts a seal. Then the range IIIa no longer exists; only Range IIIb sustains (i.e., only L-type e-vendors that adopt a seal can establish a trade).

Analysis w.r.t. ε

Figure 4 presents the relationship among the parameters from another perspective. Most of the intuitions are the same as those demonstrated in Figure 3. However, a clearer view of how the relative price advantage affects shoppers' purchasing decisions is shown in Figure 4. We define the relative price advantage as ε, where

$$\varepsilon = \frac{(P_H - P_L)}{V}.$$

When ε is relatively low, a shopper will purchase from HH-type e-vendors. As the relative price advantage is enhanced, the low reputation e-vendors with a seal start to gain customers. Similar to the discussion above, the sustainable equilibrium in Range III is IIIb.

Analysis w.r.t. V

Similarly, we draw the above relationships in terms of consumer's reservation value in Figure 5. The higher the reservation value, the lower the relative price advantage is. Therefore, when a shopper has a reservation value higher than

$$\frac{(P_H - P_L)}{(1-\alpha')\,\beta(1-\theta)},$$

he or she would like to pay the higher price and avoid any potential risk (i.e., a shopper would purchase from HH-type e-vendors). When a shopper's reservation value is between

$$\frac{(P_H - P_L)}{(1 - \alpha') \beta (1 - \theta)}$$

and

$$\frac{(P_H - P_L)}{(1 - \alpha') \beta},$$

the seal's effect emerges, and the shopper will take the price advantage and purchase from an L-type e-vendor with a seal. When a shopper's reservation value is lower than

$$\frac{(P_H - P_L)}{(1 - \alpha') \beta},$$

he or she would rather purchase from an L-type e-vendor without any seal than from an HH-type e-vendor. As discussed earlier, this range will not hold. Meanwhile, two reservation values of the cutoff points,

$$\frac{P_L}{\{\alpha' + (1 - \alpha')[\theta + (1 - \theta)(1 - \beta)]\}}$$

and

$$\frac{P_L}{[1 - (1 - \alpha') \beta]},$$

are derived from setting the expected utilities of $EU(L_{Seal})$ and $EU(L_{No\ Seal})$ equal to zero.

We assume that the reasonable orders of these four cutoff points are as presented in Figure 5. However, two of the cutoff points,

Figure 5. Shoppers' decision making w.r.t V

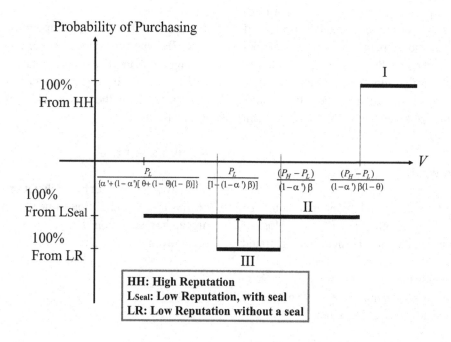

$$\frac{P_L}{[1-(1-\alpha')\,\beta]}$$

and

$$\frac{(P_H - P_L)}{(1-\alpha')\,\beta},$$

might switch places. If that is the case, Range III will be eliminated.

SOCIAL WELFARE ANALYSIS

From the afore-mentioned discussion, we see that the use of Web seals in e-markets encourages online shoppers to trade with lower priced, less-established e-vendors, and the reputation, price, and seal effects play important roles under different market conditions. In this section, we analyze the contribution of the third-party Web seals to social welfare. As Web seals help motivate some shoppers to purchase from less-established e-vendors, a lower settlement price is achieved for these shoppers, and social welfare might be enhanced as a result. We discuss three cases to clearly demonstrate how social welfare is enhanced by the participation of low reputation e-vendors and through the use of Web seals in e-markets.

Case I: Only HH-Type E-Vendors in E-Markets

When only well-established e-vendors are in e-markets, consumers can only purchase from them, with the price P_H. We assume a downward-sloping linear demand to simplify the chart formation. HH-type e-vendors will charge P_H and sell q_H for the underlying product, with a marginal cost of C. Online shoppers who have reservation value higher than P_H will purchase the product at that price.

Therefore, consumer surplus is the triangle area above the price line P_H and under the demand curve, which includes the areas from 1 to 6. The vendor's profit is the shaded area A in Figure 6.

Case II: Less-Established E-Vendors Enter E-Markets (No Seal is Introduced)

When small, less-established e-vendors enter e-markets, consumers can either purchase from HH-type e-venders or from L-type e-vendors. As an L-type e-vendor charges a lower price, some shoppers might take the price advantage and enjoy more consumer surplus. According to a shopper's decision-making criteria, shoppers who have reservation values higher than

$$\frac{(P_H - P_L)}{(1-\alpha')\,\beta}$$

will still purchase from HH-type e-vendors, paying the price of P_H; whereas others with reservation values from

$$\frac{P_L}{[1-(1-\alpha')\,\beta]}$$

up to

$$\frac{(P_H - P_L)}{(1-\alpha')\,\beta}$$

will purchase from low reputation e-vendors— these shoppers will take the price advantage of paying P_L but bear the potential risk.

If we momentarily set aside the potential risk and assume that all trades are carried out honestly, the social welfare chart changes to Figure 7.

Compared with Figure 6, the consumer surplus increases, the low reputation e-vendor's profit increases, and the high reputation e-vendor's profit declines. Meanwhile, more shoppers make the purchases and enjoy the products. The sales rise from

Figure 6. Social welfare with only HH-type e-vendors in e-markets

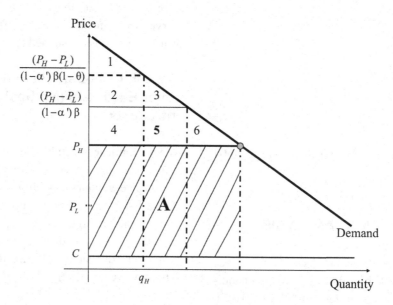

the original q_H to q_L. Social welfare increases. The total increased social welfare is shown in areas 9, 12, 16, and the bubble area under 16. However, due to the potential risks associated with trading with low reputation e-vendors, some of the trades might not be completed successfully. From a social planner's point of view, the money moved from consumers' pockets into those of the e-vendors' will not affect social welfare. However, one part of the social welfare still can be affected, which is the loss of consumer surplus. Thus, the increases in social welfare in Figure 7 should be partially discounted.

In addition, whether the increase in social welfare is positive or negative depends on the market conditions (in other words, on the parameters in e-markets). With a demand like what we project and a relatively small portion of strategic e-vendors in e-markets, social welfare is more likely enhanced by the intensification of competition due to the participation of small, less-established e-vendors. Meanwhile, even though we use the same price for the HH-type e-vendors between Case I and Case II, due to the competition brought in by low reputation

e-vendors, the price charged by HH-type e-vendors is more likely to be lowered in Case II than in Case I, yielding more consumer surplus to the shoppers.

Case III: Seal is Used by Less Established E-Vendors in E-Markets

When seals are introduced to e-markets, shoppers with reservation values higher than

$$(\frac{(P_H - P_L)}{(1 - \alpha')\beta(1 - \theta)})$$

will still purchase from an HH-type vendor and pay the price of P_H. Shoppers with lower reservation values will purchase from a low reputation e-vendor with a seal and pay the price of P_L. According to the assumed orders of the four cutoff points shown in Figure 5, we can draw the new social welfare in Figure 8.

Figure 8 indicates that only those shoppers who have high reservation values will purchase from HH-type e-vendors, and the quantity demanded

Figure 7. Social welfare with L-type e-vendors in e-markets (before seal is introduced)

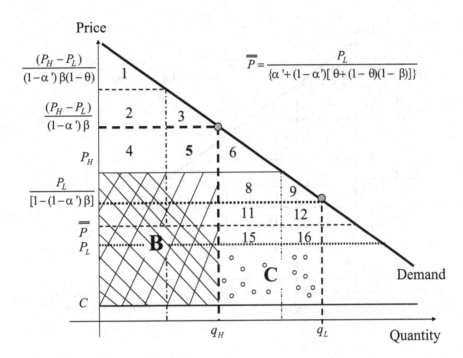

is q_H. For those shoppers, the consumer surpluses are the areas 1, 2, and 4. The e-vendor's profit is the area D. Other shoppers purchase from the low reputation e-vendors with a seal, pay P_L, and the consumer surpluses are the areas 3 and 5 through 17. The e-vendor's profit is the bubble area E.

Comparing Figures 8 and 7, consumer surplus is definitely enhanced; the vendor profit is reallocated, shifting from HH-type e-vendors to L-type e-vendors. The social welfare has been increased due to the introduction of seals.

Meanwhile, uncertainty about low reputation e-vendors still exists. The increased social welfare is also subject to some degree of discount. However, as all of the trades are conducted with either HH-type e-vendors or L-type e-vendors that adopt a seal, the potential risks are relatively low. Therefore, we believe that the social welfare is enhanced significantly by the services provided by third-party Web seals.

CONCLUSION AND FUTURE RESEARCH

Due to the nature of e-markets, it is difficult for consumers to assess the trustworthiness of an e-vendor. The issue is more prominent when an e-vendor is small and less-established. The display of a third-party-assured Web seal has been adopted by small e-vendors as a trust-building practice. Though seals of approval have long existed offline, the use of such seals on the Web is a recent phenomenon. The literature needs a theoretical analysis to examine how online trading is impacted when seals of approval are used in e-markets.

In this article, we establish a decision-making model for online shoppers which examines when they would choose to purchase from a small, less-established e-vendor rather than from a well-established one. This model indicates that when

Figure 8. Social welfare when seal is employed by L-type e-Vendors

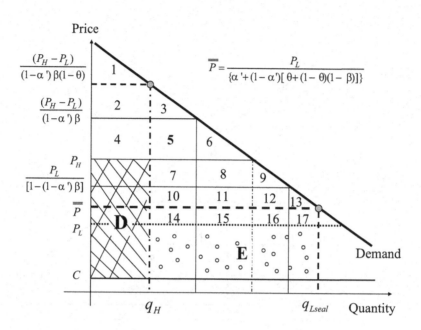

the same product can be purchased from either a less-established e-vendor or a well-established e-vendor, relative price advantage is a key factor in attracting consumers to the less-established e-vendors. Small e-vendors in e-markets compete with big names through price. When third-party Web seals are introduced to e-markets, the competition structure starts to change. Web seals, due to their scrutiny functions and the reputation of the seal issuers, can signal online shoppers of the trustworthiness of the e-vendor, thus enhancing both the online shoppers' trust of the e-vendor and the likelihood of purchasing from it. Consequently, a small e-vendor with a seal enjoys a competitive advantage over other small e-vendors that have no seal. In addition, small e-vendors with seals are able to compete more efficiently with well-established e-vendors. Besides price advantage, the effect of assurance seals in preventing e-vendors from behaving strategically also plays an important role.

Based on the analytical results, this research presents how and when the price effect, the seal effect, and the reputation effect play a major role in an online shopper's decision making. When the online environment is perceived to be risky, reputation effect plays a major role, and shoppers purchase from well-established e-vendors only. As the perceived proportion of honest e-vendors among less-established ones increases and the use of Web seals converts a great number of strategic e-vendors into honest businesses, the seal effect starts to play a major role. Small e-vendors with seals start to win shoppers from the well-established e-vendors. In fact, when the relative price advantage is high and when online trading is perceived to be less risky, shoppers would rather purchase from a less-established e-vendor with no seal than from a well-established e-vendor.

Throughout the analysis, price effect is a key factor that attracts consumers to small e-vendors. From a social planner's point of view, participation of small e-vendors and the use of Web seals directly or indirectly fosters competition in e-markets, which, in turn, enhances social welfare. As a result, shoppers enjoy lower prices, low reputation e-vendors obtain a better chance to compete in e-markets, and the overall social welfare is enhanced as e-markets become more competitive and secure.

However, the current research has its limitations as well. We applied a representative model in the shopper's decision-making process. We assumed all shoppers are the same and we intentionally ignored the possible distribution of the reservation values for the underlying merchandise of all shoppers. In reality, shoppers might possess differentiated reservation values. Thus, their purchase decisions might not be exactly the same as presented in Figures 3 through 5. Meanwhile, shoppers reflect a different risk aversion, which will induce differentiated decision making when facing the same market situation. In addition, the model is presented in an abstract form. If we gather empirical data to support the model setting, it will benefit online shoppers, small e-vendors, and social planners in understanding the model.

Future research can be conducted to enrich the current model and research stream. Three streams are identified. First, we can allow consumers to have different risk perceptions toward online shopping. Based on their risk tolerance, consumers can be risk-seeking, risk-neutral, or risk-averse. A consumer's risk perception could affect his or her purchasing decision, and this factor could be incorporated into the decision-making model. Meanwhile, the price charged for a specific product by a less-established e-vendor with a seal or one with no seal can be projected as being different. A seal may earn a premium and an e-vendor with a seal might charge a higher price than one without a seal. Future research can study how the price premium changes the decision-making criteria of online shoppers and the competition structure of the e-markets. Finally, e-vendors themselves are active decision makers as well. Their decision with

regard to seal adoption is based on their analyses of the benefits provided vs. the expenses incurred by the seal, as well as the overall condition of the e-markets. Exploration of a decision-making model from an e-vendor's perspective could also be a future research direction.

For practitioners and academic researchers to gain a fuller understanding of the role of Web seals in online trading, more research needs to be done in this area. As discussed, the extent to which Web seals impact online shopper's decision making is still a debated topic, but past research (Kovar et al., 2000; Odom et al., 2002) agrees that the effectiveness of a Web seal in affecting a consumer's purchasing decision is related to the consumer's knowledge and familiarity with the seal and the seal issuer. Thus, an important task for seal-issuing organizations and small e-vendors that adopt those seals is to educate online shoppers about the benefits of the seals. In the meantime, selecting a well-known Web seal can also help small e-vendors win more consumers. As the use of Web seals gains in popularity, better understanding of how e-vendors can take full advantage of these benefits is compelling enough to warrant more research.

REFERENCES

Bhatnagar, A., Misra, S., & Rao, H. R. (2000). On risk, convenience, and Internet shopping behavior. Communications of the ACM, 43(11), 98-105.

Bhimani, A. (1996). Securing the commercial Internet. *Communications of the ACM, 39(6),* 29-31.

Cook, D. P., & Luo, W. (2003). The role of third-party seals in building trust online. *E-Service Journal, 2(3),* 71-84.

Cunningham, S. M. (1967). The major dimensions of perceived risk. In *Risk taking and information handling in consumer behavior* (pp. 82-108). Boston: Harvard University Press.

Ford, W., & Baum, M. S. (1997). *Secure electronic commerce*. Upper Saddle River, NJ: Prentice Hall.

Gefen, D. (2002). Customer loyalty in e-commerce. *Journal of the Association for Information Systems, 3*(1), 27-51.

Gefen, D., Karahanna, E., & Straub, D. W. (2003). Trust and TAM in online shopping: An integrated model. *MIS Quarterly, 27*(1), 51-90.

Griffin, K., Ladd, P., & Whitehead, R. (1997). Internet commerce: Security is still a concern. *The Review of Accounting Information Systems, 2*(1), 67-71.

Hu, X., Lin, Z., & Zhang, H. (2003). Trust promoting seals in electronic markets: An exploratory study of their effectiveness for online sales promotion. *Journal of Promotion Management, 9*(1/2), 163-180.

Internet Crime Complaint Center. (2007). *The Internet crime complaint center hits 1 million!* Retrieved February 13, 2008, from http://www.ic3.gov/media/2007/070613.htm

Internet Fraud Watch. (2005). *Internet fraud statistics report*. Retrieved September 24, 2007, from http://www.fraud.org/internet/intstat.htm

Internet Fraud Watch. (2007). *Internet fraud tips*. Retrieved February 13, 2008, from http://www.fraud.org/tips/internet/general.htm

Jarvenpaa, S., Tractinsky, L. N., & Vitale, M. (2000). Consumer trust in an Internet store. *Information Technology and Management, 1*(1/2), 45-71.

Kau, A. K., Tang, Y. E., & Ghose, S. (2003). Typology of online shoppers. *The Journal of Consumer Marketing, 20*(2/3), 139-156.

Kimery, K. M., & McCord, M. (2006). Signals of trustworthiness in e-commerce: Consumer understanding of third-party assurance seals. *Journal of Electronic Commerce in Organizations, 4*(4), 52-74.

Kovar, S. E., Burke, K. G., & Kovar, B. R. (2000). Consumer responses to the CPA WEBTRUST assurance. *Journal of Information Systems, 14*(1), 17-35.

Lasica, J. D. (1999). *The confidence game*. Retrieved September 24, 2007, from http://www.jdlasica.com/idrive/TIS/confidence.html

Lee, M. K. O., & Turban, E. (2001). A trust model for consumer Internet shopping. *International Journal of Electronic Commerce, 6*(1), 75-91.

McKnight, D. H., Choudhury, V., & Kacmar, C. (2002). The impact of initial consumer trust on intentions to transact with a Web site: A trust building model. *Journal of Strategic Information Systems, 11*, 297-323.

Metzger, M. J. (2006). Effects of site, vendor, and consumer characteristics on Web site trust and disclosure. *Communication Research, 33*(3), 155-179.

Miyazaki, A. D., & Fernandez, A. (2001). Consumer perceptions of privacy and security risks for online shopping. *The Journal of Consumer Affairs, 35*(1), 27-44.

Nikitkov, A. (2006). Information assurance seals: How they impact consumer purchasing behavior. *Journal of Information System. 20*(1), 1-17.

Noteberg, A., Christiaanse, E., & Wallage, P. (2003). Consumer Trust in Electronic Channels. *E- Service Journal, 2*(2), 46-67.

Odom, M. D., Kumar, A., & Saunders, L. (2002). Web assurance seals: How and why they influence consumers' decisions. *Journal of Information Systems, 16*(2), 231-250.

Parkinson, T. L. (2002). The role of seals and certifications of approval in consumer decision-making. *Journal of Consumer Affairs, 9,* 1-14.

Peterson, R. A., Balasubramanian, S., & Bronnenberg, B. J. (1997). Exploring the implications of the Internet for consumer marketing. *Journal of the Academy of Marketing Science, 25*(4), 329-346.

Sanderson, B. (2000). Cyberspace retailing a threat to traditionalists. *Retail World, 53*(14), 6-7.

Stewart, K. J. (2003). Trust transfer on the World Wide Web. *Organization Science, 14*(1), 5-17.

Urban, G. L., Sultan, F., & Qualls W. J. (2000). Placing trust at the center of your Internet strategy. *Sloan Management Review, 42*(1), 39-48.

U.S. Census Bureau. (2007). *Quarterly retail e-commerce sales.* Retrieved February 13, 2008, from http://www.census.gov/mrts/www/ecomm.html

U.S. Department of Justice. (2007). *Internet and telemarketing fraud.* Retrieved February 13, 2008, from http://www.usdoj.gov/criminal/fraud/internet/#howtodeal

Van den Poel, D., & Leunis, J. (1999). Consumer acceptance of the Internet as a channel of distribution. *Journal of Business Research, 45,* 249-256.

Wakefield, R. L., & Whitten D. (2006). Examining user perceptions of third-party organization credibility and trust in an e-retailer. *Journal of Organizational and End User Computing, 18*(2), 1-19.

Wang, S., Beatty, S. E., & Foxx, W. (2004). Signaling the trustworthiness of small online retailers. *Journal of Interactive Marketing, 18*(1), 53-69.

Wolfingarger, M., & Gilly, M. C. (2001). Shopping online for freedom, control, and fun. *California Management Review, 43*(2), 34-55.

Yoon, S. J. (2002). The antecedents and consequences of trust in online-purchase decisions. *Journal of Interactive Marketing, 16*(2), 47-63.

This work was previously published in the International Journal of E-Business Research, edited by I. Lee, Volume 4, Issue 3, pp. 20-39, copyright 2008 by IGI Publishing (an imprint of IGI Global).

Glossary

Agent Search: In agent search, a consumer is able to evaluate more available products side by side, as is the situation in simultaneous search. In the electronic markets simultaneous search is often called agent search, because of the internet tools that makes information comparing available, is called search agents. In online settings, a consumer can use various tools (for example: comparison sites, search agents or comparison agents) to collect information that is available on the internet on a particular product or service.

Balance Theory (http://en.wikipedia. org/wiki/Balance_theory): First proposed by Fritz Heider (http://en.wikipedia.org/wiki/Fritz_ Heider) to explain and describes the relationships between people and objects/other people. Heider proposed that positive and negative feeling/beliefs/ relationships must be in psychological balance.

BargainFinder Experiment: In 1995, a shopbot named BargainFinder was launched by a group of researchers in then Andersen Consulting to test the reaction of consumers and online vendors. It received major media coverage and became one of the first shopbots that came into public attention.

Bargain-Oriented Shoppers: Buyers that search for the best existing offers, attempting to maximise the rapport between quality and price for the product/services they buy.

Bundled Comparison: A feature of comparison-shopping service that allows shoppers to compare price for multiple products as a whole offered by different online vendors

Channel Selection: The strategy online vendors employ to maximum their ROI on customer acquisition. For example, an online vendor could select only the most popular shopbot to list their product or select a few specialized shopbots to list their products.

Choice Overload: A scenario when a consumer is being overwhelmed and hesitating to make decisions when facing with too many choices.

Comparison-Shopping Market: The shopbot-mediated electronic commerce market consisting of online shoppers, online vendors and shopbots in which online shoppers are referred to online vendors by the comparison-shopping services.

Comparison-Shopping Services: The Web-based services that online shoppers use when they try to find product prices and other related information aggregated from multiple vendor sites.

Convenience-Oriented Consumers: Consumers who value convenience value more than price reductions and often prefer to pay a premium for shopping online rather than travelling to brick-and-mortar outlets. These consumers do not wish to negotiate with several sellers when shopping, because of the increased search effort.

Cost Per Click: A revenue model by comparison-shopping service providers that charge the online vendors for each customers it refers to the vendor. For example, online shoppers want to buy an iPod and searched shopping.com. Shopping.com provides a list of online vendors that offer the iPod model requested by the online shopper. The online shopper find one vendor from the list and click through to the vendor site to buy the product. The vendor paid shopping.com for this referral based on the agreed rate regardless whether the purchase is complete or not.

Customer Satisfaction/dissatisfaction (http://en.wikipedia.org/wiki/Customer_satisfaction): Is a measure of how satisfied a customer is with your products and services. Customer satisfaction/dissatisfaction is a predictor of the degree to which customer will remain loyal, repurchase products and services, and tell others (see also netpromoter) (http://www.netpromoter.com)

Data Feeding: A data retrieval technique that allow users to feed information into a shopbot database in a pre-defined format. Data feeding was widely used in popular shopbots.

Data Wrapping: A data retrieval technique that can be either automatically or manually created to identify information contained in a HTML web page and then transform them into a consistent format for further processing. Data wrapping technology was widely used in early shopbots.

E-Commerce: The process of buying and selling goods and/or services using the Internet.

Electronic Customer Relationship Management (eCRM): eCRM (http://en.wikipedia.org/wiki/ECRM) is the use of the information technologies and the Internet to manage relationships with the customer. Examples of e-CRM include frequently asked questions (FAQ's) , chat, e-mail, mobile, sales force management, customer database.

Electronic Markets: Electronic market is the markets in the internet. The word Electronic market means the same as digital markets, internet markets, virtual markets or online markets.

E-Retailing (www.internetretailer.com): A storefront on the Internet (also known as Internet retailing). An e-retailer can be part of a chain of retail stores (e.g., Walmart* has 3500+ stores as well as a website) or the only access a consumer has to your business.

General Shopbots: Shopbots that provide price comparison information for products from multiple and unrelated product categories. For example, shopping.com provides price comparison for electronics, books, computers, furniture, toys, etc.

Hedonic Shopping Motivations: This term reflects the value found in the shopping experience itself independent of task-related activities. Hedonic motivations refer to experiential benefits and sacrifices, such as entertainment and escapism or social interaction. Individuals who focus on hedonic motivations prefer to be stimulated by internal gratifications such as emotions, entertainment and contact with other consumers rather than convenience or price reductions.

Individualised Marketing: A marketing strategy in which the firm adapts its commercial and promotional activities to the specific characteristics of individual customers.

Information Search: Consumers look for information of products with desired qualities and sellers offering these products at competitive prices in an attempt to decide what, when, and from whom to purchase. Consumer's pre-purchase information search is an essential part of consumer decision making process (Bettman 1979; Bettman et al. 1990; Engel et al. 1990; Howard and Sheth 1969; Olhavsky 1985, Schmidt and Spreng 1996).

Iterative Search: An iterative search begins just as a sequential query to the product information. The query results are compared to each other, and then outputs or results are reported or at least noted. The difference in the sequential search is that after finding the outputs, a consumer will make the query again, and the process is then repeated. The possibility to return to price / product information that was previously searched, but not chosen, can be called iterative search. Iterative search allows back-and-forth-movement as consumers compare product and service offerings.

Mass Marketing: A marketing strategy in which the firm attempts to attract one or more large customer segments with a standardised offer or products/services.

M-Commerce Customer Perception of Convenience: The ease of access to and use of the services offered by m-commerce service providers.

M-Commerce Service Features: Specific services provided by mobile commerce vendors. Examples include order placement, payment, security and privacy measures, inquiry, etc.

M-Commerce: Using mobile communication devices and the Internet to complete business transactions

Megabrand: A brand of products and or services that is widely known, recognised and bought by consumers, generating a large and constant amount of revenues.

Mobile Comparison: A feature of comparison-shopping service that allows a shopper to interact with shopbot via mobile devices

Multi Attribute Utility Theory: A decision-making theory that assume human beings can subjectively assign a weight to each attribute and calculate the utility of each choice by multiplying the weight and value of each attribute then adding them together. As a result, each alternative has a corresponding utility. Comparison and a decision can be made by choosing the alternative that has the highest utility.

Multichannel: Multichannel retailing/marketing is the use of different marketing channels to reach a customer. A multichannel retailer (http://www.mckinsey.com/practices/retail/knowledge/knowledge_multichannel.asp) might have stores, catalogs, an Internet site, kiosks, direct mail, e-mail access for the customer.

Online Marketing Channel: The way an online vendor reaching the customer. There are several ways an online vendor can reach the potential customer. They could launch a website and established a brand name like Amazon.com so customers could go to them directly. They could also list their product in popular auction sites like eBay.com or list them in comparison-shopping sites like shopping.com.

Online Shopping: Process consumers go through to purchase products or services over the Internet.

Price-Oriented Shoppers: Consumers who see price as an important cost component and compare prices between different alternatives before purchasing. Price is the most important choice criteria used by these consumers in deciding where to shop online. Price-oriented consumers constantly compare offers with those of competitors, changing the supplier when there is the least reduction in price for the products and services they need.

Search Agent: We define, the internet tools that make information *comparing* available, for consumers purchase decision, search agents. Search agents are made to help consumers to make purchase decision most efficiently. Search agents include information of product prices and product qualities in the same internet site. In search agent site, information is in comparable form.

Search Behavior: In recent years, there have been many studies into consumer search behavior in a digital environment (Chiang 2006, Jansen 2006, Johnson et al. 2004, Lauraeus-Niinivaara et al. 2007, 2008, Smith and Spreng 1996, Spink et al. 2005, Öörni 2002, 2003). When we are writing about search behavior, we mean the situation when Consumers are seeking, or looking for, information of products for decision making purposes. There are nearly 60 factors that have been found to influence the consumer pre-purchase information search behaviour (Schmidt and Spreng 1996; Srinivasan and Ratchford 1991).

Search Engine: Web application that gathers information from the web using different strategies (crawlers or spiders) and then performs the basic retrieval task, accepting a query, comparing a query with the records in a database, and producing a retrieval set as output.

Search Engine: When we are writing about the tools in the internet, search engine is different than search agent. We define the internet tools that make information available for different purposes, search engines.

Search Engine Marketing: Form of Internet marketing that seeks to promote websites by increasing their visibility in search engine result pages

Search Patterns: Search pattern means the shape of the consumer search process. In other words, search pattern is the search strategy consumer employed, when seeking for information for buying decision. Consumers employ different search patterns in their pre-purchase search. We identified three types of search patterns in our experiment: sequential, agent search, and iterative search.

Sequential Search: Sequential search occurs when a consumer consecutively visits or contacts sellers. Each visit is composed of an information gathering and a buying decision phase. The consumer familiarizes her/himself with the products available and decides whether to purchase a product or to visit the next store. The consumer can compare the products in various stores, yet s/he has to resort to her/his memory as a source of product information to evaluate those products not in the current store.

Service Failure: The failure of a business to meet the expectations of a customer.

Service Recovery: The identification of points of customer pain and be willing to address these issues to achieve customer satisfaction. The ability to recover after a service failure is important because customers are more loyal if a company has addressed a failure than if they never address the failure or never had the failure at all. (http://www.amazon.com/Knock-Your-Socks-Service-Recovery/dp/081447084X)

SERVQUAL: A theoretical model developed by Zeithaml, Parasuraman and Berry which can be used to evaluate service quality.

Shopbot: The software agent powered the comparison-shopping service. Though there are variations in design and implementation for different services, the basic functions include data gathering, storage, and presentation. There are two main data retrieval methods: data wrapping and data feeding.

Shopbots: Web-based software agents that help online shoppers search price and related product information from multiple vendor sites.

Shopping Agent: Specialised software application that can be interactively used by customers to search for and compare Stores, Products/Services or Prices, on the basis of specific selection criteria.

Simultaneous Search: Product comparison could be more efficient, if the consumer were able to evaluate more available products side by side. This is the essence of simultaneous search. All information needed for the evaluation is readily available, and consumer has no need to resort to secondary information sources. Thus, there are only two phases in the consumer decision making process: information gathering and buying decision. In the electronic markets simultaneous search is often called agent search, because of the internet tools that makes information comparing available is called search agents. In offline circumstances, a consumer might collect a simultaneous search sample based on either internal information formed by experience of repeated purchases (internal search), or by, for example, acquainting her/himself with special issues of consumer journals that compare products the consumer is interested in (external search).

Small Online Vendors: Online vendors without an established brand name and mainly depend on third party technology to operate their online store.

Specialized Shopbots: Shopbots that provide price comparison information for products from one or a few related categories. For example, ad-dall.com provides price comparison for books, CDs, and DVDs.

The Least Effort Principle: A decision-making theory that human beings always try to minimize their effort in decision-making as long as the decision quality meets the minimum criteria.

Traffic Rank: The number of hits a website receives in a specific time period. It is an indicator for the popularity of the site.

Utilitarian Shopping Motivations: This term reflects the task-related value of a shopping experience. In particular, they refer to time savings and the chance to avoid shopping tasks that Internet offers. Search engines allow consumers to achieve some utilitarian shopping orientation goals such as: convenience, time saving, variety seeking and price reductions.

Variety-Seekers: Consumers who like to compare among a wide range and assortment of products before purchasing. These consumers also like to find detailed information online.

Compilation of References

Aaker, J. L., & Williams, P. (1998). Empathy Versus Pride: The Influence of Emotional Appeals Across Cultures. *Journal of Consumer Research, 25*(December), 241-261.

Adamic, L. A., Huberman, B. A., Barabasi, A. L., Albert, R., Jeong, H., & Bianconi, G. (2000). Power-Law Distribution of the World Wide Web. *Science, 287*(5461), 2115a-.

AECE (Asociación Española de Comercio Electrónico) (2005). Estudio sobre Comercio Electrónico B2C. Retrieved February 14, 2006, from http://www.aece.es.

Aggarwal, P., & Vaidyanathan, R. (2003). The perceived effectiveness of virtual shopping agents for search vs. experience goods. *Advances in Consumer Research, 30*, 347-348.

Agrawal M., Hariharan G., Kishore R., & Rao H. R. (2005). Matching intermediaries for information goods in the presence of direct search: an examination of switching costs and obsolescence of information. *Decision Support Systems, 41*(1), 20 – 36.

Ahn, T., Ryu, S., & Han, I. (2004). The impact of the online and offline features on the user acceptance of Internet shopping malls. *Electronic Commerce Research and Applications, 3*(4), 405–420.

Ahuja, V. (2000). Building Trust in Electronic Commerce. *IT Professional, 2*(1), pp. 61-63.

AIMC (Asociación de Investigación de los Medios de Comunicación) (2008), Estudio General de Medios. Tercera ola 2007, Madrid. Retrieved July 2, 2008, from http://www.aimc.es.

Ajzen, I. (1991). The theory of planned behavior. *Organizational Behavior & Human Decision Processes, 50*(2), 179–211.

Ajzen, I., & Fishbein, M. (1980). *Understanding attitudes and predicting social behavior.* Englewood Cliffs, NJ: Prentice Hall.

Akhter, F., & Kaya, L. (2008). Building Secure e-Business Systems: Technology and Culture in the U.A.E. *In E-Business Applications Track of ACM SAC.* Fortaleza, Brazil, March 16-20.

Akhter, F., Hobbs, D., & Maamar Z. (2005). A fuzzy logic-based system for assessing the level of business-to-consumer (B2C) trust in electronic commerce. *Expert Systems with Applications, 28*, 623–628.

Aladwani, A. M., & Palvia, P. (2002). Developing and validating an instrument for measuring user-perceived Web quality. *Information & Management, 39,* 467-476.

Alatovic, T. (2002). *Capabilities aware planner/optimizer/executioner for context interchange project.* M.S. thesis, MIT.

Alba, J. W., & Hutchinson, J. W. (1987). Dimensions of consumer expertice. *Journal of Consumer Research,* 13 March, 411-54.

Alba, J., & Hutchinson, J. (1987). Dimensions of Consumer Expertise. *Journal of Consumer Research, 13*(4), 411-454.

Alba, J., Lynch, J, Weitz, B., Janiszewski, C., Lutz, R., Sawyer, A., et al. (1997). Interactive home shopping: Consumer, retailer, and manufacturer incentives to participate in electronic marketplaces. *Journal of Marketing, 61*(3), 38–53.

Alptekinoglu, A., & Tang, C.S. (2005). A model for analyzing multi-channel distribution systems. *European Journal of Operational Research, 163*(3), 802–824.

Amazon. (2008). See http://www.amazon.com.

Andarajan, M., Simmers, C., & Igbaria, M. (2000). An exploratory investigation of the antecedents and impact of Internet usage: an individual perspective. *Behaviour and Information Technology, 19*(1), 69-85.

Anderson, J., & Gerbing, D. (1988). Structural equation modeling in practice: A review and recommended two-step approach. *Psychological Bulletin, 103*(3), 411-423.

Anderson, J.C., & Gerbing, D.W. (1984). The effect of sampling error on convergence, improper solutions, and goodness-of-fit indices for maximum likelihood confirmatory factor analysis. *Psychometrika, 49*(2), 155–173.

Anderson, P. L., McLellan, R., Overton, J. P., & Wolfram, G. (1997). *The Universal Tuition Tax Credit: A Proposal to Advance Parental Choice in Education.* Retrieved July 9, 2008, from http://www.mackinac.org/archives/1997/s1997-04.pdf.

Anderson, R. E., & Srinivasan, S. S. (2003). E-Satisfaction and E-Loyalty: A Contingency Framework. *Psychology & Marketing, 20*(2), 123-138.

Anderson, W. T. Jr. (1972). Convenience Orientation and Consumption Behavior. *Journal of Retailing, 48*(Fall), 49-71.

Andreassen, T. W. (2000). Antecedents to satisfaction with service recovery. *European Journal of Marketing, 34(1/2), 156-175.*

Andrews, P. (2003). Christmas clicking. *U.S. News & World Report, 135*(21), 42.

Angwin, J. (2001, July 16). Consumer adoption rate slows in replay of TV's history; bad news for online firms. *Wall Street Journal,* p. B1.

Arbuckle, J.L. (1999). *Amos user's guide, version 4.0.* Chicago, IL: Smallwaters Cooperation.

Ariely, D. (2000). Controlling the information flow: effects on consumers, decision making and preferences. *Journal of Consumer Research, 27,* 233-248.

Ariely, D. (2000). Controlling the Information Flow: Effects on Consumers, Decision Making and Preferences. *Journal of Consumer Research, 27*(2), 233-248.

Arlitt, M., Krishnamurthy, D., & Rolia, J. (2001). Characterizing the scalability of a large Web-based shopping system. *ACM Transactions on Internet Technology, 1*(1), 44-69.

Armstrong, A., & Hagel, J. III. (1996). The real value of online communities. *Harvard Business Review, 74*(3), 134–141.

Aron, D. (2001). Consumer grudgeholding: Toward a conceptual model and research agenda. *Journal of Consumer Satisfaction, Dissatisfaction, and Complaining Behavior, 14,* 108-119.

Athanassopoulos, A., Gounaris, S., & Stathakopoulos, V. (2001). Behavioural Responses to Customer Satisfaction: An Empirical Study. *European Journal of Marketing, 35*(5/6), 687-707.

Babin, B., & Attaway, J. (2000). Atmospheric affect as a tool for creating value and gaining share of customer. *Journal of Business Research, 49*(2), 91-99.

Babin, B., Darden, W., & Griffin, M. (1994). Work And/Or Fun: Measuring Hedonic and Utilitarian Shopping Value. *Journal of Consumer Research, 20*(4), 644-656.

Bailey, J. P., Faraj, S., & Yuliang, Y. (2007). The Road More Travelled: Web Traffic and Price Competition in Internet Retailing. *Electronic Markets, 17*(1), 56-67.

Bakos, J. Y. (1997). Reducing buyer search cost: Implications for electronic marketplaces. *Management Science, 43*(12), 1676-1692.

Balabanis, G., & Reynolds, N.L. (2001). Consumer attitudes towards multi-channel retailer's Web sites: The role of involvement, brand attitude, Internet knowledge, and visit duration. *Journal of Business Strategies, 18*(2), 105–131.

Balasubramanian, S. (1998). Mail versus mall: A strategic analysis of competition between direct marketers and conventional retailers. *Marketing Science, 17*(3), 181–195.

Balasubramanian, S., Konana, P., & Menon, N. (2003). Customer satisfaction in virtual environments: A study of online trading. *Management Science, 49*, 871-889

Bandura, A. (1977). Self-efficacy: Toward a unifying theory of behavioral change. *Psychological Review, 84*(2), 191-215.

Bansal, H. S., McDougall, G. H. G., Dikalli, S. S., & Sedatole, K. L. (2004). Relating e-satisfaction to behavioral outcomes: An empirical study. *Journal of Services Marketing, 18*(4), 290-302.

Baron, R. M., & Kenny, D. A. (1986, December). The moderator-mediator variable distinction in social psychological research: Conceptual, strategic, and statistical considerations. *Journal of Personality and Social Psychology, 51*(6), 1173-82.

Bart, Y., Shankar, V., Sultan, F., & Urban, G. L. (2005). Are the drivers and role of online trust the same for all Web sites and consumers? A large-scale exploratory empirical study. *Journal of Marketing, 69*(4), 133-152.

Baty, J. B., & Lee, R. M. (1995). InterShop: Enhancing the vendor/customer dialectic in electronic shopping. *Journal of Management Information Systems, 11*(4), 9-31.

Baumohl, B. (2000). Can you really trust those bots? *TIME Magazine, 156,* 80.

Beatty, S. E., & Smith, S. M. (1987). External search effort: an investigation across several product categories. *Journal of Consumer Research,* 14 June, (pp. 83-95).

Belanger, F., Hiller, J. S., & Smith, W. J. (2002). Trustworthiness in e-commerce: The role of privacy, security, and site attributes. *Journal of Strategic Information Systems, 11,* 245-270.

Bellman, S., & Lohse, G. (1999). Predictors of online buying behavior. *Communications of the ACM, 42*(12), 32-39.

Bellman, S., Lohse, G., & Eric, J. (1999). Predictors of online buying behavior. *Communications of the ACM, 42*(12), 32-38.

Belsley, D. A., Kuh, E., & Welsch, R. E. (1980). *Regression Diagnostics.* New York, NY: John Wiley and Sons.

Bentler, P. M. (1990). Comparative fit indices in structural models. *Psychological Bulletin, 107*(2), 238-246.

Bergadaa, M. (1990). The Role of Time in the Action of the Consumer. *Journal of Gonsumer Research, 17*(December), 289-302.

Bergan, M., Dutta, S., & Shugan, S.M. (1996). Branded variants: A retail perspective. *Journal of Marketing Research, 33*(1), 9-19.

Berlyne, D. E. (1960). *Conflict, Arousal and Curiosity.* New York: McGraw-Hill.

Berman, B., & Evans, J.R. (2001). *Retail management—A strategic approach.* Upper Saddle River, NJ: Prentice-Hall.

Berman, B., & Thelen, S. (2004). A guide to developing and managing a well-integrated multi-channel retail strategy. *International Journal of Retail & Distribution Management, 32*(3), 1147-156.

Berman, B., & Thelen, S. (2004). A guide to developing and managing a well-integrated multi-channel retail strategy. *International Journal of Retail & Distribution Management, 32*(2/3), 147–156.

Berners-Lee, T., Hendler, J. & Lassila, O. (2001). The Semantic Web. *Scientific American*, May 2001, 29-37.

Berry, L. L., Seiders, K., & Grewal, D. (2002). Understanding Service Convenience. *Journal of Marketing, 66*(3), 1-17.

Bettman, J. R. (1979). *An Information Processing Theory of Consumer Choice*. Reading, MA: Addison-Wesley., (p. 218).

Bettman, J. R., & Sujan, M. (1987). Effects of Framing on Evaluation of Comparable and Noncomparable Alternatives by Expert and Novice Consumers. *Journal of Consumer Research, 14,* 141-154.

Bettman, J. R., Johnson, E. J., & Payne, J. W. (1990). A componential analysis of cognitive effort in choice. *Organizational Behaviour Human Decision Processes, 45,* 111-39.

Bettman, J., & Park, W. (1980). Effects of Prior Knowledge and Experience and Phase of the Choice Process on Consumer Decision Processes: A Protocol Analysis. *Journal of Consumer Research, 7*(3), 234-248.

Betts, M. (2001). Turning browsers into buyers. *Sloan Management Review, 42*(2), 8-9.

Bharati, P., & Chaudhury, A. (2004). Using choiceboards to create business value. *Communications of the ACM, 47*(12), 77-81.

Bhargava, H., & Power (2001). Decision support systems and web technologies: a status report. *Seventh Americas Conference on Information Systems*.

Bhatnagar, A, Misra, S., & Rao, R. (2000). On risk, convenience, and Internet shopping behavior. *Communications of the ACM, 43*(11), 98-105.

Bhattacherjee, A. (2002). Individual trust in online firms: Scale development and initial tests. *Journal of Management Information Systems, 19*(1), 211–242.

Bhimani, A. (1996). Securing the commercial Internet. *Communications of the ACM, 39*(6), 29-31.

Birzan, D.G., & Tansel, A.U. (2006). A survey of entity resolution and record linkage methodologies. *Communications of the IIMA, 6*(3), 41-50.

Biswas, D. (2004), Economics of information in the Web economy towards a new theory? *Journal of Business Research, 57,* 724-733

Biswas, D. (2004). Economics of information in the Web economy towards a new theory? *Journal of Business Research, 57,* 724-733

Bitner, M. J., Booms, B. H., & Tetreault, M. S. (1990). The service encounter: Diagnosing favorable and unfavorable incidents. *Journal of Marketing, 54*(1), 71-84.

Blanchard, K., & Bowles, S. (1993). *Raving fans: A revolutionary approach to customer service*. NY: William Morrow.

Blattberg, R. C., & Deighton, J. (1996). Manage Marketing by the Customer Equity Test. *Harvard Business Review, 74*(4), 136-144.

Blattberg, R. C., Glazer, R., & Little, J.D.C. (eds.) (1994). Introduction. *The Marketing Information Revolution, 1.* Boston: Harvard Business School Press.

Blodgett, J. G., Hill, D. J., & Tax, S. S. (1997). The effects of distributive, procedural, and interactional justice on postcomplaint behavior. *Journal of Retailing, 73*(2), 185-210.

Boyle, R., & Ruppel, C. (2004, February 27-28). Online purchase intent: The effect of personal innovativeness, perceived risk, and computer self-efficacy. In R. Papp (Ed.), *Proceedings of the Seventh Annual Conference of the Southern Association for Information Systems* (pp. 131-137).

Brassington, F., & Petitt, S. (1997). *Principles of Marketing*. London: Pitman Publishing.

Brengman, M., Geuens M., Weijters, & Swinyard, W. (2005). Segmenting Internet shoppers based on their Web-usage-related lifestyle: a cross-cultural validation. *Journal of Business Research, 58*(1), 79-88.

Brian Grow and Ben Elgin, w. M. H. (2006). Click Fraud. *Business Week*(4003), 46.

Brin, S., & Page, L. (1998). The Anatomy of a Large-Scale Hypertextual Web Search Engine. *WWW7/Computer Networks, 30*(1-7), 107-117.

Brown, J. R., & Goolsbee, A. (2002). Does the Internet make markets more competitive? Evidence from the Life Insurance Industry. *Journal of Political Economy, 110*(3), 481-507.

Brown, J. R., & Goolsbee, A. (2002). Does the Internet make markets more competitive. *Journal of Political Economy, 110*(3), 481-507.

Brown, L. G. (1989). The Strategic and Tactical Implications of Convenience in Consumer Product Marketing. *Journal of Consumer Marketing, 6*(Summer), 13-19.

Brown, L. G. (1990). Convenience in Services Marketing. *Journal of Service Marketing, 4*(Winter), 53-59.

Brown, M., Pope, N., & Voges, D. (2003), Buying or browsing? An exploration of shopping orientation and online purchase intention. *European Journal of Marketing, 37*(11/12), 1666-1684.

Brown, M.W., & Cudeck R. (1993). Alternative ways of assessing model fit. In K.A. Bollen, & S. Long (Eds.), *Testing structural equation models* (pp. 136–162). Newbury Park, CA: Sage Publications.

Brucks, M. (1985). The Effect of Product Class Knowledge on Information Search Behavior. *Journal of Consumer Research, 12*(June), 1-16.

Brucks. M. (1985).The Effects of Product Class Knowledge on Information Search Behavior, *Journal of Consumer Research,* June 1985, *12.*

Brynjolfsson, E., & Smith, M. (1999). *Frictionless commerce? A comparison of Internet and conventional retailers* (Working paper). Massachusetts: MIT Sloan School of Management, Cambridge.

Brynjolfsson, E., & Smith, M. D. (2000). Frictionless commerce? A comparison of Internet and conventional retailers. *Management Science, 46*, 563-585.

Brynjolfsson, E., & Smith, M. D. (2000). Frictionless commerce? A comparison of Internet and conventional retailers. *Management Science, 46*(4), 563-585.

Brynjolfsson, E., & Smith, M. D. (2000). Frictionless commerce? A comparison of Internet and conventional retailers. *Management Science, 46*(4), 563-585.

Brynjolfsson, E., & Smith, M. D. (2000). The great equalizer? consumer choice behavior at Internet shopbots. *Working Paper.*

Brynjolfsson, E., & Smith, M. D.(2000). Frictionless commerce? A comparison of Internet and conventional retailers. *Management Science 46*, 563-585.

Brynjolfsson, E., & Smith, M.D. (2000). *The great equalizer?. Consumer choice behaviour at Internet shopbots* (Working paper). Massachusetts: MIT Sloan School of Management, Cambridge.

Brynjolfsson, E., Dick, A.A., & Smith, M.D. (2004). Search and product differentiation at an Internet Shopbot. *Working paper*, MIT Sloan School of Management, July. Cambridge, Massachusetts.

Burke, R. (2000). *Creating the ideal shopping experience: What consumers want in the physical and virtual store.* NY: KPMG. Available at www.kelley.iu.edu/retail/research/iukpmg00b.pdf

Burke, R.R. (2002). Technology and the customer interface: What consumers want in the physical world and virtual store. *Journal of the Academy of Marketing Science, 30*(4), 411–432.

Burroughs, R. E., & Sabherwal, R. (2002). Determinants of retail electronic purchasing: A multi-period investigation. *INFOR, 40*(1),.

Burroughs, R.E., & Sabherwal, R. (2002). Determinants of retail electronic purchasing: A multi-period investigation. *Journal of Information System Operation Research,* *40*(1), 35–56.

Burton, D. (2000). Postmodernism, social relations and remote shopping. *European Journal of Marketing,* *36*(7/8), 792–810.

Byrne, B.M. (2001). *Structural equation modeling with AMOS.* Mathwah, NJ: Lawrence Erlbaum Associates.

Carter, D. (1996). THE FUTURE OF Interactive MARKETING. *Harvard Business Review, 74*(6), 157-157.

Casillas, J., & Martínez-López, F. J. (2009). *Expert Systems with Applications, 36*(2) PART 1, 1645-1659

Caudill, E. M., & Murphy, P. E. (2000, Spring). Consumer online privacy: Legal and ethical issues. *Journal of Public Policy & Marketing, 19,* 7-19.

Center for the Digital Future (2004). *USC Annenberg School, The digital future report.* www.digitalcenter.org/downloads/ DigitalFutureReport-Year4-2004.pdf

Ceri, S., Gottlob, G., & Tanca, L. (1989). What you always wanted to know about Datalog (and never dared to ask). *IEEE Transactions on Knowledge and Data Engineering, 1*(1), 146-166.

Cespedes, F.V., & Corey, E.R. (1990). Managing multiple channels. *Business Horizons, 33*(3), 67–77.

Chan, C. O. (2005). Toward a unified view of customer relationship management. *Journal of American Academy of Businmess, 6*(1), 32-38.

Chang, C.H., Kaye, M., Girgis, M.R., & Shaalan, K.F. (2006). A survey of Web information extraction system. *IEEE Transactions on Knowledge and Data Engineering, 18*(10), 1411-1428.

Chang, J., & Samuel, N. (2004). Internet shopper demographics and buying behavior in Australia. *Journal of the Academy of Business, 5*(1/2), 171–176.

Chang, M. K., Cheung, W., & Lai,V. S. (2005). Literature derived reference models for the adoption of online shopping. *Information & Management, 42*(4), 543-559.

Chen, F. Y., Jian, C., & Yongbo, X. (2007). Optimal Control of Selling Channels for an Online Retailer with Cost-per-Click Payments and Seasonal Products. *Production & Operations Management, 16*(3), 292-305.

Chen, P. Y., & Hitt, L. M. (2002). Measuring switching costs and the determinants of customer retention in Internet-enabled businesses: A study of the online brokerage industry. *Information Systems Research, 13*(3), 255-274.

Chen, Q., & Chen, H. (2004). Exploring the success factors of eCRM strategies in practice. *Database Marketing & Customer Service Strategy Management, 11,* 333-343.

Cheung, M.K., & Limayem, M. (2005). The role of habit and the changing nature of the relationship between intention and usage. In *Proceedings of the 13th European Conference of Information Systems,* Regensburg, Germany.

Chiang K-P. (2006). Clicking Instead of Walking: Consumers Searching for Information in the Electronic Marketplace, *Bulletin,* December/January 2006

Chiu, Y. C., Shyu, J. Z., & Tzeng, G. H. (2004). Fuzzy MCDM for evaluating e-commerce Strategy. *International Journal of Computer Applications in Technology, 19*(1), 12-22.

Choi, J. D., Choi, J. S., Park, C., & Kim, D. (1998). A cell-based shared virtual world management mechanism in the cyber mall system. *Computer Networks and ISDN Systems, 30,* 1865-1874.

Christensen, E., Curbera, F., Meredith, G., & Weerawarana, S. WSDL. (2001). Web Services Description Language. See http://www.w3.org/TR/wsdl.

Chu, J., & Pike, T. (2002). *Integrated multichannel retailing (IMCR): A roadmap to the future.* IBM Institute for Business Value. Available at http://www-1.ibm.com/services/strategy/e_strategy/integrated_multi_channel.html

Chu, W., Choi, B., & Song, M. R. (2005). The role of on-line retailer brand and infomediary reputation in increasing consumer purchase intention. *International Journal of Electronic Commerce, 9*(3) 115-127.

Churchill, G.A.J., & Iacobucci, D. (2002). *Marketing research: Methodological foundations.* Mason, OH: South-Western Publishing.

Citrin, A., Stern, D., Spangenberg, E., & Clark, M. (2003). Consumer need for tactile input. An Internet retailing challenge. *Journal of Business Research, 56*(11), 915-922.

Clark, D. (2000). Shopbots: help or hindrance? *IEEE Expert Intelligent Systems & Their Applications, 15*(2), 8-9.

Clark, I. III. (2001). Emerging Value Propositions for M-Commerce. *Journal of Business Strategy, 18*(2), 133-148.

Close, W. (2002). CRM at work: Eight Characteristics of CRM Winners. *Defying the Limits, 3,* 66-68.

Coelho, F., & Easingwood, C. (2003). Multiple channel structures in financial services: A framework. *Journal of Financial Services Marketing, 8*(1), 22-34.

Coelho, F., Easingwood, C., & Coelho, A. (2003). Exploratory evidence of channel performance in single vs. multiple channel strategies. *International Journal of Retail and Distribution Management, 31*(11/12), 561-573.

Compeau, E. R., & Higgins, C. A. (1995). Computer self-efficacy: Development of a measure and initial test. *MIS Quarterly, 19*(2), 189-211.

Cook, D. P., & Luo, W. (2003). The role of third-party seals in building trust online. *E-Service Journal, 2*(3), 71-84.

Cooke, A. D. J., Sujan, H., Sujan, M., & Weitz, B.A. (2002). Marketing the Unfamiliar: The Role of Context and Item-Specific Information in Electronic Agent Recommendations. *Journal of Marketing Research, 39*(4), 488-497.

Copeland, M. T. (1917). Relation of consumers buying habits of marketing methods. *Harvard Business Review,* 1 April, 282-289.

Copeland, M. T. (1923). Relation of Consumers' Buying Habits to Marketing Methods. *Harvard Business Review,* April, 282-289.

Corner, J. L., Thompson, F., Dillon, S., & Doolin, B. (2005). Perceived risk, the Internet shopping experience and online purchasing behavior: A New Zealand perspective. *Journal of Global Information Management, 13*(2), 66-86.

Coughlan, A. T., Anderson, E., Stern, L. W., & El-Ansary, A. I. (2001). *Marketing Channels* (6th ed.). Upper Saddle River, New Jersey: Prentice Hall.

Cournot, A. (1838). *Researches into the Mathematical Principles of the Theory of Wealth.* New York: Macmillan.

Crescenzi, V., Mecca G., & Merialdo, P. (2001). RoadRunner: Towards automatic data extraction from large web sites. *Proceedings of the 27th International Conference on Very Large Databases (VLDB 2001),* (pp. 109-118).

Cronin, J. J., Brady, M. K., & Hult, G. T. M. (2000). Assessing the effects of quality, value, and customer satisfaction on consumer behavioral intentions in service environments. *Journal of Retailing, 76*(2), 193-218.

Cross, S., & Madson, L. (1997). Models of the self: self-constructuals and gender. *Psychological Bulletin, 122,* 5-37.

Crowston, K. (1997). *Price Behavior In a Market With Internet Buyer's Agents.* Paper presented at the International Conference on Information Systems, Atlanta, GA.

Crowston, K., & MacInnes, I. (2001). The effects of market-enabling Internet agents on competition and prices. *Journal of Electronic Commerce Research, 2*(1), 1-22.

Csikszentmihalyi, M. (1990). *Flow: The psychology of optimal experience.* New York: Harper and Row.

Cuieford, J. P. (1965). *Fundamental Statistics in Psychology and Education, 4th Edition.* New York: McGraw Hill.

Cunningham, S. M. (1967). The major dimensions of perceived risk. In *Risk taking and information handling in consumer behavior* (pp. 82-108). Boston: Harvard University Press.

Curbera, F., Khalaf, R., Mukhi, N., Tai, S., & Weerawarana, S. (2003). The next step in Web services. *Communications of the ACM, 46*(10), 29-34.

Dahlen, M. (2002). Learning the web: Internet User Experience and Response to Web Marketing in Sweden. *Journal of Interactive Advertising, 3*(1). Retrieved September 10, 2004, from http://www.jiad.org/vol3/no1/dahlen/index.html.

Damanpour, F. (1991). Organizational innovation: A meta-analysis of effects of determinants and moderators. *Academy of Management Journal, 34*(3), 555-590.

DAML. (2006).The DARPA Agent Markup Language. See http://www.daml.org.

Danaher, P. J., Wilson, I. W., & Davis, R. A. (2003). A Comparison of Online and Offline Consumer Brand Loyalty. *Marketing Science, 22*(4), 461-476.

Darian, J. (1987). In home shopping: Are there consumer segment? *Journal of Retailing, 63*(2), 163-186.

Davis, F. D. (1989). Perceived Usefulness, Perceived Ease of Use and User Acceptance of Information Technology. *MIS Quarterly, 13*(3), 319-339.

Dawson, M. (2001). Land in Sicht. *Lebensmittelzeitung Spezial E-Business, 1*, 60–61.

De Wulf, K., Schillewaert, N., Muylle, S., & Rangarajan, D. (2006). The role of pleasure in Web site success. *Information & Management, 43*(4), 434-446.

Degeratu, A., Rangaswamy, A., & Wu, J. (2000). Consumer choice behavior in online and traditional supermarkets: the effects of brand name, price and other search attributes. *International Journal of Research in Marketing, 17*(1), 55-78.

Dell Computer Timeline. (2004). *Processor, 26*(2), 7. Retrieved April 2, 2007, from http://www.processor.com/articles//P2602/24p02/24p02timeline.pdf.

Dellaert, B.G.C., & Kahn, B.E. (1999). How tolerable is delay? Consumer's evaluation of Internet Web sites after waiting. *Journal of Interactive Marketing, 13*(1), 41–54.

Devi, C. (2001, December 6). Guidelines to ensure safe Internet use. *New Straits Times*, p. 6.

Dholakia, R., & Uusitalo, O. (2002). Switching to Electronic Stores: Consumer Characteristics and the Perception of Shopping Benefits. *International Journal of Retail & Distribution Management, 30*(10), 459-469.

Dholakia, R.R., Zhao, M., & Dholakia, N. (2005). Multichannel retailing: A case study of early experiences. *Journal of Interactive Marketing, 19*(2), 63–74.

Dickerson, M. D., & Gentry, J. W. (1983, September). Characteristics of adopters and non-adopters of home computers. *Journal of Consumer Research, 10*, 225-235.

Dignum, F., & Siera, C. (Eds.) (2001). *Agent Mediated Electronic Commerce: The European AgentLink Perspective*. London: Springer.

Dinev, T., & Hart, P. (2005–2006). Internet privacy concerns and social awareness as determinants of intention to transact. *International Journal of Electronic Commerce, 10*(2), 7-29.

Dolan, R. J. (1990). *Conjoint Analysis: A Manager's Guide, Note 9-590-059*. Boston, MA: Harvard Business School.

Dolan, R. J. (2001). *Analyzing Consumer Preferences, Note 9-599-112*. Boston, MA: Harvard Business School.

Doney, P.M., & Cannon, J.P. (1997). An examination of the nature of trust in the buyer-seller relationship. *Journal of Marketing, 61*(2), 35–51.

Doorenbos, R. B., Etzioni, O., & Weld, D. S. (1997). *A scalable comparison-shopping agent for the World Wide Web*. Paper presented at the International Conference on Autonomous Agents, Marina del Rey, California.

Doorenbos, R. B., Etzioni, O., & Weld, D. S. (1997). A scalable comparison-shopping agent for the World-Wide

Web. In *Proceedings of the First International Conference on Autonomous Agents (Agents-97)* (pp.39-48).

Doorenbos, R.B., Etzioni, O., & Weld, D.S. (1997). A scalable comparison-shopping agent for the World-Wide Web', *Proceedings of the First International Conference on Autonomous Agents (Agents'97)*, (pp. 39-48).

Drake, M. A. (2003). *Encyclopedia of Library and Information Science*. New York, NY: Marcel Dekker.

Drèze, X., & Zufryden, F., (2004). Measurement of Online visibility and its impact on Internet traffic. *Journal of Interactive Marketing, 18*(1), 20-37.

Dudek, D., Mastora, A., & Landoni, M. (2007). Is Google the answer? A study into usability of search engines. *Library Review, 56*(3), 224-233.

Duffy, D.L. (2004). Using online retailing as a springboard for catalog marketing. *Journal of Consumer Marketing, 21*(3), 221–225.

Duncan, C. P., & Olshavsky, R. W. (1982). External search: The role of consumer beliefs. *Journal of Marketing Research*, 19 Feb, (pp. 32-43).

Eastlick, M., Lotz, S. L., & Warrington, P. (2006). Understanding online B-to-C relationships: An integrated model of privacy concerns, trust, and commitment. *Journal of Business Research, 59*(8), 877-886.

Eastlick, M.A., & Feinberg, R.A. (1994). Gender differences in mail-catalog patronage motives. *Journal of Direct Marketing, 8*(2), 37–44.

Eastlick, M.A., & Feinberg, R.A. (1999). Shopping motives for mail catalog shopping. *Journal of Business Research, 45*(3), 281–290.

Eastman, J., & Iyer, R. (2004). The elderly's uses and attitudes towards the Internet. *Journal of Consumer Marketing, 21*(3), 208-220.

Edwards, J. (2000). Is that your best offer? Shopbots search the web for bargains. CIO Magazine. See http://www.cio.com/archive/110100/et.html.

Edwards, L. (2004) Reconstructing consumer privacy protection on-line: A modest proposal. *International Review of Law Computers, 18*(3), 313–344.

Egger, F. N. (2003). Deceptive Technologies: Cash, Ethics & HCI. *SIGCHI Bulletin, 35*(2). ACM Press.

Einhorn, H. J. (1970). The use of nonlinear, noncompensatory models in decision making. *Psychological Bulletin, 73*(211-230).

Ellison, G., & Ellison, S. F. (2001). *Search, obfuscation and price elasticities on the Internet* (Working paper). Massachusetts: MIT Sloan School of Management, Cambridge.

Engel, J. F., Blackwell, R. D., & Miniard, P. W. (1990). *Consumer Behavior*. Chigago: The Dryden Press, 6th edition.

Engel, J., Blackwell, R., & Kollatt, D. (1978). *Consumer Behavior*. Hinsdale, IL: Dryden Press.

Engledow, J. L., Anderson, R. D., & Becker, H. (1978). Comparative Product Tests in the Consumer Decision Process: Correlates of Use and Impact on Satisfaction. *Decision Sciences, 9*(4), 627.

Ernst & Young (2003). Global Online Retailing. http://www.ey.com/GLOBAL

Ethier, J., Hadaya, P., Talbot, J., & Cadieux, J. (in press). B2C Web site quality and emotions during online shopping episodes: An empirical study. *Information & Management*.

Everard, A., & Galletta, D. F. (2005). How presentation flaws affect perceived site quality, trust, and intention to purchase from an online store. *Journal of Management Information Systems, 22*(3), 55-95.

Faber, R. J., & Christenson, G. A. (1996). In the mood to buy: Differences in the mood states experienced by compulsive buyers and other consumers. *Psychology & Marketing, 13*(8), 803-819.

Fain, D. (1994). *Consumers navigating channels: Behavior motivations for direct vs. retail*. Unpublished manuscript, New York University, New York.

Fasli, M. (2006). Shopbots: A syntactic present, a semantic future. *IEEE Internet Computing, 10*(6), 69-75.

Fasli, M. (2006). Shopbots: A syntactic present, a semantic future. *IEEE Internet Computing, 10*(6), 69-75.

Fasli, M. (2007). *Agent Technology for e-Commerce.* Chichester: John Wiley and Sons.

Fasli, M. (2007). On Agent Technology for E-commerce: Trust, Security and Legal Issues. *Knowledge Engineering Review, 22*(1), 3-35.

Federal Trade Commission. (2000). *Privacy online: Fair information practices in the electronic marketplace* (Report to Congress). Retrieved from http://www.ftc.gov/privacy/index.html

Feeny, D. (2001). Making business sense of the e-opportunity. *Sloan Management Review, 42*(2), 41-51.

Feinberg, R. (2001). Customer service and service quality. In G. Salvendy (Ed.). *Handbook of Industrial Engineering.* NY: John Wiley and Sons, Inc., (pp. 651-664).

Feinberg, R., & Trotter, M. (2003). The customer access evolution: Leveraging touch points for customer acquisition, retention, and wallet share. *Defying the Limits, 2,* 30-35.

Feinberg, R., Trotter, M., & Anton, J. (2000). At any time- From anywhere- In any form. *Defying the Limits: 1,* 296- 304.

Feinberg, R.A., Kadam, R., Hokama, L., & Kim, I. (2002). The state of electronic customer relationship management in retailing. *International Journal of Retail & Distribution Management, 30*(10), 470-481.

Feldman, S., & Spencer, M. (1965). The effect of personal influence in the selection of consumer services. In P. Bennett (Ed.). *Marketing and Economic Development* (pp. 440-452). Chicago: American Marketing Association.

File, K., Judd, B., & Prince, R. (1992). Interactive marketing: the influence of participation on positive word-of-mouth referrals. *The Journal of Services Marketing, 6*(4), 5-11.

Filson, D., & Willimson, K. (2001). The impact of e-commerce strategies on firm value: Lessons from Amazon.com. Working paper.

Firat, A. (2003). *Information integration using contextual knowledge and ontology merging.* Massachusetts Institute of Technology, Cambridge, MA'.

Firat, A., Madnick, S., & Siegel, M. (2000). The Cameleon Web wrapper engine. *Proceedings of the Workshop on Technologies for E-Services,* September 14-15, 2000, Cairo, Egypt.

Fitchard, K. (2004). The Two M's of Commerce. *Telephony, 245*(8). P.26.

Fitzgerald, K. (2004). Another Life for Internet Ads. *Credit Card Management, 17*(7), 64-67.

Flavin, C., Guinaliu, M., & Gurrea, R. (2006). The role played by perceived usability, satisfaction, and consumer trust on Web site loyalty. *Information & Management, 43*(1), 1-14.

Focus on Internet News and Data. (2006). Retrieved on 03/17/2006 from http://www.find.org.tw/find/home.aspx?page=news&id=4185.

Ford, W., & Baum, M. S. (1997). *Secure electronic commerce.* Upper Saddle River, NJ: Prentice Hall.

Forman, A. M., & Sriram, V. (1991). The depersonalization of retailing: Its impact on the "lonely" consumer. *Journal of Retailing, 67*(2), 226-243.

Fornell, C., & Larcker, D. (1981). Evaluating structural equation models with unobservable variables and measurement error. *Journal of Marketing Research, 18*(3), 39-50.

Fornell, C., Johnson, M. D., Anderson, E. W., Cha, J., & Bryant, B. E. (1996). The American Customer Satisfaction Index: nature, purpose, and findings, *Journal of Marketing, 60,* 7-18.

Forrester Research. (2002). See http://www.forrester.com/ER/Press/ForrFind/0,1768,0,00.html.

Freed, L. (2003). *The insiders view of e-retailing 2003.* www.foreseereults.com

Frolick, M. N., & Chen, L. (2004). Assessing M-Commerce Opportunities. *Information Systems Management, 21*(2), 53-61.

Frühwirth, T. (1998). Theory and practice of constraint handling rules. *Journal of Logic Programming, 37*(1-3), 95-138.

Furse, D., Punj, G., & Stewart, D. (1984). A typology of individual search strategies among purchasers of new automobiles. *Journal of Consumer Research, 10*(4), 417-431.

Gabrielsson, M., Kirpalani, V.H.M., & Luostarinen, R. (2002). Multiple channel strategies in the European personal computer industry. *Journal of International Marketing, 10*(3), 73–95.

Gagliano, K., & Hathcote, B. J. (1994). Customer Expectations and Perceptions of Service Quality in Retail Apparel Specialty Stores. *Journal of Services Marketing, 8*(1), 60-69.

Gallaugher, J.M. (2002). E-commerce and the undulating distribution channel. *Communications of the ACM, 45*(7), 89–95.

Garbarino, E., & Strahilevitz, M. (2004). Gender differences in the perceived risk of buying online and the effects of receiving a site recommendation. *Journal of Business Research, 57*(7), 768-775.

Garcia-Molina, H., Hammer, J., Ireland, K., Papakonstantinou, Y., Ullman, J., & Widom., J. (1995). Integrating and accessing heterogeneous information sources in TSIMMIS. *AAAI Symposium on Information Gathering,* Stanford, California, (pp. 61-64).

Gay, R., Charlesworth, A., & Esen, R. (2007). *Online Marketing: A Customer-Led Approach.* Oxford: Oxford University Press.

Gefen, D. (2000). E-commerce: The role of familiarity and trust. *Omega: The International Journal of Management Science, 28*(6), 725–737.

Gefen, D. (2002). Customer loyalty in e-commerce. *Journal of the Association for Information Systems, 3*(1), 27-51.

Gefen, D., & Straub, D. (2000). *The Relative Importance of Perceived Ease of Use in IS Adoption: A Study of E-Commerce Adoption.* Retrieved from http://jais.isworld.org/articles/1-8/article.htm.

Gefen, D., & Straub, D. W. (2004). Consumer trust in B2C e-commerce and the importance of social presence: Experiments in e-products and e-services. *Omega, 32*(6), 407-425.

Gefen, D., Karahanna, E., & Straub, D. W. (2003). Trust and TAM in online shopping: An integrated model. *MIS Quarterly, 27*(1), 51–90.

Gehrt, K. C., & Yale, L. J. (1993). The Dimensionality of the Convenience Phenomenon: A Qualitative Reexamination. *Journal of Business and Psychology, 8*(2), 163-180.

Gehrt, K.C., & Yan, R.-N. (2004). Situational, consumer, and retailer factors affecting Internet, catalog, and store shopping. *International Journal of Retail and Distribution Management, 32*(1), 5–18.

Gimein, M. (1999). Why won't Amazon help you compare prices? Retrieved January 5, 2005, 2005, from http://www.salon.com/tech/log/1999/08/05/amazon/

Girard, T., Silverblatt, R., & Korgankoar, P. (2002). Influence of product class on preference for shopping on the Internet. *Journal of Computer Mediated Communications, 8*(1). Retrieved August 21, 2005, from http://www.ascusc.org/jcmc/vol8/issue1/girard.html.

Goh, C. H., Bressan, S., Madnick, S., & Siegel, M. (1999). Context interchange: New features and formalisms for the intelligent integration of information. *ACM Transactions on Information Systems, 17*(3), 270-293.

Goi, C. L. (2008). Review of the Implementation of Mobile Commerce in Malaysia. *Journal of Internet Banking and Commerce, 13*(2), 1-11.

Gonsalves, A. (2004, January 26). Online retail sales to climb. *InformationWeek, 973*, 16.

Google Product Search. (2008). See http://www.google.com/products.

Grant, I. C., & Waite, K. (2003). Following the yellow brick road — Young adults' experiences of the information superhighway. *Qualitative Market Research: An International Journal, 6*(1), 48-57.

Grewal, D, Gopalkrishnana, R., Iyer, R. K., & Sharma, A. (2003). The Internet and the price-value-loyalty. *Journal of Business Research, 56*(5), 391-398.

Grewal, D., & Marmorstein, H. (1994). Market price variation, perceived price variation, and consumers' price search decisions for durable goods. *Journal of Consumer Research, 21*(3), 453-460.

Griffin, K., Ladd, P., & Whitehead, R. (1997). Internet commerce: Security is still a concern. *The Review of Accounting Information Systems, 2*(1), 67-71.

Gronroos, C. (1988). Service quality: The six criteria of good perceived service. *Review of Business, 9*(3), 10-13.

Gross, B. L., & Sheth, J. N. (1989). Time-Oriented Advertising: A Content Analysis of *United States Magazine Advertising*, 1890-1988. *Journal of Marketing, 53*(October), 76-83.

Grosso, C., McPherson, J., & Shi, C. (2004). Retailing: What's working online. *McKinsey Quarterly, 2005*(3), 18–20.

Gulati, R., & Garino, J. (2000). Get the right mix of bricks & clicks. *Harvard Business Review, 78*(3), 107-114.

Guo, C. (2002, March/April). Competing in high growth markets: The case of e-commerce. *Business Horizons, 45*, 77-83.

Gupta, A. (1998). *Junglee: integrating data of all shapes and sizes.* Paper presented at the Fourteenth International Conference on Data Engineering, Orlando, FL.

Gupta, A., Su, B., & Walter, Z. (2004). Risk profile and consumer shopping behavior in electronic and traditional channels. *Decision Support Systems, 38*(3), 347–367.

Guttman, A. G., Moukas, R. H., & Maes, P. (1999). Agent-mediated integrative negotiation for retail electronic commerce. In *Agent Mediated Electronic Commerce, First International Workshop on Agent Mediated Electronic Trading (AMET'98)* (pp. 70-90). Berlin: Springer.

Guttman, R. H., Moukas, A. G., & Maes, P. (1998). Agents as Mediators in Electronic Commerce. *International Journal of Electronic Markets, 8*(1), 22-27.

Hackman, D., Gundergan, S. P., Wang, P., & Daniel, K. (2006). A service perspective on modeling intentions of on-line purchasing. *The Journal of Services Marketing, 20*(7), 459.

Haeberle, M. (2003). On-line retailing scores big. *Chain Store Age, 79*(7), 48.

Hair, J. F., Anderson, R. E., Tatham, R. L., & Black, W. C. (1998). *Multivariate data analysis* (5th ed). Upper Saddle River, NJ: Prentice Hall.

Hancock, B. (2000). American Express creates disposable credit card numbers. *Computers & Security, 19*(7), 571-572.

Hansen, T. (2005). Understanding consumer online grocery behavior: Results from a Swedish study. *Journal of Euromarketing, 14*(3), 31–58.

Haskin, D. (1999). *Analysts: Smart phones to lead e-commerce explosion.* All-NetDevices. Retrieved from http://www.allnetdevices.com/news/9911/991103ecomm/991101ecomm.html.

Haubl, G., & Murray, K. B. (2003). Preference construction and persistence in digital marketplaces: The role of electronic recommendation agents. *Journal of Consumer Psychology, 13*(1&2), 75-91.

Haubl, G., & Murray, K. B. (2003). Preference Construction and Persistence in Digital Marketplaces: The Role of Electronic Recommendation Agents. *Journal of Consumer Psychology, 13*(1&2), 75-91.

Haubl, G., & Trifts, V. (2000). Consumer decision making in online shopping environments: the effects of interactive decision aids. *Marketing Science, 19*(1), 4-21.

Haubl, G., & Trifts, V. (2000). Consumer Decision Making in Online Shopping Environments: The Effects of Interactive Decision Aids. *Marketing Science, 19*(1), 4-21.

Heijden, H. (2003). Factors influencing the usage of Websites: The case of a generic portal in the Netherlands. *Information & Management, 40,* 541-549.

Heijden, H. V. D., Verhagen, T., & Creemers, M. (2003). Understanding online purchase intentions: Contributions from technology and trust perspectives. *European Journal of Information Systems, 12*(1), 41-49.

Henderson-Sellers, B., & Giorgini, P. (2005). *Agent-oriented Methodologies.* Hershey: IDEA Group Publishing.

Herman, S. W. (2000). Fixed Assets and Consumer Durable Goods. Retrieved July 10, 2008, from http://www.bea.gov/scb/account_articles/national/0400niw1/maintext.htm

Hirschman, E. C. (1980, December). Innovativeness, novelty seeking, and consumer creativity. *Journal of Consumer Research, 7,* 283-295.

Hitwise.com. (2008). Hitwise US holiday 2007 retail recap report. See http://www.hitwise.com.

Hoffer, J., George, J., & Valacich, J. (2004). *Modern System Analysis and Design* (Fourth ed.). Upper Saddle River, NJ Prentice Hall.

Hoffman, D. L., & Novak, T. P. (1996). Marketing in Hypermedia Computer-Mediated Environments: Conceptual Foundations. *Journal of Marketing, 80*(4), 50-68.

Hoffman, D. L., Novak, T. P., & Peralta, M. (1999). Building consumer trust online. *Communications of the ACM, 42*(4), 80-86.

Hoffman, K. D., & Kelley, S. W. (2000). Perceived justice needs and recovery evaluation: A contingency approach. *European Journal of Marketing, 34*(3/4), 418-432.

Hofstede, G. (1980). *Culture's consequences: International differences in work relates values.* Newbury Park (CA): Sage Publications.

Holbrook, M. (1999). Introduction to Customer Value. In Holbrook, M. (Ed.) *Costumer Value: a Framework for Analysis and Research* (pp. 1-28). New York: Routledge.

Holzwarth, M., Janiszewski, C., & Neumann, M. M. (2006). The influence of avatars on online consumer shopping behavior. *Journal of Marketing, 70*(4), 19-36.

Hong, W., Thong, J.Y.L., & Tam, K.Y. (2004). The effects of information format and shopping task on consumers' online shopping behavior: A cognitive fit perspective. *Journal of Management Information Systems, 21*(3), 149–184.

Hoque, A. Y., & Lohse, G. L. (1999). An information search cost perspective for designing interfaces for electronic commerce. *Journal of Marketing Research, 36,* 387-394.

Howard, J. A. (1977). *Consumer Behavior: Application of Theory.* New York: McGraw-Hill.

Howard, J. A., & Jadish, N. S. (1969). *The Theory of Buyer Behavior.* New York, NY: Wiley.

Howcroft, D. (2001). After the goldrush: Deconstructing the myths of the dot.com market. *Journal of Information Technology, 16*(4), 195-204.

Hsu, M., & Chiu, C. (2004). Internet self-efficacy and electronic service acceptance. *Decision Support Systems, 38*(3), 369-381.

Hu, X., Lin, Z., & Zhang, H. (2003). Trust promoting seals in electronic markets: An exploratory study of their effectiveness for online sales promotion. *Journal of Promotion Management, 9*(1/2), 163-180.

Huhns, M. N., & Stephens, L. M. (1999). Multiagent Systems and Societies of Agents. In G. Weiss, (Ed.), *Multiagent Systems: A Modern Approach to Distributed Artificial Intelligence* (pp. 79-120). Cambridge, MA: The MIT Press.

Huizingh, E. (2000). The content and design of Web sites: An empirical study. *Information & Management, 37*(3), 123-134.

Hummel, M. (2005). *E-commerce—Eine Sonderform des Versandhandels?* Master's thesis, Vienna University of Economics and Business Administration, Vienna.

Ibbotson, P., & Fahy, M. (2004). The impact of e-commerce on small Irish firms. *International Journal of Services Technology & Management, 5*(4), 317–331.

Igbaria, M. (1993). User acceptance of microcomputer technology: an empirical test. *International Journal of Management Science, 21*, 73-90.

Igbaria, M., Parasuraman, S., & Baroudi, J. (1996). A motivational model of microcomputer usage. *Journal of Management Information Systems, 13*, 127-143.

Inman, J., Shankar, V., & Ferraro, R. (2004). The roles of channel-category associations and geodemographics in channel patronage. *Journal of Marketing, 68*, 51-71.

Integral. (2006). Austrian Internet Monitor Internet-Entwicklung 3. *Quartal 2005.* Retrieved February 22, 2006, from http://www.integral.co.at/dImages/AIM-C_3.%20Quartal2005.pdf

Internet Crime Complaint Center. (2007). *The Internet crime complaint center hits 1 million!* Retrieved February 13, 2008, from http://www.ic3.gov/media/2007/070613.htm

Internet Fraud Watch. (2005). *Internet fraud statistics report.* Retrieved September 24, 2007, from http://www.fraud.org/internet/intstat.htm

Internet Fraud Watch. (2007). *Internet fraud tips.* Retrieved February 13, 2008, from http://www.fraud.org/tips/internet/general.htm

Introna, L. (2001). Defining the virtual organization. In S. Barnes & B. Hunt (Eds.), *E-commerce & v-business* (pp. 143-152). Oxford: Butterworth-Heinemann.

Iwaarden, J. V., & Wiele, T. V. D. (2003). Applying SERVQUAL to Web sites: An exploratory study. *International Journal of Quality, 20*(8), 919-935.

Iwaarden, J. V., Wiele, T. V. D., Ball, L., & Millen, R. (2004). Perceptions about the quality of Websites: A survey amongst students at Northeastern University and Erasmus University. *Information & Management, 41*(8), 947–959.

Iyengar, S. S., & Lepper, M. R. (2000). When Choice is Demotivating: Can One Desire Too Much of a Good Thing? *Journal of Personality and Social Psychology, 79*(6), 12.

Iyer, G. A., & Pazgal, A. (2003). Internet shopping agents: Virtual co-location and competition. *Marketing Science, 22*(1), 85-106.

Jain, S. C. (1990). *Marketing Planning & Strategy* Cincinnati, OH: Thomson South-Western.

Jansen, B. J. (2006, July). Paid Search. *IEEE Computer.*

Jansen, B. J., & Pooch, U. (2001). Web user studies: a review and Framework for future work. *Journal of the American Society of Information Science and Technology, 52*(3), 235-246.

Jansen, P. G. W., van der Velde, M. E. G., & Telting, I. A. (2001). The effectiveness of human resource practices on advancing men's and women's ranks. *Journal of Management Development, 20*(4), 318-331.

Januz, L. R. (1983). It's helpful to know who is purchasing through the mail. *Marketing News, 17*, 4.

Jarvenpaa, S. L., & Todd, P. A. (1997a). Is there a future for retailing on Internet? In R. A. Peterson (Ed.), *Electronic marketing and consumer* (pp. 139-154). Thousand Oaks, CA: Sage.

Jarvenpaa, S. L., & Todd, P. A. (1997b). Consumer reactions to electronic shopping on the World Wide Web. *International Journal of Electronic Commerce, 1*(2), 59-88.

Jarvenpaa, S. L., Tractinsky, N. M., & Vitale, M. (2000). Consumer trust in an Internet store. *Information Technology and Management,* (pp. 45–71).

Jarvenpaa, S.L., & Todd P.A. (1997). Consumer reactions to electronic shopping on the World Wide Web. *International Journal of Electronic Commerce, 1*(2), 59–88.

Jarvenpaa, S.L., Tractinsky, N., & Vitale, M. (2000). Consumer trust in an Internet store. *Information Technology and Management, 1*, 45–71.

Jasper, C.R., & Lan, P.-N.R. (1992). Apparel catalog patronage: Demographic, lifestyle and motivational factors. *Psychology and Marketing, 9*(4), 275–296.

Jih, W. J., & Lee, S. F. (2004). Relationship between Online Shoppers' Motivation and Life Style Indicators. *Journal of Computer Information Systems, XLIV*(2), 65-73.

Johnson, C. (2004). The growth of multichannel retailing: A Forrester document prepared for: National Governor's Association and the National Conference of State Legislatures. Available at www.nga.org/cda/files/0407MULTICHANNEL.PDF

Johnson, E. J., Moe, W., Fader, P., Steven, B., & Lohse, J. (2004). On the depth and dynamics of online search behavior. *Management Science, 50*, 299-308.

Joines, J., Scherer, C., & Scheufele, D. (2003). Exploring motivations for consumer Web use and their implications for E-commerce. *Journal of Consumer Marketing, 20*(2), 90-108.

Kakas, C., Michael, A., & Mourlas, C. (2000). ACLP: Integrating abduction and constraint solving. *Journal of Logic Programming, 44*(1-3), 129-177.

Kantor, A. (2007, June 14). Internet suffering from information overload. *USA Today.*

Karlsson, T., Kuttainen, C., Pitt, L., & Spyropoulou, S. (2005). Price as a variable in online consumer trade-offs. *Marketing Intelligence & Planning, 23*(4/5), 350.

Kasiran, M. K., & Meziane, F. (2002). An information framework for a merchant trust agent in electronic commerce. In H. Yin, N. Allinson, R. Freeman, J. Keane, & Hubbard S. (Eds), *Intelligent data engineering and automated learning,* (pp. 243-248). Springer

Kau, A. K., Tang, Y. E., & Ghose, S. (2003). Typology of online shoppers. *The Journal of Consumer Marketing, 20*(2/3), 139-156.

Kaufman-Scarborough, C., & Lindquist, J.D. (2002). E-shopping in a multiple channel environment. *Journal of Consumer Marketing, 19*(4/5), 333–350.

Kayak. (2008). See http://www.kayak.com.

Keen, C., Wetzels, M., de Ruyter, K., & Feinberg, R. (2004). E-tailers versus retailers: Which factors determine consumer preferences. *Journal of Business Research, 57*, 685-695

Kelley, S. W., Hoffman, K. D., & Davis, M. A. (1993). A typology of retail failures and recoveries. *Journal of Retailing, 69*(4), 429-452.

Kelly, D., & Teevan, J. (2003). Implicit feedback for inferring user preference: A bibliography. *SIGIR Forum, 37*(2), 18–28.

Kephart, J. O., & Greenwald, A. R. (1999). *Shopbot economics.* Paper presented at the International Conference on Autonomous Agents, Seattle, Washington, United States.

Kephart, J. O., & Greenwald, A. R. (2000). When Bots Collide. *Harvard Business Review, 78*(4), 17-18.

Kephart, J. O., Hanson, J. E., & Greenwald, A. R. (2000). Dynamic pricing by software agents. *Computer Networks, 32*(6), 731-752.

Kerlinger, F. N. (1986). *Foundations of Behavioral Research.* 3rd Edition, New York□McGraw-Hill.

Kerstetter, J. (1999). New generation of shopping 'bots swarms in. *ZFDnet.co.uk.* Retrieved June 2007, from http://news.zdnet.co.uk/internet/0,1000000097,2073092,00.htm.

Kiani, R. G. (1998). Marketing opportunities in the digital world. *Internet Research: Networking Applications and Policy, 8*(2), 185-194.

Kiel, G. C., & Layton, R. A. (1981). Dimensions of Consumer Information Seeking Behavior. *Journal of Marketing Research*, 18 May, 233-239.

Kiely, T. (1997). The Internet: Fear and shopping in cyberspace. *Harvard Business Review, 75*(4), 13-14.

Kiffer, M., Laussen, G., & Wu, J. (1995). Logic foundations of object-oriented and frame-based languages. *Journal of the ACM, 42*(4), 741-843.

Kim, C., & Galliers, R. D. (2004). Deriving a diffusion framework and research agenda for Web based shopping systems. *Journal of Electronic Commerce Research, 5*(3), 199-215.

Kim, C., & Galliers, R. D. (2006). The development and application of a configuration model of Web-based shopping systems. *International Journal of Electronic Business, 4*(1), 1-17.

Kim, C., Galliers, R. D., & Yang, K. H. (2005). Comparison of Web-based shopping systems in the UK and Korea. *International Journal of Global Information Technology Management, 8*(4), 49-66.

Kim, E. Y., & Kim, Y.-K. (2004), Predicting online purchase intentions for clothing products. *European Journal of Marketing, 38*(7), 883-897.

Kim, J., Oard, D., & Romanik, K. (2000). *Using implicit feedback for user modeling in internet and intranet searching.* Technical Report, College of Library and Information Services, University of Maryland at College Park. Available at http://www.clis.umd/edu/research/reports/.

Kim, S., & Stoel, L. (2004). Apparel retailers: Website quality dimensions and satisfaction. *Journal of Retailing and Consumer Services, 11*(2), 109–117.

Kim, W., Choi, D., & Park, S. (2005). Product information meta-search framework for electronic commerce through ontology mapping. *The Semantic Web: Research and Applications, LNCS 3532,* 408-422

Kim, W., Choi, D., Kim, J., & Jin, J. (2005). Development of a meta product search engine with web services. In *Proceedings of the Second Asia Information Retrieval Symposium (AIRS 2005)* pp.571-576. Berlin: Springer.

Kimery, K. M., & McCord, M. (2006). Signals of trustworthiness in e-commerce: Consumer understanding of third-party assurance seals. *Journal of Electronic Commerce in Organizations, 4*(4), 52-74.

Kitchin, J. (1923). Cycles and Trends in Economic Factors. *The Review of Economics and Statistics, 5*(1), 10-16.

Kline, R.B. (1998). *Principles and practice of structural equation modeling.* New York: Guilford.

Kocas, C. (2002). Evolution of prices in electronic markets under diffusion of price-comparison shopping. *Journal of Management Information Systems, 19*(3), 99.

Koças, C. (2005). A model of internet pricing under price-comparison shopping. *International Journal of Electronic Commerce, 10*(1), 111-134.

Kohn M. G., & Shavell, S. (1974). The theory of search. *Journal of Economic Theory, 9,* 93– 123.

Korgaonkar, P., & Wollin, L. (1999). A multivariate analysis of Web usage. *Journal of Advertising Research, 39*(2), 53-68.

Korgaonkar, P.K. (1984). Consumer shopping orientations, non-store retailers, and consumers' patronage intentions: A multivariate investigation. *Journal of the Academy of Marketing Science, 12*(1), 11–22.

Koufaris, M. (2002). Applying the technology acceptance model and flow theory to online consumer behavior. *Information Systems Research, 13*(2), 205-212.

Koufaris, M., & Hampton-Sosa, W. (2004). The development of initial trust in an online company by new customers. *Information & Management, 41*(3), 377-397.

Kovar, S. E., Burke, K. G., & Kovar, B. R. (2000). Consumer responses to the CPA WEBTRUST assurance. *Journal of Information Systems, 14*(1), 17-35.

Koyuncu, C., & Lien, D. (2003). E-commerce and consumer's purchasing behavior. *Applied Economics, 35*(6), 721-726.

Kraemer, K. L., Dedrick, J., & Yamashiro, S. (2000). Refining and extending the business model with information technology: Dell computer corporation. *Information Society, 16*(1), 5-21.

Krulwich, B. (1996). The BargainFinder Agent: Comparison Price Shopping on the Internet. In J. Williams (Ed.), *Bots, and Other Internet Beasties* (pp. 257-263). Indianapolis: Macmillan Computer Publishing.

Kulviwat, S., Guo C., & Engchanil (2004). Determinants of online information search: a critical review and assessment. *Internet research* 2004, *14*(3), 245-253.

Kumar, P., Kalwani, M. U., & Dada, M. (1997). The Impact of Waiting Time Guarantees on Consumer Waiting Experiences. *Marketing Science, 16*(4), 295-314.

Lain, L.C., Chen, Z., & Ichalkaranje, N. (Eds.) (2002). *Intelligent Agents and Their Applications.* Heidelberg: Physica-Verlag.

Landy, P. J., Rastegary, H., Thayer, J., & Colvin, C. (1991). Time Urgency: The Construct and Its Measurement. *Journal of Applied Psychology, 76*(5), 644-657.

Lasica, J. D. (1999). *The confidence game.* Retrieved September 24, 2007, from http://www.jdlasica.com/idrive/TIS/confidence.html

Lauraeus-Niinivaara T., Saarinen T., & Öörni A. (2007). Knowledge and Choice Uncertainty Affect Consumer Search and Buying Behavior, *HICSS Conference paper* 3.- 7.1.Jan.2007

Lauraeus-Niinivaara, T., Saarinen, T., Sunikka, A., & Öörni, A. (2008). Relationship between uncertainty and patterns of pre-purchase search in electronic markets. *HICSS Conference paper* (2008) 7.- 10. Jan.

Lazonder, A., Biemans, J., & Wopereis, G. (2000). Differences between novice and experienced users in searching information on the world wide web. *Journal of the American Society for Information Science, 51*(6), 576-581.

Lederer, A.L., Maupin, D.J., Sena, M.P., & Zhuang, Y. (2000). The technology acceptance model and the World Wide Web. *Decision Support Systems, 29*(3), 269–282.

Lee, B.-K., & Lee, W.-N. (2004). The Effect of Information Overload on Consumer Choice Quality in an On-Line Environment. *Psychology & Marketing, 21*(3), 159-183.

Lee, G., & Lin, H. (2005). Customer perceptions of e-service quality in online shopping. *International Journal of Retail & Distribution Management, 33*(2), 161-176.

Lee, H. G. (1998, January). Do electronic marketplaces lower the price of goods? *Communication of ACM, 41*, 73.

Lee, J. W., & Lee, J. K. (2006). Online advertising by the comparison challenge approach. *Electronic Commerce Research and Applications, 5*(4), 282-294.

Lee, M. K. O., & Turban, E. (2001). A Trust Model for Consumer Internet Shopping. *International Journal of Electronic Commerce, 6*(1), 75-91.

Lepkowska-White, E. (2004). Online store perceptions: How to turn browsers into buyers? *Journal of Marketing Theory & Practice, 12*(3), 36–47.

Levinson, H., Price, C. R., Munden, K. J., Mandl, H. J., & Solley, C. M. (1962). *Men, management, and mental health.* Cambridge, MA: Harvard University Press.

Levy, M., & Weitz, B. (2003). *Retail Management,* 5th edition . NY: McGraw Hill

Levy, S. J. (2001). The psychology of an online shopping pioneer. *Advances in Consumer Research, 28*(1), 222-226.

Lewis, T. (1999). Ubiner: The ubiquitous Internet will be wireless. *IEEE Computer, 32*(10), 56-63.

Li, H., Kuo, C., & Russell, M. (1999). The impact of perceived channel utilities, shopping orientations, and demographics on the consumer's online buying behaviour. *Journal of Computer Mediated Communications* 5(2). Retrieved March 15, 2002, from http://www.ascusc.org/jcmc/vol5/issue2/hairong.html.

Liand, T. P., & Huang, J. S. (2000). A framework for applying intelligent agents to support electronic trading. *Decision Support Systems, 28(*4).

Liao, Z., & Cheung, T. (2001). Internet-based e-shopping and consumer attitudes: An empirical study. *Information & Management, 38*(5), 299-306.

Lightner, N. J., & Eastman, C. (2002). User preference for product information in remote purchase environments. *Journal of Electronic Commerce Research, 3*(3), 174-186.

Lin, C. E., & Bi, L. Y. (2008). A Model Electronic Toll Collection for E-Commerce Applications. *Journal of Theoretical and Applied Electronic Commerce Research, 3*(2), 111-129.

Lin, S., Chen, Y. J, & Lin, T. T. (2001). A Study of College Students' Usage of and Satisfaction with Mobile Phones – The Cases of Taipei University and Chiao-Tung University. *Seventh Internet Conference – Taiwan.* Tanet.net.

Lisa, H., & Geraldine, C. (2003). Marketing in the Internet age: What can we learn from the past? *Management Decision, 41*(9), 944.

Litan, R., & Rivlin, A. M. (2001). Project the Economic Impact of the Internet. *The American Economic Review, 91*(2), 313-317.

Liu, C., & Arnett, K. P. (2000). Exploring the factors associated with Web site success in the context of e-commerce. *Information & Management, 38*(1), 23-33.

Liu, F., Geng, H., & Zhang, Y. (2005). Interactive Fuzzy Interval Reasoning for smart Web shopping. *Applied Soft Computing, 5*(4), 433-439.

Liu, J., & Ye, Y. (Eds.) (2001). *E-Commerce Agents: Marketplace Solutions, Security Issues, and Supply and Demand.* London: Springer.

Lohse, G. L., & Spiller, P. (1999). Internet retail store design: How the user interface influences traffic and sales. *Journal of Computer Mediated Communication, 5*(2). Retrieved from www.ascusc.org/jcmc/vol5/issue2/

Lohse, G., Bellman, S., & Johnson, E. (2000). Consumer buying behavior on the Internet: findings from panel data. *Journal of Interactive Marketing, 14*(1), 15-29.

Loiacono, E., Watson, R., & Goodhue, D. (2002). WebQual: A Web site quality instrument. *American marketing association. Winter Marketing Educators' Conference, Austin, TX,* 432-438.

Looney, C. A., & Chatterjee, D. (2002). Web-enabled transformation of the brokerage industry. *Communication of the ACM, 45*(8), 75-81.

Loveman, G. (1998). Employee satisfaction, customer loyalty, and financial performance: an empirical examination of the service project chain in retail banking. *Journal of Service Research, 1,* 18-31.

Lukasiewicz, J. (1970). Philosophical remarks on many-valued systems of propositional logic. Reprinted in Selected Works, ed. Borkowski, Studies in Logic and the Foundations of Mathematics (North-Holland, Amsterdam, 1970) (pp. 153-179).

Lumpkin, G. T., Droege, S. B., & Dess, G. G. (2002). E-commerce strategies: Achieving sustainable competitive advantage and avoiding pitfalls. *Organizational Dynamics, 30*(4), 325-340.

Luqmani, M., Yavas, U., & Quraeshi, Z. A. (1994). A Convenience-Oriented Approach to Country Segmentation: Implications for Global Marketing Strategies. *Journal of Consumer Marketing, 11*(4), 29-40.

Lynch, J., & Ariely, D. (2000, Winter). Wine online: Search costs affect competition on price, quality, and distribution. *Marketing Science, 19,* 83-103.

Maamar, Z. (2003). Commerce, E-Commerce, and M-Commerce: What Comes Next? *Communications of the ACM, 46*(12).

Madlberger, M. (2004). *Electronic retailing.* Wiesbaden, Germany: Deutscher Universitaetsverlag.

Madlberger, M. (2006). Multi-channel retailing in B2C e-commerce. In M. Khosrow-Pour (Ed.), *Encyclopedia of e-commerce, e-government, and mobile commerce.* Hershey, PA: Idea Group Reference.

Madnick, S. E., & Siegel, M. D. (2002). Seizing the opportunity: Exploiting Web aggregation', *MISQ Executive, 1*(1), 35-46.

Madnick, S. E., & Wang Y. R. (1989). The inter-database instance identification problem in integrating autonomous systems. *Proceedings of the Fifth International Data Engineering Conference*, February 1989, Los Angeles, CA.

Madnick, S.E. (2001). The misguided silver bullet: What XML will and will NOT do to help information integration. *Proceedings of the Third International Conference on Information Integration and Web-based Applications and Services* (IIWAS2001), September 2001, Linz, Austria, (pp. 61-72).

Maes, P., Guttman, R., & Moukas, A. (1999). Agents that buy and sell: transforming commerce as we know it. *Communications of the ACM, 42*(3), 81-83.

Mahajan, V., & Wind, J. (1989, August). Market discontinuities and strategic planning: A research agenda. *Technological Forecasting and Social Change, 36*, 185-99.

Maier, P. (2005). A "Global Village" without borders? International price differentials at eBay. Netherlands Central Bank Working Paper, #044.

Malone, T. W., Yates, J., & Benjamin, R. I. (1987). Electronic Markets and Electronic Hieratchies. *Communications of the ACM, 30*(6), 484-497.

Mann, T. (1987). *A Guide to Library Research Methods.* New York, NY: Oxford University Press.

Manning, R., & Morgan, P. (1982). Search and Consumer Theory. *Review of Economic Studies* 1982, XLIX, (pp. 203–216).

Markopoulos, P. M., & Kephart, J. O. (2002). How valuable are shopbots? In *Proceedings of the First International Joint Conference on Autonomous Agents and Multiagent Systems, AAMAS'02* (pp. 1009-1016). New York, NY: ACM.

Markus, H., & Oyserman, D. (1989). Gender and thought: the role of the self-concept. In M. Cradfort, & M. Gentry (Ed.), *Gender and thought: psychological perspectives,* (pp.100-127). New York: Springer-Verlag.

Marmorstein, H., Grewal, D., & Fishe, R. P. H. (1992). The value of time spent in price comparison shopping: Survey and experimental evidence. *Journal of Consumer Research, 9*(June), 52-61.

Martin, J. (1996). *Cybercorp: The New Business Revolution.* New York: AMACOM.

Mauldin, E., & Arunachalam, V. (2002). An experimental examination of alternative forms of Web assurance for business-to-consumer e-commerce. *Journal of Information Systems, 16*, 33-54.

McCarthy, J., & Buvac S. (1994). *Formalizing context (expanded notes).* Stanford University.

McCleary, K. W., & Whitney, D. L. (1994). Projecting western consumer attitudes toward travel to six Eastern European countries. *Journal of International Consumer Marketing, 6*(3/4), 239-256.

McCloskey, D. (2004). Evaluating electronic commerce acceptance with the technology acceptance model. *Journal of Computer Information Systems, 44*(2), 49–57.

Mcguire, W. (1974). Psychological motives and communication gratifications. In: Blumler, JF. and Katz, J. (Eds.) *The uses of mass communications: current perspectives on gratification research* , (pp. 106-167), Beverly Hills (CA): Sage.

McKenna, R. (1995). Real-Time Marketing. *Harvard Business Review, 73*(4), 87-96.

McKnight, D. H., Choudhury. V., & Kacmar, C. (2002). The impact of initial consumer trust on Intentions to transact with a website: A Trust building model. *Journal of Strategic Information Systems, 11*, 297-323.

McKnight, D.H., Choudhury, V., & Kacmar, C. (2002). Developing and validating trust measures for e-commerce: An integrative typology. *Information Systems Research, 13*(3), 334–359.

Menczer, F., Street, W. N., & Monge, A. E. (2002). Adaptive Assistants for Customized E-Shopping. *IEEE Intelligent Systems, 17*(6), 12-19.

Metaxiotis, K., Psarras, J., & Samouilidis, J. (2004). New applications of fuzzy logic in decision support systems. *International Journal of Management and Decision Making, 5*(1), 47 – 58.

Metzger, M. J. (2006). Effects of site, vendor, and consumer characteristics on Web site trust and disclosure. *Communication Research, 33*(3), 155-179.

Meziane, F., & Kasiran, M. K. (2003). Extracting unstructured information from the WWW to support merchant existence in e-commerce. In A. Dusterhoft & B. Thalheim (Eds.), *Lecture Notes in Informatics, Natural Language Processing and Information Systems, GI-Edition*, (pp. 175-185). Bonn, Germany.

Michelson, M. J. (2005). *Building queryable datasets from ungrammatical and unstructured sources.* M.S. thesis, University of Southern California.

Michelson, M. J., & Knoblock, C. A. (2007). An automatic approach to semantic annotation of unstructured, ungrammatical sources: A first look. *IJCAI'07 Workshop on Analytics for Noisy Unstructured Text Data*, January 8, Hyderabad, India, (pp. 123-130).

Midgley, D. F., & Dowling, G. R. (1978). Innovativeness: The concept and its measurement. *Journal of Consumer Research, 4*, 229-242.

Miyazaki, A. D., & Fernandez, A. (2001). Consumer perceptions of privacy and security risks for online shopping. *Journal of Consumer Affairs, 35*(1), 27-44.

Modahl, M. (2000). *Now or never.* New York: Harper Collins.

Mohanty, B. K., & Bhasker, B. (2005). Product classification in the Internet Business: a fuzzy approach. *Journal of Decision Support Systems, 38*, 611-619.

Molenaar, C. (2002). *The future of marketing: Practical strategies for marketers in the post-Internet age.* London: Financial Times Prentice Hall.

Monsuwé, T.P.Y., Dellaert, B.G.C., & deRuyter, K. (2004). What drives consumers to shop online? A literature review. *International Journal of Service Industry Management, 15*(1), 102–121.

Montgomery, A. L., Hosanagar, K., Krishnan, R., & Clay, K. B. (2004). Designing a Better Shopbot. *Management Science, 50*(2), 189-206.

Montgomery, L. A., Hosanagar, K., Krishnan, R., & Clay, K. B. (2003). Designing a Better Shopbot. *Management Science, 50*(2), 189-206.

Moon, J.W., & Kim, Y.-G. (2001). Extending the TAM for a World-Wide-Web context. *Information & Management, 38*(4), 217–230.

Moore, G., & Benbasat, I. (1991). Development of an instrument to measure the perceptions of adopting an information technology innovation. *Information Systems Research, 2*(3), 192-223.

Moorthy, S., Ratchford, B., & Talukdar, D. (1997). Consumer information search revisited: theory and empirical analysis. *Journal of Consumer Research*, March, (pp. 263–77).

Morgan, R., & Hunt, S., (1994). The commitment-trust theory of relationship marketing. *Journal of Marketing, 58*, 20-38.

Moriarty, R., & Moran, U. (1990). Managing hybrid marketing systems. *Harvard Business Review, 68*(6), 146–155.

Moshe, D. (2003). Have you heard the word? The effect of word of mouth on perceived justice, satisfaction and repurchase intentions following complaint handling. *Journal of Consumer Satisfaction, Dissatisfaction, and Complaining Behavior, 16*, 67-80.

Mulhern, F. (1997). Retail Marketing: From distribution to integration. *International Journal of Research in Marketing, 14*(2), 103-124.

Muslea, I., Minton, S., & Knoblock, C. (2001). Hierarchical wrapper induction for semistructured information source. *Journal of Autonomous Agents and Multi-Agent Systems, 4*(1-2), 93-114.

Myers, J.B., Pickersgill, A.D., & Van Metre, E.S. (2004). Steering customers to the right channels. *McKinsey Quarterly, 2004*(4), 36–47.

Myerscough, M.A. (2002, August). Information systems quality assessment: Replicating Kettinger and Lee's USIF/SERVQUAL combination. In *Proceedings of the 8th Americas Conference on Information Systems*, Dallas, Texas, USA (pp. 1104–1115).

Mylene, M. (2006). E-Commerce; Ad Vantage: New tools help marketers figure out which campaigns are worth it -- and which aren't. *Wall Street Journal*, p. R.11.

MySimon. (2000). See http://www.mysimon.com.

Napier, H. A, Judd, P. J., Rivers, O. N., & Adams, A. (2003). *E-Business Technologies*. Boston, Massachusetts: Course Technology.

Nelson, R. A., Cohen, R., & Rasmussen, F. R. (2007). An analysis of pricing strategy and price dispersion on the internet. *Eastern Economic Journal, 33*(1), 95-110.

Newman, J. W., & Staelin, R. (1972). Prepurchase information seeking for new cars and major household appliances. *Journal of Marketing Research, 9* (August), 249-257.

Newman, J., & Staelin, R. (1971). Multivariate analysis of differences in buying decision time. *Journal of Marketing Research*, 8 May, (pp. 192-8).

Ngai, E., & Wat, F. (2005). *Fuzzy decision support system for risk analysis in e-commerce development*.

Ng-Kruelle, G., Swatman, P. A., Rebme, D. S., & Hampe, J. F. (2002). The Price of Convenience: Privacy and Mobile Commerce. *Quarterly Journal of Electronic Commerce, 3*(3), 273-285.

Nielsen Media Research. (2008). Over 875 million consumers have shopped on line. See http://www.nielsenmedia.com. January 2008.

Nielsen//NetRatings (2007). Search Engine Strategies conference 2007, 13-15 February. Retrieved July 2, 2008, from http://www.searchenginesstrategies.com.

Nikitkov, A. (2006). Information assurance seals: How they impact consumer purchasing behavior. *Journal of Information System. 20*(1), 1-17.

Nohria, N., & Leestma, M. (2001) A Moving Target: The Mobile-Commerce Customer. *Sloan Management Review, 42*(3), 104-115.

Noteberg, A., Christiaanse, E., & Wallage, P. (2003). Consumer Trust in Electronic Channels. *E- Service Journal, 2*(2), 46-67.

Nour, M. A., & Fadlalla, A. (2000). A framework for Web marketing strategies: The e-commerce revolution. *Information Systems Management, 17*(22), 41-50.

Novak, T., Hoffman, D. L., & Yung, Y. (2000). Measuring the customer experience in online environments: A structural modeling approach. *Marketing Science, 19*(1), 22-42.

Nunnally, J. (1978). *Psychometric Theory*. New York: McGraw-Hill.

Nyongesa, H., Shicheng, T., Maleki-Dizaji, S., Huang, S. T., & Siddiqi, J. (2003). Adaptive Web Interface Design Using Fuzzy Logic. *IEEE/WIC International Conference on Web Intelligence, 13*(17), 671- 674.

O'Dea, F. (2000). Mobile-Commerce – Trend in Wireless Interactions. *Anderson Consulting Report*.

Odom, M. D., Kumar, A., & Saunders, L. (2002). Web assurance seals: How and why they influence consumers' decisions. *Journal of Information Systems, 16*(2), 231-250.

Office of Workers' Compensation Programs (OWCP). (2008). Retrieved July 12, 2008, from http://www.dol.gov/esa/owcp/dlhwc/NAWWinfo.htm

Olla, P., Atkinson, C., & Gandceha, R. (2003). Wireless Systems Development Methodologies: An Analysis of Practice Using Actor Network Theory. *Journal of Computer Information Systems, XXXXIV*(1), 102-119.

Olshavsky, R. W. (1985). Towards a more comprehensive theory of choice. In E. Hirschman and M. T. Holbrook (Eds.), *Advances in Consumer Research, 12*, 465-470.

Online shopping still causes anxiety. (2004, January). *Credit Management*, 12.

Öörni, A, (2003).Consumer Search in Electronic Markets. *European Journal of Information Systems,* (2003) *12*, 30-40.

Öörni, A. (2002). *Consumer Search in Electronic Markets,* Dissertation in Helsinki School of Economics, Acta Universitatis Oeconomicae Helsingiensis, A-197.

Öörni, A. (2002). Dominant search pattern in electronic markets: Sequential or agent search search, *HSE Working papers,* W-31

OWL-S. (2004). Semantic Markup for Web Services. See http://www.w3.org/Submission/OWL-S/.

Padgham, L., & Winikoff, M. (2004). *Developing Intelligent Agent Systems: A Practical Guide.* Chichester: Wiley & Sons.

Pal, N., & Rangaswamy, A. (2006). *The Power of One: Gaining Business Value from Personalization Technologies.* Penn State University: eBRC Press.

Paolucci, M., & Sycara, K. (2003). Autonomous Semantic Web Services. *IEEE Internet Computing, 7*(5), 34-41.

Paper, D., Pedersen, E., & Mulbery, K. (2003). An e-commerce process model: Perspectives from e-commerce entrepreneurs. *Journal of Electronic Commerce in Organizations, 1*(3), 28-47.

Parasuraman, A., & Zinkham, G. (2002). Marketing and serving customers through the internet: An overview and research agenda. *Journal of the Academy of Marketing Science, 30,* 286-295.

Parasuraman, A., Zeithaml, V. A, & Berry, L. L. (1988). SERVQUAL: a multiple-item scale for measuring consumer perceptions of quality. *Journal of Retailing, 64*(1), 12-40.

Parasuraman, A., Zeithaml, V. A., & Berry, L. L. (1985). A conceptual model of service quality and its implications for future research. *Journal of Marketing, 49*(4), 41-50.

Park, C. W., & Lessig, P. V. (1981). Familiarity and Its Impact on Consumer Decision Biases and Heuristics. *Journal of Consumer Research, 8*(2), 223.

Park, C. W., Mothersbaugh, D. L., & Feick, L. (1994). Consumer Knowledge Assessment. *Journal of Consumer Research, 21*(1), 71-82.

Park, C., & Kim, Y. (2003). Identifying key factors affecting consumer purchase behaviour in an online shopping context. *International Journal of Retail and Distribution Management, 31*(1), 16-29.

Parkinson, T. L. (2002). The role of seals and certifications of approval in consumer decision-making. *Journal of Consumer Affairs, 9,* 1-14.

Pastore, M. (2000). *Future of E-tail lies with multichannel retailers.* http://cyberatlas.internet.com/markets/retailing/article/0,1323,6061_417411,00.html

Pavlou, P. A. (2003). Consumer acceptance of electronic commerce integrating trust and risk with the technology acceptance model. *International Journal of Electronic Commerce, 7*(3), 101-134.

Payne, J. W., Bettman, J. R., & Johnson, E. J. (1993). *The adaptive decision maker.* Cambridge: Cambridge University Press.

Payne, J. W., Bettman, J. R., & Johnson, E. J. (2003). *The Adaptive Decision Maker.* New York, NY: Cambridge University Press.

Pechtl, H. (2003). Adoption of online shopping by German grocery shoppers. *The International Review of Retail, Distribution and Consumer Research, 13*(2), 145-159.

Petersen, S. A., Divitini, M., & Matskin, M. (2001). An Agent-based approach to modelling virtual enterprises. *Production, Planning and Control, 12*(3), 224-233.

Peterson, R. A., Balasubramanian, S., & Bronnenberg, B. J. (1997). Exploring the implications of the Internet for consumer marketing. *Journal of the Academy of Marketing Science, 25*(4), 329-346.

Peterson, R., & Merino, M. (2003). Consumer information search behavior and the Internet. *Psychology & Marketing, 20*(2), 99-122.

Peterson, R., Balasubramanian, S. A., & Bronnenberg, B. J. (1997). Exploring the implications of the Internet for consumer marketing. *Journal of the Academy of Marketing Science, 25*(4), 329-346.

Peterson, R.A., Albaum, G., & Ridway, N.M. (1989). Consumer who buy from direct sales companies. *Journal of Retailing, 65*(3), 273-286.

Pflughoeft, K.A., Ramamurthy, K., Soofi, E.S., Yasai-Ardekani, M., & Zahedi, F. (2003). Multiple conceptualizations of small business Web use and benefit. *Decision Sciences, 34*(3), 467–512.

Piercy, N. F., & Cravens, D. W. (1995). The network paradigm and the marketing organization. *European Journal of Marketing, 29*(3), 7-34.

Pinker, E. J., Seidmann, A., & Foster, R. C. (2002). Strategies for transitioning "old economy" firms to e-business. *Communications of the ACM, 45*(5), 77-83.

Plitch, P. (2002). Are Bots Legal? *Wall Street Journal, 240*(54), R13.

Plitch, P. (2002). E-Commerce (A Special Report): The Rules --- Law: Are Bots Legal? --- Comparison-shopping sites say they make the Web manageable; Critics say they trespass. *Wall Street Journal, 240*(54), R.13.

Porter, M. E. (1980). *Competitive Strategy.* New York, NY: Free Press.

Porter, M. E. (1985). *The Competitive Advantage: Creating and Sustaining Superior Performance.* N.Y.: Free Press,

Porter, M. E. (2001). Strategy and the Internet. *Harvard Business Review, 79*(3), 63-76.

Preston, D. (1998). Business Ethics and Privacy in the Workplace. *ACM Computers and Society*, (pp. 12-18).

PriceGrabber. (2008). See http://www.pricegrabber.com.

Producer Price Indexes Introduced for the Wholesale Trade Sector—NAICS 423, 424, and 425120. (2006). from http://www.bls.gov/ppi/ppiwholesale.htm

Punj, G., & Staelin, R. (1983). A model of consumer information search for new automobiles. *Journal of Consumer Research, 9*(4), 336-380.

Punj, G., & Staelin, R. (1983). A Model of Consumer Information Search Behavior for New Automobiles. *Journal of Consumer Research*, March, 9.

Quality and Its Implications for Future Research. *Journal of Marketing, 49*(4), 41-50.

Quelch, J. A., & Klein, L. R. (1996, February). The Internet and international marketing. *Sloan Management Review, 37*, 60-75.

Rackoff, N., Wiseman, C., & Ullrich, W. (1985). Information systems for competitive advantage: Implementation of a planning process. *MIS Quarterly, 9*(4), 285-294.

Rahman, S.M., & Bignall, R.J. (2001). *Internet Commerce and Software Agents: Cases, Technologies and Opportunities.* Hershey: IDEA Group Publishing.

Raiffa, H., & Keeney, R. L. (1976). *Decisions with Multiple Objectives.* New York: Wiley.

Rajiv, V., & Aggarwal, P. (2002). The impact of shopping agents on small business ecommerce strategy. *Journal of Small Business Strategy, 13*(1), 62-79.

Ranchhod, A., & Gurau, C. (1999). Internet-enabled distribution strategies. *Journal of Information Technology, 14*(4), 333-346.

Randall, T., Ulrich, K., & Reibstein, D. (1998). Brand equity and vertical product line extension. *Marketing Science, 12*, 356-379.

Ranganathan, C., & Ganapathy, S. (2002). Key dimensions of business-to-consumer Web sites. *Information & Management, 39*(6), 457-465.

Rayport, J. F., & Sviokla, J. J. (1995). Exploiting the Virtual Value Chain. *Harvard Business Review, 73*(6), 75-85.

Red.es (2007). Estudio sobre Comercio Electrónico B2C. Retrieved May 14 2007, from http://www.red.es.

Reibstein, D. (2002). What attracts customers to online stores and what keeps them coming back? *Journal of the Academy of Marketing Science, 30*(4), 465-473.

Reichheld, F., & Schefter, P. (2000). E-loyalty: Your secret weapon on the Web. *Harvard Business Review, 78*(4), 105–113.

Resnick, P., Kuwabara, K., Zeckhauser, R., & Friedman, E. (2000). Reputation systems. *Communications of the ACM, 43*(12), 45-48.

Resource Library - Dictionary. (2008). Retrieved April 4, 2008, from http://www.marketingpower.com/_layouts/Dictionary.aspx?dLetter=P

Reynolds, F.D. (1974). An analysis of catalog buying behavior. *Journal of Marketing, 38*(3), 47–51.

Rheault, M. (2004). The Kiplinger monitor. *Kiplinger's Personal Finance, 58*(2), 22.

Rifkin, G., & Kurtzman, J. (2002). Is your e-business plan radical enough? *Sloan Management Review, 43*(3), 91-95.

Rodgers, S., & Harris, M.A. (2003). Gender and e-commerce: An exploratory study. *Journal of Advertising Research, 43*(3), 322–329.

Rogers, E. M. (1995). *Diffusion of innovations* (4th edition). New York: The Free Press.

Rogers, E. M., & Rogers, E. (2003). *Diffusion of innovations* (5th edition). New York: The Free Press.

Rogers, E. M., & Shoemaker, F. F. (1971). *Communication of innovations: A cross-cultural approach*. New York: The Free Press.

Rohm, A., & Swaminathan, V. (2004). A typology of online shoppers based on shopping motivations. *Journal of Business Research, 57*(12), 748-757.

Rosen, E. (2000). *The anatomy of buzz: how to create word-of-month marketing* (First Edition ed.). New York: Random House.

Routray, S., Sherry, A. M., & Reddy, B. V. R. (2208). Wireless ATM: A Technological Framework to m-

Banking. *Journal of Internet Banking and Commerce 13*(1), 1-11.

Rowley, J. (1998). *The Electronic Library*. London: Facet Publishing.

Rowley, J. (2000). Product searching with shopping bots. *Internet Research, 10*(3), 203-215.

Rowley, J. (2000). Product search in e-shopping: a review and research propositions. *Journal of Consumer Marketing, 17*(1), 20-35.

Rowley, J. (2000). Product searching with shopping bots, *Internet Research: Eletronic Networking Applications and Policy, 10*(3), 203-214.

Rowley, J. (2002). 'Window' shopping and browsing opportunities in cyberspace. *Journal of Consumer Behaviour, 1*(4), 369-378.

Russell, S., & Norvig, P. (2002). *Artificial Intelligence: A Modern Approach* (2nd ed.). Upper Saddle River, NJ Prentice Hall.

Rust, R., & Zahorik, A., (1993). Customer satisfaction, customer retention, and market share. *Journal of Retailing, 69*, 193-215.

Rust, R., Zeithaml, V., & Lemon, K. (2000). *Driving customer equity: How customer lifetime value is reshaping corporate strategy*. NY: Free Press.

Sadeh, N. M., & Lee, J. K. (2003). Advances in B2B e-commerce and e-supply chain management. *Journal of Organizational Computing & Electronic Commerce, 13*(3/4), 163-165.

Saeed, K. A., Hwang, Y., & Grover, V. (2003). Investigating the Impact of Web Site Value and Advertising on Firm Performance in Electronic Commerce. *International Journal of Electronic Commerce, 7*(2), 119-141.

Salaun, Y., & Flores, K. (2001). Information quality: Meeting the needs of the consumer. *International Journal of Information Management, 21*, 21-37.

Salisbury, W.D., Pearson, R.A., Pearson, A.W., & Miller, D.W. (2001). Perceived security and World Wide Web purchase intention. *Industrial Management & Data Systems, 101*(3/4), 165-176.

Sanderson, B. (2000). Cyberspace retailing a threat to traditionalists. *Retail World, 53*(14), 6-7.

Sandhusen, R. L. (2000). *Marketing.* Hauppauge, NY: Barron's Educational Series.

Santos, S. C., Angelim, S., & Meira, S. R. (2001). Building comparison-shopping brokers on the Web. *Proceedings of the Second international Workshop on Electronic Commerce* November 16-17, L. Fiege, G. Mühl, and U. G. Wilhelm, Eds. *LNCS 2232,* 26-38.

SCCI. (2006). *Amazon timeline history Q3 2006.* Retrieved April 2, 2007, from http://media.corporate-ir.net/media_files/irol/17/176060/TimelineHistoryQ32006.pdf.

Schiesel, S. (1997, January 2). Payoff still elusive on Internet gold rush. *The New York Times,* p. C17.

Schlosser, A. E., White, T. B., & Lloyd, S. M. (2006). Converting Web site visitors into buyers: How Web site investment increases consumer trusting beliefs and online purchase intentions. *Journal of Marketing, 70*(2), 133-148.

Schoenbachler, D.D., & Gordon, G.L. (2002). Multi-channel shopping: Understanding what drives channel choice. *The Journal of Consumer Marketing, 19*(1), 42–53.

Schwartz, B. (2004). *The Paradox of Choice.* New York: HarperCollins.

Seager, A. (2003). M-Commerce: An Integrated Approach. *Telecommunications International, 37*(2), 36-38.

Seiders, K., & Berry, L. L. (1998). Service Fairness: What It Is and Why It Matters. *Academy Management Executive, 12*(2), 8-21.

Seiders, K., Berry, L. L., & Gresham, L. G. (2000). Attention, retailers! How convenient is your convenience strategy? *Sloan Management Review, 41*(3), 79-89.

Selnes, F. (1998). Antecedents and consequences of trust and satisfaction on buyer-seller relationships. *European Journal of Marketing, 3,* 305-322.

Sen, R., King, R. C., & Shaw, M. J. (2006). Buyers' Choice of Online Search Strategy and Its Managerial Implications. *Journal of Management Information Systems, 23*(1), 211-238.

Sewell, C., & Brown, P. (2002) *Customers for life: How to turn that one buyer into a customer for life.* NY: Doubleday.

Shapiro, C., & Varian, H. R. (1998). *Information Rules: A Strategic Guide to the Network Economy.* Cambridge, MA: Harvard Business School Press.

Shaw, M., Blanning, R., & Strader, T. (Eds.) (2000). *Handbook on Electronic Commerce.* London: Springer.

Sheppard, B., Hartwick, J., & Warshaw, P. (1988). The theory of reasoned action: A meta-analysis of past research with recommendations for modifications and future research. *Journal of Consumer Research, 15*(3), 325-344.

Sheth, J.N. (1983). An integrative theory of patronage preference and behavior. In W.R. Darden, & R.F. Lusch (Eds.), *Patronage behavior and retail management* (pp. 9–28). New York: Elsevier Science Publishing.

Shih, H. P. (2004). An empirical study on predicting user acceptance of e-shopping on the Web. *Information & Management, 41*(3), 351-368.

Shop.org. (2002). See at http://www.shop.org/learn/stats_usshop_general.asp.

Shopping.com. (2008). See http://www.shopping.com.

Siau, K., & Shen, Z. (2002). Mobile Commerce Applications in Supply Chain Management. *Journal of Internet Commerce, 1*(3), 3-14.

Sidestep (2008). See http://www.sidestep.com.

Sieber, J. E., & Lanzetta, J. T. (1964). Conflict and Conceptual Structure as Determinants of Decision making Behavior. *Journal of Personality, 32*(4), 622-641.

Sim, L., & Koi, S. (2002). Singapore's Internet shoppers and their impact on traditional shopping patterns. *Journal of Retailing and Consumer Services, 9*(2), 115-124.

Simon, H. A. (1955). A behavioral model of rational choice. *Quarterly Journal of Economics, 69*(1), 20.

Simon, H. A. (1956). Rational choice and the structure of the environment. *Psychological Review, 63*, 129-138.

Singh, I. (2000, March/April). Cost transparency: The net's real threat to prices and brands. *Harvard Business Review, 78*, 3.

Singh, M. P. (2000). The Service Web. *IEEE Internet Computing, 4*(4), 4-5.

Singh, M. P., & Huhns, M. N. (2005). *Service-oriented computing: Semantics, Processes, Agents.* Chichester: John Wiley and Sons.

Smith, J. B., & Spreng, R. (1996). A proposed model of external consumer information search, Journal of the *Academy of Marketing Science, 24*, Summer, 246-56.

Smith, M. (2002). The impact of shopbots on electronic markets. *Journal of the Academy of Marketing Science, 30*(4), 446-454.

Smith, M., & Brynjolfsson, E. (2001). Consumer decision making at an Internet shopbot: Brand still matters. *The Journal of Industrial Economics, 49*(4), 541-558.

SOAP. (2003). Simple Object Access Protocol. See http://www.w3.org/TR/soap/.

Solomon, M. R. (1986). The Missing Link: Surrogate Consumers in the Marketing Chain. *Journal of Marketing, 50*(October), 208-218.

Spiller, P., & Lohse, G. L. (1998). A classification of Internet retail stores. *International Journal of Electronic Commerce, 2*(2), 29-56.

Spink, A., Koshman, S., & Jansen, B. J. (2005). Multitasking on the Vivisimo Web Search Engine. *IEEE ITCC International Conference on Information Technology, 2005*, LA.

Spreng, R. A., & Olshavsky, R. W. (1993). A Desires Congruency Model of Consumer Satisfaction. *Journal of the Academy of Marketing Science, 21*(3), 169-177.

Sproule, S., & Archer, N. (2000). A buyer behaviour framework for the development and design of software agents in e-commerce. *Internet Research: Electronic Networking Applications and Policy, 10*(5), 396-405.

Srinivasan, N., & Ratchford, B. (1991). An Empirical test of a model of external search for automobiles. *Journal of Consumer Research, 18.*

Srinivasan, N., Paolucci, M., & Sycara, K. (2004). An Efficient Algorithm for OWL-S Based Semantic Search in UDDI. In *Semantic Web Services and Web Process Composition, First International Workshop, SWSWPC 2004, Revised Selected Papers* (pp. 96-110). Berlin: Springer.

Srinivasan, S., Anderson, R., & Ponnavolu, K. (2002). Customer loyalty in e-commerce: an exploration of its antecedents and consequences. *Journal of Retailing, 78*(1), 41-50.

Stallings, W. (2003). *Network Security Essentials: Applications and Standards.* Upper Saddle River, NJ: Prentice Hall.

Stauss, B. (2002). The dimensions of complaint satisfaction: Process and outcome, complaint satisfaction versus cold fact and warm act complaint satisfaction. *Managing Service Quality, 12*(3), 173-183.

Steckel, J. (2000). *On-line shopping: how many will come to the party? And when they will get there?* (Working paper). New York: University of New York, Stern School of Business.

Steenkamp, J., Hofstede, G., & Wedel, M. (1999). A cross-national investigation into the individual and national antecedents of consumer innovativeness. *Journal of Marketing, 63* (April), 55-69.

Steinfield, C., Bouwman, H., & Adelaar, T. (2002). The dynamics of click-and-mortar electronic commerce: Opportunities and management strategies. *International Journal of Electronic Commerce, 7*(1), 93–119.

Stewart, K. J. (2003). Trust transfer on the World Wide Web. *Organization Science, 14*(1), 5-17.

Stigler, G. (1961). The economics of information. *The Journal of Political Economy, 49*(3), 213-225.

Sugumaran, V. (2007). *International Journal of Intelligent Information Technologies, 3*(4), *Support Systems, 2*(40), 235-255. IGI Global.

Suh, B., & Han, I. (2003). The impact of customer trust and perception of security control on the acceptance of electronic commerce. *International Journal of Electronic Commerce, 7*(3), 135–162.

Tan, C. H. (2003, December). *Comparison-Shopping websites: An Empirical Investigation on the Influence of Decision Aids and Information Load on Consumer Decision-Making Behavior.* Paper presented at the The 24th Annual International Conference on Information Systems (ICIS), Seattle, WA.

Tan, P., Madnick, S. E., & Tan, K. L (2004). Context mediation in the semantic Web: Handling OWL ontology and data disparity through context interchange. Processing of Semantic Web and Database (SWDB), (pp. 140-154).

Tanenbaum, A. S. (2002). *Computer Networks* (Fourth ed.). Upper Saddle River, NJ Prentice Hall PTR.

Tarafdar, M., & Zhang, J. (2005). Analyzing the influence of Web site design parameters on Web site usability. *Information Resources Management Journal, 18*(4), 62-80.

Tax, S. S., & Brown, S. W. (1998). Recovering and learning from service failure. *Sloan Management Review, 40*(1), 75-88.

Tax, S. S., Brown, S. W., & Chandrashekaran, M. (1998). Customer evaluations of service complaint experiences: Implications for relationship marketing. *Journal of Marketing, 6292*, 60-76.

Taylor, J. W. (1977). A striking characteristic of innovators. *Journal of Marketing Research, 14*(1), 104-107.

Taylor, S., & Todd, P. (1995). Understanding information technology usage: A test of competing models. *Information Systems Research, 6*(2), 144-176.

Taylor, S., & Todd, P.A. (1995). Understanding information technology usage: A test of competing models. *Information Systems Research, 6*(2), 144–176.

Teo, T.S.H., & Yeong, Y.D. (2003). Assesing the consumer decision process in the digital marketplace. *The International Journal of Management Science, 31*, 349-363.

Thayer, G. (2002a). M-Commerce: Long Trek to the Promised Land. *Pen Computing 9*(45), 17.

Thompson, B. (2003). Multi-Channel service: Boosting customer value and loyalty. *RightNow Technologies. Available* for download at http://www.rightnow.com/resource/crm-whitepapers.html

Timiraos, N. (2006, December 23). Web Can Pay Off for Traditional Retailers. *Wall Street Journal.*

Todd, P. A. (1988). *An Experimental Investigation of the Impact of Computer Based Decision Aids on the Process of Preferential Choice.* The University of British Columbia, Vancouver.

Todd, P., & Benbasat, I. (1992). The Use of Information in Decision Making: An Experimental Investigation of the Impact of Computer-Based Decision Aids. *MIS Quarterly, 16*(3), 373-393.

Todd, P., & Benbasat, I. (1999). Evaluating the Impact of DSS, Cognitive Effort, and Incentives on Strategy Selection. *Information Systems Research, 10*(4), 356-374.

Torkzadeh, G., & Dhillon, G. (2002). Measuring factors that influence the success of Internet commerce. *Information Systems Research, 13*(2), 187-204.

Tornatzky, L. G., & Klein, R. J. (1982). Innovation characteristics and innovation adoption-implementation: A metaanalysis of findings. *IEEE Transactions on Engineering Management, 29*(1), 28-45.

Trevino, L. K., & Webster, J. (1992). Flow in computer-mediated communication: Electronic mail and voice mail evaluation and impacts. *Communication Research,* *19*(5), 539-573.

Trocchia, P., & Janda, S. (2000). A phenomenological investigation of Internet usage among older individuals. *Journal of Consumer Marketing, 17*(7), 605-616.

Trocchia, P., & Janda, S. (2003). How do consumers evaluate Internet retail service quality? *Journal of Services Marketing, 17*(3), 243-253.

Tversky, A. (1972). Elimination by aspects: A theory of choice. *Psychological Review, 79*(281-299).

U.S. Census Bureau News. (2008). Quarterly retail e-commerce sales 2nd quarter 2008. See http://www.census.giv/mrts/www/data/html/08Q2.html, August 2008.

U.S. Census Bureau. (2007). *Quarterly retail e-commerce sales.* Retrieved February 13, 2008, from http://www.census.gov/mrts/www/ecomm.html

U.S. Department of Justice. (2007). *Internet and telemarketing fraud.* Retrieved February 13, 2008, from http://www.usdoj.gov/criminal/fraud/internet/#howtodeal

UDDI. (2006). Universal Description, Discovery and Integration protocol. See http://www.uddi.org/.

Ulfelder, S. (2000). Undercover Agents. Computer World, See http://65.221.110.98/news/2000/story/0,11280,45452,00.html, June 2000.

Urban, G. L., Sultan, F., & Qualls W. J. (2000). Placing trust at the center of your Internet strategy. *Sloan Management Review, 42*(1), 39-48.

Urbany, J. E. (1986). An Experimental Examination of the Economics of Information. *Journal of Consumer Research, 13*, Sep 1986.

Urbany, J., Dickson, P., & Wilkie, W. (1989). Buyer Uncertainty and Information Search. *Journal of Consumer Research*, September 1989, *16*.

Vahidov, K., & Fazlollahi, R. (2004). Multi-agent DSS for supporting e-commerce decisions. *Journal of Computer Information Systems, 44*(2).

Van den Poel, D., & Leunis, J. (1999). Consumer acceptance of the Internet as a channel of distribution. *Journal of Business Research, 45,* 249-256.

Van Slyke, C., & Belanger, F. (2004). Factors influencing the adoption of Web-based shopping: The impact of trust. *Database for Advances in Information Systems, 35*(2), 32- 49.

Van Slyke, C., Comunale, C. L., & Belanger, F. (2002). Gender differences in perceptions of Web-based shopping. *Communications of the ACM, 45*(7), 82-86.

Varadarajan, R., & Yadav, M. (2002). Marketing strategy and the Internet: An organizing framework. *Journal of the Academy of Marketing Science, 30,* 296-312.

Vatanasombut, B., Stylianou, A.C., & Igbaria, M. (2004). How to retain online customers. *Communications of the ACM, 47*(6), 64-70.

Venkatraman, N. (1989). The concept of fit in strategy research: Toward verbal and statistical correspondence. *Academy of Management Review, 14*(3), 423–444.

Verma, K., Sivashanmugam, K., Sheth, A., Patil, A., Oundhakar, S., & Miller, J. (2005). METEOR-S WSDI: A scalable P2P infrastructure of registries for semantic publication and discovery of web services. *Information Technology and Management, 6*(1), 17-39.

Vijayasarathy, L. R. (2004). Predicting consumer intentions to use on-line shopping: The case for an augmented technology acceptance model. *Information & Management, 41*(6), 747-762.

Vulkan, N. (2003). *The Economics of E-commerce.* Princeton, NJ: Princeton University Press.

Wakefield, R. L., & Whitten D. (2006). Examining user perceptions of third-party organization credibility and trust in an e-retailer. *Journal of Organizational and End User Computing, 18*(2), 1-19.

Wallace, D.W., Giese, J.L., & Johnson, J.L. (2004). Customer retailer loyalty in the context of multiple channel strategies. *Journal of Retailing, 80*(4), 249–263.

Wan, H. A. (2000). Opportunities to enhance a commercial Website. *Information & Management, 38*(1), 15-21.

Wan, Y. (2005). *The Impact of Web-based Product Comparison Agent on Choice Overload in Online Individual Decision-Making.* University of Illinois at Chicago, Chicago.

Wan, Y., Menon, S., & Ramaprasad, A. (2003). A classification of product comparison agents. In *Proceedings of the Fifth International Conference on Electronic Commerce, ICEC'03* (pp.498-504). New York, NY: ACM.

Wan, Y., Menon, S., & Ramaprasad, A. (2007). A Classification of Product Comparison Agents. *Communications of the ACM, 50*(8), 65-71.

Wang, S., Beatty, S. E., & Foxx, W. (2004). Signaling the trustworthiness of small online retailers. *Journal of Interactive Marketing, 18*(1), 53-69.

Webb, H. W., & Webb, L. A. (2004). SiteQual: An integrated measure of Web site quality. *Journal of Enterprise Information Management, 17*(6), 430-440.

Weinberg, B. D. (2000). *24/7 Internet Shopping Diary.* Retrieved from http://www.internetshopping 247.com

Weinberg, B. D. (2001). The three faces of e-commerce: Insight into online consumer behavior through the interpretation of an Internet consumer's experiences. *Advances in Consumer Research, 28*(1), 218-221.

Wen, H. J., & Gyires, T. (2002). The Impact of Wireless Application Protocol (WAP) on M-Commerce Security. *Journal of Internet Commerce, (3),* 15-27.

West, P., Ariely, D., Bellman, S., Bradlow, E., Huber, J., Johnson, E., Kuhn, B., Little, J., & Schkade, D. (1999). Agents to the rescue? *Marketing letters, 10,* 285-301.

Westbrook, R. (1987). Product/consumption-based affective responses and postpurchase processes. *Journal of Marketing Research, 24* (March), 258-270.

Whinston, A. B., Stahl, D. O. et al. (1997). *The Economics of Electronic Commerce.* Indianapolis, Macmillan Technical Publishing.

White, C. (2004) *Data Communiations and Computer Networks* (3rd ed.). Boston, Massachusetts: Course Technology.

White, E. (2000). E-Commerce (A Special Report): The Lessons We've Learned --- Comparison Shopping: No Comparison --- Shopping `bots' were supposed to unleash brutal price wars. Why haven't they? . *Wall Street Journal*, R.18.

White, H. (1980). A Heteroskedasticity-Consistent Covariance Matrix estimator and a Direct Test for Heteroskedasticity. *Econometrica., 48,* 817-838.

Whitt, W. (1999). Improving Service by Informing Customers about Anticipated Delays. *Management Science, 45*(2), 192-207.

Wiederhold, G. (1992). Mediators in the architecture of future information systems. *Computer, 25*(3), 38-49.

Wilkie, W. (1975). *How consumers use product information: An assessment of research in relation to public policy needs*, Washington, D.C.: National Science Foundation.1985.

Williamson, R. (2001). Creating a better brighter smarter Internet. *Interactive Week, 8*(39), 26-29.

Winkler, W.E. (2006). Overview of Record Linkage and Current Research Directions, Research Report, Statistics #2006-2, US Census Bureau, available at http://www.census.gov/srd/papers/pdf/rrs2006-02.pdf.

Wireless Business Forecast. (2005). Wireless in the Driver's Seat. *Wireless Business Forecast, 13*(4), Feb. 24, 1.

Wolfingarger, M., & Gilly, M. C. (2001). Shopping online for freedom, control, and fun. *California Management Review, 43*(2), 34-55.

Wollin, L.D. (2003). Gender issues in advertising- An oversight synthesis of research: 1970-2002. *Journal of Advertising Research*, March, (pp. 111-129).

Wong, H. C., & Sycara, K. (2000). A taxonomy of middle-agents for the Internet. In *Proceedings of the Fourth International Conference on MultiAgent Sys-*

tems, ICMAS-00 (pp.465-466). Washington, DC: IEEE Computer Society.

Wooldridge, M., & Jennings, N. R. (1995). Intelligent Agents: Theory and Practice. *Knowledge Engineering Review, 10*(2), 115-152.

Worthington, S. L. S., & Boyes, W. (2001). *E-business in manufacturing: Putting the Internet to work in the industrial enterprises*. Research Triangle Park, NC: Instrumentation, Systems and Automation Society.

Wotruba, T., & Privoba, M. (1995). Direct selling in an emerging market economy: A comparison of central Europe with the U.S. In T. Wotruba (Ed.), *Proceedings of the International Academic Symposium on Direct Selling in Central and Eastern Europe* (pp. 87-193). Washington, DC: Direct Selling Education Foundation:

Wu, C. H. (2006). *Portio Research: Half of World Population will be Pan-Pacific Mobile Phone Users in Ten Years*. Retrieved from http://www.find.org.tw/find/home. aspx?page=news&id=4117 .

Wu, D., Ray, G., Geng, X., & Whinston, A. (2004). Implications of reduced search cost and free riding in e-commerce. *Marketing Science, 23*, 255-262.

Wu, F., Mahajan, V., & Balasubramanian, Sridhar (2003). An analysis of e-business adoption and its impact on business performance. *Journal of the Academy of marketing Science, 31*, 425-447.

Xin, W., Xiaojun, S., & Georganas, N. D. (2006). A Fuzzy Logic Based Intelligent Negotiation Agent (FINA) in Ecommerce. Electrical and Computer Engineering, Canadian Conference (pp. 276–279).

Yahoo!Shopping. (2008). See http://shopping.yahoo. com.

Yale, L., & VenKatseh, A. (1986). Toward the Construct of Convenience in Consumer Research. *Advances in Consumer Research, 13*, 403-408.

Yang, B., & Lester, D. (2004). Attitudes toward buying online. *Cyber Psychology & Behavior, 7*(1), 85–91.

Yoh, E., Damhorst, M. L., Sapp, S., & Laczniak, R. (2003). Consumer adoption of the Internet: The case of apparel shopping. *Psychology & Marketing, 20*(12), 1095–1118.

Yoon, D., Cropp, F., & Cameron, G. (2002). Building relationships with portal users: the interplay of motivation and relational factors. *Journal of Interactive Advertising, 3*(1). Retrieved July 13, 2005, from http://jiad. org/vol3/no1/yoon.

Yoon, S. J. (2002). The antecedents and consequences of trust in online-purchase decisions. *Journal of Interactive Marketing, 16*(2), 47-63.

Yousafzai, S.Y., Pallister, J.G., & Foxall, G.R. (2003). A proposed model of e-trust for electronic banking. *Technovation, 23*(11), 847–860.

Yuan, F.-C, (2009). *Expert Systems with Applications, 36*(2), PART 1, 1155–1163.

Zeithaml, V. (1988). Consumer perceptions of price, quality, and value: a means-end model and synthesis of evidence. *Journal of Marketing, 52* (January), 2-22.

Zeithaml, V. A., Parasuraman, A., & Malhotra, A. (2001). A conceptual framework for understanding e-service quality: implications for future research and managerial practice. *MSI Working Paper Series*, No 00-115, Cambridge MA, 1-49.

Zeithaml, V. A., Parasuraman, A., & Malhotra, A. (2002). Service quality delivery through Web sites: a critical review of extant knowledge. *Journal of the Academy of Marketing Science, 30*(4), 362-375.

Zhang, J. J., Yuan, Y., & Archer, N. (2002). Driving Forces for M-Commerce. *Journal of Internet Commerce, 1*(3), 81-106.

Zhang, P., & von Dran, G. M. (2000). Satisfiers and dissatisfiers: A two-factor model for Website design and evaluation. *Journal of the American Society for Information Science, 51*(14), 1253-1268.

Zhang, X., Prybutok, V. R., & Koh, C. E. (2006). The role of impulsiveness in TAM-based online purchasing behavior. *Information Resources Management Journal, 19*(2), 54-68.

Zhu, H. (2002). A technology and policy analysis for global e-business. M.S. thesis, Massachusetts Institute of Technology.

Zhu, H., & Madnick, S. (2006). A lightweight ontology approach to scalable interoperability. *VLDB Workshop on Ontologies-based techniques or DataBases and Information Systems (ODBIS'06)*, September 11, 2006, Seoul, Korea.

Zhu, H., & Madnick, S. E. (2006). Reutilization and legal protection of non-copyrightable database contents. *Proceedings of the Fourth IASTED International Con-*

ference on Law and Technology (LawTech'06), October 9-11, Cambridge, MA, USA.

Zhu, H., Siegel, M., & Madnick, S. (2001). *Information aggregation. A value–added E-service.* Paper presented at the International Conference on Technology, Policy and Innovation: Critical Infraestructures (paper 106), The Netherlands.

Zipf, G. K. (1949). *Human Behavior and the Principle of Least Effort: An introduciton to Human Ecology.* Cambridge: Addison-Wesley Press.

Zviran, M., Glezer, C., & Avni, I. (2006). User satisfaction from commercial Web sites: The effect of design and use. *Information & Management, 43*(2), 157-178.

About the Contributors

Yun Wan is an assistant professor in computer information systems and the Master of Science in Computer Information Systems (MS-CIS) graduate program advisor at the University of Houston, Victoria. His research interests include decision support systems, especially software agents, and e-commerce. Wan has a BS in management and a BE in computer science from the University of Science and Technology of China, and a PhD in management information systems from the University of Illinois at Chicago. Contact him at wany@uhv.edu.

* * *

Dr. Fahim Akhter received his BSc in Management Information Systems from the University of Missouri - St. Louis (USA), M.B.A. from the Lindenwood University (USA), and Ph.D. in Informatics from the University of Bradford (England). Dr. Akhter has more than fifteen years of academic experience in lecturing, curriculum design, and research at the Colgate University of New York, Baruch College at City University of New York and Zayed University. Dr. Akhter's research activities are in the areas of e-commerce, web services, and information security. He has written numerous papers in the areas of information technology and e-business, which have been published in international journals and proceedings such as Information & Software Technology - Elsevier, International Journal of E-Business Research, IEEE and ACM. He has served in program committees, advisory boards, and editorial review boards for various international Journals and conferences.

Maria Fasli is a Senior Lecturer at the Department of Computing and Electronic Systems of the University of Essex. She obtained her Ph.D. in Computer Science in 2000. Her current research interests lie in agents and their theoretical foundations and practical applications, web service discovery and composition, and social networks. She has published papers on logics for reasoning agents, formal models of multi-agent systems, trading agents and platforms, trust, and web search assistants. She is the author of "Agent Technology for E-commerce" (John Wiley and Sons, 2007). Her interests extend to technology-enhanced learning and she was also awarded a National Teaching Fellowship for her innovative approaches to learning and teaching.

Richard Feinberg, PhD is a consumer psychologist and professor in the Department of Consumer Sciences and Retailing and the director of the Center for Customer-Driven Quality at Purdue University and was head of the Department of Consumer Sciences and Retailing (1989-1998; 2001-2002). He teaches courses in consumer behaviour, retailing, "e"-retailing, customer relationship management and leadership. He has directed over 85 PhD and masters theses. He is responsible for the development and delivery of executive education programs and has been a consultant for many companies on customer service/satisfaction. He is the author of over 200 research and trade articles, and hundreds of presentations and seminars. With Jon Anton and others he is the author of *Customer Relationship Management* and with Ko deRuyter and Lynne Bennington *"Call Center Management: Great Ideas Th(at) work."* He is consulting editor and reviewer for professional journals and has been a member of the advisory board for OneBlue World, an Internet start-up, and was a member of the board of directors for Paul Harris Stores, the Purdue University Press, Benchmarkportal and the FightBack Foundation. He has consulted with tens of companies (some big ones) and has served as an expert witness and consultant on some extremely interesting law suits.

Bob Galliers is provost of Bentley College, USA, formerly professor of information systems at the London School of Economics, UK where he was research professor in the Department of Information Systems. He retains his link with the LSE as a visiting professor. He was previously professor of information management at Warwick Business School, where he was dean for the period 1994-1998. His research is transdisciplinary in nature and currently focuses on information technology and business innovation, knowledge creation and management, and intra- and extra-organisational impacts of the Internet. He is editor-in-chief of the *Journal of Strategic Information Systems* and co-author of a number of books.

Dr. Călin Gurău is Associate Professor of Marketing at GSCM - Montpellier Business School, France, since September 2004. He is a Junior Fellow of the World Academy of Art and Science, Minneapolis, USA. He worked as Marketing Manager in two Romanian companies and he has received degrees and distinctions for studies and research from University of Triest, Italy; University of Vienna, Austria; Duke University, USA; University of Angers, France; Oxford University and Southampton Business School and Heriot-Watt University, United Kingdom. His present research interests are focused on Marketing Strategies for High-Technology Firms and Internet Marketing. He has published more than 30 papers in internationally refereed journals, such as International Marketing Review, Journal of Consumer Marketing, Journal of Marketing Communications, etc.

Chiquan Guo is an assistant professor of marketing and international business at the University of Texas-Pan American. His research interests include marketing strategy and management, market orientation, and e-commerce.

Adam Hagen is a graduate Ph.D. student in Consumer Behavior in the Department of Consumer Sciences and Retailing at Purdue University. His area of expertise is CRM with a specialty in service recovery management.

Nan Hu is an Assistant Professor of Information Systems at the Singapore Management University. Prior to joining SMU, Dr. Hu works as a senior analyst for Capital One Auto Finance at USA. His research interests are in the economics of information, user behavior mining, capital market, online word of mouth, and firm information environment. Dr. Hu's work has cross-discipline nature and he has published at various Computer Science, Information System , Marketing Science, and Accounting related conferences. Dr. Hu received his PhD in management science from the University of Texas at Dallas. Contact him at nanhu2010@yahoo.com.

Xiaorui Hu is an associate professor of decision sciences and information technology management at the John Cook School of Business at Saint Louis University. She received her PhD in economics from the University of Texas at Austin. Her research focuses on trust related issues in electronic commerce, B2B markets, telecommunication market evolution, information security, and culture impact on international business. Her work has appeared in Information Systems Research, Decision Support Systems, IEEE Computer, Journal of Organizational Computing and Electronic Commerce, International Marketing Review, Journal of Global Information Management, and Journal of Promotion Management, and other outlets.

Sanjeev Jha is a doctoral student at the Department of Information & Decision Sciences at the College of Business Administration, University of Illinois at Chicago (UIC). His research interests include sustained innovation, innovation management, organizational learning, information technology adoption, and strategic information systems. He has published in journals such as *Communications of the ACM* and *IEE Engineering Management,* and proceedings of several conferences including the Academy of Management, International Conference in Information Systems, Americas Conference in Information Systems, among others.

Wen-Jang (Kenny) Jih is a professor of computer information systems of the Jennings A. Jones College of Business, Middle Tennessee State University. He obtained his doctorate degree in business computer information systems from the University of North Texas in 1985. His recent research interests include: e-commerce, m-commerce, knowledge management, customer relationship management, and innovative instructional methods in information systems.

Changsu Kim is assistant professor in electronic commerce at Yeungnam University, Korea. He received his PhD in information systems from London School of Economics (LSE). His research interests include ubiquitous computing, electronic commerce, ICT innovation diffusion, and IS strategy.

Jaekyung Kim is a PhD candidate in management at the University of Nebraska-Lincoln. He received his MBA from Miami University of Ohio. His research focuses on knowledge management, decision support systems, and electronic commerce. His work has been published in journals such as *Decision Support Systems, Omega, International Journal of Electronic Commerce, Expert Systems with Applications* and *International Journal of Knowledge Management.*

Songpol Kulviwat is assistant professor of marketing and international business at Hofstra University. He received his PhD in marketing from Southern Illinois University. His research interests include Internet marketing, high-tech marketing, international business (cross-cultural research), and information technology. His scholarly works have been published or accepted for publication in the *Journal of the Academy of Marketing Science and Journal of Internet Research.*

Theresa Lauraeus-Niinivaara is PhD Candidate and Researcher in Information Systems Science at the Helsinki School of Economics. She is finishing her dissertation about "Uncertainty Affects Consumer Decision Making and Buying Behaviour in E-Market". Her research interests include consumer buying behavior, decision making, information search processes and uncertainty in e-Market. She is also interested in the household robots, the future electronic services. She have published a book article, several conference papers and working papers about these areas. Before doctoral studies she worked as Leading Consultant and Director of a Finnish internet office, Key Account Manager and Project Leader in the electronic commerce field.

Dr. Zakaria Maamar has published several papers in well-known journals such as Communications of the Association for Computing Machinery (ACM) and the Institute for Electronic and Electrical Engineers (IEEE)'s Internet Computing, and conference proceedings such as "Mobile Data Management and Advanced Information Systems." Dr. Zakaria Maamar also received two IEEE awards in 1999 and 2001. He regularly co-organizes international workshops on various topics including ubiquitous computing, context-aware Web services, and handheld computing

Maria Madlberger (maria.madlberger@wu-wien.ac.at) is assistant professor at the Institute for Management Information Systems at the Vienna University of Economics and Business Administration. She received her PhD in commerce from this university in 2002. Her research focuses on how information systems can be used as a basis for efficiency gains in distribution and interfirm networks. Her current areas of interest are interorganizational information sharing in supply chain management, strategic and operational benefits of electronic data interchange, multi-channel retailing, distribution in B2C e-commerce, and Internet marketing. Dr. Madlberger has published in journals and refereed conferences in the fields of e-commerce, marketing, and supply chain management.

Dr. Stuart Madnick is the John Norris Maguire Professor of Information Technology in the MIT Sloan School of Management and Professor of Engineering Systems in the MIT School of Engineering. He received his MBA and Ph.D. in Computer Science from MIT and has been an MIT faculty member since 1972 and head of IT Group for more than twenty years. He is co-Director of PROductivity From Information Technology and Total Data Quality Management research programs. He is the author/co-author of over 250 books, articles, or reports. His research interests include integrating information systems, data semantics, and strategic use of IT.

Makoto Nakayama is Associate Professor at the College of Computing and Digital Media in DePaul University. He holds a Ph.D. from University of California, Los Angeles and an MBA from University of Texas at Austin. Prior to moving into academe, he served as a product marketing manager at Novell Japan. He also worked on business planning and operating system developments at Yokogawa Electric Corporation in Tokyo. His current research interests are in IT use in marketing channels and IT skills portfolio management. His papers appeared in Information & Management, Journal of Information Technology, International Journal of Information Systems and Change Management, and proceedings of international conferences.

Anssi Öörni is assistant professor of information systems at the Helsinki School of Economics. He received his M.Sc. and Ph.D. in economics at the Helsinki School of economics. He has published in the *European Journal of Information Systems, Information Technology and Tourism, and the Journal of Travel Marketing.* His current research interests include consumer adoption of information technology and diffusion of mobile services.

Carla Ruiz-Mafé (PhD in Business and Economics, Universitat de València, Spain) is Assistant Professor in the Department of Marketing, Faculty of Economics, Universitat de València. Her primary research interests include e-commerce, mobile commerce, communication, interactive marketing and consumer behaviour and she has articles published in Internet Research, Online Information Review, Journal of Electronic Commerce Research, Journal of Consumer Marketing, Journal of Theoretical and Applied Electronic Commerce Research and the best Spanish refereed Journals. She has also presented some papers at AM and EMAC Conferences.

C. Ranganathan is associate professor of information systems at the Liautaud Graduate School of Business, University of Illinois at Chicago. His research interests include e-business transformation, strategic management of information systems, management of IT outsourcing and business value of IT investments. His research has been published or is forthcoming in journals including *Communications of the ACM, Decision Sciences Journal, IEEE Transactions on Engineering Management, Information & Management, Information Systems Research, MIS Quarterly Executive, International Journal of Electronic Commerce,* among others. Ranga holds a doctorate from the Indian Institute of Management of Management, Ahmedabad and a master's degree from BITS, Pilani, India.

Timo Saarinen is a professor of information systems and electronic commerce at the department of Business Technology and a Vice-Rector for research at the Helsinki School of Economics. He holds a Ph.D. in information systems form the Helsinki School of Economics. Timo Saarinen has published in major journals as *MIS Quarterly, Journal of Management Information Systems, Information & Management and Journal of Strategic Information Systems.* His research interests include economics of information systems and the development of efficient market-driven services, with the focus on the multi-channel environment of electronic commerce.

Silvia Sanz-Blas (PhD in Business and Economics, Universitat de València, Spain) is Associate Professor in the Department of Marketing, Faculty of Economics, Universitat de València. Her primary research interests include communication, sales, e-commerce, interactive marketing and consumer behaviour she has articles published in Internet Research, Online Information review, Journal of Electronic Commerce Research, Journal of Consumer Behaviour, Journal of Consumer Marketing, Journal of Vacation Marketing and the best Spanish refereed Journals. She has also presented numerous papers at AM, AMS and EMAC Conferences.

Anne Sunikka is PhD Candidate and Researcher in Information Systems Science at the Helsinki School of Economics. She has M.Sc.'s from both international marketing and information systems. Her research interests include personalization, multi-channel management, information search, and electronic commerce. She has extensive work experience in financial industry, in information systems and education. She has presented research papers in several conferences (ECIS, HICSS, EMAC, IAREP). She expects to finalize her thesis on customer activation in financial industry in 2009.

Norma Sutcliffe is Associate Professor at the College of Computing and Digital Media in DePaul University. She holds a Ph.D. as well as an MBA from University of California, Los Angeles. With extensive experience in industry, Dr. Sutcliffe has been a consultant for many Fortune 500 firms in evaluating IT needs, IT implementations, and IT strategies. Dr. Sutcliffe has worked as systems developer on mainframe and client/server systems as well. Her current research interests are in IT enabled organizational change, IT leadership behavior, and IT skills portfolio management. Her papers appeared in Information & Management, Journal of Information Systems Education, International Journal of Information Systems and Change Management, and proceedings of international conferences.

Ramendra Thakur is an assistant professor at UVSC. He received his PhD in marketing from Southern Illinois University. His research interests are in customer relationship management, e-commerce, high-tech marketing, marketing strategies on shareholder value, marketing models, and international marketing. His publications have appeared in the *Journal of the Academy of Marketing Science,* the *Marketing Management Journal*, and the *Journal of Website Promotion*.

Dr. Patricia T. Warrington is an assistant professor of merchandising at Texas Christian University in Fort Worth, Texas. Her research focuses on consumer patronage behavior, particularly as it relates to multichannel retailing and technology. Dr. Warrington's industry experience includes positions in department store buying, retail financial planning/analysis, and small business consulting. Her publications appear in *Journal of Retailing, Psychology & Marketing, Journal of Business Research*, and other publications. Dr. Warrington holds an MBA from Texas Christian University and a PhD in retailing and consumer sciences from The University of Arizona.

Yuhong Wu was an assistant professor of marketing at Christos M. Cotsakos College of Business, William Paterson University. She received her PhD degree in marketing from the University of Texas at Austin. Her research interests lie in the areas of internet marketing and e-commerce, strategies in network market, and new product development and management. Her works has appeared in *Journal of Marketing* and other outlets.

Kyung Hoon Yang is currently an assistant professor in the Department of Information Systems at the University of Wisconsin-La Crosse. He received his PhD in management information systems from Purdue University in 1989 and has been a full professor at the Chungang University in Korea from 1989 to 2004. His major research interests include knowledge transfer and knowledge based organization. He has published more than 20 journal articles including *Decision Support Systems, Expert Systems with Applications*.

Hongwei Zhu is an Assistant Professor of Information Technology at the College of Business and Public Administration, Old Dominion University. He holds a Ph.D. in Technology, Management and Policy from MIT. His research interests include data integration and reuse technologies, data quality management, data mining, information policy analysis, and information economics.

Index